Professional Review Guide for the CCA Examination
2014 Edition

Professional Review Guide for the CCA Examination
2014 Edition

Patricia J. Schnering, RHIA, CCS

Toni Cade, MBA, RHIA, CCS, FAHIMA

Lisa M. Delhomme, MHA, RHIA

Lauralyn Kavanaugh-Burke, DrPH, RHIA, CHTS-IM

Leslie Moore, RHIT, CCS

CENGAGE
Learning®

Australia • Brazil • Japan • Korea • Mexico • Singapore • Spain • United Kingdom • United States

CENGAGE
Learning®

Professional Review Guide for the CCA Examination, 2014 Edition
Patricia J. Schnering, RHIA, CCS

Vice President, GM Skills & Product Planning: Dawn Gerrain

Product Manager: Jadin B. Kavanaugh

Director, Development-Career and Computing: Marah Bellegarde

Product Development Manager: Juliet Steiner

Content Developer: Amy Wetsel

Product Assistant: Courtney Cozzy

Marketing Director: Michele McTighe

Marketing Manager, Special Markets: Erica Glisson

Senior Production Director: Wendy Troeger

Production Manager: Andrew Crouth

Content Project Management: Bharathi Sanjeev / S4Carlisle

Art Direction: Laurie Entringer / S4Carlisle

Media Editor: Deborah Bordeaux

Cover Image: Donald Nausbaum/ Photographer's Choice/Getty Images

The 2014 versions of CPT, ICD-10-CM, and ICD-10-PCS were used in preparation of this product.

CPT Copyright 2013 American Medical Association. All rights reserved.

CPT is a registered trademark of the American Medical Association.

For product information and technology assistance, contact us at
Cengage Learning Customer & Sales Support,
1-800-354-9706

For permission to use material from this text or product, submit all requests online at **www.cengage.com/permissions.**

Further permissions questions can be e-mailed to
permissionrequest@cengage.com

Library of Congress Control Number: 2013954336
ISBN-13: 978-1-285-73550-4
ISBN-10: 1-285-73550-1

Cengage Learning
200 First Stamford Place, 4th Floor
Stamford, CT 06902
USA

Cengage Learning is a leading provider of customized learning solutions with office locations around the globe, including Singapore, the United Kingdom, Australia, Mexico, Brazil, and Japan. Locate your local office at: **www.cengage.com/global**

Cengage Learning products are represented in Canada by Nelson Education, Ltd.

To learn more about Cengage Learning, visit **www.cengage.com**

Purchase any of our products at your local college store or at our preferred online store **www.cengagebrain.com**

Notice to the Reader

Printed in the United States of America
1 2 3 4 5 6 7 18 17 16 15 14

ABOUT THE AUTHORS

Patricia J. Schnering, RHIA, CCS

Patricia J. Schnering was the founder of PRG Publishing, Inc. and Professional Review Guides, Inc. She works as an author and editor for PRG products. Mrs. Schnering is a 1995 graduate of the Health Information Management program at St. Petersburg College in St. Petersburg, Florida, and received her RHIT certification in 1995. In 1998, she was certified as a CCS, and in 1999 she received her RHIA certification. Her education includes a bachelor's degree from the University of South Florida in Tampa, Florida, with a major in Business Administration. Since 1993, her work in Health Information Services includes supervisory positions, as an HIM consultant and as an adjunct HIM instructor at St. Petersburg College. She was the recipient of the Florida Health Information Management Association (FHIMA) Literary Award in 2000 and 2006.

Lisa M. Delhomme, MHA, RHIA

Lisa M. Delhomme is an Instructor in the Health Information Management Department at the University of Louisiana at Lafayette, located in Lafayette, Louisiana. She has a bachelor's degree in Health Information Management and a master's degree in Health Services Administration. She teaches several courses, including CPT coding, legal aspects for health care, and computers in health care organizations. Prior to teaching, she held a management position at a physician practice and ambulatory surgery center. Mrs. Delhomme has been an active member of the American Health Information Management Association for 12 years. In addition, she has been involved with committees and projects for the Louisiana Health Information Management Association and Louisiana Medical Group Management Association.

Lauralyn Kavanaugh-Burke, DrPH, RHIA, CHTS-IM

After receiving a BS degree in Medical Record Administration with a minor in biology from York College of Pennsylvania, Dr. Burke worked in several hospitals in Virginia and Maryland in various management positions, including DRG Analyst, Assistant Director, and Director of the Medical Record / Health Information departments. During this time, her interest in pathophysiology intensified after working with several physicians in their research endeavors. She started teaching at an associate's degree Health Information Technology (HIT) program at Fairmont State College in West Virginia where she was able to strengthen her anatomy and pathophysiology skills, not only instructing HIT students, but also working with the medical laboratory and veterinary technology programs there. This position gave her the chance to complete her MS degree in Community Health Education from West Virginia University, which perfectly blended health information management and education. She achieved her Certified Health Education Specialist (CHES) credential shortly afterward. She then moved back to Pennsylvania and returned to the hospital arena as a DRG and coding consultant. Dr. Burke had the opportunity to teach at her alma mater and lay the foundation for an associate's degree program in HIT at a local community college.

Subsequent to relocating to Florida, she became a faculty member at Florida A&M University's BS degree program in Health Informatics & Information Management Division. She continued her pursuit of more training in pathophysiology, and soon after received her Doctor of Public Health (DrPH) with a concentration in epidemiology from Florida A&M University. Dr. Burke's main areas of interest are in disaster preparedness for hospitals, and bioterrorism and infectious diseases. She recently achieved certification as a Health Information Technology Implementation Manager (CHTS-IM) after completing her HITECH training through Santa Fe College.

Toni Cade, MBA, RHIA, CCS, FAHIMA

Toni Cade is a tenured Associate Professor in the Health Information Management Department at the University of Louisiana at Lafayette. She teaches several courses, including health care reimbursement methodologies (MS-DRGs, APCs, RUGs, etc.), hospital statistics, case management, performance improvement, medical terminology, and health care risk management. Mrs. Cade is also the Management Internship Site Coordinator, coordinating affiliation sites throughout the United States.

Mrs. Cade has 31 years' experience with previous positions, including Data Analyst for the QIO, Utilization Review Supervisor, and Coding Supervisor in a large acute care hospital. She holds a bachelor's degree in Medical Record Science and a master's degree in Business Administration. Her credentials include RHIA (Registered Health Information Administrator) and CCS (Certified Coding Specialist). She was also awarded the designation of Fellow (FAHIMA) by the American Health Information Management Association.

She is listed in *Marquis' Who's Who in Medicine and Health Care* and serves on the Editorial Advisory Board of Health Information Management Manual and For the Record. She has reviewed and authored publications on topics including medical terminology, billing and reimbursement, and health care statistics.

As an independent consultant, Mrs. Cade has extensive experience conducting seminars in coding and reimbursement. She also consults at acute care hospitals and works as an expert health care data analyst and expert witness with attorneys involved in medical malpractice cases.

Mrs. Cade has served AHIMA in various positions, including Delegate, Nominating Committee member, and Fellowship Review Committee member. She was nominated for AHIMA's Champion Award and Educator's Award. She has served her state association, the Louisiana Health Information Management Association, in many capacities, including serving on the Board of Directors, as President and Secretary, and as Project Manager of various projects. She was awarded the Distinguished Member Award in 2003, and also received the Outstanding Volunteer Award for her efforts as Coding Roundtable Coordinator in Louisiana in 2003–2004. In 2009, she received the Outstanding Volunteer Award for her efforts in creating a Central Office Coordinator position for LHIMA.

Leslie A. Moore, RHIT, CCS

Leslie A. Moore has been Director of Operations for Charts In Time, Inc. since 2007. Ms. Moore oversees and manages the performance, productivity, and quality of the coding staff at Charts In Time. She is an AHIMA-certified ICD-10 trainer and has developed all the education service lines for CIT. Leslie's experience spans over 26 years as Corporate Coding Director, adjunct coding faculty, and as Independent Coding Consultant in both inpatient and outpatient settings, with extensive experience in physician coding and documentation.

ACKNOWLEDGMENTS

First and foremost, I would like to express my gratitude to all of the authors who have worked on the educational materials PRG Publishing has produced. They are seasoned professionals and excellent educators. They inspire me to work harder to produce better products. Each of these educators presents a facet of HIM practice necessary to view the HIM arena as a whole.

I thoroughly enjoy working with the authors. They are experts in the HIM field. They go all out to keep the quality of HIM education at an increasingly higher level. The superb quality of work they produce keeps me motivated. It is a pleasure to be able to call them friends and professional peers.

There have been very special people in my family who always knew I could do it when I wasn't sure I could. My late husband, Bob, always continued to keep me grounded when I tended to spin off in space as I worked on the books. My mother has always been my role model for perseverance leading to success. She embodied grace, courage, strength, and endurance. I have been blessed to have had both of them in my life.

The Cengage Learning family has been extremely patient and helpful in guiding me through the publishing system. Thank you all very much!

My thanks would not be complete without acknowledging all the HIM/HIT educators and students who support our efforts by purchasing PRG Publishing products.

My reward is knowing that the materials you study here may assist you in preparing for the challenge of the examination. Thank you for the letters and words of encouragement.

I wish you the very best now and throughout your career.

Until we meet....

Patricia J. Schnering, RHIA, CCS

PJSPRG@AOL.COM

TABLE OF CONTENTS

Introduction

Patricia J. Schnering, RHIA, CCS

INTRODUCTION TO THE PROFESSIONAL REVIEW GUIDE FOR THE CCA EXAMINATION

The Certified Coding Associate (CCA) Certification is for entry-level coders.

Source: *Certified Coding Associate (CCA) candidate handbook from AHIMA.*

This examination review guide represents a renewed effort to provide materials for HIM students and professionals. In reviewing the results of past examinations, we found that it would be beneficial for examination candidates to have additional practice in answering multiple-choice questions. We have selected questions to cover the broad topic of HIM categories necessary for sitting for the CCA Certification Examination. Researching the questions and cases as you study should increase your knowledge such that, when you encounter similar questions, you can arrive at the correct answer. We believe that this review material will jog your memory and build on information you have already gained through your education and professional experiences. This book provides you with a mix of coding questions to both increase your coding skills and provide you with testing that mimics the exam format.

The questions in this examination review guide are based on the broad competencies listed in the AHIMA Candidate Handbook for the CCA Examination. Review the latest candidate information and handbook when preparing for the exam. It can be found on AHIMA's Web site (http://www.AHIMA.org).

The beginning of this book offers suggestions for studying and test-taking strategies and a coding review section. The following chapters contain multiple-choice questions covering the competencies for the exam. Then there is a quiz with 35 multiple-choice questions and mock examination containing 100 multiple-choice questions. The backmatter of the book contains appendices with information on pharmacology and laboratory testing. Table 1 displays the major content areas of this book by sections.

Table 1 Content Areas for the Professional Review Guide for the CCA Examination

Content Area	Number of Questions
Health Data Content, Requirements, and Standards	73
Medical Sciences	145
Classification Systems and Secondary Data Sources	87
Medical Billing and Reimbursement Systems	114
ICD-10-CM/PCS Coding	203
CPT Coding	217
CCA Quiz	35
Mock Exam	100
TOTAL QUESTIONS	974

ABOUT THE COMPETENCIES FOR THE CCA EXAMINATION

We suggest that you start by examining the competencies for the Certified Coding Associate. The Domains and Task Statement Competencies were created to reflect the entry-level competencies for HIM professional practice. A detailed copy of the entry-level competencies is provided in the AHIMA Candidate Handbook Examination.

It is the responsibility of the American Health Information Management Association's (AHIMA) Commission on Certification for Health Informatics and Information Management (CHIIM) to assess what job tasks are frequently executed by newly certified practitioners. In addition, the CHIIM determines the job tasks that are critical to entry-level practice—in other words, which job tasks, if done incorrectly, could create a negative impact. The task statements are also referred to as the test specifications.

The process of identifying those critical job functions was accomplished by conducting a job analysis. The objective was to determine how entry-level practice is evolving and to develop the test specifications and a certification examination to correspond with changes that are occurring in the field. The data that were collected as a result of this research provided the essential elements that were necessary to establish the test specifications for the certifying exam. The CHIIM is responsible for developing and administering the certification examination and determining the eligibility of applicants to write the exam.

The entry-level task statements for the Certified Coding Associate from the AHIMA Certification are grouped into six domains:
- ☑ Clinical Classification Systems
- ☑ Reimbursement Methodologies
- ☑ Health Records and Data Content
- ☑ Compliance
- ☑ Information Technologies
- ☑ Confidentiality and Privacy

These six domains are divided further into task statements. See the Candidate Handbook for a complete listing of the task statements.

Weights for each domain are assigned. Each weight correlates to the degree of emphasis, or importance, given to each domain as it relates to the health information practice. Table 2 displays the weights that were assigned to each of the domains.

Table 2 CCA Examination Content with Percentage Questions by Domain

Domain	Percentage of Exam
Domain 1: Clinical Classification Systems	32
Domain 2: Reimbursement Methodologies	23
Domain 3: Health Records and Data Content	15
Domain 4: Compliance	14
Domain 5: Information Technology	8
Domain 6: Confidentiality and Privacy	8
TOTAL	100

Source: AHIMA Candidate Handbook for the CCA Examination. Reminder: Monitor AHIMA's Web site for updates on the testing information.

Although we have no way of knowing exactly what questions will be on the examination, the authors have tried to cover the competencies and content areas as comprehensively as possible. Researching the questions as you study should expand your knowledge such that, should you encounter similar questions, you can arrive at the correct answer. We believe this review material will serve to help you build on information you have already gained through your experience and education.

Crosswalks between the competencies for the CCA Certification Examination and the questions in the chapters are provided in Table 3. In addition to the competencies, the questions are written in three cognitive levels of testing, which are explained after Table 3.

Table 3 Crosswalk of CCA Competencies to Chapter Questions

Crosswalk of the CCA Examination Competencies to Chapters							
	1	2	3	4	5	6	Total
Health Data Content and Standards	1	0	68	1	2	1	73
Medical Science	145	0	0	0	0	0	145
Classification Systems and Secondary Data Sources	63	1	12	7	4	0	87
Medical Billing and Reimbursement Systems	35	66	0	6	6	1	114
ICD-10-CM/PCS Coding	203	0	0	0	0	0	203
CPT Coding	217	0	0	0	0	0	217
CCA Quiz	35	0	0	0	0	0	35
CCA Mock Examination	10	3	77	4	4	2	100
Totals	709	70	157	18	16	4	974

The key to success on the exam is a thorough knowledge of coding, which can only be achieved through extensive use of and familiarity with the code books. Having to use the code books to answer questions will help increase your speed in the use of both coding books.

This book is only one of many tools available to you to prepare. Use a variety of review methodologies (multiple-choice questions, case studies, review of theory, mock exams, etc.) as an effective means of reviewing. These tools can help prepare you for the challenge of the CCA coding exam.

In the following chapters there are a myriad of suggested resources.

ABOUT THE COGNITIVE LEVELS OF TESTING FOR THE CCA EXAMINATION

The examination questions test your knowledge on three cognitive levels:
- Recall (RE)
- Application (AP)
- Analysis (AN)

The recall level tests your memory of basic facts, such as being able to identify terms, methods, and procedures. The application level tests your ability to interpret data and information, to be able to apply concepts and principles, to recognize relationships among data, and to calculate mathematical problems. The analysis level measures your ability to solve specific problems by evaluating, comparing, and selecting appropriate solutions for action and to evaluate information and perform multiple calculations to assemble various elements into a total picture. There are sample questions provided on the AHIMA Web site (http://www.AHIMA.org) so that you can experience the testing situation.

The general format of the exam is primarily designed to engage your problem-solving and critical thinking skills. These types of questions require you to translate and apply what you have learned as well as interpret information. There are sample questions provided on the AHIMA Web site so that you can experience the testing situation (http://www.AHIMA.org).

CCA EXAMINATION CONTENTS

The CCA examination is in a computer-based format. Carefully read the latest Candidate Handbook for the CCA Examination and continue to monitor AHIMA's Web site to look for updated information on the examination format. The handbook is available for downloading in PDF format on the AHIMA Web site (http://www.AHIMA.org).

The CCA examination has 100 questions (90 questions scored and 10 that are not scored for the exam). The 90 scored questions are the basis for scoring your examination. The 10 unscored questions on the CCA examination are used in obtaining statistical information to help in the construction of questions for future examinations. These 10 questions will not be identified in the exam, nor will they count toward the examination pass/fail score.

Pass rates for the CCA examination for 2010 through 2012 are shown in Table 4.

Table 4 Pass Rates for the CCA Examination (2010–2012)

CCA Examination Pass Rates for the First-Time Test Takers			
Year	Number of Test Takers	Pass Rate	Number of Credentials Awarded
2012	2,798	57.8%	1,617
2011	2,799	56.6%	1,586
2010	2,510	60.5%	1,519

Examination pass rates are based on the calendar year (January 1 through December 31).

Source: http://www.ahima.org

ADDITIONAL INSIGHTS ABOUT THE CCA EXAMINATION

1. **Computerized testing.** You will be able to review questions on the computer screen to check your answers before you close the exam file on the computer.

2. **On-screen information.** Any additional information needed to complete the questions will be provided on the screen in the testing software.

3. **Medical sciences.** These questions tend to be interspersed throughout the other topic categories. Medical terminology, pathophysiology, and anatomy and physiology are part of the general knowledge base for health information management, coding, and reimbursement.

4. **National exam.** Keep in mind that this is a national examination. Concentrate on federal legislation, statutes, and legal issues that would be appropriate nationally in all 50 states.

5. **Be prepared to shift gears quickly throughout the exam.** Questions on the examinations are scrambled and change topics from question to question. Therefore, you may have a health care data question, followed by a coding question, followed by a reimbursement question, etc.

6. **You will need to bring your ICD-10-CM and ICD-10-PCS coding books and the AMA CPT-4 coding book to the test. AHIMA has a list of allowable code books in the Candidate Guide.** It is necessary that the entry-level coding practitioner be adept at using code books. Although some questions are in a narrative form and any necessary codes and/or code narratives will be supplied in the answer options on the computer screen for you to choose from, you will need to use your code books to answer other questions or verify the answer you choose. Practicing coding using your coding books will help increase your speed in finding the codes. Remember, the test is timed. The faster you code, the more time you have to choose your answers. It may be the difference in being able to successfully complete the examination in the time allotted.

7. **Review the latest candidate handbook.** The AHIMA Candidate Handbook for the CCA Examination contains information on the exam, how to apply for the examination, what to bring, and other pertinent information you need.

8. **Make sure that you have the necessary items for admission for testing**. You will need to bring your Authorization to Test (ATT), two forms of identification (one with your photograph), and your coding books. Verify that you have correct versions of the coding books. *Candidates that do no present the correct versions of codebooks will forfeit their exam fees.*

I. Examination Study Strategies and Resources

Patricia J. Schnering, RHIA, CCS

FORMAT OF THE EXAMINATION

The multiple-choice questions developed for the examinations are based on specifications currently referred to as domains and task statements. A complete copy of these entry-level specifications is provided in the AHIMA Candidate Handbook. The handbook is available for downloading in PDF format from the AHIMA Web site (http://www.AHIMA.org).

The general format of the exam is primarily designed to engage your problem-solving and critical thinking skills. These types of questions require you to translate what you have learned and apply it to a situation. There are sample questions provided on the AHIMA Web site (http://www.AHIMA.org) so that you can experience the testing situation.

How to Use This Book

We suggest you answer the multiple-choice questions in the review section of the book before taking the mock examination. It will give you a baseline to begin your CCA examination preparation. Your strengths and weaknesses will become more apparent, allowing you to plan your study time more effectively and focus on your problem areas.

After working through the review questions, take the mock examination. It will provide you an opportunity to assess your speed in answering multiple-choice questions.

STUDY STRATEGIES

BEGIN BY BUILDING YOUR STUDY STRATEGIES

First, you must get organized
You must be deliberate about making sure that you develop and stick to a regular study routine. Find a place where you can study, either at home or at the library.

How you schedule your study time during the week is an individual decision. However, we recommend that you avoid all-nighters and other unreasonably long study sessions. The last thing you want to do is burn yourself out by working too long and too hard at one time. Try to do a little bit at a time, and maintain a steady pace that is manageable for you.

Second, develop your individual study program
Write the exam topics and subjects in a list. Outline the chapters in your coding textbooks, and review the sections in your code books. Pinpoint your weakest subjects. Pause at each chapter outline and recall basic points. Do you draw a blank, recall them more or less, or do you feel comfortable with your recall? By using this approach, you can see where you stand.

Then, weigh the importance of each subject
How are the topics emphasized in the examination competencies, textbooks, professional journal articles, coding guidelines, and coding books? Take a look at the top MS-DRGs and APCs. Try to pick out concepts that would make good examination questions.

Create a topic list: Look at the competencies you are responsible for, and write the topics and subjects in a list. Do you draw a blank, recall them more or less, or feel comfortable with your recall? Pinpoint your weakest subjects. By using this approach, you can see where you stand. Weigh the importance of each subject and try to pick out concepts that would make good exam questions.

Personalize your list: Avoid trying to make a head-on attack by giving equal time and attention to all topics. Use the outline you have made to identify your weakest topics. Determine which topics you believe will require a significant amount of study time and which will only require a brief review. Some experts suggest that you begin your plan with your strongest topics and concentrate on your weaknesses as you get closer to your exam date. That way they will be fresh in your mind. Reorganize your list of the topics in the order that you plan to study them.

Use your list: Your list will give you a clear mental picture of what you need to do and will keep you on track. There are three additional advantages to a list.

1. It builds your morale as you steadily cross off items that you have completed, and you can monitor your progress.
2. Glancing back at the list from time to time serves to reassure you that you are on target.
3. You can readily see that you are applying your time and effort where they are most needed.

Keep the list conspicuously in view. Carefully plan your pre-exam study time and stick to your plan.

Design a 10-week study program: Make your study process a systematic review of all topic categories, followed by achieving mastery of strategically selected subjects within the topic categories. To facilitate this effort, we recommend that you design a 10-week study program. You should plan on spending an average of 10–12 hours per week studying. The idea is to study smart, not to bulldoze through tons of material in a haphazard way.

Consider a study group: Everyone has his or her own particular study style. Some people prefer to study alone; others work best in a group. Regardless of your preference, we strongly recommend that you take advantage of group study at least some of the time. Studying with others can prove very helpful when working through your weakest areas. Each member of the study team will bring strengths and weaknesses to the table, and all can benefit from the collaboration. So, even if you are a solitary learner, you may occasionally want to work with a group for those topics you find more challenging. If you do not have easy access to a study group for the examination, you may want to study with other HIM professionals over the Internet. The AHIMA Communities of Practice (CoP) on the Internet is an excellent avenue to find others who are in the same position.

Increase your endurance: Preparing for a major exam is similar to preparing for a marathon athletic event. Know the time allotted for your certification examination. One suggestion is to use your study process to slowly build up your concentration time until you can focus your energy for the appropriate period. This is like the runner who begins jogging for 30 minutes and builds up to 1 hour, then 1½ hours, and so on, and gradually increases the endurance time to meet the demands of the race. Try this strategy; it could work for you!

Go to the exam like a trained and disciplined runner going to a marathon event!

SAMPLE STUDY SCHEDULE

Week 1
Review your resources for domains and tasks relating to:
> Health Data Content, Requirements and Standards
> Information and Communications Technologies
> Privacy, Confidentiality, Legal, and Ethical Issues

Work on the questions in the Health Data chapter in this book.

Week 2
Review your resources for medical sciences:
> Medical Terminology
> Anatomy and Physiology
> Pathophysiology (disease process and pharmacology)

Review Appendix A and Appendix B in this book.
Work on the questions in the Medical Science chapter in this book.

Week 3
Review your resources for regulatory requirements for health information.
Work on the questions in the Classification Systems and Secondary Data Sources chapter in this book.

Week 4
Review your Billing and Reimbursement resources.
Work on the questions in the Billing and Reimbursement chapter in this book.

Week 5
Review your ICD-10-CM/PCS coding resources, including:
> ICD-10-CM and ICD-10-PCS Official Coding Guidelines
> ICD-10-CM Outpatient Coding Guidelines

Read the ICD-10-CM/PCS section in the Coding Review provided in the front of this book.
Begin working on the questions in the ICD-10-CM/PCS Coding chapter in the book.

Week 6
Continue your review and work on the ICD-10-CM/PCS Coding chapter.
Work on areas in which you have weaknesses.

Week 7
Review your resources on CPT/HCPCS Coding.
Read the CPT section in the Coding Review provided in the front of this book.
Begin working on the questions in the CPT chapter in this book.

Week 8
Continue to review CPT/HCPCS Coding materials.
Finish working on the questions in the CPT chapter in this book.
Work on areas in which you have weaknesses in CPT.

Week 9
Work on the questions in the Mock Quiz.
Take the Mock Examination in the back of this book.

Week 10
Do an overall review of areas in which you feel you have weaknesses.

STUDY RESOURCES

Don't spend time trying to memorize something you do not understand. The main issue is to understand the materials so you can use the knowledge in a practical way. Search for additional information that will help make the subject clear to you. There are four basic sources of information: books, people, educational programs/colleges, and Internet resources.

Books and other written resources

➤ A different textbook may use another style of presentation that you are more receptive to and may be all you need to gain a better insight into the subject. It can offer a fresh point of view, provide relief from boredom, and encourage critical thinking in the process of comparing the texts. There are a variety of books and workbooks available to use in studying for your coding certification.

➤ Periodical literature in the field provides well-written articles that may open up the subject to you and turn your study into an adventure in learning. AHIMA publishes authoritative and insightful information on every aspect of coding. In addition to the ongoing coding articles in the *Journal of AHIMA*, *Advance for Health Information Professionals* and *For the Record* have articles on coding in each issue. Sometimes an article can help put the subject material into practical perspective and pull it together so that you gain a deeper understanding. Don't forget to use *Coding Clinics* and *CPT Assistant* to refresh your memory and learn more about specific coding guidelines. Journals will help you keep updated on new information on coding issues that may be incorporated into the exams.

➤ Take advantage of the local college library by using reserved materials specifically set aside for HIM student study purposes.

Your HIM community

➤ Interaction with others can be truly beneficial in keeping you motivated and on track.

➤ Professional contacts can also be helpful in your study effort. Most people in our field are eager to share their knowledge and are flattered by appeals for information. Schedule a conference with the director of the HIM/Coding program at your local college. These educators may have current information and resources you are not aware of. Talking to those who have recently taken the examination can also be of great assistance.

➤ Collaborating with other test applicants can reveal fresh viewpoints, stimulate thought by disagreement, or at least let you see that you are not alone in your quest. Organize study groups and set aside specific times to work together. This interaction can be truly beneficial in keeping you motivated and on task.

Classes, workshops, seminars, and coding teleconferences

These can present opportunities to learn and review the subject matter in a new light and to keep you updated on changes. Take advantage of any coding review sessions available in your area.

Internet resources

➢ Use the Internet to connect with others who are preparing for the examination. In this dynamic, changing environment, the most up-to-date materials may not be available in a book. Don't overlook the power of AHIMA's Web site. The AHIMA online resources are extensive and quite easy to access at www.ahima.org. In addition, the Communities of Practice (CoPs) are a phenomenal source of contact with HIM professionals and other students preparing for the examination on a myriad of subjects. AHIMA is available online for members. You may find other examination applicants to work with by using e-mail.

➢ There are innumerable resources for coding and reimbursement on the Internet. **Just be aware that you may want to verify the information, as it is only as good as the source.**

Some Suggested Study Resources

1. **Mandatory:** AHIMA Candidate Handbook for the CCA Examination
2. **Mandatory:** *ICD-10-CM* and *ICD-10-PCS Code Books* (refer to instructions from AHIMA for the appropriate version)
3. **Mandatory:** *ICD-10-CM Official Guidelines for Coding and Reporting* (2014) is available online at http://www.cdc.gov/nchs/data/icd/icd10cm_guidelines_2014.pdf
4. **Mandatory:** *ICD-10-PCS Official Guidelines for Coding and Reporting* (2014); online at http://www.cms.gov/Medicare/Coding/ICD10/Downloads/PCS-2014-guidelines.pdf
5. **Mandatory:** AMA CPT Code Book (refer to instructions from AHIMA for the appropriate version)
6. *HCPCS Level II Code Book* (refer to instructions from AHIMA for the appropriate version)
7. "Documentation Guidelines for Evaluation and Management Services," *CPT Assistant* (May 1997) as well as other *CPT Assistant* issues
8. Professional journal articles on coding
   Journal of AHIMA
   Advance for Health Information Professionals
   For the Record
9. Medical dictionaries (check for the latest edition)
10. Coding class, seminar, workshop notes, and tests
11. Study groups or partners
12. On-the-job experience
13. Examination review sessions
14. Review books written for CCA examination
15. Various online computer resources. For online coding practice sites as well as those for information and Internet interaction with others, visit the following examples:
    MANDATORY: http://www.AHIMA.org
    http://www.cms.hhs.gov
    http://www.cms.gov/Medicare/Coding/ICD10/
    http://www.hospitalconnect.com
    http://www.cdc.gov/nchs/icd/icd10cm.htm
    http://www.icd10data.com/
    http://icd10cmcode.com/icd10cmpcscodes.php
16. HIM textbooks and Class textbooks: There is a large variety of textbooks for HIM and coding available on the market. Both Cengage Delmar Learning (www.cengage.com) and AHIMA (www.ahima.org) have a variety of HIM products. For example, see the partial listing of books available through Delmar Cengage Learning.

Those resources marked **MANDATORY** are essential for you to have in order to prepare for the examination.

Contact Information for Resources for CCA Examination Review Studies

AMA CPT Code Book 2014
American Medical Association (AMA): Phone: (800) 621-8335
website: http://www.ama-assn.org/ama
https://www.amacatalog@ama-assn.org.

HCPCS II, Code Book 2014 Edition
American Medical Association: Phone: (800) 621-8335

AMA CPT Assistant
American Medical Association: Phone: (800) 621-8335 Fax: (312) 464-5600
Documentation Guidelines for E & M Coding
Published May 1995 and revised November 1997
American Medical Association (AMA) and HCFA
Printed in the *CPT Assistant* May 1997 and November 1997
Online at Centers for Medicare and Medicaid Services:
   http://www.cms.hhs.gov/
   http://go.cms.gov/MLNGenInfo

ICD-10-CM and ICD-10-PCS Code Books with October 2014 updates
OptumInsight, website https://www.optumcoding.com/

ICD-10-CM Official Guidelines for Coding and Reporting
Central Office on ICD-10-CM of the American Hospital Association (AHA)
Phone: (312) 422-3000 or it can be accessed online at the
Web site for National Center for Health Statistics (NCHS) http://www.cdc.gov/nchs

ICD-10-PCS Official Guidelines for Coding and Reporting
Centers for Medicare and Medicaid Services:
http://www.cms.hhs.gov/
http://www.cms.gov/Medicare/Coding/ICD10/Downloads/PCS-2014-guidelines.pdf

AHIMA has developed a series of HIM and coding resources
To place an order: call (800) 335-5535
For additional resources and information about the coding certification examinations, visit the
AHIMA Web site at http://www.ahima.org

OptumInsight has an array of coding, reimbursement, and compliance products
Contact them at 1-800-464-3649, choose Option 1 for speedier service.
Visit their Web site at https://www.optumcoding.com/

Delmar Cengage Learning has a multitude of HIM products. In addition, they have partnered with
OptumInsight so that you can order your OptumInsight resources through Delmar Cengage Learning
also.

For a complete list, contact:
Cengage Learning, Inc.
Email: esales@cengage.com
Web site: http://www.cengagebrain.com/
Phone: 866-994-2427
For additional information on these Health Information resources, visit Delmar Cengage Learning at
www.cengage.com\delmar.

The following is a partial listing of Cengage products for Health Information.

3-2-1 Code It! (4th Edition)
Green, Michelle A.

A Guide to Health Insurance Billing
(Includes Optum EncoderPro Trial Printed Access Card and Premium Web Site Printed Access Card)
Moisio, Marie A.

Basic Allied Health Statistics and Analysis
Koch, G.

Case Studies for Health Information Management
McCuen, Charlotte; Sayles, Nanette; and Schnering, Patricia

Coding Basics: Medical Billing and Reimbursement Fundamentals
Richards, Cynthia

Coding Basics: Understanding Medical Collections
Rimmer, Michelle

Coding for Medical Necessity in the Physician Office
Kelly-Farwell, Deborah and Favreau, Cecile

Coding Surgical Procedures: Beyond the Basics
Smith, Gail I.

Coding Workbook for the Physician's Office
Covell, Alice

Comparative Health Information Management
Peden, Ann

Essentials of Health Information Management Principles and Practices (2nd Edition)
Green, M. A. and Bowie, M. J.

Essentials of Healthcare Compliance
Safian, Shelly

Ethics Case Studies for Health Information Management
Grebner, Leah

Guide to Coding Compliance
Becker, Joanne M.

Health Services Research Methods
Shi, L.

HIPPA for Medical Office Personnel
Krager, Dan and Krager, Carole

ICD-10: A Comprehensive Guide: Education, Planning and Implementation
Dawlish, Carline

ICD-10-CM Diagnostic Coding System: Education, Planning and Implementation
Dagleish, Carline

ICD-10-PCS Coding System: Education, Planning and Implementation
Dagleish, Carline

Legal and Ethical Aspects of Health Information Management
McWay, Dana C.

Medical Terminology for Insurance and Coding
Moisio, Marie A.

Today's Health Information Management: An Integrated Approach
McWay, D. C.

Understanding Health Insurance: A Guide to Billing and Reimbursement
Green, Michelle A. and Rowell, Jo Anne

Understanding Hospital Billing and Coding: A Worktext
Diamond, Marsha S.

Understanding ICD-9-CM: A Worktext
Bowie, Mary Jo and Schaffer, Regina M.

Understanding ICD-9-CM Coding
Bowie, Mary Jo and Schaffer, Regina M.

Understanding ICD-10-CM and ICD-10-PCS: A Worktext
Bowie, Mary Jo and Schaffer, Regina M.

Understanding Medical Coding: A Comprehensive Guide
Johnson, Sandra L. and Linker, Robin

Understanding Procedural Coding: A Worktext
Bowie, Mary Jo and Schaffer, Regina M.

Using the Electronic Health Record in the Healthcare Provider Practice
Eichenwald Maki, Shirley and Petterson, Bonnie

For additional information on these Health Information resources, visit Cengage Learning at **www.cengage.com**

A SUMMARY OF TIPS FOR ORGANIZING YOUR TIME AND MATERIALS

1. **Make a list of exam topics.**
   Review the major topic categories and determine what your areas of strength are and what areas are in need of improvement.

2. **Focus on your weaknesses.**
   Using the list, identify your weaknesses. It's natural to spend time on the areas where you feel confident. However, it's important to spend more time and energy studying your areas of weakness. Remember, every question counts toward that passing score!

3. **Set up a realistic study schedule**.
   Refer to the sample schedule provided in this book and customize it to meet your needs. Consider having a study group that meets regularly.

4. **Organize and review all of the following items:**
   a. The latest AHIMA Candidate Handbook for the Examination
   b. Official Coding Guidelines for Inpatient and Outpatient
   c. Coding textbooks and any coding course syllabi, outlines, class notes, and tests
   d. Coding books
   e. *Coding Clinic* from the past 3–4 years
   f. *CPT Assistant* from the past 3–4 years
   g. Professional journal articles on documentation, reimbursement, and coding issues
   h. List of pertinent Web sites for research and review

5. **Organize and enter valuable coding information directly into your code books.**
   You will not be allowed to have loose materials in your books. However, information that is permanently attached or written into the code book is acceptable.

6. **Practice taking timed tests.**
   One of the best ways to study for an examination is to take tests. Practice answering questions and working coding cases as much as possible. Time yourself so that you become accustomed to taking, on average, less than 1 minute per each multiple-choice question. Work with your watch in front of you.

7. **MANDATORY! Read the certification guide.**
   Carefully read the latest AHIMA Candidate Handbook for the Certified Coding Associate. If anything in the Certification Guide is unclear, seek assistance from AHIMA. You are held accountable for the important information, deadlines, and instructions addressed in this material.

THE DAY BEFORE AND THE MORNING OF THE EXAM

1. **Know the exam location.** Take a practice drive. If necessary, spend the night before the examination in a hotel or motel near the exam test site if it is a great distance from your home.

2. **Avoid studying the night before the exam.** Last-minute studying tends to increase your anxiety level. However, you may want to allocate a small amount of time to review any information that you feel you must look at one more time.

3. **Organize in advance all the materials you need to take with you to the exam.** Review the candidate handbook carefully and be sure to have all the items that are required, especially the admission card and proof of identity and your code books.

4. **Get a good night's sleep.**
   Taking a 4-hour test with little rest the night before may prevent you from having the energy and stamina you need to complete the exam.

5. **Have a healthy meal before your exam.**
   Four hours is a long time to go on an empty stomach. Try to eat a nutritious meal, for instance, cereal and fruit, bagel and fruit or juice, or a meal with protein such as cheese and crackers or eggs and toast. You need something to give you energy to keep going. Take a healthy snack bar to munch on if you get hungry and need to take a short break at the testing center.

6. **Dress comfortably.** Plan for possible variations in room temperature. Dressing in layers may prove helpful.

7. **Arrive early.** Allow yourself plenty of time so that you arrive at the test site early.

TAKING THE EXAMINATION

You have stuck to your study schedule and have conditioned yourself to be in the best physical and mental shape possible. Now comes the "moment of truth": the examination pops up on the screen before your eyes. Every paratrooper knows that in addition to having a parachute, one must know how to open it. You have mastered the major topics; you have the parachute. Now, you need to utilize good test-taking techniques to apply the knowledge you have gained; open the parachute!

1. **Taking the practice test.** Prior to starting the exam, you will be given a chance to practice taking an examination on the computer. Time will be allotted for this practice test. However, you may quit the practice test and begin the actual exam when you are comfortable with the computerized testing process.

2. **Read all directions and questions carefully.** Try to avoid reading too much into the questions. Be sensible and practical in your interpretation. Read ALL of the possible answers, because the first one that looks good may not be the best one.

3. **Scan the screen quickly for general question format.** Like the marathon runner, pace yourself for the distance. A good rule of thumb is 1–1.5 minutes per question. You may wish to keep the timer displayed on the computer to check your schedule throughout the exam. For example, at question 30, about one-half hour will have elapsed, etc.

4. **Coming back to questions.** Some people answer all questions that they are certain of first, and then go back through the exam a second time to answer any questions they were uncertain about. Others prefer not to skip questions, but make their best choice on encountering each question and go on. Both can be good approaches. Choose the one that works best for you. You can "mark" questions that you have left unanswered and/or those questions you may want to review. Before you sign off of the exam or run out of time, you will have the ability to go back to those questions for a final review.

5. **Answer all the questions.** There are no penalties for guessing, but not choosing an answer is definitely a wrong answer.

6. **Process of elimination.** Use deductive reasoning and the process of elimination to arrive at the most correct answer. Some questions may have more than one correct answer. You will be asked to select the "best" possible answer based on the information presented.

7. **Determine what is being asked.** If the question is written in a scenario format, first identify the question being asked and then review the entire question for the information needed to determine the correct answer.

8. **Use all the time available to recheck your answers.** However, avoid changing your answers unless you are absolutely certain it is necessary. Second-guessing yourself often results in a wrong answer.

9. **Getting your score.** A huge advantage to taking the computerized exam is that before you leave the testing center, you will be able to get your final test score instead of having to wait up to 6 weeks to receive the score by mail.

AFTER THE EXAM

Our advice is to reclaim your life and focus on your career. One good way to start is to plan a special reward for yourself at some point immediately following or shortly after the exam. Schedule a family vacation or a relaxing weekend getaway. Just find some way of being good to yourself. You certainly deserve it! You have worked hard, so relish your success.

Now Available - All New Professional Review Guide Series Online Quizzing Software

For 2014, we are providing you with new dynamic quizzing software for more effective study results. Follow the instructions on the Printed Access Card bound into this text to access the online quizzing software for this title.

Features include:
- All of the quizzes and mock exams available in the text, customizable by subject area
- Immediate feedback options by subject area and competency for better self-assessment
- Flashcards for self-review
- Case Studies available as Adobe PDF documents in the quizzing software for independent review

For Instructors:
- Ability to track student and class progress by domain or subject area in real-time for better classroom focus
- Excel ™ exporting feature for gradebooks

Go to www.cengagebrain.com to create a unique instructor user login. Contact your sales representative for more information.

II. Coding Review

Patricia Schnering, RHIA, CCS

Leslie Moore, RHIT, CCS

Lisa Delhomme, MHA, RHIA

ICD-10-CM PREFACE
2014

This 2014 update of the International Statistical Classification of Diseases and Related Health Problems, 10th revision, Clinical Modification (ICD-10-CM) is being published by the United States Government in recognition of its responsibility to promulgate this classification throughout the United States for morbidity coding. The International Statistical Classification of Diseases and Related Health Problems, 10th Revision (ICD-10), published by the World Health Organization (WHO), is the foundation of ICD-10-CM. ICD-10 continues to be the classification used in cause-of-death coding in the United States. The ICD-10-CM is comparable with the ICD-10. The WHO Collaborating Center for the Family of International Classifications in North America, housed at the Centers for Disease Control and Prevention's National Center for Health Statistics (NCHS), has responsibility for the implementation of ICD and other WHO-FIC classifications and serves as a liaison with the WHO, fulfilling international obligations for comparable classifications and the national health data needs of the United States. The historical background of ICD and ICD-10 can be found in the Introduction to the International Classification of Diseases and Related Health Problems (ICD-10), 2008, World Health Organization, Geneva, Switzerland.

ICD-10-CM is the United States' clinical modification of the World Health Organization's ICD-10. The term "clinical" is used to emphasize the modification's intent: to serve as a useful tool in the area of classification of morbidity data for indexing of health records, medical care review, and ambulatory and other health care programs, as well as for basic health statistics. To describe the clinical picture of the patient, the codes must be more precise than those needed only for statistical groupings and trend analysis.

Characteristics of ICD-10-CM
ICD-10-CM far exceeds its predecessors in the number of concepts and codes provided. The disease classification has been expanded to include health-related conditions and to provide greater specificity at the sixth and seventh character level. The sixth and seventh characters are not optional and are intended for use in recording the information documented in the clinical record.

ICD-10-CM extensions, interpretations, modifications, addenda, or errata other than those approved by the Centers for Disease Control and Prevention are not to be considered official and should not be utilized. Continuous maintenance of the ICD-10-CM is the responsibility of the aforementioned agencies. However, because the ICD-10-CM represents the best in contemporary thinking of clinicians, nosologists, epidemiologists, and statisticians from both public and private sectors, when future modifications are considered, advice will be sought from all stakeholders.

All official authorized addenda through October 1, 2013, have been included in this revision. The complete official authorized addenda to ICD-10-CM, including the "ICD-10-CM Official Guidelines for Coding and Reporting," can be accessed at the following website:
http://www.cdc.gov/nchs/icd/icd10cm.htm#10update
A description of the ICD-10-CM updating and maintenance process can be found at the following website:
http://www.cdc.gov/nchs/icd/icd9cm_maintenance.htm

Reference: http://www.cdc.gov/nchs/data/icd/2014_icd10cm_preface.pdf

ICD-10-CM and ICD-10-PCS

The compliance date for implementation of ICD-10-CM/PCS is October 1, 2014, for all Health Insurance Portability and Accountability Act (HIPAA)-covered entities.

ICD-10-CM, including the "ICD-10-CM Official Guidelines for Coding and Reporting," will replace ICD-9-CM Diagnosis Codes in all health care settings for diagnosis reporting with dates of service, or dates of discharge for inpatients, that occur on or after October 1, 2014.

ICD-10-PCS, including the "ICD-10-PCS Official Guidelines for Coding and Reporting," will replace ICD-9-CM Procedure Codes.

BENEFITS OF ICD-10-CM

ICD-10-CM incorporates much greater clinical detail and specificity than ICD-9-CM. Terminology and disease classification are updated to be consistent with current clinical practice. The modern classification system will provide much better data needed for:
- Measuring the quality, safety, and efficacy of care;
- Reducing the need for attachments to explain the patient's condition;
- Designing payment systems and processing claims for reimbursement;
- Conducting research, epidemiological studies, and clinical trials;
- Setting health policy;
- Operational and strategic planning;
- Designing health care delivery systems;
- Monitoring resource use;
- Improving clinical, financial, and administrative performance;
- Preventing and detecting health care fraud and abuse; and
- Tracking public health and risks.

Non-specific codes are still available for use when medical record documentation does not support a more specific code.

ICD-10-CM Diagnosis Codes:
There are 3–7 digits;
Digit 1 is alpha;
Digit 2 is numeric;
Digits 3–7 are alpha or numeric (alpha characters are not case sensitive); and a decimal is used after the third character.
Examples:
A78–Q   fever;
A69.21   Meningitis due to Lyme disease; and
S52.131A   Displaced fracture of neck of right radius, initial encounter for closed fracture.

NEW FEATURES IN ICD-10-CM

The following new features can be found in ICD-10-CM:

1) *Laterality (Left, Right, Bilateral)*
   Examples:
   > C50.511 – Malignant neoplasm of lower-outer quadrant of right female breast;
   > H16.013 – Central corneal ulcer, bilateral; and
   > L89.012 – Pressure ulcer of right elbow, stage II.

2) *Combination Codes for Certain Conditions and Common Associated Symptoms and Manifestations*
   Examples:
   > K57.21 – Diverticulitis of large intestine with perforation and abscess with bleeding;
   > E11.341 – Type 2 diabetes mellitus with severe nonproliferative diabetic retinopathy with macular edema; and
   > I25.110 – Atherosclerotic heart disease of native coronary artery with unstable angina pectoris.

3) *Combination Codes for Poisonings and Their Associated External Cause*
   Example:
   > T42.3x2S – Poisoning by barbiturates, intentional self-harm, sequela.

4) *Obstetric Codes Identify Trimester Instead of Episode of Care*
   Example:
   > O26.02 – Excessive weight gain in pregnancy, second trimester.

5) *Character "x" Is Used as a 5th Character Placeholder in Certain 6 Character Codes to Allow for Future Expansion and to Fill in Other Empty Characters (For Example, Character 5 and/or 6) When a Code that Is Less than 6 Characters in Length Requires a 7th Character*
   Examples:
   > T46.1x5A – Adverse effect of calcium-channel blockers, initial encounter; and
   > T15.02xD – Foreign body in cornea, left eye, subsequent encounter.

6) *Two Types of Excludes Notes*
   Excludes 1 Indicates that the code excluded should never be used with the code where the note is located (do not report both codes).
   Example:
   > Q03 – Congenital hydrocephalus.
   > Excludes 1: Acquired hydrocephalus (**G91.-**).

   Excludes 2 Indicates that the condition excluded is not part of the condition represented by the code, but a patient may have both conditions at the same time, in which case both codes may be assigned together (both codes can be reported to capture both conditions).
   Example:
   > L27.2 – Dermatitis due to ingested food.
   > Excludes 2: Dermatitis due to food in contact with skin (L23.6, L24.6, L25.4).

7) *Inclusion of Clinical Concepts that Do Not Exist in ICD-9-CM (For Example, Underdosing, Blood Type, Blood Alcohol Level)*

Examples:

T45.526D – Underdosing of antithrombotic drugs, subsequent encounter;

Z67.40 – Type O blood, Rh positive; and

Y90.6 – Blood alcohol level of 120 – 199 mg/100 ml.

8) *A Number of Codes Are Significantly Expanded (For Example, Injuries, Diabetes, Substance Abuse, Postoperative Complications)*

Examples:

E10.610 – Type 1 diabetes mellitus with diabetic neuropathic arthropathy;

F10.182 – Alcohol abuse with alcohol-induced sleep disorder; and

T82.02xA – Displacement of heart valve prosthesis, initial encounter.

9) *Codes for Postoperative Complications Are Expanded and a Distinction Is Made Between Intraoperative Complications and Postprocedural Disorders*

Examples:

D78.01 – Intraoperative hemorrhage and hematoma of spleen complicating a procedure on the spleen; and

D78.21 – Postprocedural hemorrhage and hematoma of spleen following a procedure on the spleen.

ADDITIONAL CHANGES IN ICD-10-CM

The additional changes that can be found in ICD-10-CM are as follows:

- Injuries are grouped by anatomical site rather than by type of injury;
- Category restructuring and code reorganization occur in a number of ICD-10-CM chapters, resulting in the classification of certain diseases and disorders that are different from ICD-9-CM;
- Certain diseases are reclassified to different chapters or sections to reflect current medical knowledge;
- New code definitions (for example, definition of acute myocardial infarction is now 4 weeks rather than 8 weeks); and
- The codes corresponding to ICD-9-CM V codes (Factors Influencing Health Status and Contact with Health Services) and E codes (External Causes of Injury and Poisoning) are incorporated into the main classification (in ICD-9-CM, they were separated into supplementary classifications).

USE OF EXTERNAL CAUSE AND UNSPECIFIED CODES IN ICD-10-CM

Similar to ICD-9-CM, there is no national requirement for mandatory ICD-10-CM external cause code reporting. Unless you are subject to a State-based external cause code reporting mandate or these codes are required by a particular payer, you are not required to report ICD-10-CM codes found in Chapter 20, External Causes of Morbidity.

If you have not been reporting ICD-9-CM external cause codes, you will not be required to report ICD-10-CM codes found in Chapter 20 unless a new State or payer-based requirement about the reporting of these codes is instituted. If such a requirement is instituted, it would be independent of ICD-10-CM implementation.

In the absence of a mandatory reporting requirement, you are encouraged to voluntarily report external cause codes, as they provide valuable data for injury research and evaluation of injury prevention strategies.

In both ICD-9-CM and ICD-10-CM, sign/symptom and unspecified codes have acceptable, even necessary, uses. While specific diagnosis codes should be reported when they are supported by the available medical record documentation and clinical knowledge of the patient's health condition, in some instances signs/symptoms or unspecified codes are the best choice to accurately reflect the health care encounter.

Each health care encounter should be coded to the level of certainty known for that encounter. If a definitive diagnosis has not been established by the end of the encounter, it is appropriate to report codes for sign(s) and/or symptom(s) in lieu of a definitive diagnosis. When sufficient clinical information is not known or available about a particular health condition to assign a more specific code, it is acceptable to report the appropriate unspecified code (for example, a diagnosis of pneumonia has been determined, but the specific type has not been determined). In fact, unspecified codes should be reported when they are the codes that most accurately reflect what is known about the patient's condition at the time of that particular encounter. It is inappropriate to select a specific code that is not supported by the medical record documentation or conduct medically unnecessary diagnostic testing to determine a more specific code. Reference: MLM Matters CMS Website

2014 release of ICD-10-CM

These files have been created by the National Center for Health Statistics (NCHS), under authorization by the World Health Organization.

These files linked below are the 2014 update of the ICD-10-CM. Content changes to the full ICD-10-CM files are described in the respective addenda files. This year, in addition to PDF (Adobe) files, the XML format is also being made available. Most files are provided in a compressed zip format for ease in downloading. These files have been created by the National Center for Health Statistics (NCHS), under authorization by the World Health Organization.

Although this release of ICD-10-CM is now available for public viewing, the codes in ICD-10-CM are not currently valid for any purpose or use. As noted earlier, the effective implementation date for ICD-10-CM (and ICD-10-PCS) is October 1, 2014. Updates to this version of ICD-10-CM are anticipated prior to its implementation.

- Preface [PDF - 35 KB]
- ICD-10-CM Guidelines [PDF - 512 KB]
- Detailed List of Codes Exempt from Diagnosis Present on Admission Requirement PDF Format
- Detailed List of Codes Exempt from Diagnosis Present on Admission Requirement XLSM Format
- ICD-10-CM PDF Format
- ICD-10-CM XML Format
- ICD-10-CM List of Codes and Descriptions (updated 7/3/2013)
- General Equivalence Mapping Files

To download these files, go to: http://www.cdc.gov/nchs/icd/icd10cm.htm#10update

Content source: CDC/National Center for Health Statistics
Page maintained by: Office of Information Services
http://www.cdc.gov/nchs/icd/icd10cm.htm

Development of the ICD-10 Procedure Coding System (ICD-10-PCS)

Richard F. Averill, M.S., Robert L. Mullin, M.D., Barbara A. Steinbeck, RHIT, Norbert I. Goldfield, M.D, Thelma M. Grant, RHIA, Rhonda R. Butler, CCS, CCS-P

The International Classification of Diseases 10th Revision Procedure Coding System (ICD-10-PCS) has been developed as a replacement for Volume 3 of the International Classification of Diseases 9th Revision (ICD-9-CM). The development of ICD-10-PCS was funded by the U.S. Centers for Medicare and Medicaid Services (CMS). ICD-10-PCS has a multiaxial, seven-character, alphanumeric code structure that provides a unique code for all substantially different procedures, and allows new procedures to be easily incorporated as new codes. ICD-10-PCS was under development for over five years. The initial draft was formally tested and evaluated by an independent contractor; the final version was released in the Spring of 1998, with annual updates since the final release. The design, development, and testing of ICD-10-PCS are discussed.

Introduction

Volume 3 of the International Classification of Diseases 9th Revision Clinical Modification (ICD-9-CM) has been used in the U.S. for the reporting of inpatient procedures since 1979. The structure of Volume 3 of ICD-9-CM has not allowed new procedures associated with rapidly changing technology to be effectively incorporated as new codes. As a result, in 1992 the U.S. Centers for Medicare and Medicaid Services (CMS) funded a project to design a replacement for Volume 3 of ICD-9-CM. After a review of the preliminary design, CMS in 1995 awarded 3M Health Information Systems a three-year contract to complete development of the replacement system. The new system is the ICD-10 Procedure Coding System (ICD-10-PCS).

Attributes Used in Development

The development of ICD-10-PCS had as its goal the incorporation of four major attributes:

• Completeness

There should be a unique code for all substantially different procedures. In Volume 3 of ICD-9-CM, procedures on different body parts, with different approaches, or of different types are sometimes assigned to the same code.

• Expandability

As new procedures are developed, the structure of ICD-10-PCS should allow them to be easily incorporated as unique codes.

• Multiaxial

ICD-10-PCS codes should consist of independent characters, with each individual axis retaining its meaning across broad ranges of codes to the extent possible.

• Standardized Terminology

ICD-10-PCS should include definitions of the terminology used. While the meaning of specific words varies in common usage, ICD-10-PCS should not include multiple meanings for the same term, and each term must be assigned a specific meaning.

If these four objectives are met, then ICD-10-PCS should enhance the ability of health information coders to construct accurate codes with minimal effort.

General Development Principles

In the development of ICD-10-PCS, several general principles were followed:

- *Diagnostic Information Is Not Included in Procedure Description*

When procedures are performed for specific diseases or disorders, the disease or disorder is not contained in the procedure code. There are no codes for procedures exclusive to aneurysms, cleft lip, strictures, neoplasms, hernias, etc. The diagnosis codes, not the procedure codes, specify the disease or disorder.

- *Not Otherwise Specified (NOS) Options Are Restricted*

ICD-9-CM often provides a "not otherwise specified" code option. Certain NOS options made available in ICD-10-PCS are restricted to the uses laid out in the ICD-10-PCS official guidelines. A minimal level of specificity is required for each component of the procedure.

- *Limited Use of Not Elsewhere Classified (NEC) Option*

ICD-9-CM often provides a "not elsewhere classified" code option.

Because all significant components of a procedure are specified in ICD-10-PCS, there is generally no need for an NEC code option. However, limited NEC options are incorporated into ICD-10-PCS where necessary. For example, new devices are frequently developed, and therefore it is necessary to provide an "Other Device" option for use until the new device can be explicitly added to the coding system. Additional NEC options are discussed later, in the sections of the system where they occur.

- *Level of Specificity*

All procedures currently performed can be specified in ICD-10-PCS. The frequency with which a procedure is performed was not a consideration in the development of the system. Rather, a unique code is available for variations of a procedure that can be performed.

ICD-10-PCS has a seven-character, alphanumeric code structure. Each character contains up to 34 possible values. Each value represents a specific option for the general character definition (e.g., stomach is one of the values for the body part character). The ten digits 0–9 and the 24 letters A–H, J–N, and P–Z may be used in each character. The letters O and I are not used in order to avoid confusion with the digits 0 and 1.

Procedures are divided into sections that identify the general type of procedure (e.g., medical and surgical, obstetrics, imaging). The first character of the procedure code always specifies the section. The sections are shown in Table 1.

Table 1: ICD-10-PCS Sections

0	Medical and Surgical
1	Obstetrics
2	Placement
3	Administration
4	Measurement and Monitoring
5	Extracorporeal Assistance and Performance
6	Extracorporeal Therapies
7	Osteopathic
8	Other Procedures
9	Chiropractic
B	Imaging
C	Nuclear Medicine
D	Radiation Oncology
F	Physical Rehabilitation and Diagnostic Audiology
G	Mental Health
H	Substance Abuse Treatment

The second through seventh characters mean the same thing within each section, but may mean different things in other sections. In all sections, the third character specifies the general type of procedure performed (e.g., resection, transfusion, fluoroscopy), while the other characters give additional information such as the body part and approach. In ICD-10-PCS, the term "procedure" refers to the complete specification of the seven characters.

ICD-10-PCS 2014 Version
Update Summary / **Change Summary Table**

2013 Total	New Codes	Revised Titles	Deleted Codes	2014 Total
71,920	7	0	3	**71,924**

ICD-10-PCS Code 2013 Totals, by Section

Medical and Surgical	**61,898**
Obstetrics	300
Placement	861
Administration	**1,388**
Measurement and Monitoring	339
Extracorporeal Assistance and Performance	41
Extracorporeal Therapies	42
Osteopathic	100
Other Procedures	60
Chiropractic	90
Imaging	2,934
Nuclear Medicine	463
Radiation Oncology	1,939
Rehabilitation and Diagnostic Audiology	1,380
Mental Health	30
Substance Abuse Treatment	59
Total	**71,924**

ICD-10-PCS Code Changes

Four codes added under new technology application, valid October 1, 2013

- **08H005Z** Insertion of Epiretinal Visual Prosthesis into Right Eye, Open Approach
- **08H105Z** Insertion of Epiretinal Visual Prosthesis into Left Eye, Open Approach
- **30280B1** Transfusion of Nonautologous 4-Factor Prothrombin Complex Concentrate into Vein, Open Approach
- **30283B1** Transfusion of Nonautologous 4-Factor Prothrombin Complex Concentrate into Vein, Percutaneous Approach

Three new codes added and three codes deleted, to correct body part value for temporary occlusion of abdominal aorta

- New: **04V00DJ** Restriction of Abdominal Aorta with Intraluminal Device, Temporary, Open Approach
- New: **04V03DJ** Restriction of Abdominal Aorta with Intraluminal Device, Temporary, Percutaneous Approach
- New: **04V04DJ** Restriction of Abdominal Aorta with Intraluminal Device, Temporary, Percutaneous Endoscopic Approach
- Deleted: **02VW0DJ** Restriction of Thoracic Aorta with Intraluminal Device, Temporary, Open Approach
- Deleted: **02VW3DJ** Restriction of Thoracic Aorta with Intraluminal Device, Temporary, Percutaneous Approach
- Deleted: **02VW4DJ** Restriction of Thoracic Aorta with Intraluminal Device, Temporary, Percutaneous Endoscopic Approach

Revised Section Title

Title for Radiation Oncology section revised to Radiation Therapy in response to public comment. Because the phrase "Radiation Oncology" is not used in code titles, no code titles were revised as a result of the section title change.

New Index Addenda

- New file showing new, revised, and deleted index entries in response to public comment
- First discussed at September 2012 Coordination and Maintenance Committee, proposed format shown at March 2013 Coordination and Maintenance Committee
- See list of updated files for details

New Definitions Addenda

- New file showing new, revised, and deleted PCS definitions entries (e.g., Body Part Key) in response to public comment
- First discussed at September 2012 Coordination and Maintenance Committee, proposed format shown at March 2013 Coordination and Maintenance Committee
- See list of updated files for details

List of Updated Files
2014 Official ICD-10-PCS Coding Guidelines
- Downloadable PDF file
- Revised in response to public comment and review by the cooperating parties

2014 ICD-10-PCS Code Tables and Index (Zip file)
- Downloadable PDF file, file name is **PCS_2014.pdf**
- Downloadable xml files for developers, file names are:
  icd10pcs_tabular_2014.xml
  icd10pcs_index_2014.xml
  icd10pcs_definitions_2014.xml
- Accompanying schema for developers, file names are:
  icd10pcs_tabular_2014.xsd
  icd10pcs_index_2014.xsd
  icd10pcs_definitions_2014.xsd

2014 ICD-10-PCS Code Titles, Long and Abbreviated (Zip file)
- Tabular order file defines an unambiguous order for all ICD-10-CM/PCS codes
- Text file format, file name is:
  icd10pcs_order_2014.txt
  Provides a unique five-digit "order number" for each ICD-10-PCS table and code
- Accompanying documentation, file name is:
  ICD10OrderFiles.pdf

2014 ICD-10-PCS Final Addenda (Zip file)
- New code titles for FY2014 shown as ICD-10-PCS table entries. File name is:
  PcsAddendaAdditionsNewLabels.pdf
- Deleted code titles for FY2014 shown as ICD-10-PCS table entries. File name is:
  PcsAddendaDeletionsOldLabels.pdf
- Downloadable xml format for developers. File names are:
  PcsAddendaAdditionsNewLabels.xml, PcsAddendaDeletionsOldLabels.xml
- Accompanying documentation. File name is:
  pcs_addenda_readme2014.pdf
- Index addenda in downloadable PDF. File name is:
  index_addenda_2014.pdf
- PCS Definitions addenda in downloadable PDF. File name is:
  definitions_addenda_2014.pdf
- Index and Definitions addenda in machine-readable text format for developers. File names are:
  index_addenda_2014.txt, definitions_addenda_2014.txt

2014 ICD-10-PCS Reference Manual (Zip file)
- Downloadable PDF file. File name is:
  ICD-10-PCS Reference Manual.pdf
  Revised in response to public comment and internal review
- Addenda to 2014 version of reference manual specifies the changes. File name is:
  pcs_ref_addenda_2014.pdf

2014 ICD-10-PCS and ICD-9-CM General Equivalence Mappings (Zip file)
- Downloadable text format. File names are:
  gem_i9pcs.txt, gem_pcsi9.txt
  Contain entries for the new FY2014 ICD-9-CM and ICD-10-PCS codes and entries revised in response to public comment and internal review
- Documentation for general users and technical users. File name is:
  pcs_gemguide_2014.pdf
- Documentation for technical users. File name is:
  GemsTechDoc.pdf

2014 ICD-10 Reimbursement Mappings (Zip file)
- Downloadable text format. File names are:
  reimb_map_dx_2014.txt
  reimb_map_pr_2014.txt
  FY2014 version uses the FY2014 GEM files.
- Accompanying documentation includes rules used in the mapping. File name is:
  reimb_map_guide_2014.pdf

HEALTH RECORD CODING REVIEW
CODING PROCESS

Fine-tune your coding skills by seeking complete documentation and selecting the most detailed codes.

1. Assess the case by performing a quick review of the record's demographic information and the first few lines of the History and Physical.

2. Get an overview of key reports because they contain valuable detailed information.
   A. The discharge summary sums up the patient's hospital course and confirms conditions or complications. In ambulatory records, look at the final progress note and/or discharge instructions.
   B. Review the physician orders for treatment protocols. The orders may indicate chronic or acute conditions for which the patient is receiving treatment.
   C. Review the history and physical to complete the clinical picture. Social and family history, as well as past and present illnesses, may have clinical implications.
   D. Read the progress notes to track the course of hospitalization or outpatient treatment. These provide information concerning daily status, reactions, or postoperative complications.
   E. Study the operative reports. Additional procedures may be identified in the body of the operative report.

3. Check all data from clinical reports.
   A. Laboratory reports may show evidence of conditions such as anemia, renal failure, infections, and metabolic imbalances.
   B. Radiology reports may confirm diagnosis of pneumonia, COPD, CHF, degenerative joint diseases, and traumatic injuries.
   C. Medication Administration Reports (MARs) indicate all drugs that were administered to the patient. Look for documentation of diagnoses elsewhere in the medical record to correlate with each drug. If uncertain why a medication was administered, query the physician.
   D. Respiratory therapy notes document the use of mechanical ventilation and describe severity of respiratory disorders.
   E. Physical therapy reports detail useful information for coding musculoskeletal dysfunctions.
   F. Dietary reports describe nutritional deficiencies (e.g., malnutrition).
   G. Speech pathology reports give information on dysphasia, aphasia, and other speech-related conditions.
   H. Pathology reports are essential for accurate coding of conditions where excised tissue has been submitted for interpretation.

4. Perform a coding evaluation.
   A. Establish the principal diagnosis and formulate secondary diagnoses codes.
   B. Exclude all conditions not relevant to the case. Abnormal lab and X-ray findings and previous conditions having no effect on current management of the patient are not coded.

5. Take time to review and refine your coding.
   A. Review all diagnoses and procedures to confirm the selections of appropriate principal and secondary diagnoses and all procedure codes.
   B. For inpatient records, determine if each diagnosis was present on admission (POA) to adequately identify the POA indicator.
   C. Refine code assignments, where necessary, to make changes to more accurately classify the diagnoses and procedure codes selected.

Sample 10-Step Inpatient ICD-10-CM Coding Process
1. **Locate Patient's Gender, Age, and Discharge Date.**

2. **Locate Discharge Status (Disposition). Some examples include:**
    01: Home
    02: Short-term hospital
    03: Skilled nursing facility
    04: Facility providing custodial or supportive care
    05: Cancer or child hospital
    06: Home health services
    07: Against medical advice
    20: Expired
    30: Still a patient
    61: Swing bed
    62: Inpatient rehab facility or distinct rehab unit
    63: Long-term care hospital
    65: Psychiatric hospital or distinct psych unit
    66: Critical access hospital

3. **List consultants** as you go through the consults. **Write down pertinent diagnoses** (histories and present illnesses).
4. **Locate and list all procedures.** Review description of each procedure performed.
5. **Go through the physician orders and medication administration orders.** This is where you will find drugs ordered and administered. Make sure that you look for the diagnosis that corresponds with each medication. If not, query the physician.
6. **Read the H&P, ER record, and progress notes.** **Write down all diagnoses that meet criteria for principal and secondary diagnosis:** If a diagnosis is ruled out, just cross it off the list.
7. **Select the Principal Diagnosis.** UHDDS Definition: The condition established *after study* to be chiefly responsible for occasioning the admission of the patient to the hospital for care.

Sample 10-Step Inpatient ICD-10-CM Coding Process (continued)

8.	**Select Other Diagnoses and indicate whether each was present on admission (POA) or not.** UHDDS Definition: All conditions that coexist at the time of admission, develop subsequently, or affect the treatment received and/or the length of stay. Diagnoses that relate to an earlier episode of care that have no bearing on the current hospital stay are to be excluded. **Complication** UHDDS Definition: A condition arising during hospitalization, which increases the patient's length of stay by 1 day in 75% of cases. **Comorbidity** UHDDS Definition: Condition present at admission, in addition to the principal diagnosis, which increases the patient's length of stay by 1 day in 75% of cases. For reporting purposes, the definition of "other diagnoses" is interpreted as additional conditions that affect patient care in terms of requiring: • clinical evaluation • therapeutic treatment • diagnostic procedures • extended length of hospital stay • increased nursing care and/or monitoring
9.	**Principal Procedure.** UHDDS Definition: One performed for definitive treatment (rather than performed for diagnostic or exploratory purposes) or one that was necessary to care for a complication. If two or more procedures appear to meet the definition, then the one most closely related to the principal diagnosis should be selected as the principal procedure.
10.	**Other Procedures** UHDDS Definition for significant procedures: One that meets any of the following conditions: is surgical in nature, carries an anesthetic risk, carries a procedural risk, or requires specialized training.

Some Additional Tips for Coding

1. When a patient is admitted with or develops a condition during his or her stay, look to see if there is documentation to differentiate if the complication is acute, chronic, or both acute and chronic.

2. When a patient presents with or develops infectious conditions, seek documentation of any positive cultures (urine, wound, sputum, blood) pertaining to that condition. If the positive cultures are available for that condition (e.g., sepsis due to Pseudomonas), it will help in being more specific in coding the diagnoses and may increase reimbursement in some cases. For example, in a case of pneumonia due to Pseudomonas, the MS-DRG may increase considerably. According to coding guidelines, if the culture is not documented, even though present in laboratory reports, the condition is to be coded as unspecified, which can affect reimbursement. Examples: sepsis, cellulitis, UTI, pneumonia, etc.

3. If a condition is due to surgery, ask the physician to verify and document that it is due to the procedure. If the patient has been discharged, and you are not sure but believe it was due to the procedure, seek verification that it is possibly due to the procedure by querying the physician.

4. If the patient had outpatient surgery for removal of a lesion, look for documentation of the size of the lesion that may have been removed. It should be documented in the operative report.
   The American Medical Association's publication, *CPT Assistant* (issues from Fall 1995 and August 2000) states, "Since the physician can make an accurate measurement of the lesion(s) at the time of the excision, the size of the lesion should be documented in the OP (operative) report. A pathology report is likely to contain a less accurate measurement due to the shrinking of the specimen or the fact that the specimen may be fragmented."

   Reimbursement is based on the diameter of the lesion(s). Even 1 millimeter (mm) off in the diameter calculation can mean fewer dollars for the hospital and the physician. The documentation in the record ensures appropriate reimbursement.

5. Look for documentation in the final diagnoses in the discharge summary for clarification or to differentiate whether specific conditions are currently present, or if the patient only has a history of the condition.

   Examples: 1. Acute CVA versus history of CVA
   2. Current drug or alcohol abuse versus history of drug or alcohol abuse
   3. Current neoplasm being treated versus history of malignancy

6. Verify if a condition is a manifestation of an existing condition.
   Example: CRF secondary to DM or CRF due to HTN

7. Look for documentation of conditions that are secondary to previous conditions.
   Examples: 1. Quadriplegia due to fall
   2. Dysphagia due to previous CVA

ICD-10-CM Outpatient/Ambulatory Coding Guidelines

Note: This is a brief overview. ICD-10-CM codes are used for diagnoses. CPT codes are used for procedures for billing purposes.

1. Documentation should include specific diagnoses as well as symptoms, problems, and reasons for visits.

2. First-listed diagnosis is listed first with other codes following.

3. Chronic diseases may be coded as long as the patient receives treatment.

4. Code all documented conditions that coexist at the time of the visit and are treated or affect treatment. History codes may be used if they impact treatment.

5. Diagnosis coding for Diagnostic Services: Code the diagnosis chiefly responsible for the service. Secondary codes may follow.

   Instructions to Determine the Reason for the Test: The referring physicians are required to provide diagnostic information to the testing entity at the time the test is ordered. All diagnostic tests "must be ordered by the physician who is treating the beneficiary." An order by the physician may include the following forms of communication:
   1. A written document signed by the treating physician/practitioner, which is hand delivered, mailed, or faxed to the testing facility.
   2. A telephone call by the treating physician/practitioner or his or her office to the testing facility.
   3. An electronic mail by the treating physician or practitioner or his or her office to the testing facility.
   Note: Telephone orders must be documented by both the treating physician or practitioner office and the testing facility.
   If the interpreting physician does not have diagnostic information as to the reason for the test, and the referring physician is unavailable, it is appropriate to obtain the information directly from the patient or patient's medical record. Attempt to confirm any information obtained from the patient by contacting the referring physician.

6. Diagnosis coding for Therapeutic Services: Code the diagnosis chiefly responsible for the service. Secondary codes may follow.

7. Diagnosis coding for Ambulatory Surgery: Code the diagnosis for which surgery was done. Use the postoperative diagnosis if it is available and more specific.

Commonly Missed Complications and Comorbidities (CCs)

Depending on the patient's principal diagnosis, this list of commonly missed complications and comorbidities (CCs) and major complications and comorbidities (MCCs) may or may not help the MS-DRG when documented and coded. If any of these conditions are being managed while the patient is being hospitalized, it may change the MS-DRG to a higher paying one. Some MS-DRGs will not change even if these are present. The MS-DRG may or may not change if the patient has a major procedure performed. Some of these conditions may be considered CCs, while others may be considered Major CCs.

Acidosis
Alcoholism acute/chronic
Alkalosis
Anemia due to blood loss, acute/chronic (e.g., from GI bleed, or surgery)
Angina pectoris (stable or unstable angina)
Atrial fibrillation/flutter
Atelectasis
Cachexia
Cardiogenic shock
Cardiomyopathy
Cellulitis
CHF
Combination of both acidosis/alkalosis
COPD
Decubitus ulcer
Dehydration (volume depletion)
Diabetes: If DM is uncontrolled (type 1 or 2)
Electrolyte imbalance
Hematuria
Hematemesis
Hypertension (HTN) accelerated or malignant HTN only qualifies (not uncontrolled, hypertensive urgency or hypertensive crisis)
Hypertensive heart disease with CHF
Hyponatremia ($\downarrow$ Na)
Hypernatremia ($\uparrow$ Na)
Hypochloremia ($\downarrow$ Cl)
Hyperchloremia ($\uparrow$ Cl)
Hyperpotassemia ($\uparrow$ K)
Malnutrition
Melena
Pleural effusion (especially if it has to be treated by a procedure, e.g., thoracentesis)
Pneumonia
Pneumothorax
Postoperative complications
Renal failure, acute or chronic (not renal insufficiency)
Respiratory failure
Septicemia
Urinary retention
UTI (e.g., urosepsis): If urosepsis is documented, it will be coded as a UTI unless otherwise specified.

Note: This is not an all-inclusive listing of possible complications and comorbidities.

SOME AREAS OF SPECIAL INTEREST

Adhesions

- When minor adhesions are present, but do not cause symptoms or increase the difficulty of an operative procedure, coding a diagnosis of adhesions and a lysis procedure is inappropriate.
- When adhesions are dense or strong or create problems during a surgical procedure, it is appropriate to code both the diagnosis of adhesions and the operative procedure to lyse the adhesions.

Anemia

- The coder must distinguish between chronic blood loss anemia and acute blood loss anemia because the two conditions are assigned to different category codes.
- Acute blood loss anemia occurring after surgery may or may not be a complication of surgery.
  The physician must clearly identify postoperative anemia as a complication of the surgery in order to use the complication code.
- Depending on the primary reason for admission, anemia of chronic disease can be used as the principal diagnosis (if the reason for admit is to treat the anemia) or as the secondary diagnosis.
- When assigning code D63.1(anemia in chronic kidney disease), also assign a code from category N18.3 (chronic kidney disease) to identify the stage of chronic kidney disease.

Asthma

- Acute exacerbation of asthma is increased severity of asthma symptoms, such as wheezing and shortness of breath.
- Terms suggesting status asthmaticus include intractable asthma, refractory asthma, severe intractable wheezing, and airway obstruction not relieved by medication. It is a life-threatening complication that requires emergency care.
- The coder must not assume status asthmaticus is present. The physician must document the condition in order to code it.

Body Mass Index (BMI)

- The code(s) for body mass index should only be reported as secondary diagnoses and must meet the definition of a reportable additional diagnosis.
- Documentation from clinicians (such as dieticians) may be used for code assignment as long as the physician has documented the diagnosis of obesity.
- If there is conflicting documentation, query the attending physician.

Burns

- When coding multiple burns, assign separate codes for each site and sequence the burn with the highest degree first.
- When coding burns of the same site with varying degrees, code only the highest degree.
- Necrosis of burned skin is coded as a nonhealing burn. Nonhealing burns are coded as acute burns.

Cellulitis

- Coders must not assume that documentation of redness at the edges of a wound represents cellulitis. Rely on physician documentation of cellulitis.
- Coding of cellulitis with an injury or burn requires one code for the injury and one for the cellulitis. Sequencing will depend on the circumstances of admission.
- When the patient is seen primarily for treating the original injury, sequence that code first. When the patient is seen primarily for treatment of the cellulitis, the code for cellulitis is the principal diagnosis.

Complications

- When coding complications of surgical and medical care, if the code fully describes the condition, no additional code is necessary. If it does not fully describe the condition, an additional code should be assigned. Codes for medical and surgical care are found within the body system chapters.

Congenital Anomalies

- Congenital anomaly codes have been assigned to categories Q00–Q99 and may be used for a principal or secondary diagnosis.
- When there is a code that identifies the congenital anomaly, do not assign additional codes for the inherent manifestations. Do assign additional codes for manifestations that are not an inherent component.
- For the birth admission, category Z38 is still the principal diagnosis followed by any congenital anomaly code (Q00–Q99).
- Codes from Chapter 17, Congenital Anomalies, can be reported for patients of any age. Many congenital anomalies do not manifest any symptoms until much later in life.

Diabetes Mellitus

- When the type of diabetes mellitus is not documented, code it as type 2.
- Diabetes with a manifestation or complication requires documentation of a causal relationship to be coded. Assign as many codes from the diabetes category as needed to identify all associated conditions.
- Even if the patient is using insulin, it does not necessarily mean that the patient is type 1.
- Most patients with type 1 diabetes develop the condition before reaching puberty. That is why type 1 diabetes mellitus is also referred to as juvenile diabetes.
- For type 2 patients who routinely use insulin, code (long-term, current use of insulin) should also be assigned. Do not use this code if the patient receives insulin to temporarily bring a type 2 patient's blood sugar under control.
- An underdose of insulin due to an insulin pump failure should be assigned T85.6- (mechanical complications due to insulin pump) as the principal diagnosis code, followed by a code from categories E08-E13.
- When the patient has an insulin pump malfunction resulting in an overdose of insulin, assign a code from the T85.6- category as the principal diagnosis code with an additional code of T38.3- (poisoning by insulin and antidiabetic agents). Also code the appropriate diabetes mellitus code from E08–E13.
- Use codes from category E08.9- (secondary diabetes mellitus) to identify diabetes caused by another condition or event. Category code E08.9- is listed first followed by the code for the associated condition.

  The patient may be admitted for treatment of the secondary diabetes or one of its associated conditions OR for treatment of the condition causing the secondary diabetes. Code the primary reason for the encounter as the principal diagnosis, which will be a code from category E08.9 followed by the code for the associated condition or a code for the cause of the secondary diabetes.

- Assign code E89.1 for post-pancreatectomy diabetes mellitus. Assign a category code from E08.9 for secondary diabetes mellitus. Also assign Z90.410 for acquired absence of the pancreas. Also code any diabetes manifestations.

Dysplasia of the Vulva and Cervix

- A diagnosis of cervical intraepithelial neoplasia (CIN) III or vulvar intraepithelial neoplasia
  (VIN) III is classified as carcinoma in situ of the site.
- A diagnosis of CIN III or VIN III is made only on the basis of pathological evaluation of tissue.

Elevated Blood Pressure vs. Hypertension

- A diagnosis of high or elevated blood pressure without a firm diagnosis of hypertension is reported using code R03.0.
- This code is never assigned on the basis of a review of blood pressure readings; the physician must document elevated blood pressure/hypertension.

Fracture

- Traumatic fractures are coded as long as the patient is receiving active treatment.
- Subsequent care of traumatic fractures are coded to the acute fracture code with the appropriate 7th character. Aftercare Z codes should not be reported for aftercare of traumatic fractures.
- An open fracture is one in which there is communication with the bone. The following terms indicate open fracture: compound, infected, missile, puncture, and with foreign body.
- A closed fracture does not produce an open wound. Some types of closed fractures are impacted, comminuted, depressed, elevated, greenstick, spiral, and simple.
- When a fracture is not identified as open or closed, the code for a closed fracture is used.
- Internal fixation devices include screws, pins, rods, staples, and plates.
- External fixation devices include casts, splints, and traction device (Kirschner wire) (Steinman pin).

Gastrointestinal Hemorrhage

- Patients may be admitted for an endoscopy after a history of GI bleeding. It is acceptable to use a code for GI hemorrhage even if there is no hemorrhage noted on the current encounter.

Hematuria

- Blood in the urine discovered on a urinalysis is not coded as hematuria but as R82.3, Hemoglobinuria.
- Hematuria following a urinary procedure is not considered a postoperative complication.

Human Immunodeficiency Virus (HIV)

- Documentation of HIV infection as "suspected," "possible," "likely," or "questionable": physician must be queried for clarification. Code only confirmed cases of HIV infection. Confirmation does not require documentation of positive test results for HIV. A physician's documentation is sufficient.
- B20: Patients with symptomatic HIV disease or AIDS. If HIV test results are positive and the patient has symptoms. Patients with known diagnosis of HIV-related illness should be coded to B20 on every subsequent admission.
- Z21: Patients with physician-documented asymptomatic HIV infection who have never had an HIV-related illness. If HIV results are positive and the patient is without symptoms. Do not use this code if the term "AIDS" is used or if the patient is being treated for HIV-related conditions. In these cases, use code B20.

- Patients previously diagnosed with HIV-related illness (B20) should never be assigned Z21 Z11.4: Patient seen to determine his or her HIV status (screening).
- Patients admitted with an HIV-related condition are assigned code B20 as the principal diagnosis followed by additional diagnosis codes for all reported HIV-related conditions.
- Patients admitted for a condition unrelated to the HIV (such as traumatic injury) are assigned the code for the unrelated condition as the principal diagnosis, then code B20.
- When an obstetric patient has the HIV infection, a code from subcategory O98.7 is sequenced first with either code B20 (symptomatic) or V08 (asymptomatic) used as an additional code.

Hypertension

- Hypertensive heart disease I11. Physician must document causal relationship between hypertension and heart disease that is stated as "due to hypertension" or implied by documenting "hypertensive." Use an additional code from category I50 to identify the type of heart failure, if present. If the heart disease is stated as occurring "with hypertension," do not assume a cause-and-effect relationship and code it separately.
- Hypertensive chronic kidney disease I12-. ICD-10-CM assumes a causal relationship between hypertension and chronic kidney disease. There is no causal relationship with acute renal failure. Use an additional code from category N18 to identify the stage of CKD.
- Hypertensive heart and chronic kidney disease I13.0-. Physician must document causal relationship with the heart disease, but you may assume a causal relationship with chronic kidney disease. Assign an additional code for category I50 to identify the type of heart failure, if present. More than one code for category I50 may be assigned if the patient has systolic or diastolic failure and congestive heart failure. Use an additional code from category N18 to identify the stage of CKD.

Injuries

- Superficial injuries (e.g., abrasions, contusions) are not coded when there are more severe injuries of the same site.

Mechanical Ventilation

- Codes for intubation or tracheostomy should also be assigned.
- It is possible for a patient to be placed back on mechanical ventilation, thus necessitating two codes for mechanical ventilation on the same admission.

Methicillin-Resistant Staphylococcus Aureus (MRSA)

- To code a current infection due to MRSA when that infection does not have a combination code that includes MRSA, code the infection first, and then add code A49.02; B95.62 (MRSA).
- Use code Z22.321 for MSSA (Methicillin-Susceptible *Staphylococcus aureus*) colonization.
- Use code Z22.322 for MRSA (Methicillin-Resistant *Staphylococcus aureus*) colonization.
- Use code Z22.31; Z22.39 for other types of *Staphylococcus* colonization.

Myocardial Infarction (MI)

- An MI that is documented as acute or with a duration of 4 weeks or less is coded to category I21, Acute MI.
- When a patient has a subsequent infarction at the time of the encounter for the original infarction, both the initial and the subsequent AMI should be reported with codes from categories I21.- and I22.-
- Subcategory codes I21.0–I21.2 are used for "ST elevation MI" (STEMI).

- Subcategory I21.4 is used for "non-ST elevation MI" (NSTEMI) and nontransmural MI.
- If only STEMI or transmural MI without the documentation of the site, query the physician.
- If an AMI is documented as transmural or subendocardial, but the site is provided, it is still coded as subendocardial AMI.
- If STEMI converts to an NSTEMI due to thrombolytic therapy, it is still coded as STEMI.

Neoplasms

- Neoplasms are listed in the Alphabetic Index in two ways:
  - The Table of Neoplasms provides code numbers for neoplasms by anatomic site. For each
    site, there are six possible code numbers according to whether the behavior of the
    neoplasm is malignant primary, malignant secondary, malignant in situ, benign, of uncertain behavior, or of unspecified nature.
  - Histological terms for neoplasms (e.g., adenoma, adenocarcinoma, and sarcoma) are listed as main terms in the appropriate alphabetic sequence and are usually followed by a cross reference to the neoplasm table.
- In sequencing neoplasms, when the treatment is directed toward the malignancy, then the malignancy of that site is designated as the principal diagnosis, unless the patient is admitted for one of the reasons listed next.
- When the patient has a primary neoplasm with metastasis and the treatment is directed toward the secondary site only, the secondary site is sequenced as the principal diagnosis.
- When a patient is admitted solely for chemotherapy, immunotherapy, or radiation therapy, a code from category V58 (V58.11, V58.12, or V58.0) is assigned as the principal diagnosis with the malignant neoplasm coded as an additional diagnosis.
- Codes from category Z85.00–Z85.89 are used when the primary neoplasm is totally eradicated and the patient is no longer having treatment and there is no evidence of any existing primary malignancy. Codes from category Z85 can only be listed as an additional code, not as a principal diagnosis. If extension, invasion, or metastasis is mentioned, code secondary malignant neoplasm to that site as the principal diagnosis.
- When a patient is admitted for pain management associated with the malignancy, code G89.3 as the principal diagnosis followed by the appropriate code for the malignancy. When a patient is admitted for management of the malignancy, code the malignancy as the principal diagnosis with code G89.3 as an additional code.
- When a patient is admitted for management of an anemia associated with the malignancy, and the treatment is only for anemia, code the anemia code D63.0 as the principal diagnosis followed by the appropriate code for the malignancy. Code D63.0 can be used as a secondary code if the patient has anemia and is being treated for the malignancy.
- When a patient is admitted for management of dehydration associated with the malignancy or the therapy, or both, and only the dehydration is being treated (intravenous rehydration), the dehydration is sequenced first, followed by the code(s) for the malignancy.
- If the patient is admitted for surgical removal of a neoplasm followed by chemotherapy or radiation therapy, code the neoplasm (primary or secondary) as the principal diagnosis.
- If the patient has anemia associated with chemotherapy, immunotherapy, or radiotherapy and the only treatment is for the anemia, code anemia due to antineoplastic chemotherapy, and then code the neoplasm as an additional code.
- If the patient is admitted for chemotherapy, immunotherapy, or radiation therapy and then complications occur (such as uncontrolled nausea and vomiting or dehydration); assign the appropriate code for chemotherapy, immunotherapy, or radiation therapy as the principal diagnosis followed by any codes for the complications.

- If the primary reason for admission is to determine the context of the malignancy or for a procedure, even though chemotherapy or radiotherapy is administered, code the malignancy (primary and secondary site) as the principal diagnosis.
- When a malignant neoplasm is associated with a transplanted organ, assign a code from category T86 (complications of transplanted organ), followed by code C80.2 (malignant neoplasm associated with transplanted organ) followed by a code for the specific malignancy.

Newborn

- Newborn (perinatal) codes P00–P96 are never used on the maternal record.
- The perinatal period is defined as before birth through the 28th day following birth.
- A code from category Z38.0 is assigned as the principal diagnosis for any live birth.
- Other diagnoses may be coded for significant conditions noted after birth as secondary diagnoses.
- Insignificant or transient conditions that resolve without treatment are not coded.
- Assign codes from subcategories P00–P04 for evaluation of newborns and infants for suspected condition not found, is used when a healthy baby is evaluated for a suspected condition that proves to not exist. These codes are used when the baby exhibits no signs or symptoms.

Obstetrics

- Chapter 15 codes take sequencing precedence over other chapter codes, which may be assigned to provide further specificity as needed.
- The postpartum period begins immediately after delivery and continues for 6 weeks after delivery.
- The peripartum period is defined as the last month of pregnancy to 5 months.
- Codes from Chapter 15 can continue to be used after the 6-week period if the doctor documents that it is pregnancy related.
- When the mother delivers outside the hospital prior to admission and no complications are documented, code Z39.0 (postpartum care and examination immediately after delivery) as the principal diagnosis. If there are complications, the complications would be coded instead. Do not code a delivery diagnosis code because she delivered prior to admission.
- Principal diagnosis is determined by the circumstances of the encounter or admission.
- Complications: Any condition that occurs during pregnancy, childbirth, or the puerperium is considered to be a complication unless the physician specifically documents otherwise.
- A code from category Z37 is assigned as an additional code to indicate the outcome of delivery on the maternal chart. Z38 codes are not to be used on subsequent records or on the newborn record.
- Code O80, normal delivery, is used only when a delivery is perfectly normal and results in a single live birth. No abnormalities of labor or delivery or postpartum conditions can be present; therefore, there can be no additional code from Chapter 16. Z38.0-, single liveborn, is the only outcome of delivery code appropriate for use with O80.
- Z-codes from category Z34 are used when no obstetric complications are present and should not be used with any codes from Chapter 16.
- When the fetal condition is responsible for modifying the management of the mother (requires diagnostic studies or additional observation, special care, or termination of pregnancy), use codes from categories O35 and O36. The mere fact that the condition exists does not justify assigning a code from categories O35 and O36.

- When in utero surgery is performed on the fetus, assign codes from category O35. No code from Chapter 16 (the perinatal codes) should be used on the mother's record to identify fetal conditions.
- Patients with an HIV-related illness during pregnancy, childbirth, or the puerperium should have codes O98.7- and B20.
- Patients with asymptomatic HIV infection status during pregnancy, childbirth, or the puerperium should have codes O98.7- and V08.
- Patients with diabetes during pregnancy, childbirth, or puerperium should have codes O24 and categories E08-E13. Also code Z79.4 (long-term, current use of insulin), if the diabetes is being treated with insulin.

Pain

- Use a code from category G89 in addition to other codes to provide more detail about whether the pain is acute, chronic, or neoplasm-related.
- If pain is not specified as acute or chronic, do not assign a code from category G89 except for postthoracotomy pain, postoperative pain, neoplasm-related pain, or central pain syndrome.
- A code from subcategories G89.1 and G89.2 should not be used if the underlying diagnosis is known unless the primary reason for admission is pain control.
- A code from category G89 can be the principal or first-listed diagnosis code when pain control or management is the reason for the admission or encounter. Code the underlying cause of the pain as an additional diagnosis.
- When a patient is admitted for a procedure for purposes of treating the underlying condition (e.g., spinal fusion), code the underlying condition (e.g., spinal stenosis) as the principal diagnosis. Do not code the pain from category G89.
- When a patient is admitted for the insertion of a neurostimulator for pain control, assign the code for pain as the principal diagnosis.
- If the patient is admitted primarily for a procedure to treat the underlying condition and a neurostimulator is inserted for pain, code the underlying condition as the principal diagnosis, followed by a code for the pain.
- If a code describes the site of the pain, but does not indicate whether the type of pain is acute or chronic (category G89), use two codes (one for the site and one for the type). If the admission is for pain control, assign category code G89 (acute or chronic) as the principal diagnosis. If the admission is not for pain control and a related definitive diagnosis is not documented, assign the code for the specific site of the pain as the principal diagnosis.
- Routine or expected postoperative pain immediately after surgery should not be coded.
- Postoperative pain not associated with a specific postoperative complication is coded using the appropriate code in category G89.
- Postoperative pain can be listed as the principal diagnosis when the reason for admission is pain control.

Pleural Effusion

- Pleural effusion is almost always integral to the underlying condition and therefore is usually not coded.
- When the effusion is addressed and treated separately, it can be coded.
- Pleural effusion noted only on an X-ray is not coded.

Pneumonia

- There are many combination codes that describe the pneumonia and the infecting organism.
- In some situations, the pneumonia is a manifestation of an underlying condition. In this situation, two codes are needed—one for the underlying condition and the other for the pneumonia.
- Lobar pneumonia does not refer to the lobe of the lung that is affected. It is a particular type of pneumonia.
- Gram-negative pneumonias are much more difficult to treat than gram-positive pneumonias. If the findings suggest a gram-negative pneumonia, and it is not documented as such, query the physician.
- Signs of gram-negative pneumonia include: worsening of cough, dyspnea, fever, purulent sputum, elevated leukocyte count, and patchy infiltrate on chest X-ray.
- When the physician has documented Ventilator Associated Pneumonia (VAP), use code J95.851.
  Add an additional code to identify the organism. Do not assign an additional code from categories J12–J18 to identify the type of pneumonia. Do not use code J95.851 just because the patient is on a ventilator and has pneumonia. The physician must document that the pneumonia is attributed to the ventilator.

Postoperative Complications

- Physician must document that a condition is a complication of the procedure before assigning a complication code.
- "Expected" conditions occur in the immediate post-op period. These are not reported unless they exceed the usual post-op period and meet the criteria for reporting as an additional diagnosis.

Pressure Ulcers

- When the patient has multiple pressure ulcers at different sites and each is at different stages, code each of the sites and each of the different stages.
- When the patient has pressure ulcers documented as "healed," no code is assigned.
- When the patient has pressure ulcers documented as "healing," code the site(s) and the stage(s).
- When the patient has a pressure ulcer at one stage at the time of admission, but then it progresses to a higher stage, assign the code for the highest stage.

Pulmonary Edema

- Pulmonary edema can be cardiogenic or noncardiogenic.
- Pulmonary edema is a manifestation of heart failure and, as such, is included in heart failure, hypertension, or rheumatic heart disease. Therefore, it is not coded separately.
- Noncardiogenic acute pulmonary edema occurs in the absence of heart failure or other heart disease.

Respiratory Failure (Acute)

- Careful review of the medical record is required for the coding and sequencing of acute respiratory failure. If it meets the definition of principal diagnosis, it is coded as such. If it does not, it is coded as a secondary diagnosis.
- When a patient is admitted with acute respiratory failure and another acute condition, the principal diagnosis will depend on the individual patient's condition and the chief (main) reason that caused the admission of the patient to the hospital.

Septicemia

- A diagnosis of bacteremia R78.81 refers to the presence of bacteria in the bloodstream following a relatively minor injury or infection.
- Septicemia and sepsis are often used to mean the same thing, but they have two distinct and separate meanings.
- Septicemia is a systemic condition associated with pathogenic microorganisms or toxins in the blood (such as bacteria, viruses, fungi, or other organisms). Most septicemias are classified to category A41.-. Additional codes are assigned for any manifestations, if present.
- Negative blood cultures do not preclude a diagnosis of septicemia or sepsis. Query the physician.
  A code for septicemia is used only when the physician documents a diagnosis of septicemia.
- Urosepsis is not a condition that is classified in ICD-10-CM. A physician query should be initiated for clarification of the condition under treatment.
- Systemic Inflammatory Response Syndrome (SIRS) refers to the systemic response to infection, trauma, burns, or other insult (such as cancer) with symptoms (such as fever, tachycardia, tachypnea, and leukocytosis).
- When a patient has SIRS with no subsequent infection, and is a result of a noninfectious disease (such as trauma, cancer, or pancreatitis), code the noninfectious disease first, and then code R65.10 or R65.11. If an acute organ dysfunction is documented, code that also.
- Sepsis generally refers to SIRS due to infection.
- Severe sepsis generally refers to sepsis with associated acute organ dysfunction.
- If sepsis or severe sepsis is present on admission and meets the definition of principal diagnosis, the systemic infection code should be coded first, followed by the appropriate code from subcategory R65.2-. Codes from subcategory R65.2- can never be assigned as a principal diagnosis. An additional code should be added for any localized infection, if present.
- If sepsis or severe sepsis develops during admission, assign the code for the systemic infection and a code from subcategory R65.2- as a secondary code.
- Septic shock is defined as sepsis with hypotension, which is a failure of the cardiovascular system. Septic shock is used as an additional code when the underlying infection is present.
- For all cases of septic shock, code the systemic infection first (such as A40.-; A41.-; B37.7) followed by code R65.21. Any additional codes for other acute organ dysfunction should also be assigned.

Substance Abuse

- Substance abuse and dependence are classified as mental disorders in ICD-10-CM.
- Alcohol dependence is classified to category F10.2, and nondependent alcohol use is coded to category F10.1.
  The physician documentation must indicate the pattern of use.
- There are codes for alcohol withdrawal and drug withdrawal symptoms. These codes are used in conjunction with the dependence codes.
- When a patient is admitted in withdrawal or when withdrawal develops after admission, the withdrawal code is principal.
- There are procedure codes for rehabilitation, detoxification, and combination rehabilitation and detoxification for both alcohol and drug dependence.

Z-Codes

Z-Codes (Z00–Z99) characterize the purpose for an encounter when a disease or injury is not the reason a patient is seeking healthcare services. Z codes can be used in any healthcare setting. Certain Z-codes can be assigned as the principal or first listed diagnosis.

- Special main terms for Z-Codes in the Alphabetic Index of Diseases include:

Abnormal	Foreign Body
Admission	Healthy
Aftercare Anomaly	History (family)
Attention to	History
(personal) Boarder	Maintenance
Care of	Maladjustment
Carrier	Observation
Checking	Problem with
Complication	Procedure (surgical)
Contraception	Prophylactic
Counseling	Replacement
Delivery	Screening
Dialysis	Status
Donor	Supervision (of)
Examination	Test
Exposure to	Transplant
Fitting of	Unavailability of medical facilities
Follow-up	Vaccination

OUTPATIENT PROCEDURE CODING REVIEW

CMS (Centers for Medicare and Medicaid Services, formerly HCFA, Health Care Financing Administration) administers Medicare and Medicaid.

HCPCS (Healthcare Common Procedure Coding System)
- A coding system describing the physician and nonphysician patient services covered by the government's Medicare and Medicaid programs.
- Designed by CMS and used primarily to report reimbursable services rendered to the patient.
- Consists of two levels of HCPCS codes for ambulatory (outpatient) patients.

LEVEL I—CPT (Current Procedural Terminology) is a coding system developed by the American Medical Association (AMA) to convert descriptions of medical, surgical, and diagnostic services rendered by health care providers into five-digit numerical codes. The codes are updated annually by AMA.

The CPT coding system:
- provides uniform language to accurately designate medical, surgical, and diagnostic services.
- provides effective means of reliable, nationwide communication between physicians, patients, and third-party payers.
- allows for the ability to compare reimbursements for procedures.

Justification for listing of a procedure:
- The procedure is commonly performed by physicians nationally.
- The procedure must be consistent with modern medical practice.

LEVEL II—National Codes
- Updated by CMS
- Five-digit alphanumeric codes
- Codes exist for products, supplies, and services not included in CPT.

Rules for Coding CPT

1. Determine the service provided by analyzing the statement provided by the physician.
2. Identify the main term(s) in the Alphabetic Index.

    To locate a code in the index, the coder should first look up the procedure or service provided. If the procedure is not listed, look under the anatomic site involved, the condition, the synonym, or the eponym. Follow the guidance of the index in locating the code most accurately describing the service.
3. Write down or note the code number(s) found for the term.
    *   If a single code number is given, locate the code in the body of the CPT book. Verify the code and its description against the statement, ensuring they match.
    *   If two or more codes separated by a comma are given, locate each code in the body of the CPT book. Read the description of each and select the appropriate code matching the statement.
    *   If a range of codes is given, locate the range of codes in the body of the CPT book. Review the description of each entry prior to selecting a code.
4. NEVER code from the Alphabetic Index; look up the codes to verify accuracy.
5. Read all notes that apply to the code selected.
    Notes may appear at the beginning of a section, subsection, before or after a code, or within the code description. Notes are utilized throughout the CPT, requiring special attention and review by the coder. Some of these notes define terms, such as *simple, intermediate,* and *complex wound repair.* Other notes provide specific coding instruction applicable to specific codes.
6. Select the appropriate modifier, if applicable, to complete the code description.
7. Code multiple procedures from highest resource intensive to lowest (most complicated to least complicated).

Common Errors That Prevent Payment to Physicians

1. No documentation or incomplete documentation for services billed
2. Missing signatures
3. Consistently assigning the same level of services
4. Billing of a consult instead of an office visit
5. Using invalid codes in the bill due to use of old coding resources or forms
6. Unbundling procedure codes
7. Not listing the chief complaint
8. Abbreviations that are misinterpreted
9. Billing of services included in global fee as a separate professional fee
10. Not using a modifier or use of an inappropriate modifier for accurate payment of a claim

CPT Code Book Format Information

Guidelines provide specific instructions about coding for each section. The guidelines contain definitions of terms, explanations of notes, subsection information, unlisted services, and special reports information.

Sections: There are eight major areas into which all CPT codes and descriptions are categorized. The majority of CPT codes are arranged in numerical order in each section. The first six sections are comprised of five-digit numerical codes. The codes in the last two sections, Category II and Category III Codes, are comprised of five-digit codes—four numbers and a letter.

> Evaluation and Management
> Anesthesia
> Surgery
> Radiology
> Pathology/Laboratory
> Medicine
> Category II Codes
> Category III Codes

Category II Codes are optional tracking codes used to measure performance.

Category III Codes are temporary codes for emerging technology, services, and procedures. These codes can be used for data collection purposes or possibly in the FDA approval process. If a Category III code is available, this code must be reported instead of a Category I unlisted code.

Subsections, subcategories, and headings divide the sections into smaller units, based on anatomy, procedure, condition, description, or approach.

Symbols used in CPT coding: The following symbols are special guides that help the coder compare codes and descriptors with the previous year's CPT edition, or that provide additional coding guidance.

- • Bullet is used to indicate a new procedure or service code added since the previous edition of the CPT manual.

- ▲ Triangle indicates that the code has been changed or modified since the last CPT manual edition.

- + A plus sign is used to indicate an add-on code.

- ⦸ Null symbol is used to identify a modifier -51 exempt code.

- ►◄ A right and left triangle indicates the beginning and end of the text changes.

- ⊙ A circled bullet indicates the code includes moderate sedation.

- ⟶ Reference to CPT Assistant, Clinical Examples in Radiology, and CPT Changes
- \# The number sign is used to identify codes that have been resequenced and are not placed numerically.
- ○ Indicates a reinstated/recycled code.

Modifiers: Two-character codes added to CPT codes to supply more specific information about the services provided.

Special reports: Detailed reports that include adequate definitions or descriptions of the nature, extent, and need for the procedure, and the time, effort, and equipment necessary to provide the service.

Unlisted procedures: Procedures that are considered unusual, experimental, or new and do not have a specific code number assigned. Unlisted procedure codes are located at the end of the subcategories, or headings, and may be used to identify any procedure that lacks a specific code and requires a "special report" submitted at the time of billing.

CPT Index: Located at the back of the CPT manual and arranged alphabetically. To locate terms in the alphabetic index, look under the

Service/procedure

Anatomic site/body organ

Condition/disease/problem

Synonym

Eponym (procedure named after someone)

Abbreviation or acronym (e.g., CBC)

Notations:

"see"—sends you to a more appropriate section.

"see also"—cross-reference to refer to another main term.

CPT Appendices in back section of the CPT manual:

Appendix A: Lists all modifiers with complete explanations for use

Appendix B: Contains a complete list of additions to, deletions from, and revisions of the previous year's edition

Appendix C: Provides clinical examples of Evaluation and Management (E&M) codes

Appendix D: Contains a listing of the CPT add-on codes

Appendix E: Contains a list of modifier-51 exempt codes

Appendix F: Contains a list of modifier-63 exempt codes

Appendix G: Summary of CPT codes that include moderate (conscious) sedation

Appendix I: Genetic testing code modifiers

Appendix J: Electrodiagnostic medicine listing of sensory, motor, and mixed nerves

Appendix K: Product pending FDA approval

Appendix L: Vascular families

Appendix M: Crosswalk to deleted CPT codes

Appendix N: Summary of resequenced CPT codes

Appendix O: Multianalyte Assays with Algorithmic Analyses

General E&M Coding Guidelines

1. Determine place of service: office, emergency room, or nursing home.

2. Determine type of service: consult, admission, newborn.

3. Determine patient status: new unless seen in last 3 years by the physician or another physician of the same specialty in the same group.

4. Determine the level of each of the three key components:
   A. **History:** problem focused, expanded problem focused, detailed, comprehensive
   B. **Physical examination:** problem focused, expanded problem focused, detailed, comprehensive
   C. **Medical decision making:** straightforward, low, moderate, high
      - New patients, consultations, emergency department services, and initial care: generally require all three key components.
      - Established patients and subsequent care: usually require two of the three key components.
      - Some codes are based on time: critical care, prolonged services.

5. Read Critical Care guidelines carefully. Watch for the procedures that are included in the codes.

6. Read Inpatient Neonatal and Pediatric Critical Care Services and intensive (noncritical) low birth weight services guidelines carefully. Watch for procedures that are inclusive in this area.

7. Be sure to read the coding guidelines for E&M coding carefully.

8. Review definition for "consultations" and determine when consult codes are more appropriate than office visit codes.

9. There are specific codes used for hospital observation services (initial care, subsequent care, and discharge services) and codes for same-day admissions and discharges.

10. When a patient is admitted as an inpatient on the same day that services are provided at another site (office, ER, observation, etc.), only the inpatient services are reported. The E&M services provided in these outpatient settings can be used to determine the level of inpatient services provided.

11. Preventive Care codes are based on the patient's age.

Some Additional Areas of Interest When Coding with CPT

Abortion

"Incomplete Abortions" and "Miscarriages" are alternate terms for missed and spontaneous abortions.

Spontaneous abortion that occurs during any trimester and is completed surgically, assign 59812.

Missed abortion that occurs during the first trimester, assign 59820.

Induced abortion, which combines curettage and evacuation, assign 59851.

Induced abortion by dilation and evacuation, code 59841.

Induced abortion by dilation and curettage, code 59840. Code 58120 is used for a nonobstetrical D&C.

Angioplasty

Determination of the site and whether it is open or percutaneous.

Open transluminal angioplasty of renal or other visceral arteries, aortic, brachiocephalic, or venous sites code from 35450 to 35460.

Percutaneous transluminal angioplasty of renal or other visceral arteries, aortic, brachiocephalic, or venous sites code from 35471 to 35476.

Endovascular revascularization (open or percutaneous, transcatheter) of lower extremies code from 37220 to 37235.

PTCA: Percutaneous transluminal coronary angioplasty: assign code appropriately from 92920 and 92921.

Percutaneous transluminal angioplasty of the peripheral arteries and visceral arteries:
75962–75968 (Radiology Section) for the radiological supervision and interpretation

Codes 92928 and 92929 for stent placement include the PTCA and thus the PTCA is not coded separately.

Appendectomy

There are several codes that are used to describe appendectomies: open surgical appendectomy (including incidental), laparoscopic appendectomy, appendectomy done for a ruptured appendix, and appendectomy done for a specified purpose at the time of other major surgery.

Auditory

Simple mastoidectomy is also called a transmastoid antrotomy (69501).

Apicetomy is the excision of the tip of the petrous bone. This is often performed with a radical mastoidectomy (69530). It would be inappropriate to code 69511 in addition.

Tympanostomy (requiring insertion of ventilating tube). Code 69436, Tympanostomy (requiring insertion of ventilating tube) general anesthesia, and 69433, Tympanostomy (requiring insertion of ventilating tube), local or topic anesthesia, are used for "insertion of tubes."

Removal of impacted cerumen from one or both ears, use code 69210.

Some Additional Areas of Interest When Coding with CPT (continued)

Bronchoscopy and Biopsy

Surgical bronchoscopy includes a diagnostic bronchoscopy.

Code appropriate endoscopy for each anatomic site examined.

Endobronchial biopsy, code 31625.

Review for types of specimen collection:

- **Biopsy** forceps used to remove tissue
- **Bronchial brush** used to obtain surface cells
- **Bronchial alveolar lavage (BAL)** used to collect cells from peripheral lung tissue
- **Cell washings** used to exfoliate cells from crevices

   Note: Cell washings or brushings are NOT biopsies.

Transbronchial biopsy is performed by positioning the scope in the bronchus nearest to the lesion. A hole is punctured through the bronchus into the lung tissue where the lesion is located. The lesion is then biopsied. Transbronchial lung biopsy is reported with code 31628.

Transbronchial needle aspiration biopsy (31629).

Catheter aspiration of tracheobronchial tree at bedside (31725).

CABG

To report combined arterial-venous grafts, it is necessary to report two codes:

1. The appropriate combined arterial-venous graft code (33517–33523)
2. The appropriate arterial graft code (33533–33536)

Procurement of the saphenous vein graft is included in the description of the work for 33517–33523 and is not reported separately.

Procurement of an upper extremity artery is reported separately.

Casting and Strapping

Services in the musculoskeletal system include the application or removal of the first cast or traction device only. Subsequent replacement of casts, traction devices, or removals is reported using codes from the 29000–29750 series of codes.

The codes in the 29000–29750 series of codes have very specific guidelines directing the use of the codes.

Endoscopy

Codes specify the purpose and site of application.

Dx endoscopy is coded only if a surgical procedure was not done. Surgical endoscopy always includes a diagnostic endoscopy.

Code as far as the scope is passed.

Stomach endoscopy is included with UGI endoscopy, not separately.

Multiple codes may be necessary to cover one endoscopic episode.

Removal of gastrostomy tube by endoscopy, code 43247.

Colonoscopy: first determine the route the procedure follows (via colostomy, colotomy, or rectum).

Colonoscopy with dilation of rectum or anorectum, code 45999.

Biliary endoscopy (47550) is only used with 47420 or 47610.

EGDs are coded to 43235–43259.

Some Additional Areas of Interest When Coding with CPT (continued)

Eye and Ocular

Preliminary iridectomy is not coded separately if performed as part of a cataract extraction or prior to lens extraction. It is included in the code for the lens extraction.

Two types of cataract extraction:

- ICCE: Intracapsular cataract extraction
- ECCE: Extracapsular cataract extraction

Do not code medication injections used in conjunction with cataract surgery. Injections are considered part of the procedure.

Cataract removal includes the following in codes 66830–66984.

DO NOT CODE THE FOLLOWING PROCEDURES SEPARATELY: anterior capsulotomy, enzymatic zonulysis, iridectomy, iridotomy, lateral canthotomy, pharmacological agents, posterior capsulotomy, viscoelastic agents, subconjunctival, and subtenon injections.

Female Genital System

Codes 57452–57461 are used to report various cervical colposcopic procedures.

Code 57455 describes colposcopy with single or multiple biopsies of the cervix.

Code 58150 describes total abdominal hysterectomy with or without removal of tube(s) or ovary(s).

Code 58611 is an add-on code that describes tubal ligation or transection when done at the time of Cesarean delivery or intra-abdominal surgery.

Fractures/Dislocations

- Treatment of fractures/dislocations can be open or closed.
- Closed treatment means that the fracture or dislocation site is not surgically opened. It is used to describe procedures that treat fractures by three methods: without manipulation, with manipulation, and with or without traction.
- Open treatment implies that the fracture is surgically opened and the fracture is visualized to allow treatment.
- Skeletal fixation is neither open nor closed treatment. Usually pins are placed across the fracture using X-ray guidance.
- Manipulation is used to indicate the attempted reduction or restoration of a fracture or dislocation.

Genitourinary

Many of the procedures in the urinary system are performed endoscopically—cystoscopy, urethroscopy, cystourethroscopy, ureteroscopy, pyeloscopy, and renal endoscopy.

Most cystourethroscopy codes are unilateral. When a cysto is performed bilaterally, modifier -50 should be appended.

Codes in the 52320–52355 series include the insertion and removal of a temporary stent during diagnostic or therapeutic cystourethroscopic intervention(s).

Cystourethroscopy with removal of a self-retaining/indwelling ureteral stent, planned or staged during the associated normal postoperative follow-up period of the original procedure, is reported by means of code 52310 or 52315 with the modifier -58 appended as appropriate.

Be careful to differentiate between codes for ureteral and urethral procedures.

Some Additional Areas of Interest When Coding with CPT (continued)

GI Biopsy

Code only the biopsy if a single lesion is biopsied but not excised.

Code only the biopsy and list only one time if multiple biopsies are done (from the same or different lesions) and none of the lesions are excised.

Code only the excision if a biopsy of a lesion is taken and the balance of the same lesion is then excised.

Code both the biopsy and the excision if both are performed and if the biopsy is taken from a lesion different from that which is excised, and the code for the excision does not include the phrase "with or without biopsy." If such a phrase is in the code narration, then a separate biopsy code should not be used.

Surgical endoscopy always includes a diagnostic endoscopy.

Modifier -59 may be used to explain unusual circumstances when coding both biopsy and removal of a different lesion.

Hernia Repair

- Hernia repair codes are categorized by type (inguinal, femoral, etc.).
- Hernias are further categorized as "initial" or "recurrent" based on whether or not the hernia has required previous repair.
- Age and clinical presentation (reducible versus strangulated).
- Code 49568 is used only with nonlaparscopic incisional or ventral hernia repairs.

Immunizations

Codes 90460–90474 are used to report the administration of vaccines/toxoids.

Codes 90476–90749 identify the vaccine PRODUCT alone.

If a combination vaccine code is provided (MMR) it is not appropriate to report each component of the combination vaccine separately.

When the physician provides face-to-face counseling of the patient and family during the administration of a vaccine, report codes 90460–90461.

Do not append modifier -51 to the vaccine/toxoid product codes 90476–90749.

Integumentary

Three types of repairs: Add lengths of repairs together and use one code for repairs of the same location and same type.

- **Simple:** Superficial wound involving skin and/or subcutaneous tissues and requiring simple suturing.
- **Intermediate:** Involving skin, subcutaneous tissues, and fascia and requiring layer closure. May also be used when a single closure requires intensive cleaning.
- **Complex** repairs requiring reconstructive surgery or time-consuming or complicated closures.

Debridement is coded separately. When gross contamination requires cleaning, when appreciable amounts of devitalized or contaminated tissue are removed, and when debridement is carried out separately without primary closure.

Lesion size is best found on the operative report.

Benign or malignant lesion(s): Code each lesion excised separately; simple closure after excision of lesion(s) is included in the code.

Adjacent tissue transfers include excision of tissues, including lesions.

Some Additional Areas of Interest When Coding with CPT (continued)

Integumentary (continued)

Free skin grafts: Identify by size and location of the defect (recipient area) and the type of graft; includes simple debridement of granulations or recent avulsion.

There are three code ranges:

- Use 15002–15005 for initial wound preparation.
- Use 15040–15261 for autografts and tissue-cultured autografts.
- Use 15271–15278 for skin substitute grafts (homografts, allografts, and xenografts).

Repair of donor site requiring skin graft or local flaps is to be added on as an additional procedure.

Report excision of lesion(s) separately.

Excisional biopsy is used when the entire lesion, whether benign or malignant, is removed.

Breast lesion excisions performed after being identified by pre-op radiological marker (localization wires), use codes 19125 and 19126.

Placement of needle localization wires prior to biopsies, excisions, and other breast procedures, use additional codes 19281–19288.

Laryngoscopy

Many of the codes used to report laryngoscopies include the use of an operating microscope. Therefore, code 69990, microsurgical techniques, requiring the use of an operating microscope (list separately in addition to code primary procedure), would not be used with any codes that include the use of the microscope.

Maternity Care and Delivery

Antepartum care or services provided above the normally expected care (as defined in the CPT book) should be coded separately.

Medical problems complicating labor and delivery management may require additional resources and should be identified by using E&M codes in addition to the codes for maternity care.

For surgical complications of pregnancy, see services in the surgery section.

If a physician provides all or part of the antepartum and/or postpartum patient care, but does not perform delivery due to termination of pregnancy by abortion or referral to another physician for delivery, see the antepartum and postpartum care codes 59425–59426 and 59430.

Patients who have had a previous Cesarean delivery and now present with the expectation of a vaginal delivery are coded using codes 59610–59622. If the patient has a successful vaginal delivery after a previous Cesarean delivery (VBAC), use codes 59610–59614. If the attempt is unsuccessful and another Cesarean delivery is carried out, use codes 59618–59622.

Nasal Hemorrhage

Was it anterior or posterior?

- If anterior, was the hemorrhage simple or complex?
- If posterior, was the control of the hemorrhage an initial or subsequent procedure?

Anterior nasal hemorrhage has likely occurred if the physician inserts gauze packing or anterior packing or performs cauterization.

Some Additional Areas of Interest When Coding with CPT (continued)

Posterior nasal hemorrhage has likely occurred if the physician inserts nasal stents, tampons, balloon catheters, or posterior packing, or if the patient is taken to the OR for ligation of arteries to control bleeding.

Nosebleed subsequent to initial one (30906).

Neurology/Spine Surgery

The spinal and spinal cord injection codes reflect the specific spinal anatomy, such as subarachnoid or epidural; the level of the injection (cervical, thoracic, lumbar, or sacral); and the types of substances injected, such as anesthetic steroids, antispasmodics, phenol, etc.

Injection of contrast material during fluoroscopic guidance is included in codes 62263–62264, 62267, 62270–62273, 62280–62282, and 62310–62319. The fluoroscopic guidance itself is reported by code 77003. Code 62263 describes treatment involving injections of various substances over a multiple-day period. Code 62263 is not reported for each individual injection but is reported once to describe the entire series of injections or infusions.

Code 62264 describes multiple treatments performed on the same day.

Other codes in this section refer to laminectomies, excisions, repairs, and shunts. A basic distinction among the codes is the condition, such as herniated disk, as well as the approach used, such as anterior or posterior or costovertebral.

Lumbar punctures (62270) are also called spinal taps and are used to obtain cerebrospinal fluid by inserting a needle into the subarachnoid space in the lumbar area.

When coding surgery on the spine, there are many sets of guidelines for the coder to review, including those at the beginning of the subsection, as well as throughout the subsection.

Co-surgery is common in spinal surgeries. When two surgeons work together, both as primary surgeons, each surgeon should report his or her distinct operative work by adding modifier -62 to the procedure code and any associated add-on codes for that procedure as long as both surgeons continue to work together as primary surgeons.

Spinal instrumentation is used to stabilize the spinal column during repair procedures. There are two types: segmental and nonsegmental.

- Segmental instrumentation involves attachment at each end of the spinal area and at least one intermittent fixation.
- Nonsegmental instrumentation involves attachment at each end and may span several vertebral segments without intermittent fixation.

Pacemakers

1. Is it permanent or temporary?
2. What was the approach (transvenous or epicardial)?
3. What type of device (electrodes and/or pulse generator)?
4. Where were the electrodes placed (atrial, ventricle, or both)?
5. Is this an insertion of a new or replacement permanent pacemaker? Insertion or replacement of a temporary pacemaker? Repair of electrodes? Removal of a pacemaker? Repositioning?
6. Was revision of the skin pocket done?

Some Additional Areas of Interest When Coding with CPT (continued)

Sentinel Nodes

Sentinel node procedures utilize injection of a radiotracer or blue dye. After absorption of dye, the physician can visualize the node(s). Code 38792 is used for identification of sentinel nodes. For excision of sentinel nodes, see 38500–38542.

Use appropriate lymph node excision codes to report the excision.

A second sentinel node from a different lymphatic chain excised from a separate incision, report the excision and add modifier -59.

Lymphoscintigraphy, code 78195.

Injection for gamma probe node detection with imaging code 38790.

Thyroid

- **Recall** that **the thyroid has two lobes**, one on each side of the trachea. The procedure may only be unilateral (60220), but it is still considered to be a total lobectomy.
- **Thyroidectomy may be**
  - Total or complete (60240), removing both the lobes and the isthmus. It is not necessary to list the code twice.
  - Partial lobectomy (60210), unilateral, with or without isthmusectomy.
- **Thyroidectomy with neck dissection** (60252 and 60254). Do not assign these codes if an isolated lymph node is excised or biopsied.

Tonsillectomy and Adenoidectomy

- Separate codes describe tonsillectomy and adenoidectomy; tonsillectomy alone, whether primary or secondary; adenoidectomy alone, primary; adenoidectomy alone, secondary.
- Separate codes are reported for procedures performed on patients under age 12, and age 12 or older.
- A primary procedure is one in which no prior tonsillectomy or adenoidectomy has been performed. A secondary procedure is one that is performed to remove residual or regrowth of tonsil or adenoid tissue.

Wound Exploration

- Wound exploration codes (20100–20103) are used when repair of a penetrating wound requires enlargement of the existing defect for exploration, cleaning, and repair.
- If the wound does not need to be enlarged, then only repair codes from the integumentary section are used.

III. Health Data Content and Standards

Patricia J. Schnering, RHIA, CCS

1. In preparation for an EHR, you are working with a team conducting a total facility inventory of all forms currently used. You must name each form for bar coding and indexing into a document management system. The unnamed document in front of you includes a microscopic description of tissue excised during surgery. The document type you are most likely to give to this form is
   A. recovery room record.
   C. operative report.
   B. pathology report.
   D. discharge summary.

REFERENCE: Abdelhak, p 114
             Green and Bowie, pp 167
             LaTour, Eichenwald-Maki, and Oachs, pp A32–A33
             Odom-Wesley, p 171
             Sayles, p 88

2. Patient data collection requirements vary according to health care setting. A data element you would expect to be collected in the MDS but NOT in the UHDDS would be
   A. personal identification.
   C. procedures and dates.
   B. cognitive patterns.
   D. principal diagnosis.

REFERENCE: Abdelhak, pp 137–138, 141
             LaTour, Eichenwald-Maki, and Oachs, p 30
             Sayles, pp 147, 152

3. In the past, Joint Commission standards have focused on promoting the use of a facility-approved abbreviation list to be used by hospital care providers. With the advent of the Commission's national patient safety goals, the focus has shifted to the
   A. prohibited use of any abbreviations.
   B. flagrant use of specialty-specific abbreviations.
   C. use of prohibited or "dangerous" abbreviations.
   D. use of abbreviations used in the final diagnosis.

REFERENCE: Abdelhak, p 117
             LaTour, Eichenwald-Maki, and Oachs, pp 251, 264, 672
             Odom, pp 111, 230

4. A risk manager needs to locate a full report of a patient's fall from his bed, including witness reports and probable reasons for the fall. She would most likely find this information in the
   A. doctors' progress notes.
   C. incident report.
   B. integrated progress notes.
   D. nurses' notes.

REFERENCE: Abdelhak, pp 460–461, 544–545
             Davis and LaCour, pp 378–380
             Green and Bowie, p 88
             LaTour and Eichenwald-Maki, p 861
             McWay, p 132
             Odom-Wesley, p 54
             Sayles, p 613

5. For continuity of care, ambulatory care providers are more likely than providers of acute care services to rely on the documentation found in the
   A. interdisciplinary patient care plan.   C. transfer record.
   B. discharge summary.   D. problem list.

REFERENCE: Abdelhak, p 136
             Davis and LaCour, pp 10–11
             Green and Bowie, p 91
             Odom-Wesley, pp 326–327
             Sayles, p 108

6. Joint Commission does not approve of auto authentication of entries in a health record. The primary objection to this practice is that
   A. it is too easy to delegate use of computer passwords.
   B. evidence cannot be provided that the physician actually reviewed and approved each report.
   C. electronic signatures are not acceptable in every state.
   D. tampering too often occurs with this method of authentication.

REFERENCE: Green and Bowie, p 78
             LaTour, Eichenwald-Maki, and Oachs, pp 174, 897

7. As part of a quality improvement study you have been asked to provide information on the menstrual history, number of pregnancies, and number of living children on each OB patient from a stack of old obstetrical records. The best place in the record to locate this information is the
   A. prenatal record.   C. postpartum record.
   B. labor and delivery record.   D. discharge summary.

REFERENCE: Abdelhak, pp 114–115
             Green and Bowie, p 182
             Odom-Wesley, pp 180–186

8. As a concurrent record reviewer for an acute care facility, you have asked Dr. Crossman to provide an updated history and physical for one of her recent admissions. Dr. Crossman pages through the medical record to a copy of an H&P performed in her office a week before admission. You tell Dr. Crossman
   A. a new H&P is required for every inpatient admission.
   B. that you apologize for not noticing the H&P she provided.
   C. the H&P copy is acceptable as long as she documents any interval changes.
   D. Joint Commission standards do not allow copies of any kind in the original record.

REFERENCE: Abdelhak, p 109
             Green and Bowie, p 145
             Odom-Wesley, p 367

9. You have been asked to identify every reportable case of cancer from the previous year. A key resource will be the facility's
   A. disease index.
   B. number control index.
   C. physicians' index.
   D. patient index.

REFERENCE: Abdelhak, pp 486–487
LaTour, Eichenwald-Maki, and Oachs, pp 245, 250–251
McWay, p 140
Sayles, p 437

10. Discharge summary documentation must include
    A. a detailed history of the patient.
    B. a note from social services or discharge planning.
    C. significant findings during hospitalization.
    D. correct codes for significant procedures.

REFERENCE: Abdelhak, pp 111, 113
Davis and LaCour, pp 106–107
Green and Bowie, p 144
LaTour and Eichenwald-Maki, pp 200–201
Odom-Wesley, pp 200–205
Sayles, p 93

11. The performance of qualitative analysis is an important tool in ensuring data quality. These reviews evaluate
    A. quality of care through the use of preestablished criteria.
    B. adverse effects and contraindications of drugs utilized during hospitalization.
    C. potentially compensable events.
    D. the overall quality of documentation.

REFERENCE: Abdelhak, pp 130–131
Davis and LaCour, pp 374–376
LaTour, Eichenwald-Maki, and Oachs, pp 250–251
Odom-Wesley, pp 251–256

12. Ultimate responsibility for the quality and completion of entries in patient health records belongs to the
    A. chief of staff.
    B. attending physician.
    C. HIM director.
    D. risk manager.

REFERENCE: LaTour, Eichenwald-Maki, and Oachs, p 242

13. The foundation for communicating all patient care goals in long-term care settings is the
    A. legal assessment.
    B. medical history.
    C. interdisciplinary plan of care.
    D. Uniform Hospital Discharge Data Set.

REFERENCE: Abdelhak, p 109
LaTour, Eichenwald-Maki, and Oachs, pp 31, 254
Odom-Wesley, p 371
Sayles, p 83

14. As part of Joint Commission's National Patient Safety Goal initiative, acute care hospitals are now required to use a preoperative verification process to confirm the patient's true identity and to confirm that necessary documents such as x-rays or medical records are available. They must also develop and use a process for
    A. including the primary caregiver in surgery consults.
    B. including the surgeon in the preanesthesia assessment.
    C. marking the surgical site.
    D. apprising the patient of all complications that might occur.

REFERENCE: Abdelhak, p 459
                LaTour, Eichenwald-Maki, and Oachs, p 672

15. According to the Joint Commission's National Patient Safety Goals, which of the following abbreviations would most likely be prohibited?
    A. 0.04 mg Lasix
    B. 4 mg Lasix
    C. 40 mg Lasix
    D. .4 mg Lasix

REFERENCE: Odom, pp 230–231

16. Using the SOAP method of recording progress notes, which entry would most likely include a differential diagnosis?
    A. assessment
    B. plan
    C. subjective
    D. objective

REFERENCE: Abdelhak, pp 118–119
                Davis and LaCour, pp 41–43, 96–98
                Green, pp 91, 343
                LaTour, Eichenwald-Maki, and Oachs, pp 249, 256–257
                Odom, pp 215, 217
                Sayles, p 126

17. You have been asked by a peer review committee to print a list of the medical record numbers of all patients who had CABGs performed in the past year at your acute care hospital. Which secondary data source could be used to quickly gather this information?
    A. disease index   C. master patient index
    B. physician index   D. operation index

REFERENCE: LaTour, Eichenwald-Maki, and Oachs, p 369
                Sayles, p 437

18. The best example of point-of-care service and documentation is
    A. using an automated tracking system to locate a record.
    B. using occurrence screens to identify adverse events.
    C. doctors using voice recognition systems to dictate radiology reports.
    D. nurses using bedside terminals to record vital signs.

REFERENCE: Abdelhak, p 38
               LaTour, Eichenwald-Maki, and Oachs, p 96

19. Which of the following is a form or view that is typically seen in the health record of a long-term care patient but is rarely seen in records of acute care patients?
    A. pharmacy consultation   C. physical exam
    B. medical consultation   D. emergency record

REFERENCE: Abdelhak, p 141

20. In determining your acute care facility's degree of compliance with prospective payment requirements for Medicare, the best resource to reference for recent certification standards is the
    A. CARF manual.   C. Joint Commission accreditation manual.
    B. hospital bylaws.   D. Federal Register.

REFERENCE: Abdelhak, p 441
               Green and Bowie, p 29
               LaTour, Eichenwald-Maki, and Oachs, pp 301–302, 453, 466, 915
               Odom-Wesley, p 288

21. In an acute care hospital, a complete history and physical may not be required for a new admission when
    A. the patient is readmitted for a similar problem within 1 year.
    B. the patient's stay is less than 24 hours.
    C. the patient has an uneventful course in the hospital.
    D. a legible copy of a recent H&P performed in the attending physician's office is available.

REFERENCE: Abdelhak, p 109
               Green and Bowie, p 145
               LaTour, Eichenwald-Maki, and Oachs, pp 245, 252, 925
               Odom-Wesley, p 367

22. When developing a data collection system, the most effective approach first considers
    A. the end user's needs.   C. hardware requirements.
    B. applicable accreditation standards. D. facility preference.

REFERENCE: Odom-Wesley, p 230

23. A key data item you would expect to find recorded on an ER record but would probably NOT see in an acute care record is the
    A. physical findings.   C. time and means of arrival.
    B. lab and diagnostic test results. D. instructions for follow-up care.

REFERENCE: Abdelhak, pp 138–139
               Davis and LaCour, pp 95, 221–222
               Johns, p 93
               LaTour, Eichenwald-Maki, and Oachs, p 255
               Odom-Wesley, p 171
               Peden, p 37
               Sayles, p 107

24. Under which of the following conditions can an original paper-based patient health record be physically removed from the hospital?
    A. when the patient is brought to the hospital emergency department following a motor vehicle accident and, after assessment, is transferred with his health record to a trauma designated emergency department at another hospital
    B. when the director of health records is acting in response to a subpoena duces tecum and takes the health record to court
    C. when the patient is discharged by the physician and at the time of discharge is transported to a long-term care facility with his health record
    D. when the record is taken to a physician's private office for a follow-up patient visit postdischarge

REFERENCE: Abdelhak, pp 531–534
               Johns, p 804

25. Using the SOAP style of documenting progress notes, choose the "subjective" statement from the following.
    A. sciatica unimproved with hot pack therapy
    B. patient moving about very cautiously, appears to be in pain
    C. adjust pain medication; begin physical therapy tomorrow
    D. patient states low back pain is as severe as it was on admission

REFERENCE: Abdelhak, pp 111–112
               Davis and LaCour, pp 41–43, 96–98, 516–520
               Green and Bowie, p 91
               LaTour and Eichenwald-Maki, p 91
               Odom-Wesley, pp 217, 331–332

26. In 1987, OBRA helped shift the focus in long-term care to patient outcomes. As a result, core assessment data elements are collected on each SNF resident as defined in the
    A. UHDDS.   C. Uniform Clinical Data Set.
    B. MDS.   D. Uniform Ambulatory Core Data.

REFERENCE: Abdelhak, pp 141–143
               Davis and LaCour, p 231
               Green and Bowie, p 253
               LaTour, Eichenwald-Maki, and Oachs, pp 199, 435, 931
               Odom-Wesley, pp 365, 368–378
               Peden, pp 357–360
               Sayles, pp 150–152

27. Before you submit a new form to the Forms Review Committee, you need to track the field name of a particular data field and the security levels applicable to that field. Your best source for this information would be the
    A. facility's data dictionary.   C. Glossary of Health Care Terms.
    B. MDS.   D. UHDDS.

REFERENCE: Abdelhak, pp 502–503
               LaTour, Eichenwald-Maki, and Oachs, pp 202, 907, C7
               Sayles, pp 882–883

28. You notice on the admission H&P that Mr. McKahan, a Medicare patient, was admitted for disc surgery, but the progress notes indicate that due to some heart irregularities, he may not be a good surgical risk. Because of your knowledge of COP regulations, you expect that a(n) _____ will be added to his health record.
    A. interval summary
    B. consultation report
    C. advance directive
    D. interdisciplinary care plan

REFERENCE: Abdelhak, pp 111–112
                Davis and LaCour, p 106
                Green and Bowie, p 148
                LaTour, Eichenwald-Maki, and Oachs, pp 249, 905
                Odom-Wesley, pp 117–118

29. An example of objective entry in the health record supplied by a health care practitioner is the
    A. past medical history.
    B. physical assessment.
    C. chief complaint.
    D. review of systems.

REFERENCE: Abdelhak, pp 118–119
                Davis and LaCour, p 99
                Green and Bowie, p 148
                LaTour, Eichenwald-Maki, and Oachs, p 245
                Odom-Wesley, pp 217, 331–332
                Sayles, p 78

30. You have been asked to recommend time-limited documentation standards for inclusion in the Medical Staff Bylaws, Rules, and Regulations. The committee documentation standards must meet the standards of both the Joint Commission and the Medicare Conditions of Participation. The standards for the history and physical exam documentation are discussed first. You advise them that the time period for completion of this report should be set at
    A. 12 hours after admission.
    B. 24 hours after admission.
    C. 12 hours after admission or prior to surgery.
    D. 24 hours after admission or prior to surgery.

REFERENCE: Abdelhak, p 109
                Davis and LaCour, p 100
                Green and Bowie, p 145
                LaTour, Eichenwald-Maki, and Oachs, p 245
                Odom-Wesley, p 108

31. Based on the following documentation in an acute care record, where would you expect this excerpt to appear?

    "With the patient in the supine position, the right side of the neck was appropriately prepped with betadine solution and draped. I was able to pass the central line which was taped to skin and used for administration of drugs during resuscitation."

    A. physician progress notes
    B. operative record
    C. nursing progress notes
    D. physical examination

REFERENCE: Abdelhak, pp 113–114
                Davis and LaCour, p 110
                LaTour, Eichenwald-Maki, and Oachs, p 250
                Odom-Wesley, p 164
                Sayles, p 88

32. One essential item to be captured on the physical exam is the
    A. general appearance as assessed by the physician.
    B. chief complaint.
    C. family history as related by the patient.
    D. subjective review of systems.

REFERENCE: Abdelhak, p 109
                Davis and LaCour, p 99
                Green and Bowie, p 149
                LaTour, Eichenwald-Maki, and Oachs, p 245
                Odom-Wesley, p 230
                Sayles, p 80

33. An example of a primary data source for health care statistics is the
    A. disease index.   C. MPI.
    B. accession register.   D. hospital census.

REFERENCE: Abdelhak, pp 480–481
                Horton, p 4
                Koch, p 65
                LaTour, Eichenwald-Maki, and Oachs, pp 289, 368
                Odom-Wesley, p 83

34. During a retrospective review of Rose Hunter's inpatient health record, the health information clerk notes that on day 4 of hospitalization there was one missed dose of insulin. What type of review is this clerk performing?
    A. utilization review   C. legal review
    B. quantitative review   D. qualitative review

REFERENCE: Abdelhak, pp 130–131
                Green and Bowie, p 99
                LaTour, Eichenwald-Maki, and Oachs, p 943
                McWay, p 126

35. Which of the following is least likely to be identified by a deficiency analysis technician?
    A. missing discharge summary
    B. need for physician authentication of two verbal orders
    C. discrepancy between post-op diagnosis by the surgeon and pathology diagnosis by the pathologist
    D. x-ray report charted on the wrong record

REFERENCE: Abdelhak, pp 130–131
               Green and Bowie, p 99
               McWay, p 126
               Sayles, p 351

36. Which of the following reports would normally be considered a consultation?
    A. tissue examination done by the pathologist
    B. impressions of a cardiologist asked to determine whether patient is at good surgical risk
    C. interpretation of a radiologic study
    D. technical interpretation of electrocardiogram

REFERENCE: Abdelhak, pp 111–112
               Davis and LaCour, p 106
               Green and Bowie, p 148
               LaTour, Eichenwald-Maki, and Oachs, p 115
               Odom-Wesley, pp 117–118

37. The health care providers at your hospital do a very thorough job of periodic open record review to ensure the completeness of record documentation. A qualitative review of surgical records would likely include checking for documentation regarding
    A. the presence or absence of such items as preoperative and postoperative diagnosis, description of findings, and specimens removed.
    B. whether a postoperative infection occurred and how it was treated.
    C. the quality of follow-up care.
    D. whether the severity of illness and/or intensity of service warranted acute level care.

REFERENCE: Abdelhak, pp 113–114
               Davis and LaCour, p 374
               Green and Bowie, p 99
               LaTour, Eichenwald-Maki, and Oachs, pp 35, 655
               Odom-Wesley, pp 251–256

38. In your facility, the health care providers from every discipline document progress notes sequentially on the same form. Your facility is utilizing
    A. integrated progress notes.   C. source-oriented records.
    B. interdisciplinary treatment plans.   D. SOAP notes.

REFERENCE: Abdelhak, pp 118–119
               Green and Bowie, p 153
               LaTour, Eichenwald-Maki, and Oachs, p 248
               Odom-Wesley, pp 217–221

39. Which of the following services is LEAST likely to be provided by a facility accredited by CARF?
    A. chronic pain management
    B. palliative care
    C. brain injury management
    D. vocational evaluation

REFERENCE: Abdelhak, pp 26–29
                Green and Bowie, p 30
                LaTour, Eichenwald-Maki, and Oachs, p 254
                Sayles, p 679

40. Reviewing a medical record to ensure that all diagnoses are justified by documentation throughout the chart is an example of
    A. peer review.
    B. quantitative review.
    C. qualitative review.
    D. legal analysis.

REFERENCE: Abdelhak, pp 130–131
                Davis and LaCour, pp 374–376
                Green and Bowie, p 99
                LaTour, Eichenwald-Maki, and Oachs, pp 34–35
                McWay, p 126
                Odom-Wesley, pp 251–252

41. Accreditation by Joint Commission is a voluntary activity for a facility and it is
    A. considered unnecessary by most health care facilities.
    B. required for state licensure in all states.
    C. conducted in each facility annually.
    D. required for reimbursement of certain patient groups.

REFERENCE: Abdelhak, pp 113–114
                LaTour, Eichenwald-Maki, and Oachs, pp 37–38
                Odom-Wesley, p 299

42. Which of the following indices might be protected from unauthorized access through the use of unique identifier codes assigned to members of the medical staff?
    A. disease index
    B. procedure index
    C. master patient index
    D. physician index

REFERENCE: Green and Bowie, p 240
                LaTour, Eichenwald-Maki, and Oachs, pp 369–370
                Sayles, p 398

43. Which of the four distinct components of the problem-oriented record serves to help index documentation throughout the record?
    A. database
    B. problem list
    C. initial plan
    D. progress notes

REFERENCE: Abdelhak, pp 118–119
                Davis and LaCour, pp 55–56
                Green and Bowie, p 91
                LaTour, Eichenwald-Maki, and Oachs, pp 255–256
                Odom-Wesley, pp 215–216
                Sayles, p 126

44. You have been asked to report the registry's annual caseload to administration. The most efficient way to retrieve this information would be to use
    A. patient abstracts.
    B. patient index.
    C. accession register.
    D. follow-up files.

REFERENCE: LaTour, Eichenwald-Maki, and Oachs, p 371
                Sayles, p 349

45. Based on the following documentation in an acute care record, where would you expect this excerpt to appear?

    "Initially the patient was admitted to the medical unit to evaluate the x-ray findings and the rub. He was started on Levaquin 500 mg initially and then 250 mg daily. The patient was hydrated with IV fluids and remained afebrile. Serial cardiac enzymes were done. The rub, chest pain, and shortness of breath resolved. EKGs remained unchanged. Patient will be discharged and followed as an outpatient."

    A. discharge summary
    B. physical exam
    C. admission note
    D. clinical laboratory report

REFERENCE: Abdelhak, p 113
                Davis and LaCour, pp 106–107
                LaTour, Eichenwald-Maki, and Oachs, p 251
                Odom-Wesley, p 164
                Sayles, p 93

46. The best resource for checking out specific voluntary accreditation standards and guidelines for a rehabilitation facility is the
    A. Conditions of Participation for Rehabilitation Facilities.
    B. Medical Staff Bylaws, Rules, and Regulations.
    C. Joint Commission manual.
    D. CARF manual.

REFERENCE: Davis and LaCour, pp 26, 231, 351
                LaTour, Eichenwald-Maki, and Oachs, p 903
                Odom-Wesley, pp 191–196
                Sayles, p 74

47. Stage I of meaningful use focuses on data capture and sharing. Which of the following is included in the menu set of objectives for eligible hospitals in this stage?
    A. use CPOE for medication orders
    B. smoking cessation counseling for MI patients
    C. appropriate use of HL-7 standards
    D. establish critical pathways for complex, high-dollar cases

REFERENCE: Davis and LaCour, pp 82–84
                HealthIT.hhs.gov

48. Which of the following is a secondary data source that would be used to quickly gather the health records of all juvenile patients treated for diabetes within the past 6 months?
    A. disease index
    B. patient register
    C. pediatric census sheet
    D. procedure index

REFERENCE: Green and Bowie, pp 240–243
               LaTour, Eichenwald-Maki, and Oachs, p 369
               Sayles, p 436

49. Your job description includes working with agents who have been charged with detecting and correcting overpayments made to your hospital in the Medicare Fee for Service program. You will need to develop a professional relationship with
    A. the OIG.
    B. MEDPAR representatives.
    C. QIO physicians.
    D. recovery audit contractors.

REFERENCE: Green and Bowie, pp 325–326
               LaTour, Eichenwald-Maki, and Oachs, pp 851, 944
               Sayles, p 309

50. A primary focus of screen format design in a health record computer application should be to ensure that
    A. programmers develop standard screen formats for all hospitals.
    B. the user is capturing essential data elements.
    C. paper forms are easily converted to computer forms.
    D. data fields can be randomly accessed.

REFERENCE: Abdelhak, pp 119–120, 124
               LaTour, Eichenwald-Maki, and Oachs, p 51
               McWay, pp 131–132
               Odom-Wesley, p 230
               Sayles, pp 384–385

51. Before making recommendations to the Executive Committee regarding new physicians who have applied for active membership, the Credentials Committee must query the
    A. peer review organization.
    B. National Practitioner Data Bank.
    C. risk manager.
    D. Health Plan Employer Data and Information Set.

REFERENCE: Abdelhak, pp 471–472
               Green and Bowie, pp 251, 255
               LaTour, Eichenwald-Maki, and Oachs, p 16

52. The lack of a discharge order may indicate that the patient left against medical advice. If this situation occurs, you would expect to see the circumstances of the leave
    A. documented in an incident report and filed in the patient's health record.
    B. reported as a potentially compensable event.
    C. reported to the Executive Committee.
    D. documented in both the progress notes and the discharge summary.

REFERENCE: LaTour, Eichenwald-Maki, and Oachs, pp 251, 910
               Odom-Wesley, p 446

53. You recommend that the staff routinely check to verify that a summary on each patient is provided to the attending physician so that he or she can review, update, and recertify the patient as appropriate. The time frame for requiring this summary is at least every
    A. week.
    B. month.
    C. 60 days.
    D. 90 days.

REFERENCE: Abdelhak, p 143
               Odom-Wesley, pp 401–402

54. You want to review the one document in your facility that will spell out the documentation requirements for patient records; designate the time frame for completion by the active medical staff; and indicate the penalties for failure to comply with these record standards. Your best resource will be
    A. medical staff bylaws.
    B. quality management plan.
    C. Joint Commission accreditation manual.
    D. medical staff rules and regulations.

REFERENCE: Green and Bowie, p 16
               LaTour, Eichenwald-Maki, and Oachs, p 26
               Odom-Wesley, p 367

55. For inpatients, the first data item collected of a clinical nature is usually
    A. principal diagnosis.
    B. expected payer.
    C. admitting diagnosis.
    D. review of systems.

REFERENCE: Davis and LaCour, p 94
               Green and Bowie, p 140

56. In addition to diagnostic and therapeutic orders from the attending physician, you would expect every completed inpatient health record to contain
    A. standing orders.
    B. telephone orders.
    C. stop orders.
    D. discharge order.

REFERENCE: Abdelhak, p 108
               Green and Bowie, p 154
               LaTour, Eichenwald-Maki, and Oachs, p 248
               Odom-Wesley, p 115

57. When asked to explain how "review of systems" differs from "physical exam," you explain that the review of systems is used to document
    A. objective symptoms observed by the physician.
    B. past and current activities, such as smoking and drinking habits.
    C. a chronological description of patient's present condition from time of onset to present.
    D. subjective symptoms that the patient may have forgotten to mention or that may have seemed unimportant.

REFERENCE: Green and Bowie, p 147
               Odom-Wesley, p 331

58. Based on the following documentation, where would you expect this excerpt to appear?

    "The patient is alert and in no acute distress. Initial vital signs: T98, P 102 and regular, R 20 and BP 120/69…"

    A. physical exam
    B. past medical history
    C. social history
    D. chief complaint

REFERENCE: Abdelhak, p 107
              LaTour, Eichenwald-Maki, and Oachs, p 245
              Odom-Wesley, pp 108–109

59. The federally mandated resident assessment instrument used in long-term care facilities consists of three basic components, including the new care area assessment, utilization guidelines, and the
    A. UHDDS.   C. OASIS.
    B. MDS.   D. DEEDS.

REFERENCE: Peden, p 357
              Sayles, p 111

60. Skilled nursing facilities may choose to submit MDS data using RAVEN software, or software purchased commercially through a vendor, provided that the software meets
    A. Joint Commission standards.   C. HL-7 standards.
    B. NHIN standards.   D. CMS standards.

REFERENCE: Green and Bowie, p 253
              Peden, p 374

61. To enter the results of a CBC into the computer system, you would use a(n)
    A. laboratory system.   C. pharmacy system.
    B. radiology system.   D. order entry/results reporting system.

REFERENCE: Green and Bowie, pp 156, 170–171
              Johns, p 948
              Marreel and McLellan, pp 14–15, 187

62. An example of a primary data source is the
    A. disease index.   C. MPI.
    B. accession register.   D. hospital census.

REFERENCE: Abdelhak, pp 480–481
              Horton, p 4
              Koch, p 65
              LaTour, Eichenwald-Maki, and Oachs, pp 289, 368
              Odom-Wesley, p 83

63. The Recovery Audit Contractor (RAC) program identifies improper payments for
    A. Medicaid claims.
    B. Medicare claims.
    C. both B and D
    D. collection of overpayments.

REFERENCE: Davis and LaCour, pp 208, 354–355
               LaTour, Eichenwald-Maki, and Oachs, pp 855–856
               McWay, p 71
               Sayles, p 310

64. You have been asked to give an example of a clinical information system. Which one of the following would you cite?
    A. laboratory information system   C. billing system
    B. financial information system   D. admission-discharge-transfer

REFERENCE: McWay, pp 302–303

65. The PQRS is a reporting system established by the federal government for physician practices that participate in Medicare for

    A. monetary incentives.
    B. meaningful use incentives.
    C. quality measure reporting.
    D. all of the above

REFERENCE: LaTour, Eichenwald-Maki, and Oachs, p 129
               Sayles, p 968

66. Surgical case review includes all of the following EXCEPT
    A. determination of surgical justification based on clinical indication(s) in cases where no tissue has been removed.
    B. cases with elements missing in the preoperative anesthesia consultation.
    C. cases where there is a significant discrepancy between preoperative, postoperative, and pathological diagnoses.
    D. cases with serious surgical complications or surgical mortalities.

REFERENCE: LaTour, Eichenwald-Maki, and Oachs, p 665

67. While performing routine quantitative analysis of a record, a medical record employee finds an incident report in the record. The employee brings this to the attention of her supervisor. Which best practice should the supervisor follow to deal with this situation?

    A. Remove the incident report and send it to the patient.
    B. Tell the employee to leave the report in the record.
    C. Remove the incident report and have nursing personnel transfer all documentation from the report to the medical record.
    D. Refer this record to the Risk Manager for further review and removal of the incident report.

REFERENCE: Green and Bowie, p 88
               LaTour, Eichenwald-Maki, and Oachs, pp 860–863
               McWay (2008), p 110
               Sayles, pp 378–379

68. In compiling statistics to report the specific cause of death for all open-heart surgery cases, the quality coordinator assists in documenting

    A. patient care outcomes.
    B. utilization of hospital resources.
    C. delineation of physician privileges.
    D. compliance with OSHA standards.

REFERENCE: Johns, pp 644–645
               LaTour and Eichenwald-Maki, pp 21, 579
               McWay, p 153

69. Your hospital is required by the Joint Commission and CMS to participate in national benchmarking on specific disease entities for quality of care measurement. This required collection and reporting of disease-specific data is considered

    A. an environment of care.
    B. a group of sentinel events.
    C. a series of core measures.
    D. risk assessment.

REFERENCE: LaTour, Eichenwald-Maki, and Oachs, pp 201, 382, 670–671
               Sayles, pp 156, 968i, pp 538–539
               Shaw, pp 132, 359

70. Needlesticks, patient or employee falls, medication errors, or any event not consistent with routine patient care activities would require risk reporting documentation in the form of an

    A. operative report.   C. incident report.
    B. emergency room report.   D. insurance claim.

REFERENCE: Abdelhak, p 653
               Davis and LaCour, pp 378–379
               LaTour and Eichenwald-Maki, pp 860–863
               McWay, p 189
               Sayles, pp 613–620

71. The Utilization Review Coordinator reviews inpatient records at regular intervals to justify necessity and appropriateness of care to warrant further hospitalization. Which of the following utilization review activities is being performed?

    A. admission review   C. retrospective review
    B. preadmission   D. continued stay review

REFERENCE: Abdelhak, p 463
               Davis and LaCour, pp 173–175, 377
               LaTour, Eichenwald-Maki, and Oachs, pp 28–29, 331, 430, 464
               McWay, p 227
               Sayles, pp 610–611

72. Which feature is a trademark of an effective PI program?

    A. a one-time cure—all for a facility's problems
    B. an unmanageable project that is too expensive
    C. a cost-containment effort
    D. a continuous cycle of improvement projects over time

REFERENCE: Davis and LaCour, p 359
              Johns, p 610
              LaTour and Eichenwald-Maki, and Oachs, pp 650–653, 808
              McWay, pp 172, 187–189
              Sayles, p 595

73. Patient mortality, infection and complication rates, adherence to living will requirements, adequate pain control, and other documentation that describe end results of care or a measurable change in the patient's health are examples of

    A. outcome measures.   C. sentinel events.
    B. threshold level.   D. incident reports.

REFERENCE: Abdelhak, p 442
              LaTour, Eichenwald-Maki, and Oachs, pp 628–631, 670
              McWay, pp 124–128, 183
              Sayles, pp 600, 604

74. Engaging patients and their families in health care decisions is one of the core objectives for

    A. achieving meaningful use of EHRs.
    B. Joint Commission's National Patient Safety goals.
    C. HIPAA 5010 regulations.
    D. establishing flexible clinical pathways.

REFERENCE: HealthIT.hhs.gov
              LaTour, Eichenwald-Maki, and Oachs, p 286

75. Where in the health record would the following statement be located?
    "Microscopic Diagnosis: Liver (needle biopsy), metastatic adenocarcinoma"

    A. operative report   C. anesthesia report
    B. pathology report   D. radiology report

REFERENCE: Abdelhak, p 114
              Green and Bowie, p 167
              Johns, p 77
              LaTour and Eichenwald-Maki, p 200
              Odom-Wesley, p 171

76. In quality review activities, departments are directed to focus on clinical processes that are

    A. high volume.   C. problem prone.
    B. high risk.   D. all of the above

REFERENCE: LaTour, Eichenwald-Maki, and Oachs, p 652

Answer Key for Health Data Content and Standards

ANSWER   EXPLANATION

1. B   (C and D) Although a gross description of tissue removed may be mentioned on the operative note or discharge summary, only the pathology report will contain a microscopic description.

2. B   Answers A, C, and D represent items collected on Medicare inpatients according to UHDDS requirements. Only B represents a data item collected more typically in long-term care settings and required in the MDS.

3. C   The Joint Commission requires hospitals to prohibit abbreviations that have caused confusion or problems in their handwritten form, such as "U" for unit, which can be mistaken for "O" or the number "4." Spelling out the unit is preferred.

4. C   Factual summaries investigating unexpected facility events should not be treated as part of the patient's health information and therefore would not be recorded in the health record.

5. D   (A, B, and C) Patient care plans, pharmacy consultations, and transfer summaries are likely to be found on the records of long-term care patients.

6. B   Auto authentication is a policy adopted by some facilities that allows physicians to state in advance that transcribed reports should automatically be considered approved and signed (or authenticated) when the physician fails to make corrections within a preestablished time frame (e.g., "Consider it signed if I do not make changes within 7 days."). Another version of this practice is when physicians authorize the HIM department to send weekly lists of unsigned documents. The physician then signs the list in lieu of signing each individual report. Neither practice ensures that the physician has reviewed and approved each report individually.

7. A   The antepartum record should include a comprehensive history and physical exam on each OB patient visit with particular attention to menstrual and reproductive history.

8. C   Joint Commission and COP allow a legible copy of a recent H&P done in a doctor's office in lieu of an admission H&P as long as interval changes are documented in the record upon admission. In addition, when the patient is readmitted within 30 days for the same or a related problem, an interval history and physical exam may be completed if the original H&P is readily available.

9. A   The major sources of case findings for cancer registry programs are the pathology department, the disease index, and the logs of patients treated in radiology and other outpatient departments. B. The number index identifies new health record numbers and the patients to whom they were assigned. C. The physicians' index identifies all patients treated by each doctor. D. The patient index links each patient treated in a facility with the health number under which the clinical information can be located.

10. C   A. Some reference to the patient's history may be found in the discharge summary but not a detailed history. B. The attending physician records the discharge summary. D. Codes are usually recorded on a different form in the record.

11. D   A and B deal with issues directly linked to quality of care reviews. C deals with risk management. Only D points to a review aimed at evaluating the quality of documentation in the health record.

12. B   Although the nursing staff, hospital administration, and the health information management professional play a role in ensuring an accurate and complete record, the major responsibility lies with the attending physician.

13. C   Unlike the acute care hospital, where most health care practitioners document separately, the patient care plan is the foundation around which patient care is organized in long-term care facilities because it contains the unique perspective of each discipline involved.

14. C   The Joint Commission requires hospitals to mark the correct surgical site and to involve the patient in the marking process to help eliminate wrong site surgeries.

15. D   Among those abbreviations considered confusing or likely to be misinterpreted are those containing a leading decimal.

Answer Key for Health Data Content and Standards

ANSWER   EXPLANATION

16. A   The assessment statement combines the objective and subjective into a diagnostic conclusion, sometimes in the form of a differential diagnosis, such as "peritonitis versus appendicitis."

17. D   A. The disease index is a listing in diagnostic code number order. B. The physician index is a listing of cases in order by physician name or number. C. The MPI cross-references the patient name and medical record number.

18. D   A, B, and C all refer to a computer application of managing health information, but only answer D deals with the clinical application of data entry into the patient's record at the time and location of service.

19. A   Pharmacy consults are required for elderly patients who typically take multiple medications. These consults review for potential drug interactions and/or discrepancies in medications given and those ordered.

20. D   CMS publishes both proposed and final rules for the Conditions of Participation for hospitals in the daily *Federal Register*.

21. D   A. An interval H&P can be used when a patient is readmitted for the same or related problem within 30 days. B and C. No matter how long the patient stays or how minor the condition, an H&P is required.

22. A   The needs of the end user are always the primary concern when designing systems.

23. C   Answers A, B, and D are required items in BOTH acute and ER records.

24. B   A and C. In these situations a transfer summary or pertinent copies from the inpatient health record may accompany the patient, but the original record stays on the premises.

25. D   A represents the assessment statement, B the objective, and C the plan.

26. B   OBRA mandates comprehensive functional assessments of long-term care residents using the Minimum Data Set for Long-Term Care.

27. A   Answers B and D are types of data sets for collecting data in long-term (MDS) and acute care (UHDDS) facilities. A data dictionary should include security levels for each field as well as definitions for all entities.

28. B   COP requires a consultation report on patients who are not a good surgical risk as well as those with obscure diagnoses, patients whose physicians have doubts as to the best therapeutic measure to be taken, and patients for whom there is a question of criminal activity.

29. B   The medical history, including a review of systems and chief complaint, is information supplied by the patient. A physical assessment adds objective data to the subjective data provided by the patient in the history.

30. D   This meets both Joint Commission and COP standards.

31. B   This entry is typical of a surgical procedure.

32. A   The medical history (including chief complaint, history of present illness, past medical history, personal history, family history, and a review of systems) is provided by the patient or the most knowledgeable available source. The physical examination adds objective data to the subjective data provided by the patient. This exam begins with the physician's objective assessment of the patient's general condition.

33. D   Answers A, B, and C are examples of secondary data sources.

34. D   Quantitative analysis involves checking for the presence or absence of necessary reports and/or signatures, while qualitative analysis may involve checking documentation consistency, such as comparing a patient's pharmacy drug profile with the medication administration record.

35. C   A, B, and D all represent common checks performed by a quantitative analysis clerk: missing reports, signatures, or patient identification. Answer C represents a more in-depth review dealing with the quality of the data documented.

Answer Key for Health Data Content and Standards

ANSWER   EXPLANATION

36. B   A, C, and D represent routine interpretations that are not normally considered to be consultations.

37. A   B represents an appropriate job for the infection control officer. Answer C represents the clinical care evaluation process, rather than the review of quality documentation. Answer D is a function of the utilization review program.

38. A   Progress notes may be integrated or they may be separated, with nurses, physicians, and other health care providers writing on designated forms for each discipline.

39. B   The Commission on Accreditation of Rehabilitation Facilities is an independent accrediting agency for rehabilitation facilities. Palliative care (answer B) is most likely to be provided at a hospice.

40. C   A. Peer review typically involves quality of care issues rather than quality of documentation issues. D. Legal analysis ensures that the record entries would be acceptable in a court of law.

41. D   A. Advantages of accreditation are numerous and include financial and legal incentives. B. State licensure is required for accreditation but not the reverse. C. Joint Commission conducts unannounced on-site surveys approximately every 3 years.

42. D   Because information contained in the physicians' index is considered confidential, identification codes are often used rather than the physicians' names.

43. B   In a POMR, the database contains the history and physical; the problem list includes titles, numbers, and dates of problems, and serves as a table of contents of the record; the initial plan describes diagnostic, therapeutic, and patient education plans; and the progress notes document the progress of the patient throughout the episode of care, summarized in a discharge summary or transfer note at the end of the stay.

44. C   The accession register is a permanent log of all the cases entered into the database. Each number assigned is preceded by the accession year, making it easy to assess annual workloads.

45. A   The excerpt clearly indicates an overall summary of the patient's course in the hospital, which is a common element of the discharge summary.

46. D   The manual published by the Commission on Accreditation of Rehabilitation Facilities will have the most specific and comprehensive standards for a rehabilitation facility.

47. A   See all objectives for Stage I of meaningful use on the HealthIT.hhs.gov website.

48. A   The disease index is compiled as a result of abstracting patient code numbers into a computer database, allowing a variety of reports to be generated.

49. D   The RAC program is mandated to find and correct improper Medicare payments paid to health care providers participating in the Medicare reimbursement program. (A) OIG (Office of Inspector General); (B) MEDPAR (Medicare Provider Analysis and Review); (C) QIO (Quality Improvement Organization).

50. B   Both paper-based and computer-based records share similar forms and view design considerations. Among these are the selection and sequencing of essential data items.

51. B   With the passage of the Health Care Quality Improvement Act of 1986, the NPDB was established. Hospitals are required to query the data bank before granting clinical privileges to physicians.

52. D   A. Incident reports are written accounts of unusual events that have an adverse effect on a patient, employee, or facility visitor and should never be filed with the patient's record. B. PCEs are occurrences that could result in financial liability at some future time. A patient leaving AMA does not in itself suggest a PCE. C. It is not typical to report AMAs to the Executive Committee. D. Documenting the event is crucial in protecting the legal interests of the health care team and facility.

Answer Key for Health Data Content and Standards

    ANSWER   EXPLANATION

53. C This 60-day time frame is often referred to as the patient's certification period. Recertification can continue every 62 days until the patient is discharged from home health services.

54. D Although the medical staff bylaws reflect general principles and policies of the medical staff, the rules and regulations outline the details for implementing these principles, including the process and time frames for completing records, and the penalties for failure to comply.

55. C Clinical data include all health care information collected during a patient's episode of care. During the registration or intake process, the admitting diagnosis, provided by the attending physician, is entered on the face sheet. If the patient is admitted through the ED, the chief complaint listed on the ED record is usually the first clinical data collected. A. The principal diagnosis is often not known until after diagnostic tests are conducted. B. Demographic data are not clinical in nature. D. The review of systems is collected during the history and physical, which is typically done after admission to the hospital.

56. D Although many patient health records may feasibly contain all of the orders listed, only the discharge order is required to document the formal release of a patient from the facility. Absence of a discharge order would indicate that the patient left against medical advice and this event should be thoroughly documented as well.

57. D Answer A refers to the physical exam. Answer B refers to the social history. Answer C refers to the history of present illness.

58. A Answers B, C, and D represent components of the medical history as supplied by the patient, while the physical exam is an entry obtained through objective observation and measurement made by the provider.

59. B The Minimum Data Set is a basic component of the long-term care RAI. A. UHDDS is used in acute care; C. OASIS is used in home health; D. DEEDS is used in emergency departments.

60. D MDS data are reported directly to the Centers for Medicare and Medicaid Services and must conform to agency standards.

61. A

62. B

63. D

64. A

65. C

66. D

67. A Incident reports are written accounts of unusual events that have an adverse effect on a patient, employee, or facility visitor and should never be filed with the patient's record.

68. A

69. C

70. C

71. D

72. D

73. A

74. A There are several core objectives for achieving meaningful use, and engaging patients and their families is one of these objectives.

75. B

76. D

REFERENCES

Abdelhak, M., Grostick, S., Hanken, M. A., & Jacobs, E. (Eds.). (2012). *Health information: Management of a strategic resource* (4th ed.). Philadelphia: W. B. Saunders.

CMS. Fiscal Year 2009 Quality Measure Reporting for 2010 Payment Update https://www.cms.gov/HospitalQualityInits/downloads/HospitalRHQDAPU200808.pdf

Davis, N., & LaCour, M. (2014). *Health information technology* (3rd ed.). Maryland, MO: Elsevier (Saunders).

Green, M. A., & Bowie, J. (2011). *Essentials of health information management: Principles and practices.* Clifton Park, NY: Delmar Cengage Learning.

Horton, L. (2011). *Calculating and reporting health care statistics* (4th ed.). Chicago: American Health Information Management Association (AHIMA).

Koch, G. (2008). *Basic allied health statistics and analysis* (3rd ed.). Clifton Park, NY: Delmar Cengage Learning.

LaTour, K., Eichenwald-Maki, S. and Oachs, P. (2013). *Health information management: Concepts, principles and practice* (4th ed.). Chicago: American Health Information Management Association (AHIMA).

McWay, D. C. (2014). *Today's health information management, an integrated approach* (2nd ed.). Clifton Park, NY: Delmar Cengage Learning.

Odom-Wesley, B., Brown, D., & Meyers, C. (2009). *Documentation for medical records.* Chicago: American Health Information Management Association (AHIMA).

Sayles, N. (2013). *Health information management technology: An applied approach* (4th ed.). Chicago: American Health Information Management Association (AHIMA).

Competencies for Health Data Content

Question	CCA Domain					
	1	2	3	4	5	6
1			X			
2			X			
3			X			
4			X			
5			X			
6					X	
7			X			
8			X			
9			X			
10			X			
11			X			
12						X
13			X			
14			X			
15			X			
16			X			
17	X					
18			X			
19			X			
20				X		
21			X			
22					X	
23			X			
24			X			
25			X			
26			X			
27					X	
28			X			
29			X			
30			X			
31			X			
32			X			
33	X					
34			X			
35			X			
36			X			
37			X			
38			X			
39			X			
40			X			

Question	CCA Domain					
	1	2	3	4	5	6
41			X			
42			X			
43			X			
44			X			

Competencies for Classification Systems and Secondary Data Sources

Question	CCA Domain					
	1	2	3	4	5	6
45			X			
46			X			
47					X	
48			X			
49		X				
50					X	
51			X			
52			X			
53			X			
54			X			
55			X			
56			X			
57			X			
58			X			
59			X			
60					X	
61					X	
62			X			
63				X		
64				X	X	
65				x		
66			X			
67			X			
68			X			
69			X			
70			X			
71			X			
72			X			
73			X			
74			X			
75			X			
76			X			

IV. Medical Science

Lauralyn Kavanaugh-Burke, DrPH, RHIA, CHTS-IM

1. The etiology of aplastic anemia is
    A. acute blood loss.
    B. bone marrow failure.
    C. chronic blood loss.
    D. inadequate iron intake.

    REFERENCE: Jones, pp 331, 337, 340
    Moisio, p 213
    Neighbors & Tannehill-Jones, p 117
    Scott & Fong, p 250

2. The most common etiology of dementia in the United States is
    A. autism.
    B. Alzheimer's disease.
    C. alcohol abuse.
    D. anxiety disorder.

    REFERENCE: Jones, p 1084
    Neighbors & Tannehill-Jones, p 273

3. Dr. Zambrano ordered a CEA test for Mr. Logan, a 67-year-old African American male patient. Dr. Zambrano may be considering a diagnosis of
    A. cancer.
    B. carpal tunnel syndrome.
    C. cardiomyopathy.
    D. congestive heart failure.

    REFERENCE: NLM (4)

4. The prevention of illness through vaccination occurs due to the formation of
    A. helper B cells.
    B. immunosurveillance.
    C. mast cells.
    D. memory cells.

    REFERENCE: Jones, pp 350–351
    Scott & Fong, p 338

5. A bee stung little Bobby. He experiences itching, erythema, and respiratory distress caused by laryngeal edema and vascular collapse. In the emergency department where he is treated with an epinephrine injection, Bobby is diagnosed with
    A. allergic rhinitis.
    B. allergic sinusitis.
    C. anaphylactic shock.
    D. asthma.

    REFERENCE: Jones, pp 965, 974
    Neighbors & Tannehill-Jones, p 69

6. Genital warts are caused by
    A. HAV.
    B. HIV.
    C. HPV.
    D. VZV.

    REFERENCE: Jones, p 716
    Moisio, p 436
    Scott & Fong, p 468

7. A patient's history includes the following documentation:
    - Small ulcers (chancres) appeared on the genitalia and resolved after four to six weeks
    - Elevated temperature, skin rash, and enlarged lymph nodes

    Which procedure will be used to initially diagnose the patient?
    A. bone marrow test
    B. chest x-ray
    C. serology test
    D. thyroid scan

    REFERENCE: Jones, p 328
    Moisio, p 437
    Neighbors & Tannehill-Jones, p 329

8. Which of the following cells produce histamine in a type I hypersensitivity reaction?
   A. lymphocyte
   B. macrophages
   C. mast cells
   D. neutrophils

   REFERENCE: Jones, p 106
                  Neighbors & Tannehill-Jones, p 47
                  Rizzo, p 104

9. Which one of the following cells produces antibodies?
   A. A cells
   B. cytotoxic T cells
   C. helper T cells
   D. plasma cells

   REFERENCE: Neighbors & Tannehill-Jones, p 64
                  Rizzo, pp 349, 350, 352
                  Scott & Fong, p 338

10. Which of the following conditions is NOT a predisposing risk associated with essential hypertension?
    A. age
    B. cigarette smoking
    C. low dietary sodium intake
    D. obesity

    REFERENCE: Jones, p 404
                   Neighbors & Tannehill-Jones, p 134
                   Scott & Fong, pp 300–301

11. A patient, who is HIV positive, has raised red or purple lesions, appearing on the skin, in the mouth, or anywhere on the body. What is the stage of his disease process in today's medical terminology?
    A. ARC
    B. AIDS
    C. AZT
    D. HIV positive

    REFERENCE: Jones, pp 714–715
                   Neighbors & Tannehill-Jones, p 78

12. Each of the following conditions fall under the category of COPD EXCEPT
    A. chronic bronchitis.
    B. emphysema.
    C. pneumonia.
    D. smoking.

    REFERENCE: Moisio, pp 238, 240
                   Neighbors & Tannehill-Jones, pp 160–161
                   Rizzo, p 407
                   Scott & Fong, p 368

13. Which of the following is a lethal arrhythmia?
    A. atrial fibrillation
    B. atrial tachycardia
    C. bradycardia
    D. ventricular fibrillation

    REFERENCE: Jones, p 411
                   Neighbors & Tannehill-Jones, p 144

14. The drug commonly used to treat bipolar mood swings is
    A. Lanoxin.
    B. Lasix.
    C. lithium carbonate.
    D. lorazepam.

    REFERENCE: Neighbors & Tannehill-Jones, p 417
                   Woodrow, pp 358, 360

15. The leading cause of blindness in the United States is a vision-related pathology caused by diabetes. It is called
    A. retinal detachment.
    C. retinopathy.
    B. retinoblastoma.
    D. rhabdomyosarcoma.

REFERENCE: Jones, pp 569, 606–607, 1075–1077
                Moisio, p 403
                Neighbors & Tannehill-Jones, pp 254–255, 289, 294–295, 300
                Scott & Fong, pp 195, 231–232

16. Penicillin is effective in the treatment of all the following diseases EXCEPT
    A. influenza.
    C. strep throat.
    B. Lyme disease.
    D. syphilis.

REFERENCE: Jones, pp 452, 070
                Neighbors & Tannehill-Jones, pp 89–90, 190, 345, 325
                Rizzo, p 459

17. Impetigo can be
    A. spread through autoinoculation.
    C. caused by *Staphylococcus aureus.*
    B. caused by *Streptococcus pyogenes.*
    D. either A or B.

REFERENCE: Jones, pp 121, 855
                Neighbors & Tannehill-Jones, pp 344, 393
                Scott & Fong, pp 78–79

18. Diagnostic testing for meningitis usually involves
    A. blood cultures.
    C. stool C&S.
    B. cerebrospinal fluid analysis.
    D. testing urine.

REFERENCE: Jones, p 292
                Neighbors & Tannehill-Jones, p 266

19. Which disease is a malignancy of the lymphatic system?
    A. cystic fibrosis
    C. neutropenia
    B. Hodgkin's disease
    D. Von Willebrand's disease

REFERENCE: Jones, p 355
                Moisio, p 216
                Neighbors & Tannehill-Jones, pp 114, 119,121, 380
                Rizzo, p 354
                Scott & Fong, p 312

20. Which of the following is a hereditary disease of the cerebral cortex that includes progressive muscle spasticity and mental impairment leading to dementia?
    A. Huntington's disease
    C. Bell's palsy
    B. Lou Gehrig's disease
    D. Guillain–Barré syndrome

REFERENCE: Jones, pp 277–278
                Moisio, p 294
                Neighbors & Tannehill-Jones, p 280
                Scott & Fong, p 481

21. Which of the following autoimmune diseases affects tissues of the nervous system?
    A. Goodpasture's syndrome
    C. myasthenia gravis
    B. Hashimoto's disease
    D. rheumatoid arthritis

REFERENCE: Jones, pp 281–282, 356
               Neighbors & Tannehill-Jones, pp 72, 107
               Scott & Fong, p 139

22. Pain is a symptom of which of the following conditions?
    A. first-degree burn (superficial)
    B. second-degree burn (partial thickness)
    C. third-degree burn (full thickness)
    D. both A and B

REFERENCE: Jones, pp 116–117
               Neighbors & Tannehill-Jones, p 356
               Scott & Fong, pp 81–82

23. A 75-year-old patient has a sore tongue with tingling and numbness of the hands and feet. She has headaches and is fatigued. Following diagnostic workup, the doctor orders monthly injections of vitamin B_{12}. This patient most likely has which of the following conditions?
    A. aplastic anemia
    C. pernicious anemia
    B. autoimmune hemolytic anemia
    D. sickle cell anemia

REFERENCE: Jones, p 332
               Moisio, p 213
               Neighbors & Tannehill-Jones, p 116
               Scott & Fong, p 250

24. Which one of the following is NOT a pathophysiological factor in anemia?
    A. excessive RBC breakdown
    C. loss of bone marrow function
    B. lack of RBC maturation
    D. loss of spleen function

REFERENCE: Jones, pp 331–333, 338–341
               Neighbors & Tannehill-Jones, p 116
               Rizzo, p 308
               Scott & Fong, pp 250–251

25. Many bacterial diseases are transmitted directly from person to person. Which of the diseases listed below is a bacterial disease that is transmitted by way of a tick vector?
    A. Legionnaires' disease
    C. tetanus
    B. Lyme disease
    D. tuberculosis

REFERENCE: Jones, pp 228–229
               Moisio, p 434
               Neighbors & Tannehill-Jones, p 345
               Scott & Fong, p 335

26. Necrosis extending down to the underlying fascia is characteristic of a decubitus ulcer in stage
    A. one.
    C. three.
    B. two.
    D. four.

REFERENCE: Scott & Fong, p 83

27. Scabies, a highly contagious condition that produces intense pruritus and rash, is caused by
  A. pediculosis capitis.
  B. itch mites.
  C. candidiasis.
  D. ringworm.

REFERENCE: Jones, pp 124–125
  Moisio, p 108
  Neighbors & Tannehill-Jones, p 347

28. A physician prescribes a diuretic for his patient. He could be treating any of the following disorders EXCEPT
  A. congestive heart failure.
  B. mitral stenosis.
  C. pneumonia.
  D. pulmonary edema.

REFERENCE: Neighbors & Tannehill-Jones, p 162
  Scott & Fong, pp 274, 366

29. All of the following are examples of direct transmission of a disease EXCEPT
  A. contaminated foods.
  B. coughing or sneezing.
  C. droplet spread.
  D. physical contact.

REFERENCE: Neighbors & Tannehill-Jones, pp 5–6
  Scott & Fong, pp 332–336

30. _____ is the most common type of skin cancer and _____ is the most deadly type of skin cancer.
  A. Malignant melanoma, basal cell carcinoma
  B. Basal cell carcinoma, malignant melanoma
  C. Oat cell carcinoma, squamous cell carcinoma
  D. Squamous cell carcinoma, oat cell carcinoma

REFERENCE: Jones, pp 117, 122–123, 934–935, 939–940
  Neighbors & Tannehill-Jones, p 351
  Rizzo, p 132
  Scott & Fong, p 81
  Sormunen, pp 114, 115

31. John Palmer was in a car accident and sustained severe chest trauma resulting in a tension pneumothorax. Manifestations of this disorder include all of the following EXCEPT
  A. severe chest pain.
  B. dyspnea.
  C. shock.
  D. clubbing.

REFERENCE: Jones, p 454
  Neighbors & Tannehill-Jones, p 166

32. Cancer derived from epithelial tissue is classified as a(n)
  A. adenoma.
  B. carcinoma.
  C. lipoma.
  D. sarcoma.

REFERENCE: Jones, p 931
  Neighbors & Tannehill-Jones, p 26
  Rizzo, p 90
  Sormunen, p 302

33. Sex-linked genetic diseases
    A. are transmitted during sexual activity.
    B. involve a defect on a chromosome.
    C. occur equally between males and females.
    D. occur only in males.

REFERENCE: Neighbors & Tannehill-Jones, p 14
                      Rizzo, p 457
                      Scott & Fong, pp 480–485

34. A stapedectomy is a common treatment for
    A. atherosclerosis.
    B. multiple sclerosis.
    C. otosclerosis.
    D. scoliosis.

REFERENCE: Jones, p 630
                      Moisio, pp 412–413
                      Neighbors & Tannehill-Jones, p 298
                      Scott & Fong, p 201

35. In systemic circulation, which of the following vessels carries oxygenated blood?
    A. right vena cava
    B. renal arteries
    C. pulmonary arteries
    D. left ventricle

REFERENCE: Jones, pp 380–382
                      Moisio, pp 176–178
                      Neighbors & Tannehill-Jones, p 128
                      Rizzo, pp 322, 335
                      Scott & Fong, pp 286–287, 295
                      Sormunen, p 206

36. Which of the following sequences correctly depicts the flow of blood through the heart to the lungs in order for gas exchange to occur?
    A. right atrium, right ventricle, lungs, pulmonary artery
    B. right atrium, right ventricle, pulmonary artery, lungs
    C. right ventricle, right atrium, lungs, pulmonary artery
    D. right ventricle, right atrium, pulmonary artery, lungs

REFERENCE: Jones, pp 380–382
                      Moisio, pp 176–177
                      Neighbors & Tannehill-Jones, p 128
                      Rizzo, pp 322, 325
                      Scott & Fong, pp 286–288, 295
                      Sormunen, p 206

37. Diastole occurs when
    A. cardiac insufficiency is present.
    B. the atria contracts.
    C. the ventricles contract.
    D. the ventricles fill.

REFERENCE: Jones, pp 384, 387
                      Neighbors & Tannehill-Jones, p 130
                      Rizzo, p 333
                      Scott & Fong, p 295
                      Sormunen, p 207

38. The most fatal type of lung cancer is
    A. adenocarcinoma.
    B. large cell cancer.
    C. small cell cancer.
    D. squamous cell cancer.

REFERENCE: Scott & Fong, pp 368–369

39. Gas exchange in the lungs takes place at the
    A. alveoli.
    B. bronchi.
    C. bronchioles.
    D. trachea.

REFERENCE: Neighbors & Tannehill-Jones, p 154
              Rizzo, pp 402–404
              Scott & Fong, p 358
              Sormunen, p 345

40. O_2 is carried in the blood
    A. bound to hemoglobin.
    B. in the form of carbonic acid.
    C. plasma.
    D. serum.

REFERENCE: Moisio, p 208
              Neighbors & Tannehill-Jones, p 112
              Rizzo, pp 408, 413
              Sormunen, p 247

41. Which of the following anatomical parts is involved in both the respiratory and digestive systems?
    A. larynx
    B. nasal cavity
    C. pharynx
    D. trachea

REFERENCE: Moisio, p 233
              Rizzo, p 371
              Scott & Fong, pp 355–356
              Sormunen, p 344

42. A disease of the inner ear with fluid disruption in the semicircular canal that causes vertigo is
    A. labyrinthitis.
    B. mastoiditis.
    C. Meniere's disease.
    D. both A and C.

REFERENCE: Moisio, pp 411–412
              Neighbors & Tannehill-Jones, pp 300–301
              Scott & Fong, p 201

43. Softening of the bone in children is termed _____.
    A. Raynaud's disease
    B. Reye's syndrome
    C. Rickets
    D. Rubella

REFERENCE: Neighbors & Tannehill-Jones, p 92
              Rizzo, p 147
              Scott & Fong, p 112

44. A pathological diagnosis of transitional cell carcinoma is made. The examined tissue was removed from the
    A. bladder.
    B. esophagus.
    C. oral cavity.
    D. pleura.

REFERENCE: Neighbors & Tannehill-Jones, p 235
              Rizzo, pp 102–103

45. Most carbon dioxide is carried in the
    A. blood as CO_2 gas.
    B. blood bound to hemoglobin.
    C. blood plasma in the form of carbonic acid.
    D. red blood cells.

REFERENCE: Rizzo, pp 408, 413
                 Scott & Fong, p 243
                 Sormunen, p 247

46. The key diagnostic finding for typical pneumonia is
    A. abnormal chemical electrolytes.
    B. elevated WBC.
    C. lung consolidation on CXR.
    D. positive sputum culture.

REFERENCE: Neighbors & Tannehill-Jones, p 162

47. The presence of fluid in the alveoli of the lungs is characteristic of
    A. COPD.
    B. Crohn's disease.
    C. pneumonia.
    D. tuberculosis.

REFERENCE: Neighbors & Tannehill-Jones, p 163
                 Rizzo, p 407

48. Full-blown AIDS sets in as
    A. CD4 receptors increase.
    B. helper T-cell concentration decreases.
    C. HIV virus concentration decreases.
    D. immunity to HIV increases.

REFERENCE: Scott & Fong, pp 321–324
                 Sormunen, p 271

49. Which of the following BEST describes tuberculosis?
    A. a chronic, systemic disease whose initial infection is in the lungs
    B. an acute bacterial infection of the lung
    C. an ordinary lung infection
    D. a viral infection of the lungs

REFERENCE: Neighbors & Tannehill-Jones, pp 49, 392–393
                 Scott & Fong, p 366
                 Sormunen, p 272

50. A treatment for sensorineural hearing loss is
    A. cochlear implants.
    B. myringotomy.
    C. removal of impacted cerumen.
    D. stapedectomy.

REFERENCE: Jones, p 628
                 Scott & Fong, p 202

51. Mary Mulholland has diabetes. Her physician has told her about some factors that put her more at risk for infections. Which of the following factors would probably NOT be applicable?
    A. hypoxia
    B. increased glucose in body fluids
    C. increased blood supply
    D. both A and C

REFERENCE: Neighbors & Tannehill-Jones, pp 253–257

52. Most of the digestion of food and absorption of nutrients occur in the
    A. ascending colon.   C. small intestine.
    B. esophagus.   D. stomach.

REFERENCE: Neighbors & Tannehill-Jones, p 185
                 Rizzo, pp 377–378
                 Scott & Fong, pp 385–386
                 Sormunen, p 374

53. The Phalen's wrist flexor test is a noninvasive method for diagnosing
    A. carpal tunnel syndrome.   C. severe acute respiratory syndrome.
    B. Down syndrome.   D. Tourette's syndrome.

REFERENCE: NINDS

54. A chronic inflammatory bowel disease where affected segments of the bowel may be separated by
    normal bowel tissue is characteristic of
    A. appendicitis.   C. diverticulitis.
    B. Crohn's disease.   D. Graves' disease.

REFERENCE: Moisio, p 270
                 Neighbors & Tannehill-Jones, pp 193, 198
                 Rizzo, p 381
                 Sormunen, p 392

55. The patient's pathology report revealed the presence of Reed–Sternberg cells. This is indicative of
    A. Hodgkin's disease.   C. non-Hodgkin's lymphoma.
    B. leukemia.   D. sarcoma.

REFERENCE: Neighbors & Tannehill-Jones, p 119

56. The most common rickettsial disease in the United States is
    A. hantavirus.   C. Rocky Mountain spotted fever.
    B. Lyme disease.   D. syphilis.

REFERENCE: Moisio, pp 434–435
                 Neighbors & Tannehill-Jones, p 57
                 Scott & Fung, pp 331–332

57. Early detection programs apply screening guidelines to detect cancers at an early stage, which
    provides the likelihood of increased survival and decreased morbidity. Which of the following
    would NOT be a diagnostic or screening test for colorectal cancer?
    A. double contrast barium enema C. fecal occult blood test
    B. sigmoidoscopy   D. upper GI x-ray

REFERENCE: American Cancer Society
                 Neighbors & Tannehill-Jones, p 200
                 Scott & Fong, p 399

58. Prevention programs identify risk factors and use strategies to modify attitudes and behaviors to
    reduce the chance of developing cancers. Which of the following would NOT be an identified risk
    factor for colorectal cancer?
    A. alcohol use   C. high-fiber diet
    B. physical inactivity   D. obesity

REFERENCE: American Cancer Society

59. In general, excessive RBC breakdown could result in
    A. Crohn's disease.
    B. elevated BUN.
    C. high bilirubin levels.
    D. peptic ulcers.

REFERENCE: Labtestsonline (1)
               Neighbors & Tannehill-Jones, p 209
               NLM (1)

60. The most common bloodborne infection in the United States is
    A. *Helicobacter pylori.*
    B. hepatitis A.
    C. hepatitis C.
    D. hemophilia.

REFERENCE: Scott & Fong, p 397

61. The first stage of alcoholic liver disease is
    A. alcoholic hepatitis.
    B. cirrhosis.
    C. fatty liver.
    D. jaundice.

REFERENCE: Neighbors & Tannehill-Jones, p 211

62. Portal hypertension can contribute to all of the following EXCEPT
    A. ascites.
    B. dilation of blood vessels lining the intestinal tract.
    C. esophageal varices.
    D. kidney failure.

REFERENCE: Mayo Clinic (1)
               Neighbors & Tannehill-Jones, pp 211–214

63. Which of the following is a liver function test?
    A. AST (SGOT)
    B. BUN
    C. ECG
    D. TSH

REFERENCE: Neighbors & Tannehill-Jones, pp 211–214
               Sormunen, p 389

64. Which of the following is a risk factor involved in the etiology of gallstones?
    A. being overweight
    B. being an adolescent
    C. low-fat diets
    D. presence of peptic ulcer

REFERENCE: Rizzo, p 215

65. A serum potassium level of 2.8 would indicate
    A. Addison disease.
    B. anemia.
    C. diabetic ketoacidosis.
    D. hypokalemia.

REFERENCE: Mayo Clinic (2)
               NLM (3)

66. A procedure performed with an instrument that freezes and destroys abnormal tissues (including seborrheic keratoses, basal cell carcinomas, and squamous cell carcinomas) is
    A. cryosurgery.
    B. electrodesiccation.
    C. phacoemulsification.
    D. photocautery.

REFERENCE: Moisio, p 110
               Rizzo, pp 81, 469

67. Which of the organs listed below has endocrine and exocrine functions?
    A. kidney   C. lung
    B. liver   D. pancreas

REFERENCE: Moisio, p 266
                  Neighbors & Tannehill-Jones, p 252
                  Rizzo, pp 282–283, 274
                  Scott & Fong, p 386

68. Which of the following is an effect of insulin?

    A. decreases glycogen concentration in liver
    B. increases blood glucose
    C. increases the breakdown of fats
    D. increases glucose metabolism

REFERENCE: Moisio, pp 301–302, 304
                  Neighbors & Tannehill-Jones, pp 244, 252–256
                  Rizzo, pp 274–276, 282, 284–285
                  Scott & Fong, pp 225–226, 233, 504
                  Sormunen, p 554

69. The causative organism for severe acute respiratory syndrome (SARS) is a
    A. bacterium.   C. fungus.
    B. coronavirus.   D. retrovirus.

REFERENCE: Moisio, p 241
                  Neighbors & Tannehill-Jones, p 165
                  Scott & Fong, p 366

70. Before leaving the hospital, all newborns are screened for an autosomal recessive genetic disorder
    of defective enzymatic conversion in protein metabolism. With early detection and a protein-
    restricted diet, brain damage is prevented. This disease is
    A. cystic fibrosis.   C. phenylketonuria.
    B. hereditary hemochromatosis.   D. Tay–Sachs disease.

REFERENCE: Neighbors & Tannehill-Jones, p 378
                  Scott & Fong, p 481

71. Diabetic microvascular disease occurs
    A. as a direct result of elevated serum glucose.
    B. as a result of elevated fat in blood.
    C. due to damage to nerve cells.
    D. only in patients with type 1 diabetes.

REFERENCE: Neighbors & Tannehill-Jones, pp 254–255
                  Rizzo, pp 284–285
                  Scott & Fong, pp 231–232

72. Older age, obesity, and family history of diabetes are all characteristics of
    A. type 1 diabetes.   C. juvenile diabetes.
    B. type 2 diabetes.   D. IDDM.

REFERENCE: Rizzo, pp 284–285
                  Scott & Fong, p 232

73. An elevated serum amylase would be characteristic of
    A. acute pancreatitis.   C. postrenal failure.
    B. gallbladder disease.   D. prerenal failure.

REFERENCE: Neighbors & Tannehill-Jones, p 219

74. Clinical manifestations of this disease include polydipsia, polyuria, polyphagia, weight loss, and hyperglycemia. Which of the following tests would be ordered to confirm the disease?
    A. fasting blood sugar   C. glucose tolerance test
    B. glucagon   D. postprandial blood sugar

REFERENCE: Neighbors & Tannehill-Jones, pp 253–254
                  Rizzo, pp 84–85
                  Scott & Fong, pp 231, 235

75. Common kidney stone treatments that allow small particles to be flushed out of the body through the urinary system include all of the following EXCEPT
    A. extracorporeal shock wave lithotripsy.
    B. fluid hydration.
    C. ureteroscopy and stone basketing.
    D. using medication to dissolve the stone(s).

REFERENCE: Neighbors & Tannehill-Jones, p 229

76. When a decubitus ulcer has progressed to a stage in which osteomyelitis is present, the ulcer has extended to the
    A. bone.   C. muscle.
    B. fascia.   D. subcutaneous tissue.

REFERENCE: Neighbors & Tannehill-Jones, pp 92–93
                  Scott & Fong, pp 83–84

77. The 68-year-old female patient has no visible bleeding, but remains anemic. Her physician is concerned about possible gastrointestinal bleeding. Which of the following tests might be ordered?
    A. DEXA scan   C. Pap smear test
    B. guaiac smear test   D. prostatic-specific antigen test

REFERENCE: Estridge & Reynolds, pp 680–681
                  Sormunen, p 388

78. When a physician orders a liver panel, which of the following tests are NOT included?
    A. albumin   C. bilirubin
    B. alkaline phosphatase   D. creatinine

REFERENCE: Estridge & Reynolds, pp 608–609

79. Maria Giovanni is in the hospital recovering from colon resection surgery. Based on her symptoms, her doctors are concerned about the possibility that she has developed a pulmonary embolism. Which of the following procedures will provide the definitive diagnosis?
    A. chest x-ray   C. pulmonary angiography
    B. lung scan   D. none of the above

REFERENCE: Neighbors & Tannehill-Jones, p 168
                  Scott & Fong, p 369

80. A condition that involves the fifth cranial nerve, also known as "tic douloureux," causes intense pain in the eye and forehead; lower lip, the section of the cheek closest to the ear and the outer segment of the tongue; or the upper lip, nose, and cheek.
   A. Bell's palsy
   B. thrush
   C. trigeminal neuralgia
   D. Tourette's disorder

REFERENCE: Jones, pp 283, 288
                Moisio, p 396
                Scott & Fong, p 182

81. Which of the following is a congenital condition that is the most severe neural tube defect?
   A. meningocele
   B. myelomeningocele
   C. severe combined immunodeficiency
   D. spina bifida occulta

REFERENCE: Neighbors & Tannehill-Jones, p 374

82. Which of the following tubes conveys sperm from the seminal vesicle to the urethra?
   A. ejaculatory duct
   B. epididymis
   C. oviduct
   D. vas deferens

REFERENCE: Moisio, p 332
                Neighbors & Tannehill-Jones, p 481
                Rizzo, p 444

83. The most common type of vaginitis is
   A. yeast.
   B. protozoan.
   C. viral.
   D. both A and B.

REFERENCE: Neighbors & Tannehill-Jones, p 315

84. The childhood viral disease that unvaccinated pregnant women should be prevented from because it may be passed to the fetus, causing congenital anomalies such as mental retardation, blindness, and deafness, is
   A. rickets.
   B. rubeola.
   C. rubella.
   D. tetanus.

REFERENCE: Moisio, p 435
                Neighbors & Tannehill-Jones, p 389

85. In _____ anemia, the red blood cells become shaped like elongated crescents in the presence of low oxygen concentration.
   A. aplastic
   B. folic acid
   C. sickle cell
   D. vitamin B_{12}

REFERENCE: Jones, p 333
                Moisio, p 213
                Rizzo, p 308
                Scott & Fong, pp 250–251

86. _____ is usually the first symptom of benign prostate hyperplasia.
   A. Abdominal pain
   B. Burning pain during urination
   C. Difficulty in urinating
   D. Pelvic pain

REFERENCE: Neighbors & Tannehill-Jones, pp 322–324
                Rizzo, p 444
                Scott & Fong, pp 467–468

87. The hypothalamus, thalamus, and pituitary gland are all parts of the
    A. brainstem.
    B. cerebellum.
    C. exocrine system.
    D. limbic system.

REFERENCE: Rizzo, pp 157–158

88. Which of the following BEST summarizes the current treatment of cervical cancer?
    A. A new three-shot vaccination series protects against the types of HPV that cause most cervical cancer cases.
    B. All stages have extremely high cure rates.
    C. Early detection and treatment of cervical cancer does not improve patient survival rates.
    D. Over 99% of cases are linked to long-term HPV infections.

REFERENCE: CDC (1)

89. Children at higher risk for sudden infant death syndrome (SIDS) include those
    A. with sleep apnea.
    B. with respiratory problems.
    C. who are premature infants.
    D. all of the above.

REFERENCE: Jones, pp 455, 867–868
                Neighbors & Tannehill-Jones, p 395
                Scott & Fong, p 369

90. Increasing peristalsis of intestines, increasing salivation, and slowing heart rate are examples of
    A. automatic nervous system responses.
    B. higher brain function.
    C. parasympathetic nervous system responses.
    D. sympathetic nervous system responses.

REFERENCE: Jones, p 263
                Rizzo, pp 227, 251
                Scott & Fong, pp 177–179
                Sormunen, p 585

91. Photophobia or visual aura preceding a severe headache is characteristic of
    A. malnutrition.
    B. mastitis.
    C. migraines.
    D. myasthenia gravis.

REFERENCE: Jones, pp 275–276
                Neighbors & Tannehill-Jones, p 271
                Scott & Fong, p 163

92. Which of the following is characteristic of Graves' disease?
    A. is an autoimmune disease.
    B. most commonly affects males.
    C. usually cannot be treated.
    D. usually affects the elderly.

REFERENCE: Jones, p 560
                Neighbors & Tannehill-Jones, p 248
                Rizzo, pp 280, 285
                Scott & Fong, p 228

93. A "pill-rolling" tremor of the hand is a characteristic symptom of
    A. epilepsy.
    B. Guillain–Barré syndrome.
    C. myasthenia gravis.
    D. Parkinson disease.

REFERENCE: Jones, pp 282–283, 1066–1067
                Neighbors & Tannehill-Jones, p 281
                Scott & Fong, pp 162–164

94. Rheumatoid arthritis typically affects the
    A. intervertebral disks.
    B. hips and shoulders.
    C. knees and small joints of the hands and feet.
    D. large, weight-bearing joints.

REFERENCE: Jones, p 230
               Moisio, p 149
               Neighbors & Tannehill-Jones, pp 71–72, 94–95
               Rizzo, p 183
               Scott & Fong, pp 110–111

95. Henry experienced sudden sharp chest pain that he described as heavy and crushing. His pain and past medical history caused Dr. James to suspect that Henry was having an acute myocardial infarction (AMI). Which of the following tests is a more specific marker for an AMI?
    A. AST   C. LDH1
    B. CK-MB   D. Troponin I

REFERENCE: Labtestsonline (2)

96. A radiological test for bone mineral density (BMD) is a useful diagnostic tool for diagnosing
    A. osteoarthritis.   C. osteoporosis.
    B. osteomyelitis.   D. rheumatoid arthritis.

REFERENCE: Jones, p 184
               Neighbors & Tannehill-Jones, pp 90–92
               Scott & Fong, p 113

97. A 72-year-old white male patient is on Coumadin therapy. Which of the following tests is commonly ordered to monitor the patient's Coumadin levels?
    A. bleeding time   C. partial thromboplastin time
    B. blood smear   D. prothrombin time

REFERENCE: Jones, p 339
               Labtestsonline (3)
               Moisio, p 219
               Neighbors & Tannehill-Jones, p 235
               NLM (2)

98. A toxic goiter has what distinguishing characteristic?
    A. iodine deficiency   C. presence of muscle spasm
    B. parathyroid involvement   D. thyroid hyperfunction

REFERENCE: Moisio, p 304
               Neighbors & Tannehill-Jones, pp 247–248
               Rizzo, p 280
               Sormunen, p 567

99. How can Graves' disease be treated?
    A. antithyroid drugs   C. surgery
    B. radioactive iodine therapy D. all of the above

REFERENCE: Jones, pp 560–561
               Neighbors & Tannehill-Jones, pp 247–248
               Rizzo, p 285
               Sormunen, p 567

100. Fractures occur in patients with osteoporosis due to
    A. falling from loss of balance.
    B. fibrous joint adhesions tearing apart small bones.
    C. loss of bone mass.
    D. tendency to fall from lack of joint mobility.

REFERENCE: Jones, pp 174–175
                      Moisio, p 149
                      Neighbors & Tannehill-Jones, pp 90–92
                      Scott & Fong, p 113

101. United States health care providers are concerned about a possible pandemic of avian flu because
    A. there is no vaccine currently available.
    B. it is caused by a group of viruses that mutate very easily.
    C. the causative virus is being spread around the world by migratory birds.
    D. of all of the above.

REFERENCE: CDC (2)

102. A sweat test was done on a patient with the following symptoms: frequent respiratory infections, chronic cough, and foul-smelling bloody stools. Which of the following diseases is probably suspected?
    A. cystic breast disease   C. cystic lung disease
    B. cystic fibrosis   D. cystic pancreas

REFERENCE: Neighbors & Tannehill-Jones, p 380

103. Margaret Vargas needs to have her mitral valve replaced. Her surgeon will discuss which of the following issues with her before the surgery?
    A. A mechanical valve will require that she take a "blood thinner" for the rest of her life.
    B. A biological valve (usually porcine) will last 10 to 15 years.
    C. A mechanical valve increases the risk of blood clots that can cause stroke.
    D. All of the above.

REFERENCE: NHLBI

104. Cervical cerclage is a procedure used to help prevent
    A. breathing restrictions.   C. torsion.
    B. miscarriage.   D. torticollis.

REFERENCE: Jones, pp 802, 817

105. Sam Spade has been severely injured in an MVA because he was not wearing a seat belt. The organ in his body, situated at the upper left of his abdominal cavity, under the ribs, that is part of his lymphatic system has been ruptured, and he is bleeding internally. Sam needs a surgical procedure known as
    A. sequestrectomy.   C. sigmoidoscopy.
    B. sialoadenectomy.   D. splenectomy.

REFERENCE: Jones, p 345
                      Moisio, p 219
                      Rizzo, p 346
                      Sormunen, pp 275, 399

106. Henrietta Dawson presents with a chief complaint of pain and weakness in her arms and neck. After an H&P and review of diagnostic tests that include a myelogram, her doctor diagnoses a herniated nucleus pulposus at the _____ level of her spine.
    A. cervical
    B. lumbar
    C. sacral
    D. thoracic

REFERENCE: Jones, pp 160, 228, 277
               Moisio, p 147
               Neighbors & Tannehill-Jones, p 103
               Rizzo, pp 157, 170
               Scott & Fong, pp 99, 112
               Sormunen, pp 158, 161

107. Ingrid Anderson presents with a skin infection that began as a raised, itchy bump, resembling an insect bite. Within 1 to 2 days, it developed into a vesicle. Now it is a painless ulcer, about 2 cm in diameter, with a black necrotic area in the center. During the history, her doctor learns that she has recently returned from an overseas vacation and becomes concerned that she may have become infected with anthrax. He will prescribe an
    A. antibiotic.
    B. antineoplastic.
    C. antiparasitic.
    D. antiviral.

REFERENCE: Scott & Fong, pp 342, 366–367

108. Etiologies of dementia include
    A. brain tumors.
    B. ischemia.
    C. trauma.
    D. all of the above.

REFERENCE: Neighbors & Tannehill-Jones, p 414
               Rizzo, pp 937, 946
               Scott & Fong, p 164
               Sormunen, p 597

109. Carpal tunnel syndrome is caused by entrapment of the
    A. medial nerve.
    B. radial nerve.
    C. tibial nerve.
    D. ulnar nerve.

REFERENCE: Jones, p 270
               Moisio, p 142
               Neighbors & Tannehill-Jones, p 104
               NINDS
               Rizzo, p 182
               Sormunen, p 158

110. The organism transmitted by a mosquito bite that causes malaria is a
    A. bacteria.
    B. prion.
    C. protozoa.
    D. virus.

REFERENCE: Moisio, p 432
               Neighbors & Tannehill-Jones, pp 54–55, 57
               Rizzo, p 309
               Scott & Fong, p 309

111. Contributing factors of mental disorders include
    A. heredity.   C. trauma.
    B. stress.   D. all of the above.

REFERENCE: Jones, pp 1008, 1010
                Neighbors & Tannehill-Jones, p 408

112. A 13-year-old patient is brought to her pediatrician with a 2-week history of fatigue, an occasional low-grade fever, and malaise. The pediatrician indicates it is a possible infection but needs to know what type of infection. She orders a hematology laboratory test to determine the relative number and percentage of each type of leukocytes. This test is referred to as a(n)
    A. hematocrit.   C. WBC diff.
    B. CBC.   D. hemoglobin determination.

REFERENCES: Estridge & Reynolds, p 198

113. A 62-year-old female presents to her family doctor complaining of fatigue; constantly feeling cold, especially in her hands and feet; weakness; and pallor. O_2 must be transported to the cells and exchanged with CO_2, which is then transported back to the lungs to be expelled. A hematology laboratory test that evaluates the oxygen-carrying capacity of blood is referred to as a(n)
    A. hematocrit.   C. WBC diff.
    B. CBC.   D. hemoglobin determination.

REFERENCES: Estridge & Reynolds, pp 206–207
                Labtestsonline (15)

114. An African American couple are undergoing genetic counseling to determine the likelihood of producing children with a recessively genetic blood condition. The genetic tests reveal that the father carries the trait to produce abnormal hemoglobin, HbS, which causes crystallization in RBCs and deforms their shape when O_2 is low. This condition causes painful crises and multiple infarcts and is termed
    A. hemophilia.   C. sickle cell anemia.
    B. thalassemia.   D. iron-deficiency anemia.

REFERENCES: Estridge & Reynolds, pp 328–330
                Labtestsonline (4)

115. A 37-year-old female goes to her family physician complaining of dysuria, urgency, fever, and malaise. A UA is performed and upon gross examination is found to be turbid and has an unusual odor. Microscopic examination reveals a rod-shaped microorganism. A 24-hour culture produces a colony count greater than 100,000/mL of *Escherichia coli*. This would indicate a diagnosis of
    A. UTI.   C. PID.
    B. FUO.   D. KUB.

REFERENCES: Estridge & Reynolds, pp 751–753
                Labtestsonline (5)

116. A 57-year-old male patient is having his annual physical. Due to a family history of coronary artery disease and his sedentary lifestyle, his doctor orders a total blood cholesterol panel. What is the optimal level of total cholesterol in the blood for adults?
    A. < 200 mg/dL   C. 300–339 mg/dL
    B. 200–239 mg/dL   D. >500 mg/dL

REFERENCES: Estridge & Reynolds, pp 662–667
                Labtestsonline (6)

117. A pharyngeal culture is taken from a 13-year-old male patient presenting to the ER with fever, painful cervical lymph nodes, purulent tonsillar exudate, and difficulty swallowing. Blood agar culture plate shows complete hemolysis around *Streptococcus pyogenes* bacterial colonies. The patient is given a prescription for erythromycin. The diagnosis in this case is
   A. group A beta-hemolytic streptococcal throat infection.
   B. methicillin-resistant *Staphylococcus aureus* skin infection.
   C. tuberculosis with drug-resistant *Mycobacterium tuberculosis*-positive sputum.
   D. meningitis due to *Neisseria meningitidis*-positive cerebrospinal fluid.

REFERENCES: Estridge & Reynolds, pp 739–742
                Labtestsonline (7)

118. An 81-year-old male with arteriosclerosis and a long-standing history of taking Coumadin presents to his physician's office for his bi-weekly prothrombin time (PT) test. The PT test is one of the most common hemostasis tests used as a presurgery screening and monitoring Coumadin (warfarin) therapy. This test evaluates
   A. coagulation of the blood.
   B. iron-binding capacity of RBCs.
   C. oxygen-carrying capacity of RBCs.
   D. type and cross-match of blood.

REFERENCES: Estridge & Reynolds, p 394
                Labtestsonline (8)

119. A 28-year-old female presents to her general practitioner with morning nausea and vomiting, weight gain, and two missed menstrual cycles. The physician orders a pregnancy test. What chemical in the urine does this lab test detect?
   A. alpha-fetoprotein   C. carcinoembryonic antigen
   B. creatine phosphokinase   D. human chorionic gonadotropin

REFERENCES: Estridge & Reynolds, pp 471–472
                Labtestsonline (9).

120. A 19-year-old college student, who lives on campus in a dormitory, is brought to the ER by his roommates complaining of a severe headache, nuchal rigidity, fever, and photophobia. The ER physician performs an LP and orders a CSF analysis with a bacterial culture and sensitivity. The young man is admitted to the ICU with a provisional diagnosis of
   A. group A beta-hemolytic streptococcal throat infection.
   B. methicillin-resistant *Staphylococcus aureus* skin infection.
   C. tuberculosis with drug-resistant *Mycobacterium tuberculosis*-positive sputum.
   D. meningitis due to *Neisseria meningitidis*-positive cerebrospinal fluid.

REFERENCES: CDC (12)
                Labtestsonline (10)

121. Microbiological lab culture and sensitivity tests were performed on the skin scrapings of a groin lesion on a 27-year-old male patient who presented to a local health department clinic. The results confirm infection with *Treponema pallidum*. He was given a prescription for penicillin and told to return for a follow-up visit in within 2 weeks. His diagnosis is
   A. syphilis.   C. herpes.
   B. HIV.   D. HPV.

REFERENCES: CDC (13)
                Labtestsonline (11)

122. The HPV vaccine, Gardasil, is recommended for all children/young adults between the ages of 9 and 26 years. It is a quadrivalent vaccine. What is the definition of quadrivalent?
    A. It must be administered every 4 years to be effective.
    B. It is administered in a series of four shots over a 6-month period.
    C. It prevents infection from the four most prevalent types of HPV that cause cervical cancer.
    D. It reduces the risk of infection by four times.

REFERENCES: CDC (3)
               FDA (1)
               Labtestsonline (12)

123. *Mycobacterium tuberculosis* is the organism that causes tuberculosis (TB), typically a respiratory disorder. It is currently experiencing a resurgence in the United States and many other countries. What is the average time frame all patients with new, previously untreated TB must have daily antibiotic therapy?
    A. 4–7 days
    B. 6–9 months
    C. 6–9 weeks
    D. 4–7 years

REFERENCES: CDC (4)
               Labtestsonline (13)

124. A 63-year-old patient with terminal pancreatic cancer has started palliative chemotherapy. Palliative means
    A. alleviating or eliminating distressing symptoms of the disease.
    B. increasing the immune response to fight infections.
    C. quick destruction of cancerous cells.
    D. the combining of several medications to cure the cancer.

REFERENCES: ACS (3)
               Woodrow, pp 221–222

125. Why are there "black box warnings" on antidepressant medications regarding children and adolescents?
    A. Antidepressants increase the risk of suicidal thinking and behavior in some children and adolescents.
    B. Dosage requirements must be significantly higher in children and adolescents compared to adults.
    C. There is no established medical need for treatment of depression in children and adolescents.
    D. Antidepressants interfere with physiological growth patterns in children and adolescents.

REFERENCES: FDA (2)
               Woodrow, p 354

126. The positive belief in a drug and its ability to cure a patient's illness, even if this drug is an inactive or inert substance, typically positively influences a patient's perception of their outcome. This effect is termed
    A. synergistic effect.
    B. potentiation effect.
    C. placebo effect.
    D. antagonistic effect.

REFERENCES: Sormunen, pp 79, 92
               Woodrow, pp 34–36

127. A common cardiac glycoside medication that increases the force of the cardiac contraction without increasing the oxygen consumption, thereby increasing the cardiac output is typically given to patients with heart failure. However, a very narrow therapeutic window between effectiveness and toxicity and the patient must be monitored closely. This common cardiac medication is
   A. COX-2 inhibitor.
   B. nitroglycerin.
   C. digoxin.
   D. acetylsalicylic acid.

REFERENCES: NLM (9)
                Woodrow, pp 461–462

128. The interaction of two drugs working together to where each simultaneously helps the other achieve an effect that neither could produce alone is termed
   A. placebo effect.
   B. synergistic effect.
   C. potentiation effect.
   D. antagonistic effect.

REFERENCES: Woodrow, p 35

129. The opposing interaction of two drugs in which one decreases or cancels out the effects of the other is termed
   A. placebo effect.
   B. potentiation effect.
   C. synergistic effect.
   D. antagonistic effect.

REFERENCES: Woodrow, p 35

130. One of the most common causes of peptic ulcer disease is the consumption of aspirin and NSAIDs. Another common cause is the infection of *Helicobacter pylori*, and the usual treatment for this condition is with the use of
   A. antivirals.
   B. antibiotics.
   C. antifungals.
   D. antiemetics.

REFERENCES: NLM (10)
                Woodrow, p 254

131. A common contraceptive that is implanted in the uterus induces slight endometrial inflammation, which attracts neutrophils to the uterus. These neutrophils are toxic to sperm and prevent the fertilization of the ovum. This contraception is termed
   A. oral contraceptives.
   B. progestin injections.
   C. spermicides.
   D. IUD.

REFERENCES: Jones, pp 755–756
                Woodrow, p 447

132. There has been a significant increase in the number of cases and deaths from pertussis. Health care professionals attribute this disease trend to which of the following?
   A. A decrease in the number of people immunized with TDaP
   B. An increase in the virulence of the bacteria
   C. Drug-resistant strains of the bacteria
   D. All of the above

REFERENCES: CDC (5)

133. Which of the following is a severe, chronic, two-phased, bacterial respiratory infection that has become increasingly difficult to treat because many antibiotics are no longer effective against it?
   A. SARS
   B. MDR-TB
   C. MRSA
   D. H1N1

REFERENCES: CDC (6)

134. A new strain of influenza, H1N1, is a highly virulent strain that spread all over the world. This type of epidemiological disease pattern is referred to as a(n)
    A. cluster.
    B. outbreak.
    C. epidemic.
    D. pandemic.

REFERENCES: CDC (7)

135. Mary Smith, a 48-year-old patient, is receiving an IV mixture of four different medications to treat stage 2 invasive ductal breast carcinoma. Each of the medications acts upon a different aspect of the cancer cells. This mixture is typically termed a(n)
    A. amalgamation.
    B. cocktail.
    C. blend.
    D. mash-up.

REFERENCES: CDC (8)

136. Some immunizations, such as tetanus, require a second application, to strengthen or "remind" the immune system in response to antigens. The subsequent injections are termed
    A. alerting shots.
    B. warning shots.
    C. booster shots.
    D. unnecessary shots.

REFERENCES: CDC (9)

137. What common vitamin should be taken by pregnant women to substantially reduce the occurrence of neural tube defects, such as spina bifida, in a developing fetus?
    A. Folic acid   C. B_{12}
    B. Calcium   D. E

REFERENCES: CDC (10)

138. Why must influenza immunizations be developed and administered on an annual basis?
    A. The virus mutates significantly each year.
    B. People develop resistance to the vaccine.
    C. The immunization is only strong enough for one year.
    D. The pharmaceutical companies produce the lowest dosage possible.

REFERENCES: CDC (11)

139. Which of the following pieces of equipment records the electrical activity of the brain?
    A. EEG   C. ECG
    B. EMG   D. EKG

REFERENCES: Jones, p 290
               Moisio, 397
               NLM (5)

140. A surgical procedure that cuts into the skull to drain blood from a subdural hematoma in order to decrease the intracranial pressure is termed a(n)
    A. craniectomy.   C. angioplasty.
    B. craniotomy.   D. hemispherectomy.

REFERENCES: NLM (6)

141. A surgical procedure that is performed to realign and stabilize a fractured femur with a rod and screws is referred to as a(n)
    A. closed reduction with external fixation.
    B. closed reduction with internal fixation.
    C. osteotomy.
    D. open reduction with internal fixation.

REFERENCES: Jones, pp 180–181
                Moisio, p 152

142. Which of the following procedures is typically performed on children to facilitate the drainage of serous exudate behind the tympanic membrane in chronic otitis media?
    A. cochlear implants
    B. stapedectomy
    C. myringotomy with tympanostomy tubes
    D. cerumen evacuation

REFERENCES: Jones, p 624
                Moisio, p 413

143. Coronary arteries may become blocked, either partially or totally, due to athereosclerosis and lead to an AMI. Which of the following procedures would be used to improve the coronary blood flow by building an alternate route for the blood to bypass the blockage by inserting a portion of another blood vessel, typically the saphenous vein?
    A. PTCA   C. carotid endarterectomy
    B. CABG   D. cardiac catheterization

REFERENCES: Jones, p 1086
                Moisio, pp 185–186

144. A standard surgical procedure used for the treatment of early-stage breast cancer involves the removal of the cancerous tumor, skin, breast tissue, areola, nipple, and most of the axillary lymph nodes, but leaves the underlying chest muscles intact. This procedure is termed a(n)
    A. modified radical mastectomy.
    B. partial mastectomy.
    C. lumpectomy.
    D. incisional breast biopsy.

REFERENCES: Jones, pp 760, 936
                Moisio, p 361
                WebMD.com (1)

145. The least invasive restrictive gastric surgery used to reduce the size of the stomach to facilitate weight loss in obese patients is the
    A. gastric bypass.
    B. Roux-en-Y gastric surgery.
    C. laparoscopic gastric banding.
    D. biliopancreatic diversion.

REFERENCES: WebMD.com (2)

146. Which of the following procedures would be performed for the removal of the gall bladder due to excessive gallstone formation?
    A. ERCP
    B. cholangiography
    C. hemicolectomy
    D. cholecystectomy

REFERENCES: WebMD.com (3)
                NLM (7)

Answer Key for Medical Science

1.	B	50.	A	99.	D
2.	B	51.	C	100.	C
3.	A	52.	C	101.	D
4.	D	53.	A	102.	B
5.	C	54.	B	103.	D
6.	C	55.	A	104.	B
7.	C	56.	C	105.	D
8.	C	57.	D	106.	A
9.	D	58.	C	107.	A
10.	C	59.	C	108.	D
11.	B	60.	C	109.	A
12.	C	61.	C	110.	C
13.	D	62.	D	111.	D
14.	C	63.	A	112.	C
15.	C	64.	A	113.	D
16.	A	65.	C	114.	C
17.	D	66.	A	115.	A
18.	B	67.	D	116.	A
19.	B	68.	D	117.	A
20.	A	69.	B	118.	A
21.	C	70.	C	119.	D
22.	D	71.	A	120.	D
23.	C	72.	B	121.	A
24.	D	73.	A	122.	C
25.	B	74.	C	123.	B
26.	C	75.	C	124.	A
27.	B	76.	A	125.	A
28.	C	77.	B	126.	C
29.	A	78.	D	127.	C
30.	B	79.	C	128.	B
31.	D	80.	C	129.	D
32.	B	81.	B	130.	B
33.	B	82.	A	131.	D
34.	C	83.	D	132.	A
35.	D	84.	C	133.	B
36.	B	85.	C	134.	D
37.	D	86.	C	135.	B
38.	C	87.	D	136.	C
39.	A	88.	A	137.	A
40.	A	89.	D	138.	A
41.	C	90.	C	139.	A
42.	D	91.	C	140.	B
43.	C	92.	A	141.	D
44.	A	93.	D	142.	C
45.	D	94.	C	143.	B
46.	C	95.	B	144.	A
47.	C	96.	C	145.	C
48.	B	97.	D		
49.	A	98.	D		

REFERENCES

American Cancer Society (ACS). http://www.cancer.org
    ACS (1)

        http://www.cancer.org/acs/groups/cid/documents/webcontent/003096-pdf.pdf

        http://www.cancer.org/Cancer/ColonandRectumCancer/DetailedGuide/colorectal-cancer-detection

    ACS (3)

        http://www.cancer.org/Cancer/CancerofUnknownPrimary/DetailedGuide/cancer-unknown-primary-treating-palliative-care

Centers for Disease Control and Prevention (CDC). http://www.cdc.gov/index.htm
    CDC (1)

        http://www.cdc.gov/std/Hpv/STDFact-HPV-vaccine-young-women.htm#why

    CDC (2)

        http://www.cdc.gov/flu/avian/gen-info/pdf/avian_facts.pdf

    CDC (3)

        http://www.cdc.gov/Features/HPVvaccine/

    CDC (4)

        http://www.cdc.gov/tb/topic/treatment/default.htm

    CDC (5)

        http://www.cdc.gov/pertussis/outbreaks-faqs.html

    CDC (6)

        http://www.cdc.gov/tb/topic/treatment/default.htm

    CDC (7)

        http://www.cdc.gov/flu/spotlights/pandemic-global-estimates.htm

    CDC (8)

        http://www.cdc.gov/cancer/breast/basic_info/

    CDC (9)

        http://www.cdc.gov/vaccines/vac-gen/default.htm

    CDC (10)

        http://www.cdc.gov/NCBDDD/folicacid/about.html

    CDC (11)

        http://www.cdc.gov/vaccines/vac-gen/default.htm

Estridge, B. H., & Reynolds, A. P. (2012). *Basic clinical laboratory techniques* (6th ed.). Clifton Park, NY: Delmar Cengage Learning.

Food and Drug Administration (FDA). http://www.fda.gov/default.htm
    http://www.fda.gov/BiologicsBloodVaccines/Vaccines/ApprovedProducts/ucm094042.htm

Jones, B. D. (2011). *Comprehensive medical terminology* (4th ed.). Clifton Park, NY: Delmar Cengage Learning.

Labtestsonline. http://www.labtestsonline.org
    Labtestsonline (1).

        http://www.labtestsonline.org/understanding/analytes/bilirubin/glance.html

    Labtestsonline (2).

        http://www.labtestsonline.org/understanding/analytes/troponin/related.html

    Labtestsonline (3).

        http://www.labtestsonline.org/understanding/analytes/pt/test.html

    Labtestsonline (4).

        http://labtestsonline.org/understanding/conditions/sickle

REFERENCES (continued)

Labtestsonline (5).
http://labtestsonline.org/understanding/analytes/urinalysis/tab/test
Labtestsonline (6).
http://labtestsonline.org/understanding/analytes/cholesterol/tab/test
Labtestsonline (7)
http://labtestsonline.org/understanding/analytes/strep/tab/sample
Labtestsonline (8)
http://labtestsonline.org/understanding/analytes/pt/tab/sample
Labtestsonline (9)
http://labtestsonline.org/understanding/wellness/pregnancy/first-hcg
Labtestsonline (10)
http://labtestsonline.org/understanding/conditions/meningitis?start=3
Labtestsonline (11)
http://labtestsonline.org/understanding/analytes/syphilis/tab/glance
Labtestsonline (12)
http://www.cdc.gov/vaccines/vpd-vac/hpv/default.htm
Labtestsonline (13)
http://labtestsonline.org/understanding/conditions/tuberculosis/?start=4

Mayo Clinic. http://www.mayoclinic.com
Mayo Clinic (1).
http://www.mayoclinic.com/print/esophageal-varices/DS00820/
Mayo Clinic (2)
http://www.mayoclinic.com/health/diabetic-ketoacidosis/DS00674

Moisio, M. A. (2010). *Medical terminology for insurance and coding*. Clifton Park, NY: Delmar Cengage Learning.

National Library of Medicine. http://www.nlm.nih.gov/medlineplus/
NLM (1).

http://www.nhlbi.nih.gov/health/dci/Diseases/ha/ha_diagnosis.html
http://www.nlm.nih.gov/medlineplus/ency/article/003479.htm

NLM (2).
http://www.nlm.nih.gov/medlineplus/ency/article/003652.htm

NLM (3)
http://www.nlm.nih.gov/medlineplus/ency/article/003498.htm

NLM (4)
http://www.nlm.nih.gov/medlineplus/ency/article/003574.htm

NHLBI—National Heart Lung and Blood Institute. http://www.nhlbi.nih.gov
http://www.nhlbi.nih.gov/health/dci/Diseases/hvd/hvd_treatments.html

NINDS—National Institute of Neurological Disorders and Stroke.
http://www.ninds.nih.gov/disorders/carpal_tunnel/detail_carpal_tunnel.htm

Neighbors, M. and Tannehill-Jones, R. (2009). *Human DiseasesI* (3rd ed.). Clifton Park, NY: Delmar Cengage Learning.

Rizzo, D. C. (2006). *Fundamentals of Anatomy and Physiology* (2006). (2nd ed.) . Clifton Park, NY: Delmar Cengage Learning.

Scott, A. S., & Fong, P.E. (2009). *Body structures and functions* (11th ed.). Clifton Park, NY: Delmar Cengage Learning.

REFERENCES (continued)

Sormunen, C. (2010). *Terminology for allied health professionals* (6th ed.). Clifton Park, NY: Delmar Cengage Learning.

Woodrow, R. (2011). *Essentials of pharmacology for health occupations* (6th ed.). Clifton Park, NY: Delmar Cengage Learning.

Medical Sciences Competencies

Question	RHIA Domain	RHIT Domain
1–145	1	1

V. Classification Systems and Secondary Data Sources

Lisa M. Delhomme, MHA, RHIA

1. Which system is a classification of health and health-related domains that describe body functions and structures, domains of activities and participation, and environmental factors that interact with all of these components?
    A. International Classification of Primary Care (ICPC-2)
    B. International Classification on Functioning, Disability, and Health (ICF)
    C. National Drug Codes
    D. Clinical Care Classification (CCC)

REFERENCE: Latour, Eichenwald-Maki, and Oachs, p 393
                Sayles, pp 196–197

2. A physician performed an outpatient surgical procedure on the eye orbit of a patient with Medicare. Upon searching the CPT codes and consulting with the physician, the coder is unable to find a code for the procedure. The coder should assign
    A. an unlisted Evaluation and Management code from the E/M section.
    B. an unlisted procedure code located in the eye and ocular adnexa section.
    C. a HCPCS Level Two (alphanumeric) code.
    D. an ophthalmologic treatment service code.

REFERENCE: AMA (2014), p 63
                Frisch, p 254
                Green, p 384
                Smith, p 25

3. A system of preferred terminology for naming disease processes is known as a
    A. set of categories.   C. medical nomenclature.
    B. classification system.   D. diagnosis listing.

REFERENCE: Abdelhak, p 224
                Green, p 9
                Green and Bowie, p 304
                LaTour, Eichenwald-Maki, and Oachs, pp 207–208, 348, 388–389
                McWay, pp 149–150
                Sayles, p 180

4. Which of the following is NOT included as a part of the minimum data maintained in the MPI?
    A. principal diagnosis   C. full name (last, first, and middle)
    B. patient medical record number   D. date of birth

REFERENCE: Abdelhak, p 107
                Green and Bowie, pp 237–239
                LaTour, Eichenwald-Maki, and Oachs, pp 170, 271–272
                McWay, pp 139–140
                Sayles, pp 322–323

5. The Health Information Department receives research requests from various committees in the hospital. The Medicine Committee wishes to review all patients having a diagnosis of anterolateral myocardial infarction within the past 6 months. Which of the following would be the best source to identify the necessary charts?

A. operation index
B. consultation index
C. disease index
D. physician's index

REFERENCE: Green and Bowie, pp 240–243
              LaTour, Eichenwald-Maki, and Oachs, pp 369–370
              McWay, p 140
              Sayles, pp 436–437

6. One of the major functions of the cancer registry is to ensure that patients receive regular and continued observation and management. How long should patient follow-up be continued?

A. until remission occurs
B. 10 years
C. for the life of the patient
D. 1 year

REFERENCE: Abdelhak, p 485
              LaTour, Eichenwald-Maki, and Oachs, pp 370–372
              McWay, pp 142–143
              Sayles, pp 438–440

7. In reviewing the medical record of a patient admitted for a left herniorrhaphy, the coder discovers an extremely low potassium level on the laboratory report. In examining the physician's orders, the coder notices that intravenous potassium was ordered. The physician has not listed any indication of an abnormal potassium level or any related condition on the discharge summary. The best course of action for the coder to take is to

A. confer with the physician and ask him or her to list the condition as a final diagnosis if he or she considers the abnormal potassium level to be clinically significant.
B. code the record as is.
C. code the condition as abnormal blood chemistry.
D. code the abnormal potassium level as a complication following surgery.

REFERENCE: Bowie and Shaffer (2012), p 69
              Green, pp 15–16
              Johnson and Linker, pp 5–36

8. DSM-IV-TR is used most frequently in what type of health care setting?

A. behavioral health centers
B. ambulatory surgery centers
C. home health agencies
D. nursing homes

REFERENCE: Green, p 865
              LaTour, Eichenwald-Maki, and Oachs, pp 394–395
              McWay, p 152
              Sayles, pp 208–210

9. A coder notes that a patient is taking prescription Pilocarpine. The final diagnoses on the discharge summary are congestive heart failure and diabetes mellitus. The coder should query the physician about adding a diagnosis of
   A. arthritis.
   B. glaucoma.
   C. bronchitis.
   D. laryngitis.

REFERENCE: Green, pp 15–16, 174–175
               Nobles, p 689

10. The patient is diagnosed with congestive heart failure. A drug of choice is
    A. ibuprofen.
    B. oxytocin.
    C. haloperidol.
    D. digoxin.

REFERENCE: Nobles, p 329

11. ICD-10-CM utilizes a placeholder character. This is used as a 5th character placeholder at certain 6 character codes to allow for future expansion. The placeholder character is
    A. "Z."
    B. "O."
    C. "1."
    D. "x."

REFERENCE: Bowie, p 30
               Green, p 52

12. The local safety council requests statistics on the number of head injuries occurring as a result of skateboarding accidents during the last year. To retrieve this data, you will need to have the correct
    A. CPT code.
    B. Standard Nomenclature of Injuries codes.
    C. ICD-10-CM codes.
    D. HCPCS Level II codes.

REFERENCE: Frisch, pp 150–151
               Green, pp 209–220
               Johnson and Linker, pp 16, 66–69
               McWay, pp 154–155
               Schraffenberger (2013), pp 384–385

13. All children will be entered into which of the following registries at birth, and thus will continue to be monitored by the registry in their geographic area?
    A. Birth defects registry
    B. Trauma registry
    C. Cancer registry
    D. Immunization registry

REFERENCE: Latour, Eichenwald-Maki, and Oachs, p 375
               McWay, p 141
               Sayles, pp 447–449

14. In general, all three key components (history, physical examination, and medical decision making) for the E/M codes in CPT should be met or exceeded when
    A. the patient is established.
    B. a new patient is seen in the office.
    C. the patient is given subsequent care in the hospital.
    D. the patient is seen for a follow-up inpatient consultation.

REFERENCE: AMA (2014), p 10
               Green, p 414
               Johnson and Linker, p 144

15. This registry collects data on recipients of heart valves and pacemakers.
    A. Transplant registry
    B. Implant registry
    C. Cancer registry
    D. Hypertension registry

REFERENCE: LaTour, Eichenwald-Maki, and Oachs, p 374
               McWay, p 141
               Sayles, pp 445–446

16. Which classification system was developed to standardize terminology and codes for use in clinical laboratories?
    A. Systematized Nomenclature of Human and Veterinary Medicine International (SNOMED)
    B. Systematized Nomenclature of Pathology (SNOP)
    C. Read Codes
    D. Logical Observation Identifiers, Names and Codes (LOINC)

REFERENCE: Abdelhak, pp 237–239
               Latour, Eichenwald-Maki, and Oachs, pp 399–400
               McWay, p 151

17. Which classification system is used to classify neoplasms according to site, morphology, and behavior?
    A. International Classification of Diseases for Oncology (ICD-O)
    B. Systematized Nomenclature of Human and Veterinary Medicine International (SNOMED)
    C. Diagnostic and Statistical Manual of Mental Disorders (DSM)
    D. Current Procedural Terminology (CPT)

REFERENCE: Abdelhak, p 252
               Latour, Eichenwald-Maki, and Oachs, pp 392–393

18. According to the UHDDS, a procedure that is surgical in nature, carries a procedural or anesthetic risk, or requires special training is defined as a
    A. principal procedure.   C. operating room procedure.
    B. significant procedure.   D. therapeutic procedure.

REFERENCE: Green, p 263
               Latour, Eichenwald-Maki, and Oachs, p 197
               Schraffenberger (2013), p 53

19. You need to analyze data on the types of care provided to Medicare patients in your geographic area by DRG. Which of the following would be most helpful?
    A. National Practitioner Data Bank
    B. MEDPAR
    C. Vital Statistics
    D. RxNorm

REFERENCE: LaTour, Eichenwald-Maki, and Oachs, p 377
               McWay, p 187
               Sayles, pp 450–451

20. An encoder that prompts the coder to answer a series of questions and choices based on the documentation in the medical record is called a(n)
    A. logic-based encoder.
    B. automated codebook.
    C. grouper.
    D. automatic code assignment.

REFERENCE: LaTour, Eichenwald-Maki, and Oachs, p 444

21. Which of the following classification systems was designed with electronic systems in mind and is currently being used for problem lists, ICU unit monitoring, patient care assessments, data collection, medical research studies, clinical trials, disease surveillance, and images?
    A. SNOMED CT
    B. SNDO
    C. ICDPC-2
    D. GEM

REFERENCE: Abdelhak, pp 235–237
              LaTour, Eichenwald-Maki, and Oachs, pp 398–399
              McWay, pp 150–151

22. The Unified Medical Language System (UMLS) is a project sponsored by the
    A. National Library of Medicine.
    B. CMS.
    C. World Health Organization.
    D. Office of Inspector General.

REFERENCE: LaTour, Eichenwald-Maki, and Oachs, pp 405–406
              McWay, p 151
              Sayles, p 458

23. You have recently been hired as the Medical Staff Coordinator at your local hospital. Which database/registry will you utilize most often?
    A. Trauma Registry
    B. MEDPAR
    C. LOINC
    D. National Practitioner Data Bank (NPDB)

REFERENCE: LaTour, Eichenwald-Maki, and Oachs, p 377
              McWay, p 270
              Sayles, p 451

24. You need to retrieve information on a particular physician in your facility. Specifically, you need to know how many cases he saw during the month of May. What would be your best source of information?
    A. Healthcare Integrity and Protection Data Banks (HIPDB)
    B. Physician Index
    C. MEDLINE database
    D. National Practitioner Data Bank (NPDB)

REFERENCE: LaTour, Eichenwald-Maki, and Oachs, pp 369–370
              McWay, p 140
              Sayles, p 437

25. You just completed a process through which you reviewed a patient record and entered the required elements into a database. What is this process called?
    A. Case finding
    B. Staging
    C. Abstracting
    D. Nomenclature

REFERENCE: LaTour, Eichenwald-Maki, and Oachs, p 382
              McWay, p 140
              Sayles, p 394

26. Which system is used primarily to report services and supplies for reimbursement purposes?
   A. LOINC
   B. HCPCS
   C. NLM
   D. ASTM

REFERENCE: Green, pp 341–342
               LaTour, Eichenwald-Maki, and Oachs, p 394
               McWay, p 164
               Sayles, p 182

27. You are looking at statistics for your facility that include average length of stay (ALOS) and discharge data by DRG. What type of data are you reviewing?
   A. Aggregate data
   B. Patient-identifiable data
   C. MPI data
   D. Protocol data

REFERENCE: LaTour, Eichenwald-Maki, and Oachs, p 368
               McWay, p 208
               Sayles, p 41

28. In which registry would you expect to find an Injury Severity Score (ISS)?
   A. Cancer Registry
   B. Birth Defects Registry
   C. Trauma Registry
   D. Transplant Registry

REFERENCE: LaTour, Eichenwald-Maki, and Oachs, p 372
               Sayles, pp 441–442

29. A service provided by a physician whose opinion or advice regarding evaluation and/or management of a specific problem is requested by another physician is referred to as
   A. a referral.   C. risk factor intervention.
   B. a consultation.   D. concurrent care.

REFERENCE: AMA (2014), p 18–19
               Bowie and Shaffer (2013), pp 61–63
               Frisch, p 77
               Green, pp 435–436
               Johnson and Linker, pp 153–154, 644
               Smith, pp 215–216

30. Which of the following groups maintain healthcare databases in the public and private sectors?
   A. Healthcare provider organizations
   B. Healthcare data organizations
   C. Healthcare payor organizations
   D. Healthcare supplier organizations

REFERENCE: LaTour, Eichenwald-Maki, and Oachs, p 59

31. The most widely discussed and debated unique patient identifier is the
    A. patient's date of birth.
    B. patient's first and last names.
    C. patient's social security number.
    D. Unique Physician Identification Number (UPIN).

REFERENCE: LaTour, Eichenwald-Maki, and Oachs, pp 243–244

32. A nomenclature of codes and medical terms that provides standard terminology for reporting physicians' services for third-party reimbursement is
    A. Current Medical Information and Terminology (CMIT).
    B. Current Procedural Terminology (CPT).
    C. Systematized Nomenclature of Pathology (SNOP).
    D. Diagnostic and Statistical Manual of Mental Disorders (DSM).

REFERENCE: Bowie and Schaffer (2013) pp 2, 8
                  Frisch, p 5
                  Green, p 10
                  Johnson and Linker, p 110
                  Schraffenberger and Kuehn, p 10

33. A cancer program is surveyed for approval by the
    A. American Cancer Society.
    B. Commission on Cancer of the American College of Surgeons.
    C. State Department of Health.
    D. Joint Commission on Accreditation of Healthcare Organizations.

REFERENCE: Abdelhak, p 483
                  LaTour, Eichenwald-Maki, and Oachs, pp 371–372
                  Sayles, p 440

34. The nursing staff would most likely use which of the following to facilitate aggregation of data for comparison at local, regional, national, and international levels?
    A. READ codes   C. SPECIALIST Lexicon
    B. ABC codes   D. LOINC

REFERENCE: Green and Bowie, p 309
                  McWay, p 164

35. The Level II (national) codes of the HCPCS coding system are maintained by the
    A. American Medical Association.
    B. CPT Editorial Panel.
    C. local fiscal intermediary.
    D. Centers for Medicare and Medicaid Services.

REFERENCE: Bowie and Schaffer (2013), p 8
                  Green and Bowie, p 24
                  Johnson and Linker, pp 110–111

36. A patient is admitted with pneumonia. Cultures are requested to determine the infecting organism. Which of the following, if present, would alert the coder to ask the physician whether or not this should be coded as gram-negative pneumonia?
    A. pseudomonas   C. staphylococcus
    B. clostridium   D. listeria

REFERENCE: Green, pp 15–17

37. The Level I (CPT) codes of the HCPCS coding system are maintained by the
    A. American Medical Association.
    B. American Hospital Association.
    C. local fiscal intermediary.
    D. Centers for Medicare and Medicaid Services.

REFERENCE: Bowie and Schaffer (2013), pp 2, 8
                Frisch, p 5
                Green, p 10
                Green and Bowie, pp 24, 307–308
                Johnson and Linker, pp 110–111
                McWay, p 416

38. A physician excises a 3.1 cm malignant lesion of the scalp that requires full-thickness graft from the thigh to the scalp. In CPT, which of the following procedures should be coded?
    A. full-thickness skin graft to scalp only
    B. excision of lesion; full-thickness skin graft to scalp
    C. excision of lesion; full-thickness skin graft to scalp; excision of skin from thigh
    D. code 15004 for surgical preparation of recipient site; full-thickness skin graft to scalp

REFERENCE: AMA, CPT Assistant, vol. 7, no. 9, Sept. 1997, pp 1–3
                Green, pp 517–520, 527–529
                Johnson and Linker, pp 222, 227–229
                Smith, pp 61–62, 72–75

39. A patient is seen by a surgeon who determines that an emergency procedure is necessary. Identify the modifier that may be reported to indicate that the decision to do surgery was made on this office visit.
    A. −25   B. −55   C. −57   D. −58

REFERENCE: AMA (2014), pp 645–650
                Bowie and Schaffer (2013), pp 16–25
                Frisch, pp 18–19
                Green, pp 387–395
                Smith, p 212

40. A patient develops difficulty during surgery and the physician discontinues the procedure. Identify the modifier that may be reported by the physician to indicate that the procedure was discontinued.
    A. −52   B. −53   C. −73   D. −74

REFERENCE: AMA (2014), pp 645–650
                Bowie and Schaffer (2013), pp 6–25
                Frisch, p 18
                Green, pp 387–395
                Johnson and Linker, p 456
                Smith, pp 45–49

41. A barrier to widespread use of automated code assignment is
    A. inadequate technology.   C. resistance by physicians.
    B. poor quality of documentation.   D. resistance by HIM professionals.

REFERENCE: LaTour, Eichenwald-Maki, and Oachs, pp 444–445

42. In assigning E/M codes, three key components are used. These are
    A. history, examination, counseling.
    B. history, examination, time.
    C. history, nature of presenting problem, time.
    D. history, examination, medical decision making.

REFERENCE: AMA (2014), p 9
                  Bowie and Schaffer (2011), pp 39–40
                  Frisch, p 12
                  Green, p 414
                  Johnson and Linker, p 131
                  Smith, p 197

43. Mrs. Jones had an appendectomy on November 1. She was taken back to surgery on November 2 for evacuation of a hematoma of the wound site. Identify the modifier that may be reported for the November 2 visit.
    A. −58   B. −76   C. −78   D. −79

REFERENCE: AMA (2014), pp 645–650
                  Bowie and Schaffer (2011), pp 22–23
                  Frisch, pp 22, 240
                  Green, pp 387–395
                  Johnson and Linker, p 461
                  Smith, pp 48–49

44. The primary goal of a hospital-based cancer registry is to
    A. improve patient care.
    B. allocate hospital resources appropriately.
    C. determine the need for professional and public education programs.
    D. monitor cancer incidence.

REFERENCE: Abdelhak, p 486
                  McWay, pp 142–143

45. A secondary data source that houses and aggregates extensive data about patients with a certain diagnosis is a(n)
    A. disease index.   C. disease registry.
    B. master patient index.   D. admissions register.

REFERENCE: Green and Bowie, pp 240–243
                  LaTour, Eichenwald-Maki, and Oachs, p 370

46. After reviewing the following excerpt from CPT, code 27646 would be interpreted as

27645	radical resection of tumor; tibia
27646	fibula
27647	talus or calcaneus

    A. 27646   radical resection of tumor; tibia and fibula.
    B. 27646   radical resection of tumor; fibula.
    C. 27646   radical resection of tumor; fibula or tibia.
    D. 27646   radical resection of tumor; fibula, talus or calcaneus.

REFERENCE: Bowie and Schaffer (2013), pp 4–5
                  Green, p 374
                  Smith, pp 19–20

Current Procedural Terminology © 2013 American Medical Association. All Rights Reserved.

47. A population-based cancer registry that is designed to determine rates and trends in a defined population is a(n)
    A. incidence-only population-based registry.
    B. cancer control population-based registry.
    C. research-oriented population-based registry.
    D. patient care population-based registry.

REFERENCE: Abdelhak, p 487
               LaTour, Eichenwald-Maki, and Oachs, p 370
               Sayles, pp 438–440

48. Given the diagnosis "carcinoma of axillary lymph nodes and lungs, metastatic from breast," what is the primary cancer site(s)?
    A. axillary lymph nodes   C. breast
    B. lungs   D. A and B

REFERENCE: Frisch, pp 142–144
               Green, pp 156–157
               Hazelwood and Venable, p 112
               Johnson and Linker, p 63
               Schraffenberger (2013), pp 93–94

49. According to CPT, in which of the following cases would an established E/M code be used?
    A. A home visit with a 45-year-old male with a long history of drug abuse and alcoholism. The man is seen at the request of Adult Protective Services for an assessment of his mental capabilities.
    B. John and his family have just moved to town. John has asthma and requires medication to control the problem. He has an appointment with Dr. You and will bring his records from his previous physician.
    C. Tom is seen by Dr. X for a sore throat. Dr. X is on call for Tom's regular physician, Dr. Y. The last time that Tom saw Dr. Y was a couple of years ago.
    D. A 78-year-old female with weight loss and progressive agitation over the past 2 months is seen by her primary care physician for drug therapy. She has not seen her primary care physician in 4 years.

REFERENCE: AMA (2014), pp 4–5
               AMA, CPT Assistant, vol. 8, no. 10, Oct. 1998
               Bowie and Schaffer (2013), pp 37–38
               Frisch, pp 49–50
               Green, pp 411–412
               Smith, pp 195–196

50. In order to use the inpatient CPT consultation codes, the consulting physician must
    A. order diagnostic tests.
    B. document his findings in the patient's medical record.
    C. communicate orally his opinion to the attending physician.
    D. use the term "referral" in his report.

REFERENCE: AMA (2014), pp 18–21
               Frisch, pp 77–78
               Green, pp 435–438
               Smith, pp 215–216

51. The attending physician requests a consultation from a cardiologist. The cardiologist takes a detailed history, performs a detailed examination, and utilizes moderate medical decision making. The cardiologist orders diagnostic tests and prescribes medication. He documents his findings in the patient's medical record and communicates in writing with the attending physician. The following day the consultant visits the patient to evaluate the patient's response to the medication, to review results from the diagnostic tests, and to discuss treatment options. What codes should the consultant report for the two visits?
    A. an initial inpatient consult and a follow-up consult
    B. an initial inpatient consult for both visits
    C. an initial inpatient consult and a subsequent hospital visit
    D. an initial inpatient consult and initial hospital care

REFERENCE: AMA (2014), pp 18–21
               Bowie and Schaffer (2013), pp 61–63
               Frisch, pp 82–86
               Green, pp 435–438
               Smith, pp 215–216

52. According to the American Medical Association, medical decision making is measured by all of the following except the
    A. number of diagnoses or management options.
    B. amount and complexity of data reviewed.
    C. risk of complications.
    D. specialty of the treating physician.

REFERENCE: AMA (2014), p 10
               Bowie and Schaffer (2013), pp 52–54
               Frisch, p 322
               Green, pp 416–417
               Johnson and Linker, pp 139–140
               Smith, pp 205–208

53. CPT provides Level I modifiers to explain all of the following situations EXCEPT
    A. when a service or procedure is partially reduced or eliminated at the physician's discretion.
    B. when one surgeon provides only postoperative services.
    C. when a patient sees a surgeon for follow-up care after surgery.
    D. when the same laboratory test is repeated multiple times on the same day.

REFERENCE: AMA (2014), pp 645–650
               Bowie and Schaffer (2013), pp 16–25
               Frisch, pp 13–23
               Green, pp 387–395
               Johnson and Linker, pp 449–464

54. The best place to ascertain the size of an excised lesion for accurate CPT coding is the
    A. discharge summary.   C. operative report.
    B. pathology report.   D. anesthesia record.

REFERENCE: Green, pp 517–520
               Johnson and Linker, pp 220–221
               Smith, pp 61–62

55. Which of the following is expected to enable hospitals to collect more specific information for use in patient care, benchmarking, quality assessment, research, public health reporting, strategic planning, and reimbursement?
    A. LOINC
    B. ICD-10-CM
    C. NDC
    D. NANDA

REFERENCE: Abdelhak, p 249
                 Johnson and Linker, pp 82–89

56. Case definition is important for all types of registries. Age will certainly be an important criterion for accessing a case in a(n) _____ registry.
    A. implant   C. HIV/AIDS
    B. trauma   D. birth defects

REFERENCE: LaTour, Eichenwald-Maki, and Oachs, p 373

57. To gather statistics for surgical services provided on an outpatient basis, which of the following codes are needed?
    A. ICD-10-CM codes
    B. evaluation and management codes
    C. HCPCS Level II Codes
    D. CPT codes

REFERENCE: Green and Bowie, pp 240–243
                 McWay, p 164
                 Schraffenberger and Kuehn, p 10

58. The Cancer Committee at your hospital requests a list of all patients entered into your cancer registry in the last year. This information would be obtained by checking the
    A. disease index.   C. suspense file.
    B. tickler file.   D. accession register.

REFERENCE: LaTour, Eichenwald-Maki, and Oachs, p 371
                 Sayles, p 439

59. The reference date for a cancer registry is
    A. January 1 of the year in which the registry was established.
    B. the date when data collection began.
    C. the date that the Cancer Committee is established.
    D. the date that the cancer program applies for approval by the American College of Surgeons.

REFERENCE: Abdelhak, p 486

60. The abstract completed on the patients in your hospital contains the following items: patient demographics; prehospital interventions; vital signs on admission; procedures and treatment prior to hospitalization; transport modality; and injury severity score. The hospital uses these data for its
    A. AIDS registry.   C. implant registry.
    B. diabetes registry.   D. trauma registry.

REFERENCE: Abdelhak, p 496
                 LaTour, Eichenwald-Maki, and Oachs, pp 372–373
                 Sayles, pp 441–442

61. In relation to birth defects registries, active surveillance systems
    A. use trained staff to identify cases in all hospitals, clinics, and other facilities through review of patient records, indexes, vital records, and hospital logs.
    B. are commonly used in all 50 states.
    C. miss 10% to 30% of all cases.
    D. rely on reports submitted by hospitals, clinics, or other sources.

REFERENCE: Abdelhak, p 492

62. In regard to quality of coding, the degree to which the same results (same codes) are obtained by different coders or on multiple attempts by the same coder refers to
    A. reliability.   C. completeness.
    B. validity.   D. timeliness.

REFERENCE: LaTour, Eichenwald-Maki, and Oachs, pp 442–443

63. The Healthcare Cost and Utilization Project (HCUP) consists of a set of databases that include data on inpatients whose care is paid for by third-party payers. HCUP is an initiative of the
    A. Agency for Healthcare Research and Quality.
    B. Centers for Medicare and Medicaid Services.
    C. National Library of Medicine.
    D. World Health Organization.

REFERENCE: LaTour, Eichenwald-Maki, and Oachs, pp 381, 631
                McWay, p 175

64. The coding supervisor notices that the coders are routinely failing to code all possible diagnoses and procedures for a patient encounter. This indicates to the supervisor that there is a problem with
    A. completeness.   C. reliability.
    B. validity.   D. timeliness.

REFERENCE: LaTour, Eichenwald-Maki, and Oachs, pp 442–443

65. When coding free skin grafts, which of the following is NOT an essential item of data needed for accurate coding?
    A. recipient site   C. size of defect
    B. donor site   D. type of repair

REFERENCE: Bowie and Schaffer (2013), p 110
                Green, pp 527–530
                Smith, pp 72–76

66. In CPT, Category III codes include codes
    A. to describe emerging technologies.
    B. to measure performance.
    C. for use by nonphysician practitioners.
    D. for supplies, drugs, and durable medical equipment.

REFERENCE: AMA (2014), p 629
                Bowie and Schaffer (2013), p 8
                Johnson and Linker, pp 120, 130
                Smith, p 3

67. The information collected for your registry includes patient demographic information, diagnosis codes, functional status, and histocompatibility information. This type of registry is a
   A. birth defects registry.
   B. diabetes registry.
   C. transplant registry.
   D. trauma registry.

REFERENCE: LaTour, Eichenwald-Maki, and Oachs, pp 374–375

68. Patient Jamey Smith has been seen at Oceanside Hospital three times prior to this current encounter. Unfortunately, because of clerical errors, Jamey's information was entered into the MPI incorrectly on the three previous admissions and consequently has three different medical record numbers. The unit numbering system is used at Oceanside Hospital. Jamey's previous entries into the MPI are as follows:

09/03/10	Jamey Smith	MR# 10361
03/10/11	Jamey Smith Doe	MR# 33998
07/23/12	Jamie Smith Doe	MR# 36723

   The next available number to be assigned at Oceanside Hospital is 41369. Duplicate entries in the MPI should be scrubbed and all of Jamey's medical records should be filed under medical record number
   A. 10361.
   B. 33998.
   C. 36723.
   D. 41369.

REFERENCE: Green and Bowie, pp 237–240
               McWay, pp 139–140

69. The method of calculating errors in a coding audit that allows for benchmarking with other hospitals, and permits the reviewer to track errors by case type, is the
   A. record-over-record method.
   B. benchmarking method.
   C. code method.
   D. focused review method.

REFERENCE: Schraffenberger and Kuehn, p 319

70. The most common type of registry located in hospitals of all sizes and in every region of the country is the
   A. trauma registry.
   B. cancer registry.
   C. AIDS registry.
   D. birth defects registry.

REFERENCE: Green and Bowie, p 248
               McWay, p 142

71. A radiologist is asked to review a patient's CT scan that was taken at another facility. The modifier - 26 attached to the code indicates that the physician is billing for what component of the procedure?
   A. professional
   B. technical
   C. global
   D. confirmatory

REFERENCE: Bowie and Schaffer (2013), pp 17–18
               Frisch, pp 14, 16
               Green, pp 387–395
               Johnson and Linker, pp 453–454

72. When coding neoplasms, topography means
   A. cell structure and form.
   B. site.
   C. variation from normal tissue.
   D. extent of the spread of the disease.

REFERENCE: Abdelhak, p 488

73. According to CPT, antepartum care includes all of the following EXCEPT
    A. initial and subsequent history.
    B. physical examination.
    C. monthly visits up to 36 weeks.
    D. routine chemical urinalysis.

REFERENCE: Bowie and Schaffer (2013), pp 293–295
              Green, pp 687–688
              Johnson and Linker, pp 346–347
              Smith, p 146

74. The Cancer Committee at Wharton General Hospital wants to compare long-term survival rates for pancreatic cancer by evaluating medical versus surgical treatment of the cancer. The best source of these data is the
    A. disease index.
    B. operation index.
    C. master patient index.
    D. cancer registry abstracts.

REFERENCE: Abdelhak, pp 487–488
              LaTour, Eichenwald-Maki, and Oachs, pp 370–371
              McWay, pp 142–143

75. A list or collection of clinical words or phrases with their meanings is a
    A. data dictionary.
    B. language.
    C. medical nomenclature.
    D. clinical vocabulary.

REFERENCE: LaTour, Eichenwald-Maki, and Oachs, p 389

76. The main difference between concurrent and retrospective coding is
    A. when the coding is done.
    B. what classification system is used.
    C. the credentials of the coder.
    D. the involvement of the physician.

REFERENCE: Schraffenberger and Kuehn, p 30

77. A PEG procedure would most likely be done to facilitate
    A. breathing.
    B. eating.
    C. urination.
    D. none of the above.

REFERENCE: Johnson and Linker, p 89
              Schraffenberger (2013), p 253

78. CMS published a final rule indicating a compliance date to implement ICD-10-CM and ICD-10-PCS. The use of these two code sets will be effective on
    A. January 1, 2014.
    B. October 1, 2014.
    C. January 1, 2015.
    D. October 1, 2015.

REFERENCE: DeVault, Barta, and Endicott, p 3
              Bowie and Schaffer (2), p 3

79. Mappings between ICD-9-CM and ICD-10-CM were developed and released by the National Center for Health Statistics (NCHS) to facilitate the transition from one code set to another. They are called
    A. GEMS (General Equivalency Mappings).
    B. Medical Mappings.
    C. Code Maps.
    D. ICD Code Maps.

REFERENCE: DeVault, Barta, and Endicott, p 6

80. The code structure for ICD-10-CM differs from the code structure of ICD-9-CM. An ICD-10-CM code consists of
    A. five alphanumeric characters.
    B. 10 characters.
    C. three to seven characters.
    D. seven digits.

REFERENCE: DeVault, Barta, and Endicott, pp 7–8

81. The first character for all of the codes assigned in ICD-10-CM is
    A. an alphabet.
    B. a number.
    C. an alphabet or a number.
    D. a digit.

REFERENCE: DeVault, Barta, and Endicott, p 7

82. ICD-10-PCS will be implemented in the United States to code
    A. hospital inpatient procedures.
    B. physician office procedures.
    C. hospital inpatient diagnoses.
    D. hospital outpatient diagnoses.

REFERENCE: Barta, DeVault, and Endicott, p 2

83. ICD-10-PCS codes have a unique structure. An example of a valid code in the ICD-10-PCS system is
    A. L03.311.
    B. 013.2.
    C. B2151.
    D. 2W3FX1Z.

REFERENCE: Barta, DeVault, and Endicott, pp 6–10

84. ICD-10-PCS utilizes the third character in the Medical and Surgical section to identify the "root operation." The name of the root operation that describes "cutting out or off, without replacing a portion of a body part" is
    A. destruction.
    B. extirpation.
    C. excision.
    D. removal.

REFERENCE: Barta, DeVault, and Endicott, p 103

85. In ICD-10-PCS, to code "removal of a thumbnail," the root operation would be
    A. removal.
    B. extraction.
    C. fragmentation.
    D. extirpation.

REFERENCE: Barta, DeVault, and Endicott, p 111

86. In ICD-10-CM, the final character of the code indicates laterality. An unspecified side code is also provided should the site not be identified in the medical record. If no bilateral code is provided and the condition is bilateral, the ICD-10-CM Official Coding Guidelines direct the coder to
    A. assign the unspecified side code.
    B. assign separate codes for both the left and right side.
    C. not assign a code.
    D. query the physician.

REFERENCE: DeVault, Barta, and Endicott, p 24

87. An example of a valid code in ICD-10-CM is
    A. 576.212D.
    B. Z3A.34
    C. 329.6677.
    D. BJRT23x.

REFERENCE: DeVault, Barta, and Endicott, p 24

Answer Key for Classification Systems and Secondary Data Sources

NOTE: Explanations are provided for those questions that require mathematical calculations and questions that are not clearly explained in the references that are cited.

ANSWER   EXPLANATION

1. B
2. B
3. C
4. A
5. C
6. C
7. A   A coder should never assign a code on the basis of laboratory results alone. If findings are clearly outside the normal range and the physician has ordered additional testing or treatment, it is appropriate to consult with the physician as to whether a diagnosis should be added or whether the abnormal finding should be listed.
8. A
9. B   Pilocarpine is used to treat open-angle and angle-closure glaucoma to reduce intraocular pressure.
10. D   Digoxin is used for maintenance therapy in congestive heart failure, atrial fibrillation, atrial flutter, and paroxysmal atrial tachycardia. Ibuprofen is an anti-inflammatory drug. Oxytocin is used to initiate or improve uterine contractions at term, and haloperidol is used to manage psychotic disorders.
11. D
12. C   HCPCS codes (Levels I and II) would only give the code for any procedures that were performed and would not identify the diagnosis code or cause of the accident. The correct name of the nomenclature for athletic injuries is the Standard Nomenclature of Athletic Injuries and is used to identify sports injuries. It has not been revised since 1976.
13. D
14. B   All three key components (history, physical examination, and medical decision making) are required for new patients and initial visits. At least two of the three key components are required for established patients and subsequent visits.
15. B
16. D
17. A
18. B
19. B
20. A
21. A
22. A
23. D

Answer Key for Classification Systems and Secondary Data Sources

	ANSWER	EXPLANATION
24.	B	
25.	C	
26.	B	
27.	A	
28.	C	
29.	B	
30.	B	
31.	C	
32.	B	
33.	B	
34.	B	
35.	D	
36.	A	
37.	A	
38.	B	
39.	C	
40.	B	
41.	B	
42.	D	
43.	C	
44.	A	
45.	C	
46.	B	
47.	A	
48.	C	
49.	C	
50.	B	
51.	B	
52.	D	
53.	C	
54.	C	
55.	B	
56.	D	
57.	D	
58.	D	
59.	B	
60.	D	

Answer Key for Classification Systems and Secondary Data Sources

	ANSWER	EXPLANATION
61.	A	
62.	A	
63.	A	
64.	A	
65.	B	
66	A	
67.	C	
68.	A	
69.	A	
70.	B	
71.	A	With CPT radiology codes, there are three components that have to be considered. These are the professional, technical, and global components. The professional component describes the services of a physician who supervises the taking of an x-ray film and the interpretation with report of the results. The technical component describes the services of the person who uses the equipment, the film, and other supplies. The global component describes the combination of both professional and technical components. If the billing radiologist's services include only the supervision and interpretation component, the radiologist bills the procedure code and adds the modifier -26 to indicate that he or she did only the professional component of the procedure.
72.	B	
73.	C	
74.	D	
75.	D	
76.	A	
77.	B	
78.	B	
79.	A	
80.	C	
81.	A	
82.	A	
83.	D	
84.	C	
85.	B	
86.	B	
87.	A	ICD-10-CM codes begin with an alphabetical letter. There is a decimal after the third character. Codes can consist of three to seven characters.

REFERENCES

Abdelhak, M., Grostick, S., Hanken, M.A., & Jacobs, E. (Eds.). (2012). *Health information: Management of a strategic resource* (4th ed.). St. Louis, MO: Saunders Elsevier.

American Medical Association (AMA). *CPT assistant.* Chicago: AMA, CPT Assistant, vol. 7, no. 9, Sept. 1997, pp 1–3.

American Medical Association (AMA). (2013). *Physicians' current procedural terminology (CPT) 2013, Professional Edition.* Chicago: AMA, CPT Assistant, vol. 8, no. 10, Oct. 1998.

Bowie, M. J., (2014). *Understanding ICD-10-CM and ICD-10-PCS: A worktext* (2nd ed.). Clifton Park, NY: Delmar Cengage Learning.

DeVault, K., Barta, A. & Endicott, M. (2013). *ICD-10-CM Coder Training Manual.* Chicago: American Health Information Management Association (AHIMA).

Frisch, B. (2007). *Correct coding for Medicare, compliance, and reimbursement.* Clifton Park, NY: Delmar Cengage Learning.

Green, M. (2014). *3-2-1 Code it* (4th ed.). Clifton Park, NY: Delmar Cengage Learning.

Green, M. A., & Bowie, M. J. (2011). *Essentials of health information management: Principles and practices* (2nd ed.). Clifton Park, NY: Delmar Cengage Learning.

Hazelwood, A.C., & Venable, C. A. (2013). *ICD-10-CM and ICD-9-CM diagnostic coding and reimbursement for physician services.* Chicago: American Health Information Management Association (AHIMA).

Johnson, S. L., & Linker, C. S. (2013). Understanding medical coding: A comprehensive guide (3rd ed.). Clifton Park, NY: Delmar Cengage Learning.

LaTour, K., Eichenwald-Maki, S., and Oachs, P. (2013). *Health information management: Concepts, principles and practice* (4th ed.). Chicago: American Health Information Management Association (AHIMA).

McWay, D. C. (2013). *Today's health information management: An integrated approach* (2nd ed.). Clifton Park, NY: Delmar Cengage Learning.

Nobles, S. (2002). *Delmar's drug reference for health care professionals.* Clifton Park, NY: Delmar Cengage Learning.

Sayles, N. (2013). *Health information management technology: An applied approach* (4th ed.). Chicago: American Health Information Management Association (AHIMA).

Schraffenberger, L. A. (2013). *Basic ICD-10-CM/PCS and ICD-9-CM coding.* Chicago: American Health Information Management Association (AHIMA).

Schraffenberger, L. A., & Kuehn, L. (2011). *Effective management of coding services* (4th ed.). Chicago: American Health Information Management Association (AHIMA).

Smith, G. (2012). *Basic current procedural terminology and HCPCS coding 2013.* Chicago: American Health Information Management Association (AHIMA).

Question	RHIA Domain Competencies							RHIT Domain Competencies						
	1	2	3	4	5	6		1	2	3	4	5	6	7
1	X							X						
2	X								X					
3	X							X						
4			X					X						
5	X							X						
6	X							X						
7	X								X					
8	X							X						
9	X								X					
10	X							X						
11	X							X						
12	X							X						
13	X								X					
14	X							X						
15	X							X						
16	X							X						
17	X							X						
18	X								X					
19	X								X					
20			X						X					
21			X					X						
22	X							X						
23	X							X						
24	X							X						
25	X							X						
26	X								X					
27	X							X						
28	X									X				
29	X								X					
30	X							X						
31	X								X					
32	X								X					
33	X							X						
34	X							X						
35	X							X						
36	X							X						
37	X							X						
38	X							X						
39	X								X					
40	X								X					
41	X							X						
42	X								X					
43	X								X					
44	X								X					
45			X						X					
46	X								X					
47	X								X					
48	X							X						
49	X								X					
50	X							X						
51	X								X					
52	X								X					
53	X								X					

	RHIA AND RHIT COMPETENCIES BY QUESTION FOR CLASSIFICATION SYSTEMS AND SECONDARY DATA SOURCES													
Question	RHIA Domain Competencies							RHIT Domain Competencies						
	1	2	3	4	5	6		1	2	3	4	5	6	7
54	X								X					
55	X							X						
56	X								X					
57	X								X					
58	X								X					
59	X								X					
60	X								X					
61	X								X					
62	X								X					
63	X								X					
64			X					X						
65	X							X						
66	X							X						
67	X							X						
68	X							X						
69	X							X						
70	X							X						
71	X								X					
72	X							X						
73	X								X					
74	X								X					
75	X								X					
76	X							X						
77	X								X					
78	X								X					
79	X								X					
80	X								X					
81	X								X					
82	X								X					
83	X								X					
84	X								X					
85	X							X						
86	X							X						
87	X							X						
88	X								X					
89	X							X						
90	X								X					
91	X							X						
92	X							X						
93	X								X					
94	X								X					
95	X								X					
96	X								X					
97	X								X					
98	X								X					
99	X								X					
100	X								X					
101	X							X						
102	X								X					
103									X					

Question	RHIA AND RHIT COMPETENCIES BY QUESTION FOR CLASSIFICATION SYSTEMS AND SECONDARY DATA SOURCES													
	RHIA Domain Competencies							RHIT Domain Competencies						
	1	2	3	4	5	6		1	2	3	4	5	6	7
104	X								X					
105	X							X						
106	X								X					
107	X								X					
108	X								X					
109	X								X					
110	X								X					

VI. ICD-10-CM/PCS Coding

Leslie Moore, RHIT, CCS

ICD-10-CM and ICD-10-PCS

The compliance date for implementation of ICD-10-CM/PCS is October 1, 2014, for all Health Insurance Portability and Accountability Act (HIPAA)-covered entities.

ICD-10-CM, including the "ICD-10-CM Official Guidelines for Coding and Reporting," will replace ICD-9-CM Diagnosis Codes in all health care settings for diagnosis reporting with dates of service, or dates of discharge for inpatients, that occur on or after October 1, 2014.

ICD-10-PCS, including the "ICD-10-PCS Official Guidelines for Coding and Reporting," will replace ICD-9-CM Procedure Codes.

BENEFITS OF ICD-10-CM

ICD-10-CM incorporates much greater clinical detail and specificity than ICD-9-CM. Terminology and disease classification are updated to be consistent with current clinical practice. The modern classification system will provide much better data needed for:
- Measuring the quality, safety, and efficacy of care;
- Reducing the need for attachments to explain the patient's condition;
- Designing payment systems and processing claims for reimbursement;
- Conducting research, epidemiological studies, and clinical trials;
- Setting health policy;
- Operational and strategic planning;
- Designing health care delivery systems;
- Monitoring resource use;
- Improving clinical, financial, and administrative performance;
- Preventing and detecting health care fraud and abuse; and
- Tracking public health and risks.

Non-specific codes are still available for use when medical record documentation does not support a more specific code.

ICD-10-CM Diagnosis Codes:

There are 3–7 digits;
> Digit 1 is alpha;
> Digit 2 is numeric;
> Digits 3–7 are alpha or numeric (alpha characters are not case sensitive); and a decimal is used after the third character.
> Examples:
>> A78–Q   fever;
>> A69.21   Meningitis due to Lyme disease; and
>> S52.131A   Displaced fracture of neck of right radius, initial encounter for closed fracture.

NEW FEATURES IN ICD-10-CM

The following new features can be found in ICD-10-CM:

1) *Laterality (Left, Right, Bilateral)*
   Examples:
   C50.511 – Malignant neoplasm of lower-outer quadrant of right female breast;
   H16.013 – Central corneal ulcer, bilateral; and
   L89.012 – Pressure ulcer of right elbow, stage II.

2) *Combination Codes For Certain Conditions and Common Associated Symptoms and Manifestations*
   Examples:
   K57.21 – Diverticulitis of large intestine with perforation and abscess with bleeding;
   E11.341 – Type 2 diabetes mellitus with severe nonproliferative diabetic retinopathy with macular edema; and
   I25.110 – Atherosclerotic heart disease of native coronary artery with unstable angina pectoris.

3) *Combination Codes for Poisonings and Their Associated External Cause*
   Example:
   T42.3x2S – Poisoning by barbiturates, intentional self-harm, sequela.

4) *Obstetric Codes Identify Trimester Instead of Episode of Care*
   Example:
   O26.02 – Excessive weight gain in pregnancy, second trimester.

5) *Character "x" is Used as a 5th Character Placeholder in Certain 6 Character Codes to Allow for Future Expansion and to Fill in Other Empty Characters (For Example, Character 5 and/or 6) When a Code That is Less Than 6 Characters in Length Requires a 7th Character*
   Examples:
   T46.1x5A – Adverse effect of calcium-channel blockers, initial encounter; and
   T15.02xD – Foreign body in cornea, left eye, subsequent encounter.

6) *Two Types of Excludes Notes*
   Excludes 1 Indicates that the code excluded should never be used with the code where the note is located (do not report both codes).
   Example:
   Q03 – Congenital hydrocephalus.
   Excludes 1: Acquired hydrocephalus (**G91.-**).

   Excludes 2 Indicates that the condition excluded is not part of the condition represented by the code but a patient may have both conditions at the same time, in which case both codes may be assigned together (both codes can be reported to capture both conditions).
   Example:
   L27.2 – Dermatitis due to ingested food.
   Excludes 2: Dermatitis due to food in contact with skin (L23.6, L24.6, L25.4).

7) *Inclusion of Clinical Concepts That Do Not Exist in ICD-9-CM (For Example, Underdosing, Blood Type, Blood Alcohol Level)*

Examples:

T45.526D – Underdosing of antithrombotic drugs, subsequent encounter;

Z67.40 – Type O blood, Rh positive; and

Y90.6 – Blood alcohol level of 120 – 199 mg/100 ml.

8) *A Number of Codes Are Significantly Expanded (For Example, Injuries, Diabetes, Substance Abuse, Postoperative Complications)*

Examples:

E10.610 – Type 1 diabetes mellitus with diabetic neuropathic arthropathy;

F10.182 – Alcohol abuse with alcohol-induced sleep disorder; and

T82.02xA – Displacement of heart valve prosthesis, initial encounter.

9) *Codes for Postoperative Complications Are Expanded and a Distinction is Made Between Intraoperative Complications and Postprocedural Disorders*

Examples:

D78.01 – Intraoperative hemorrhage and hematoma of spleen complicating a procedure on the spleen; and

D78.21 – Postprocedural hemorrhage and hematoma of spleen following a procedure on the spleen.

ADDITIONAL CHANGES IN ICD-10-CM

The additional changes that can be found in ICD-10-CM are as follows:

- Injuries are grouped by anatomical site rather than by type of injury; Category restructuring and code reorganization occur in a number of ICD-10-CM chapters, resulting in the classification of certain diseases and disorders that are different from ICD-9-CM;
- Certain diseases are reclassified to different chapters or sections to reflect current medical knowledge;
- New code definitions (for example, definition of acute myocardial infarction is now 4 weeks rather than 8 weeks); and
- The codes corresponding to ICD-9-CM V codes (Factors Influencing Health Status and Contact with Health Services) and E codes (External Causes of Injury and Poisoning) are incorporated into the main classification (in ICD-9-CM they were separated into supplementary classifications).

USE OF EXTERNAL CAUSE AND UNSPECIFIED CODES IN ICD-10-CM

Similar to ICD-9-CM, there is no national requirement for mandatory ICD-10-CM external cause code reporting. Unless you are subject to a State-based external cause code reporting mandate or these codes are required by a particular payer, you are not required to report ICD-10-CM codes found in Chapter 20, External Causes of Morbidity.

If you have not been reporting ICD-9-CM external cause codes, you will not be required to report ICD-10-CM codes found in Chapter 20 unless a new State or payer-based requirement about the reporting of these codes is instituted. If such a requirement is instituted, it would be independent of ICD-10-CM implementation.

In the absence of a mandatory reporting requirement, you are encouraged to voluntarily report external cause codes, as they provide valuable data for injury research and evaluation of injury prevention strategies.

In both ICD-9-CM and ICD-10-CM, sign/symptom and unspecified codes have acceptable, even necessary, uses. While specific diagnosis codes should be reported when they are supported by the available medical record documentation and clinical knowledge of the patient's health condition, in some instances signs/symptoms or unspecified codes are the best choice to accurately reflect the health care encounter.

Each health care encounter should be coded to the level of certainty known for that encounter.
If a definitive diagnosis has not been established by the end of the encounter, it is appropriate to report codes for sign(s) and/or symptom(s) in lieu of a definitive diagnosis. When sufficient clinical information is not known or available about a particular health condition to assign a more specific code, it is acceptable to report the appropriate unspecified code (for example, a diagnosis of pneumonia has been determined but the specific type has not been determined). In fact, unspecified codes should be reported when they are the codes that most accurately reflect what is known about the patient's condition at the time of that particular encounter. It is inappropriate to select a specific code that is not supported by the medical record documentation or conduct medically unnecessary diagnostic testing to determine a more specific code. Reference: MLM Matters CMS Website

2014 release of ICD-10-CM

These files have been created by the National Center for Health Statistics (NCHS), under authorization by the World Health Organization.

These files linked below are the 2014 update of the ICD-10-CM. Content changes to the full ICD-10-CM files are described in the respective addenda files. This year in addition to PDF (Adobe) files XML format is also being made available. Most files are provided in compressed zip format for ease in downloading.

These files have been created by the National Center for Health Statistics (NCHS), under authorization by the World Health Organization.

Although this release of ICD-10-CM is now available for public viewing, the codes in ICD-10-CM are not currently valid for any purpose or use. As noted above, the effective implementation date for ICD-10-CM (and ICD-10-PCS) is October 1, 2014. Updates to this version of ICD-10-CM are anticipated prior to its implementation.

- Preface [PDF - 35 KB]
- ICD-10-CM Guidelines [PDF - 512 KB]
- Detailed List of Codes Exempt from Diagnosis Present on Admission Requirement PDF Format
- Detailed List of Codes Exempt from Diagnosis Present on Admission Requirement XLSM Format
- ICD-10-CM PDF Format
- ICD-10-CM XML Format
- ICD-10-CM List of codes and Descriptions (updated 7/3/2013)
- General Equivalence Mapping Files

To download these files go to: http://www.cdc.gov/nchs/icd/icd10cm.htm#10update
Content source: CDC/National Center for Health Statistics
Page maintained by: Office of Information Services
http://www.cdc.gov/nchs/icd/icd10cm.htm

Development of the ICD-10 Procedure Coding System (ICD-10-PCS)

Richard F. Averill, M.S., Robert L. Mullin, M.D., Barbara A. Steinbeck, RHIT, Norbert I. Goldfield, M.D, Thelma M. Grant, RHIA, Rhonda R. Butler, CCS, CCS-P

The International Classification of Diseases 10th Revision Procedure Coding System (ICD-10-PCS) has been developed as a replacement for Volume 3 of the International Classification of Diseases 9th Revision (ICD-9-CM). The development of ICD-10-PCS was funded by the U.S. Centers for Medicare and Medicaid Services (CMS).1 ICD-10-PCS has a multiaxial seven character alphanumeric code structure that provides a unique code for all substantially different procedures, and allows new procedures to be easily incorporated as new codes. ICD10-PCS was under development for over five years. The initial draft was formally tested and evaluated by an independent contractor; the final version was released in the Spring of 1998, with annual updates since the final release. The design, development and testing of ICD-10-PCS are discussed.

Introduction

Volume 3 of the International Classification of Diseases 9th Revision Clinical Modification (ICD-9-CM) has been used in the U.S. for the reporting of inpatient procedures since 1979. The structure of Volume 3 of ICD-9-CM has not allowed new procedures associated with rapidly changing technology to be effectively incorporated as new codes. As a result, in 1992 the U.S. Centers for Medicare and Medicaid Services (CMS) funded a project to design a replacement for Volume 3 of ICD-9-CM. After a review of the preliminary design, CMS in 1995 awarded 3M Health Information Systems a three-year contract to complete development of the replacement system. The new system is the ICD-10 Procedure Coding System (ICD-10-PCS).

Attributes Used in Development

The development of ICD-10-PCS had as its goal the incorporation of four major attributes:

• Completeness
There should be a unique code for all substantially different procedures. In Volume 3 of ICD-9-CM, procedures on different body parts, with different approaches, or of different types are sometimes assigned to the same code.

• Expandability
As new procedures are developed, the structure of ICD-10-PCS should allow them to be easily incorporated as unique codes.

• Multiaxial
ICD-10-PCS codes should consist of independent characters, with each individual axis retaining its meaning across broad ranges of codes to the extent possible.

• Standardized Terminology
ICD-10-PCS should include definitions of the terminology used. While the meaning of specific words varies in common usage, ICD-10-PCS should not include multiple meanings for the same term, and each term must be assigned a specific meaning.

If these four objectives are met, then ICD-10-PCS should enhance the ability of health information coders to construct accurate codes with minimal effort.

General Development Principles

In the development of ICD-10-PCS, several general principles were followed:

- *Diagnostic Information is Not Included in Procedure Description*

When procedures are performed for specific diseases or disorders, the disease or disorder is not contained in the procedure code. There are no codes for procedures exclusive to aneurysms, cleft lip, strictures, neoplasms, hernias, etc. The diagnosis codes, not the procedure codes, specify the disease or disorder.

- *Not Otherwise Specified (NOS) Options are Restricted*

ICD-9-CM often provides a "not otherwise specified" code option. Certain NOS options made available in ICD-10-PCS are restricted to the uses laid out in the ICD-10-PCS official guidelines. A minimal level of specificity is required for each component of the procedure.

- *Limited Use of Not Elsewhere Classified (NEC) Option*

ICD-9-CM often provides a "not elsewhere classified" code option.

Because all significant components of a procedure are specified in ICD-10-PCS, there is generally no need for an NEC code option. However, limited NEC options are incorporated into ICD-10-PCS where necessary. For example, new devices are frequently developed, and therefore it is necessary to provide an "Other Device" option for use until the new device can be explicitly added to the coding system. Additional NEC options are discussed later, in the sections of the system where they occur.

- *Level of Specificity*

All procedures currently performed can be specified in ICD-10-PCS. The frequency with which a procedure is performed was not a consideration in the development of the system. Rather, a unique code is available for variations of a procedure that can be performed.

ICD-10-PCS has a seven character alphanumeric code structure. Each character contains up to 34 possible values. Each value represents a specific option for the general character definition (e.g., stomach is one of the values for the body part character). The ten digits 0-9 and the 24 letters A-H, J-N and P-Z may be used in each character. The letters O and I are not used in order to avoid confusion with the digits 0 and 1.

Procedures are divided into sections that identify the general type of procedure (e.g., medical and surgical, obstetrics, imaging). The first character of the procedure code always specifies the section. The sections are shown in table 1.

Table 1: ICD-10-PCS Sections

0	Medical and Surgical
1	Obstetrics
2	Placement
3	Administration
4	Measurement and Monitoring
5	Extracorporeal Assistance and Performance
6	Extracorporeal Therapies
7	Osteopathic
8	Other Procedures
9	Chiropractic
B	Imaging
C	Nuclear Medicine
D	Radiation Oncology
F	Physical Rehabilitation and Diagnostic Audiology
G	Mental Health
H	Substance Abuse Treatment

The second through seventh characters mean the same thing within each section, but may mean different things in other sections. In all sections, the third character specifies the general type of procedure performed (e.g., resection, transfusion, fluoroscopy), while the other characters give additional information such as the body part and approach. In ICD-10-PCS, the term "procedure" refers to the complete specification of the seven characters.

ICD-10-PCS 2014 Version
Update Summary /Change Summary Table

2013 Total	New Codes	Revised Titles	Deleted Codes	2014 Total
71,920	7	0	3	**71,924**

ICD-10-PCS Code 2013 Totals, By Section

Medical and Surgical	**61,898**
Obstetrics	300
Placement	861
Administration	**1,388**
Measurement and Monitoring	339
Extracorporeal Assistance and Performance	41
Extracorporeal Therapies	42
Osteopathic	100
Other Procedures	60
Chiropractic	90
Imaging	2,934
Nuclear Medicine	463
Radiation Oncology	1,939
Rehabilitation and Diagnostic Audiology	1,380
Mental Health	30
Substance Abuse Treatment	59
Total	**71,924**

ICD-10-PCS Code Changes
Four codes added under new technology application, valid October 1, 2013

- **08H005Z** Insertion of Epiretinal Visual Prosthesis into Right Eye, Open Approach
- **08H105Z** Insertion of Epiretinal Visual Prosthesis into Left Eye, Open Approach
- **30280B1** Transfusion of Nonautologous 4-Factor Prothrombin Complex Concentrate into Vein, Open Approach
- **30283B1** Transfusion of Nonautologous 4-Factor Prothrombin Complex Concentrate into Vein, Percutaneous Approach

Three new codes added and three codes deleted, to correct body part value for temporary occlusion of abdominal aorta

- New: **04V00DJ** Restriction of Abdominal Aorta with Intraluminal Device, Temporary, Open Approach
- New: **04V03DJ** Restriction of Abdominal Aorta with Intraluminal Device, Temporary, Percutaneous Approach
- New: **04V04DJ** Restriction of Abdominal Aorta with Intraluminal Device, Temporary, Percutaneous Endoscopic Approach
- Deleted: **02VW0DJ** Restriction of Thoracic Aorta with Intraluminal Device, Temporary, Open Approach

- Deleted: **02VW3DJ** Restriction of Thoracic Aorta with Intraluminal Device, Temporary, Percutaneous Approach
- Deleted: **02VW4DJ** Restriction of Thoracic Aorta with Intraluminal Device, Temporary, Percutaneous Endoscopic Approach

Revised Section Title

Section title for Radiation Oncology section revised to Radiation Therapy in response to public comment. Because the phrase "Radiation Oncology" is not used in code titles, no code titles were revised as a result of the section title change.

New Index Addenda

- New file showing new, revised and deleted index entries in response to public comment
- First discussed at September 2012 Coordination and Maintenance Committee, proposed format shown at March 2013 Coordination and Maintenance Committee
- See list of updated files for details

New Definitions Addenda

- New file showing new, revised and deleted PCS definitions entries (e.g. Body Part Key) in response to public comment
- First discussed at September 2012 Coordination and Maintenance Committee, proposed format shown at March 2013 Coordination and Maintenance Committee
- See list of updated files for details

List of Updated Files
2014 Official ICD-10-PCS Coding Guidelines

- Downloadable PDF file
- Revised in response to public comment and review by the Cooperating Parties

2014 ICD-10-PCS Code Tables and Index (Zip file)

- Downloadable PDF file, file name is **PCS_2014.pdf**
- Downloadable xml files for developers, file names are:
  icd10pcs_tabular_2014.xml
  icd10pcs_index_2014.xml
  icd10pcs_definitions_2014.xml
- Accompanying schema for developers, file names are:
  icd10pcs_tabular_2014.xsd
  icd10pcs_index_2014.xsd
  icd10pcs_definitions_2014.xsd

2014 ICD-10-PCS Code Titles, Long and Abbreviated (Zip file)

- Tabular order file defines an unambiguous order for all ICD-10-CM/PCS codes
- Text file format, file name is:
  icd10pcs_order_2014.txt
  Provides a unique five-digit "order number" for each ICD-10-PCS table and code
- Accompanying documentation, file name is:
  ICD10OrderFiles.pdf

2014 ICD-10-PCS Final Addenda (Zip file)

- New code titles for FY2014 shown as ICD-10-PCS table entries, file name is: **PcsAddendaAdditionsNewLabels.pdf**
- Deleted code titles for FY2014 shown as ICD-10-PCS table entries, file name is: **PcsAddendaDeletionsOldLabels.pdf**
- Downloadable xml format for developers, file names are: **PcsAddendaAdditionsNewLabels.xml, PcsAddendaDeletionsOldLabels.xml**
- Accompanying documentation, file name is: **pcs_addenda_readme2014.pdf**
- Index addenda in downloadable PDF, file name is: **index_addenda_2014.pdf**
- PCS Definitions addenda in downloadable PDF, file name is: **definitions_addenda_2014.pdf**
- Index and Definitions addenda in machine readable text format for developers, file names are: **index_addenda_2014.txt, definitions_addenda_2014.txt**

2014 ICD-10-PCS Reference Manual (Zip file)

- Downloadable PDF file, file name is **ICD-10-PCS Reference Manual.pdf**
  Revised in response to public comment and internal review
- Addenda to 2014 version of reference manual specifies the changes, file name is: **pcs_ref_addenda_2014.pdf**

2014 ICD-10-PCS and ICD-9-CM General Equivalence Mappings (Zip file)

- Downloadable text format, file names are: **gem_i9pcs.txt, gem_pcsi9.txt**
  Contains entries for the new FY2014 ICD-9-CM and ICD-10-PCS codes and entries revised in response to public comment and internal review
- Documentation for general users and technical users, file name is: **pcs_gemguide_2014.pdf**
- Documentation for technical users, file name is: **GemsTechDoc.pdf**

2014 ICD-10 Reimbursement Mappings (Zip file)

- Downloadable text format, file names are **reimb_map_dx_2014.txt reimb_map_pr_2014.txt**
  FY2014 version uses the FY2014 GEM files
- Accompanying documentation includes rules used in the mapping, file name is: **reimb_map_guide_2014.pdf**

ICD-10-CM CODING SECTION

Infectious and Parasitic Diseases

1. The patient was admitted with AIDS-related Kaposi's sarcoma of the skin.
    A. B20, C46.1   C. B20, C46.7
    B. C46.0, B20   D. B20, C46.0

REFERENCE: AHA I-10 Coding Handbook, p 157

2. A patient was admitted with severe sepsis due to MRSA with septic shock and acute respiratory failure with hypoxia.
    A. R65.21, A41.02, J96.02
    B. A41.02, R65.21, J96.01
    C. A49.01, R65.21, J96.01
    D. J96.01, R65.21, A41.02

REFERENCE: AHA I-10 Coding Handbook, p 151

3. Patient was initially admitted and treated for an amebic abscess of the liver. During the stay the patient developed a "hospital acquired bacterial pneumonia."
    A. A06.4, J15.9, Y95   C. A06.4, J18.9, Y95
    B. A06.4, J15.8; Y95   D. A06.4, J95.89, Y95

REFERENCE: AHA I-10 Coding Handbook, pp 153, 154

4. _ A patient is admitted with fever and severe headache. The physician's diagnostic statement at discharge is: Fever and severe headache probably due to viral meningitis.
    A. A87.9, R50.9, R51   C. A87.9
    B. A87.8, R50.9, R51   D. A87.8

REFERENCE: AHA I-10 Coding Handbook, p 57

5. Positive HIV test in a patient who is asymptomatic and has a high-risk lifestyle for HIV infection.
    A. B20, Z20.6, Z72.89   C. B20, Z20.6, Z72.89
    B. B20, Z21, Z72.89   D. Z21, Z72.89

REFERENCE: AHA I-10 Coding Handbook, p 157

6. A 32-year-old female patient presents with right arm (dominant) paralysis due to childhood poliomyelitis.
    A. A80.39   C. B91, G83.21
    B. A80.39, G83.21   D. A80.39, G83.3

REFERENCE: AHA I-10 Coding Handbook, pp 6, 60, 149

Neoplasms

7. A patient is admitted for chemotherapy for treatment of breast cancer with liver metastasis. She had a mastectomy 4 months ago. Chemotherapy is given today. (Do not assign a procedure code for the chemotherapy.)
    A. C78.7, C85.3, Z51.11   C. C78.7, C85.3
    B. C85.3, C78.7, Z51.11   D. Z51.11, C78.7, Z85.3

REFERENCE: AHA I-10 Coding Handbook, pp 456, 457, 459

8. A patient with a history of malignant neoplasm of the lung status post lobectomy was admitted after experiencing a violent seizure lasting more than several minutes. During the course of the hospitalization the patient has continued to have seizures. Workup revealed metastatic lesions to the brain. The patient's seizures were treated with IV Dilantin.
    A. C79.3, Z85.118, F56.9   C. C79.31, R56.9, Z85.118
    B. C79.31, F56.9   D. F56.9 C79.32, Z85.118

REFERENCE: AHA I-10 Coding Handbook, pp 456, 457, 458

9. A patient is admitted to the hospital for treatment of dehydration following chemotherapy as treatment for right ovarian cancer.
    A. E86.0, C56.1   C. C56.1, 86.9
    B. E86.9, C56.1   D. C56.1, E86.0

REFERENCE: AHA I-10 Coding Handbook, p 458

10. A patient has malignant melanoma of the skin of the back, nose, and scalp. The patient will be scheduled to undergo a radical excision of the melanoma
    A. 173.59, 86.4, 86.63   C. 173.59, 86.3, 86.63
    B. C43.59, C43.31, C43.4   D. 172.5, 86.3, 86.63

REFERENCE: AHA I-10 Coding Handbook, pp 443, 456, 460

11. A patient is admitted with abdominal pain. A CT and MRI of the abdomen reveal a malignant neoplasm to the head of the pancreas with metastatic disease to the peritoneal cavity.
    A. C25.1, C78.6   C. C25.0, C78.6
    B. C78.89, C78.89   D. D01.7, C78.6

REFERENCE: AHA I-10 Coding Handbook, pp 456–458

12. A patient to an OP Clinic with a large growth on the left side of the neck. An MRI is performed and demonstrates metastatic disease to the lymph nodes.
    A. C77.2, C80.0   C. C77.2, R22.1, C81.1
    B. C77.0, C80.1   D. C77.8, C80.0

REFERENCE: AHA I-10 Coding Handbook, pp 459–458, 447–44/, 452–455

Endocrine, Nutritional, and Metabolic Diseases and Immunity Disorders

13. A female, 68 years old, was admitted with type 2 diabetes mellitus with a diabetic ulcer of the left heel involving the subcutaneous layer of the skin. The patient will be scheduled for wound care with whirlpool treatments.
    A. E11.621, L97.421   C. E11.621
    B. E11.620, I97.421   D. L97.421, E11.621

REFERENCE: AHA I-10 Coding Handbook, p 164

14. A 67-year-old man is admitted with acute dehydration secondary to nausea and vomiting that is due to acute gastroenteritis. He is treated with IV fluids for the dehydration.
    A. K52.9, E86.0   C. 86.0, E11.2, K52.9
    B. E11.2, 52.9, E86.0   D. E86.0, K52.9

REFERENCE: AHA I-10 Coding Handbook, pp 30–33

15. A patient was found at home in a hypoglycemic coma. This patient had never been diagnosed as being diabetic.
   A. E16.2   C. E16.1
   B. E15   D. E16.9

REFERENCE: AHA I-10 Coding Handbook, p 167

16. A patient is admitted with aplastic anemia secondary to chemotherapy administered for multiple myeloma initial encounter.
   A. D61.1, T45.1x5A, C90.00   C. C90.00, T45.1x5A, D61.1
   B. T45.1x5A, C90.00, D61.3   D. D61.1, T45.1x5A, D61.3

REFERENCE: AHA I-10 Coding Handbook, p 459

17. A male patient is admitted with gastrointestinal hemorrhage resulting in acute blood-loss anemia. A bleeding scan fails to reveal the source of the bleed.
   A. K92, D63.8   C. K92.2, D62
   B. K92.1, D62   D. K92.2, D63.8

REFERENCE: AHA I-10 Coding Handbook, pp 191, 192–196

18. A patient is admitted with severe protein calorie malnutrition.
   A. E42   C. E46
   B. E43   D. E40

REFERENCE: AHA I-10 Coding Handbook, p 168

Diseases of the Blood and Blood-Forming Organs

19. A patient is admitted with idiopathic thrombocytopenia and purpura.
   A. D61   C. D69.49
   B. D69.3, D61   D. D69.3

REFERENCE: AHA I-10 Coding Handbook, pp 191, 199

20. A patient is admitted with sickle cell anemia with crisis.
   A. D57.00, D57.3   C. D57.1
   B. D57.00   D. D57.819

REFERENCE: AHA I-10 Coding Handbook, pp 191, 196

21. A patient is admitted with sickle cell pain crisis.
   A. D57.00   C. D57.819
   B. D57.00, D57.3   D. D57.1

REFERENCE: AHA I-10 Coding Handbook, pp 191, 196

22. A patient is readmitted for post-op anemia due to acute blood loss. Patient is 5 days status post-cholecystectomy.
   A. D62, R58   C. K91.89, D62
   B. K91.840, D62   D. D62

REFERENCE: AHA I-10 Coding Handbook, pp 199, 528

23. A patient is admitted with anemia due to end-stage renal disease. The patient is treated for anemia.
   A. N18.6, D63.8
   B. D63.1, N18.6
   C. D63.1, N18.5
   D. D63.1

REFERENCE: AHA I-10 Coding Handbook, p 194

24. A patient is admitted for treatment of anemia, neutropenia, and thrombocytopenia.
   A. D70.8, D69.59, D59.2
   B. D61.810
   C. D70.8, D69.59, D59.2, D61.810
   D. D61.818

REFERENCE: AHA I-10 Coding Handbook, p 195

Mental Disorders

25. A patient is admitted with severe recurrent major depression without psychotic features.
   A. F33.0
   B. F33.3
   C. F32.2
   D. F33.2

REFERENCE: AHA I-10 Coding Handbook, p 175

26. A patient is admitted with acute alcohol intoxication with a blood alcohol level of 113 mg/100 ml.
   A. Y90.5, F10.129
   B. F10.129, Y90.5
   C. F10.129, Y90.6
   D. F10.129, Y90.4

REFERENCE: AHA I-10 Coding Handbook, pp 12, 181

27. A patient is admitted with delirium tremens with alcohol dependence.
   A. F10.221
   B. F10.222
   C. F10.121
   D. F10.231

REFERENCE: AHA I-10 Coding Handbook, p 181

28. A patient is admitted with catatonic schizophrenia.
   A. F20
   B. F14.221
   C. F20.2
   D. F14.29

REFERENCE: AHA I-10 Coding Handbook, pp 181, 182

29. A patient with chronic paranoia due to cocaine dependence with intoxication and drug delirium.
   A. F14.129
   B. F14.221
   C. F14.159
   D. F14.19, F22

REFERENCE: AHA I-10 Coding Handbook, pp 181–182

30. A patient is diagnosed with psychogenic paroxysmal tachycardia.
   A. I47.9
   B. F54
   C. I47.8, F54
   D. I47.9, F54

REFERENCE: AHA I-10 Coding Handbook, p 179

Diseases of the Nervous System and Sense Organs

31. A patient is admitted with sensorineural deafness of the left ear. The patient was fitted for a hearing aid.
    A. H90.71
    B. H90.72
    C. H90.42
    D. H90.41

    REFERENCE: AHA I-10 Coding Handbook, p 220

32. A patient is a type 2 diabetic with chronic kidney disease requiring dialysis.
    A. E09.29, N18.6, Z99.2
    B. E11.22, N18.6, Z99.2
    C. E11.21, N18.6, Z99.2
    D. E13.21, N18.6, Z99.2

    REFERENCE: AHA I-10 Coding Handbook, p 265

33. A patient has intractable status epilepticus.
    A. G40.311
    B. G40.301
    C. G40.31
    D. G40.201

    REFERENCE: AHA I-10 Coding Handbook, p 206

34. A patient is diagnosed with Alzheimer's disease and early onset dementia, and frequently wanders away from home.
    A. G30.8, F02.81, Z91.83
    B. F02.81, G30.0, Z91.73
    C. G30.0, F02.81, Z91.83
    D. G30.0, Z91.73

    REFERENCE: AHA I-10 Coding Handbook, pp 173, 206

35. A patient is admitted with poliovirus meningitis.
    A. G02, A80.9
    B. A80.9, G02
    C. A80.3, G02
    D. A80.0, G02

    REFERENCE: AHA I-10 Coding Handbook, p 205

36. A patient is admitted for pain control secondary to metastatic carcinoma of the spinal cord.
    A. G89.3, C79.49
    B. C79.51, C80.1, G89.3
    C. C79.49, C80.1 , G89.3
    D. G89.3, C79.49, C80.1

    REFERENCE: AHA I-10 Coding Handbook, p 210

Diseases of the Circulatory System

37. A patient is admitted with a thrombosis of the right middle cerebral artery, with hemiplegia affecting the right dominant side.
    A. I66.01, I69.351
    B. I63.311, I69.353
    C. I63.311
    D. I63.311, I69.351

    REFERENCE: AHA I-10 Coding Handbook, p 209

38. A patient is admitted with multiple problems. He has hypertensive kidney disease, CKD stage III, and acute systolic congestive heart failure.
    A. N18.3, I12.9, I50.21
    B. I50.21, I12.9, N18.3
    C. I12.9, N18.3, I50.21
    D. I12.9

    REFERENCE: AHA I-10 Coding Handbook, pp 394, 395, 404, 405

39. A patient is admitted with acute ST Inferolateral wall myocardial infarction. Several days later during the same episode of care, the patient sustained a subsequent non-ST subendocardial myocardial infarction.
   A. I21.09, I22.8   C. I22.2, I21.02
   B. I21.02, I22.8   D. I21.19, I22.2

REFERENCE: AHA I-10 Coding Handbook, pp 389–391

40. A patient with a diagnosis of coronary artery disease with ischemic chest pain. No history of CABG.
   A. I25.119   C. I25.9
   B. I25.119, I20.9   D. I25.10, I20.9

REFERENCE: AHA I-10 Coding Handbook, p 392

41. A patient with atherosclerotic peripheral vascular disease of the left lower leg with intermittent claudication. Past surgical history is negative.
   A. I70.219   C. I70.298
   B. I70.212   D. I70.208

REFERENCE: AHA I-10 Coding Handbook, p 407

Diseases of the Respiratory System

42. A patient presents to the outpatient department for a chest x-ray. The physician's order lists the following reasons for the chest x-ray: fever and cough, rule out pneumonia. The radiologist reports that the chest x-ray is positive for double pneumonia.
   A. J18.9   C. J18.1
   B. J18.8   D. J12.9

REFERENCE: AHA I-10 Coding Handbook, pp 140, 141

43. A patient has aspiration pneumonia with pneumonia due to *Staphylococcus aureus*.
   A. J15.211   C. J69.0, J15
   B. J69.0   D. J69.0, J15.211

REFERENCE: AHA I-10 Coding Handbook, pp 224, 227, 229

44. A patient is admitted with acute respiratory failure with hypercapnia due to acute asthmatic bronchitis with status asthmaticus. Treatment consisted of IV steroids.
   A. J45.902, J96.02   C. J45.901, J96.02
   B. J96.02, J45.902   D. J45.52, J96.02

REFERENCE: AHA I-10 Coding Handbook, pp 231, 233, 235

45. A patient is admitted for treatment of influenza and pneumonia.
   A. J11.1, J18.9   C. J11.08, J11.1
   B. J11.00   D. J11.1

REFERENCE: AHA I-10 Coding Handbook, p 228

46. A patient is admitted with acute exacerbation chronic obstructive pulmonary disease with a history of tobacco dependence.
   A. J44.1, Z87.891   C. J44.0, Z87.891
   B. J44.9, Z72.0   D. J44.1, Z72.0

REFERENCE: AHA I-10 Coding Handbook, p 230

47. A patient is admitted with extrinsic asthma with status asthmaticus with bronchospasm.
    A. J45.901   C. J45.902
    B. J45.32   D. J45.902

REFERENCE: AHA I-10 Coding Handbook, pp 230, 231

48. A patient is admitted for infection of the tracheostomy stoma secondary to cellulitis of the neck.
    A. L03.221, J95.02   C. J95.03, L03.221
    B. J95.02, L03.221   D. J95.09, L03.221

REFERENCE: AHA I-10 Coding Handbook, p 230

Diseases of the Digestive System

49. A patient is admitted to the hospital for repair of a recurrent incarcerated ventral hernia. The surgery is canceled after the chest x-ray revealed lower lobe pneumonia. The patient is placed on antibiotics for treatment of the pneumonia.
    A. K43.0, J18.9, Z53.09   C. K43.6, J18.9
    B. J18.9, K43.0, Z53.09   D. J18.9, J43.6

REFERENCE: AHA I-10 Coding Handbook, p 253

50. A patient is admitted with acute gastric ulcer with hemorrhage and perforation.
    A. K25.0, K25.1   C. K25.4, K25.6
    B. K25.6   D. K25.2

REFERENCE: AHA I-10 Coding Handbook, p 246

51. A patient has diverticulitis of the large bowel with abscess. Patient was treated with IV antibiotics.
    A. K57.92   C. K57.20
    B. K57.12   D. K57.52

REFERENCE: AHA I-10 Coding Handbook, p 247

52. A patient is admitted with acute gangrenous cholecystitis with cholelithiasis.
    A. K80.00   C. K81.0, K80.80
    B. K80.12   D. K80.32

REFERENCE: AHA I-10 Coding Handbook, p 249

53. A patient is admitted with bleeding esophageal varices with alcoholic liver cirrhosis and portal hypertension. The patient is alcohol dependent.
    A. K76.6, I85.11, K70.30   C. K70.30, I85.11, K76.6
    B. I85.11, K76.6, K70.30   D. K70.0. I85.11, K76.6

REFERENCE: AHA I-10 Coding Handbook, p 246

54. A patient is admitted for rectal bleeding. The laboratory results reveal chronic blood-loss anemia. The CT and the Bleeding Scan results of the abdomen revealed that the rectal bleeding is due to Crohn's disease of the descending colon.
    A. K50.118, D50.0   C. K50.011, D50.0
    B. K50.111, D50.0   D. K50.911, D50.0

REFERENCE: AHA I-10 Coding Handbook, p 248

Diseases of the Genitourinary System

55. A patient is admitted with acute urinary tract infection due to *E. coli.*
    A. N39.0, B96.20
    B. N11.9, B96.20
    C. N30.90, B96.20
    D. N10, B96.20

REFERENCE: AHA I-10 Coding Handbook, pp 260, 261

56. A patient admitted with gross hematuria and benign prostatic hypertrophy.
    A. R31.0, N40.0
    B. R31.0, N40.1
    C. N40.0, R31.0
    D. N40.1, R31.0

REFERENCE: AHA I-10 Coding Handbook, pp 262, 270

57. A male patient presents to the ED with acute renal failure. He is also being treated for hypertension.
    A. I12.9, N17.9
    B. N17.9, I15.9
    C. N17.9, I12.9
    D. N17.9, I10

REFERENCE: AHA I-10 Coding Handbook, p 264

58. A patient is admitted with acute hemorrhagic cystitis. The patient was treated with IV antibiotics.
    A. N30.00
    B. N30.91
    C. N30.01
    D. N30.81

REFERENCE: AHA I-10 Coding Handbook, pp 260, 261

59. A patient is admitted with chronic kidney disease stage III due to hypertension and type 1 diabetes mellitus.
    A. E11.22, I12.0, N18.3
    B. E10.22, I12.0, N18.3
    C. I12.0, E11.22, N18.3
    D. E08.22, I12.0, N18.3

REFERENCE: AHA I-10 Coding Handbook, pp 263, 264, 265

60. A patient has end-stage kidney disease, which resulted from malignant hypertension.
    A. I12.0, N18.6
    B. I10, N18.6
    C. I13.11, N18.6
    D. I15.1, N18.6

REFERENCE: AHA I-10 Coding Handbook, pp 263, 264

Complications of Pregnancy, Childbirth, and the Puerperium

61. A woman has a vaginal delivery of a full-term liveborn infant after 38 weeks gestation.
    A. O80, Z37.0, Z3A.38
    B. O80, Z37.0
    C. Z3A.38, O80, Z37.0
    D. Z37.0, Z3A.38, O80

REFERENCE: AHA I-10 Coding Handbook, pp 316, 319

62. A patient is admitted with pregnancy-induced hypertension with severe edema and 24 weeks gestation.
    A. O14.12
    B. I10, Z33.1
    C. O14.12, Z3A24
    D. O14.00, 23A24

REFERENCE: AHA I-10 Coding Handbook, p 325

63.   A patient is admitted with obstructed labor due to breech presentation. A single liveborn infant was delivered via Cesarean section. Do not assign the code for the procedure.
        A. O32.1xx0   C. 032.8xx0, Z37.0
        B. O32.1xx0, Z37.0   D. O32.6xx0, Z37.0

REFERENCE: AHA I-10 Coding Handbook, p 327

64.   A patient is admitted for gestation diabetes insulin controlled 28 weeks gestation.
        A. O24.414   C. O24.419, Z3A28
        B. E11.69, O09.892   D. O24.414, Z3A28

REFERENCE: AHA I-10 Coding Handbook, p 325

65.   A patient is seen in the ED at 22 weeks gestation who is HIV positive.
        A. B20, O98.712, Z3A.22   C. Z21, O98.712
        B. O98.712, Z21, Z3A.22   D. P98.712, B20

REFERENCE: AHA I-10 Coding Handbook, p 326

66.   A patient is admitted who is 39 weeks gestation normal delivery single full-term newborn. During the same episode of care, patient experiences a 36-hour delayed hemorrhage following the delivery.
        A. O80, O72.2, Z37.0   C. Z3A.39, O72.2, Z37.0
        B. O72.2, Z37.0   D. O72.2, Z3A.39, Z37.0

REFERENCE: AHA I-10 Coding Handbook, p 319

Diseases of the Skin and Subcutaneous Tissue

67.   A patient had a cholecystectomy 3 days ago and is now readmitted with cellulitis at the site of the operative incision.
        A. T81.4, K68.11, 95.61   C. K68.11, B95.61
        B. T81.4xxA, L03.311   D. L03.31, T81.4xxA

REFERENCE: AHA I-10 Coding Handbook, p 288

68.   A patient is admitted with a wound open to the left finger with cellulitis due to a dog bite initial encounter. The patient is given IV antibiotics for treatment of the infection.
        A. L03.012   C. S61.201A
        B. L03.011   D. L03.012, S61.201A

REFERENCE: AHA I-10 Coding Handbook, p 288

69.   A patient is admitted with Diabetes Mellitus Type II; diabetic heel ulcer with necrosis of the muscle.
        A. E11.621, L97.403   C. E11.622, L97.403
        B. E10.622, L97.403   D. E10.628, L97.403

REFERENCE: AHA I-10 Coding Handbook, pp 286, 287

70.   A patient is admitted with dermatitis due to prescription topical antibiotic cream used as directed by a physician, initial encounter.
        A. L08.89, T49.0x5   C. L02.91, T49.0x5
        B. L25.1, T49.0x5A   D. T49.0x5, L25.1

REFERENCE: AHA I-10 Coding Handbook, p 284

71. A patient is admitted with a pressure ulcer left buttock stage 2.
    A. L89.322   C. L89.152
    B. L98.411   D. L03.317

REFERENCE: AHA I-10 Coding Handbook, p 287

72. A patient is admitted with a stage 1 pressure ulcer of the sacrum. During the hospitalization, the ulcer progressed to a stage 2
    A. L89.125   C. L89.152
    B. L89.151, L89.152 D. L89.153

REFERENCE: AHA I-10 Coding Handbook, p 287

Diseases of the Musculoskeletal System and Connective Tissue

73. A patient has a pathological fracture of the left femur due to metastatic bone cancer. The past medical history is significant for lung cancer.
    A. C79.51, S72.92xG, Z85.118   C. C79.51, S72.92xS, Z85.118
    B. M84.552, C79.51, Z85.118   D. C79.51, M84.552, Z85.118

REFERENCE: AHA I-10 Coding Handbook, pp 299, 300, 460, 489

74. A patient is admitted with a back pain. A myelogram demonstrated the reason for the back pain is a herniated lumbar intervertebral disc with radiculopathy.
    A. M51.26, M54.16   C. M51.26
    B. M84.552, C79.51, Z85.118 D. M51.16

REFERENCE: AHA I-10 Coding Handbook, p 296

75. A patient is admitted with pyogenic arthritis of the right hip due to Group A *Streptococcus*. Treatment consisted of IV antibiotics.
    A. M16.11, A49.1   C. M00.251
    B. M16.7, A49.1   D. M00.851

REFERENCE: AHA I-10 Coding Handbook, p 298

76. A patient is admitted with a fracture to the L1 vertebrae secondary to postmenopausal senile osteoporosis, initial encounter.
    A. M80.08   C. M80.88xA
    B. M80.88   D. M80.08xA

REFERENCE: AHA I-10 Coding Handbook, p 300

77. A patient developed a malunion of the medical condyle humeral fracture. The original injury occurred 4 months ago.
    A. S42.462K   C. S42.462P
    B. S42.462G   D. S42.462D

REFERENCE: AHA I-10 Coding Handbook, p 484

78. A patient was admitted for removal of internal pins from the left ankle. One month ago the patient sustained a displaced bimalleolar fracture to the left ankle.
    A. S82.842K   C. S82.842S
    B. S82.842D   D. S84.842G

REFERENCE: AHA I-10 Coding Handbook, p 483

Current Procedural Terminology © 2013 American Medical Association. All Rights Reserved.

Congenital Anomalies

79. A Newborn infant is born in the hospital vaginal delivery with a unilateral hard cleft palate and cleft lip.
     A. O37.1, Z38.00   C. Z38.00, O37.1
     B. O37.2, Z38.00   D. Z38.00, O37.2

REFERENCE: AHA I-10 Coding Handbook, p 360

80. A newborn is born in the hospital vaginal delivery. Physical examination demonstrates molding of the baby's scalp, which resolved prior to discharge without treatment.
     A. Z38.00, Q82.9   C. Z38.00, L98.8
     B. Z38.00, Q82.8   D. Z38.00

REFERENCE: AHA I-10 Coding Handbook, p 367

81. A newborn infant is transferred to Community General Hospital for treatment of an esophageal atresia. What codes should be reported for Community General Hospital?
     A. Z38.00, Q39.0   C. Z38.00, Q39.1
     B. Q39.0   D. Q39.1

REFERENCE: AHA I-10 Coding Handbook, p 367

82. A patient is admitted with cervical spina bifida with hydrocephalus.
     A. Q76.0   C. Q05.0
     B. Q05   D. Q05.5

REFERENCE: AHA I-10 Coding Handbook, p 359

83. A newborn infant is born in the hospital, delivered vaginally, and sustained a fracture of the clavicle due to birth trauma.
     A. Z38.00, P13.4   C. P13.4
     B. Z38.00, S42.009A   D. Z38.00, P13.4, S42.009A

REFERENCE: AHA I-10 Coding Handbook

84. A full-term infant born in hospital vaginal delivery was diagnosed with polycystic kidneys.
     A. Z38.00, Q61.11   C. Z38.00, Q61.3
     B. Z38.00, Q61.19   D. Z38.00, Q61.8

REFERENCE: AHA I-10 Coding Handbook, p 361

Certain Conditions Originating in the Perinatal Period

85. A full-term newborn vaginal delivery was born in the hospital to a mother who is addicted to cocaine; however, the infant tested negative.
     A. Z38.00, F14.10   C. Z38.00, F14.20
     B. Z38.00, F14.129   D. Z38.00, Z03.79

REFERENCE: AHA I-10 Coding Handbook, p 373

86. A preterm infant 34 weeks gestation is born via Cesarean section and has severe birth asphyxia.
     A. Z38.01, P84, P07.37   C. Z38.01, P84, R09.02
     B. Z38.01, P84, R09.01   D. Z38.01, P84, R09.2, P07.37

REFERENCE: AHA I-10 Coding Handbook, pp 368, 369

87. A preterm infant born in the hospital vaginal delivery 36 weeks gestation is treated for neonatal jaundice.
   A. Z38.00, P59.9, P07.39
   B. Z38.00, P59.8, P07.39
   C. Z38.00, P59.29, P07.39
   D. Z38.00, P59.3, P07.39

REFERENCE: AHA I-10 Coding Handbook, pp 367, 368

88. A 1-week-old infant is admitted to the hospital with a diagnosis of urinary tract infection contracted prior to birth. The urine culture is positive for *E. coli*.
   A. P39.3
   B. P39.3, N39.0, A49.8
   C. P39.3, N30.90, A49.8
   D. P39.3, A49.8

REFERENCE: AHA I-10 Coding Handbook, p 366

89. An infant has hypoglycemia and a mother with diabetes.
   A. P70.0
   B. P70.2
   C. P70.1
   D. P70.4

REFERENCE: AHA I-10 Coding Handbook, p 373

90. A full-term newborn vaginal delivery born in the hospital. The birth is complicated by cord compression, which affected the newborn.
   A. Z38.00, P02.5
   B. P02.5
   C. Z38.00, P02.4
   D. Z38.00, P02.69

REFERENCE: AHA I-10 Coding Handbook, p 367

Symptoms, Signs, and Ill-Defined Conditions

91. A patient is admitted with right lower quadrant abdominal pain. The discharge diagnosis is listed as abdominal pain due to gastroenteritis or diverticulosis.
   A. K52.9, K57.90
   B. K57.90, K52.9
   C. R10.31, K52.9, K57.90
   D. K52.9, K57.90, R10.31

REFERENCE: AHA I-10 Coding Handbook, p 140

92. A patient was admitted with hemoptysis; a CT of the chest revealed a lung mass.
   A. R91.8
   B. R91.8, R04.2
   C. R04.2
   D. R91.8, F04.1

REFERENCE: AHA I-10 Coding Handbook, pp 140–142

93. A woman has a Pap smear that detected cervical high-risk human papillomavirus (HPV). The DNA test was positive.
   A. R87.810
   B. R87.811
   C. R87.820
   D. R87.811

REFERENCE: AHA I-10 Coding Handbook, pp 140, 141

94. A patient is admitted with malignant ascites with widespread metastatic peritoneal lesions, primary site sigmoid colon; sigmoid colon resection 6 months ago.
   A. R18.8, C78.6, Z85.038
   B. R18.8, C78.6, C18.9
   C. R18.0, C78.6, Z85.038
   D. R18.0, C78.6, C18.9

REFERENCE: AHA I-10 Coding Handbook, pp 460, 461

95. A patient is admitted with fever due to bacteremia.
    A. R78.81   C. R78.81, F50.81
    B. R50.9   D. R78.81, R50.9

REFERENCE: AHA I-10 Coding Handbook, p 150

96. A patient is admitted that has urinary retention secondary to benign prostatic hypertrophy.
    A. N40.0, R33.8   C. N40.1, R33.8
    B. N40.1, R39.11, R33.9   D. N40.3, R33.8

REFERENCE: AHA I-10 Coding Handbook, p 270

Injury and Poisoning

97. A patient is admitted with a nondisplaced fracture of the left medial malleolus, initial encounter. The fracture was treated with a cast.
    A. S82.52xB   C. S82.62xA
    B. S82.52xA   D. S82.63xA

REFERENCE: AHA I-10 Coding Handbook, p 486

98. A patient is admitted with an anaphylactic reaction due to eating strawberries, initial encounter.
    A. T78.04xA   C. T78.2
    B. T78.49   D. T78.04

REFERENCE: AHA I-10 Coding Handbook, p 494

99. A patient is admitted with a gunshot wound to the right upper quadrant of the abdomen, which involves a moderate laceration to the liver, initial encounter.
    A. S36.118A   C. S36.115A
    B. S36.115A, S31.101A   D. S36.115A, S31.600A

REFERENCE: AHA I-10 Coding Handbook, p 494

100. A woman experienced third-degree burns to her thigh and second-degree burns to her right and left foot, initial encounter. She stated that the burns were from hot liquid.
    A. T24.319A, T25.229A   C. T24.319A, T25.222A, T25.221A
    B. T24.31xA, T24.331A, T24.332A   D. T24.719A, T25.222A, T25.221A

REFERENCE: AHA I-10 Coding Handbook, pp 505, 506, 507

101. A patient is seen for a cast removal. Six weeks ago, the patient underwent open reduction internal fixation for a displaced fracture left radial styloid process.
    A. S52.512D   C. S52.515A
    B. Z47.89   D. Z47.2

REFERENCE: AHA I-10 Coding Handbook, p 484

102. A patient is admitted with a left wrist laceration, with embedded glass that involved the radical nerve, initial encounter.
    A. S64.22xA   C. S61.512, S64.22xA
    B. S62.522A   D. S61.522A, S64.22xA

REFERENCE: AHA I-10 Coding Handbook, p 494

103. A patient is admitted with a left nondisplaced comminuted patella fracture, a displaced left spiral fracture of the shaft of the fibula, and a displaced comminuted fracture of the shaft of the left tibia, initial encounter.
    A. S82.045A, S82.442A
    B. S82.045, S82.252A
    C. S82.045A, S82.442A, S82.252A
    D. S82.045A, S82.442A, S82.255A

REFERENCE: AHA I-10 Coding Handbook, p 487

104. A patient is admitted with dizziness as a result of taking phenobarbital as prescribed, initial encounter.
    A. R42, T42.4x1A
    B. R42, T42.3x5A
    C. T42.4x2A, R42
    D. T42.4x1A, R42

REFERENCE: AHA I-10 Coding Handbook, p 518

105. A patient is admitted for control of exacerbation of chronic obstructive lung disease. The patient had stopped taking the prednisone as prescribed due to gaining weight, a known side effect for this drug.
    A. J44.1, T38.0x6A, Z91.14
    B. T38.0x6A, J44.1, Z91.14
    C. J44.0, T38.0x6A, Z91.14
    D. T38.0x6A, Z91.14, J44.0

REFERENCE: AHA I-10 Coding Handbook, pp 516, 518

106. A patient is admitted for intentional overdose of valium and acute respiratory failure with hypoxia.
    A. J96.01, T42.4x2A
    B. J96.01, T42.4x2A, R09.02
    C. T42.4x2A, J96.01
    D. T42.4x2A, J96.00, R09.02

REFERENCE: AHA I-10 Coding Handbook, p 516

Z-Codes

107. A patient is being admitted for chemotherapy for primary lung cancer, left lower lobe.
    A. Z51.11
    B. Z51.11, Z85.118
    C. C34.32, Z51.11
    D. Z51.11, C34.32

REFERENCE: AHA I-10 Coding Handbook, p 127

108. The patient presents for a screening examination for lung cancer.
    A. Z03.89
    B. C78.00
    C. Z12.2
    D. C34.90

REFERENCE: AHA I-10 Coding Handbook, p 132

109. A patient is admitted for observation for a head injury. The patient was struck while playing football. The patient also suffered a minor laceration to the forehead. Head injury was ruled out.
    A. Z71.4
    B. S01.81xA, Z71.4
    C. S01.81xA
    D. Z04.3, S01.81xA

REFERENCE: AHA I-10 Coding Handbook, pp 129–131

ICD-10-PCS Coding

Identify the correct root operation for the following:

110. Excision gallbladder
    A. Resection
    B. Excision
    C. Incision
    D. Removal

    REFERENCE: AHA I-10 Coding Handbook, p 93

111. Excision descending colon
    A. Resection
    B. Excision
    C. Incision
    D. Bypass

    REFERENCE: AHA I-10 Coding Handbook, p 93

112. Removal FB right external auditory cancel
    A. Removal
    B. Extirpation
    C. Inspection
    D. Excision

    REFERENCE: AHA I-10 Coding Handbook, p 95

113. Amputation first left toe
    A. Excision
    B. Amputation
    C. Resection
    D. Detachment

    REFERENCE: AHA I-10 Coding Handbook, p 93

114. Reduction fracture right femoral shaft
    A. Transfer
    B. Reduction
    C. Reposition
    D. Reattachment

    REFERENCE: AHA I-10 Coding Handbook, p 96

115. Colon polyp fulguration
    A. Excision
    B. Destruction
    C. Extraction
    D. Detachment

    REFERENCE: AHA I-10 Coding Handbook, p 93

116. Reattachment fourth finger
    A. Reattachment
    B. Reposition
    C. Transfer
    D. Repair

    REFERENCE: AHA I-10 Coding Handbook, p 96

117. Cystoscopy
    A. Inspection
    B. Endoscopy
    C. Insertion
    D. Drainage

    REFERENCE: AHA I-10 Coding Handbook, p 101

118. Removal deep left vein thrombosis
    A. Excision
    B. Removal
    C. Resection
    D. Extirpation

    REFERENCE: AHA I-10 Coding Handbook, p 95

119. Total left knee replacement
    A. Insertion
    B. Resection
    C. Excision
    D. Replacement

    REFERENCE: AHA I-10 Coding Handbook, p 99

120. Lysis of abdominal adhesions
    A. Excision
    B. Division
    C. Incision
    D. Release

    REFERENCE: AHA I-10 Coding Handbook, p 96

121. Percutaneous angioplasty right coronary artery
    A. Dilation
    B. Restriction
    C. Insertion
    D. Excision

    REFERENCE: AHA I-10 Coding Handbook, p 98

122. Ligation right fallopian tube
    A. Restriction
    B. Occlusion
    C. Dilation
    D. Bypass

    REFERENCE: AHA I-10 Coding Handbook, p 98

123. Removal cardiac pacemaker
    A. Change
    B. Excision
    C. Revision
    D. Removal

    REFERENCE: AHA I-10 Coding Handbook, p 99

124. Creation of arteriovenous graft brachial artery left arm for hemodialysis
    A. Bypass
    B. Creation
    C. Alteration
    D. Insertion

    REFERENCE: AHA I-10 Coding Handbook, p 98

125. Lithotripsy left ureter with removal of fragment
    A. Drainage
    B. Fragmentation
    C. Removal
    D. Extirpation

    REFERENCE: AHA I-10 Coding Handbook, p 95

126. Endometrial ablation of cervical polyps
    A. Destruction
    B. Excision
    C. Removal
    D. Extraction

    REFERENCE: AHA I-10 Coding Handbook, p 93

127. Angioplasty abdominal iliac artery
    A. Dilation
    B. Repair
    C. Angioplasty
    D. Insertion

    REFERENCE: AHA I-10 Coding Handbook, p 98

128. Radiofrequency ablation right kidney
    A. Excision
    B. Removal
    C. Destruction
    D. Ablation

    REFERENCE: AHA I-10 Coding Handbook, p 93

129. Cryoablation external genital warts
    A. Destruction
    B. Cryoablation
    C. Excision
    D. Resection

    REFERENCE: AHA I-10 Coding Handbook, p 93

130. Gastric lap band for treatment of morbid obesity
    A. Dilation
    B. Occlusion
    C. Restriction
    D. Bypass

    REFERENCE: AHA I-10 Coding Handbook, p 98

131. Excisional debridement of a chronic skin ulcer
    A. Debridement
    B. Excision
    C. Incision
    D. Resection

    REFERENCE: AHA I-10 Coding Handbook, p 93

132. Application of skin graft to the nose status post excision malignant neoplasm
    A. Transfer
    B. Creation
    C. Replacement
    D. Alteration

    REFERENCE: AHA I-10 Coding Handbook, p 99

133. Spinal fusion cervical C1-C2
    A. Arthrodesis
    B. Repair
    C. Creation
    D. Fusion

    REFERENCE: AHA I-10 Coding Handbook, p 103

134. Tracheostomy
    A. Bypass
    B. Creation
    C. Reposition
    D. Insertion

    REFERENCE: AHA I-10 Coding Handbook, p 98

135. Percutaneous needle biopsy left lung
    A. Incision
    B. Excision
    C. Drainage
    D. Resection

    REFERENCE: AHA I-10 Coding Handbook, pp 92–93

136. Extraction left intraocular lens, open
    A. Extirpation
    B. Fragmentation
    C. Extraction
    D. Excision

    REFERENCE: AHA I-10 Coding Handbook, p 93

137. Uterine dilation and curettage
    A. Extraction
    B. Dilation
    C. Excision
    D. Destruction

    REFERENCE: AHA I-10 Coding Handbook, p 94

138. Excision right popliteal artery with graft replacement, open
    A. Excision
    B. Resection
    C. Replacement
    D. Repair

    REFERENCE: AHA I-10 Coding Handbook, p 99

139. Mitral valve annuloplasty using ring, open
    A. Supplement
    B. Replacement
    C. Resection
    D. Repair

    REFERENCE: AHA I-10 Coding Handbook, p 99

140. Left common carotid endarterectomy, open
    A. Excision
    B. Resection
    C. Extirpation
    D. Release

    REFERENCE: AHA I-10 Coding Handbook, p 95

141. Excision malignant lesion skin of left ear
    A. 0HB3XZZ
    B. 0HC3XZZ
    C. 0H53XZZ
    D. 0HD3XZZ

    REFERENCE: AHA I-10 Coding Handbook, pp 92, 93, 289

142. Left below the knee amputation, proximal tibia/fibula
    A. 0YBJ0ZZ
    B. 0Y6H0ZZ
    C. 0Y6J0Z1
    D. 0Y6J0Z3

    REFERENCE: AHA I-10 Coding Handbook, pp 86, 495, 496

143. Thoracoscopic pleurodesis right side
    A. 0BBN4ZZ
    B. 0BPQ40Z
    C. 0B5N4ZZ
    D. 0BCN4ZZ

    REFERENCE: AHA I-10 Coding Handbook, pp 94, 236

144. Extraction left intraocular lens without replacement, percutaneous
    A. 08DK3ZZ
    B. 08PK3JZ
    C. 08QK3ZZ
    D. 08BK3ZZ

    REFERENCE: AHA I-10 Coding Handbook, p 94

145. Routine insertion of indwelling Foley catheter
    A. 0T9B7ZZ
    B. 0T9B70Z
    C. 0T9C80Z
    D. 0T9C8ZZ

    REFERENCE: AHA I-10 Coding Handbook, p 99

146. EGD with removal FB from duodenum
    A. 0DC98ZZ
    B. 0DF98ZZ
    C. 0D898ZZ
    D. 0D798ZZ

    REFERENCE: AHA I-10 Coding Handbook, p 95

147. Facelift, open
    A. 0WQ20ZZ
    B. 0WU20KZ
    C. 0WB20ZZ
    D. 0W020ZZ

    REFERENCE: AHA I-10 Coding Handbook, p 102

148. Normal delivery with episiotomy
    A. 0W8NXZZ
    B. 0WQNXZZ
    C. 0WBNXZZ
    D. 0WMN0ZZ

    REFERENCE: AHA I-10 Coding Handbook, p 336

149. Percutaneous endoscopic clipping cerebral aneurysm
    A. 03VG4CZ
    B. 03LG0DZ
    C. 03BG0ZZ
    D. 03CG0ZZ

    REFERENCE: AHA I-10 Coding Handbook, pp 98, 436

150. Left knee arthroscopy with reposition of the anterior horn medial meniscus
    A. 0MQP4ZZ
    B. 0MQP3ZZ
    C. 0MSP0ZZ
    D. 0MSP4ZZ

    REFERENCE: AHA I-10 Coding Handbook, pp 96, 97

151. Heart transplant using porcine heart, open
    A. 02YA0Z2
    B. 02QA0ZZ
    C. 02YA0Z0
    D. 02Y0Z1

    REFERENCE: AHA I-10 Coding Handbook, p 435

152. ESWL left ureter
    A. 0TF7XZZ
    B. 0TP930Z
    C. 0TB63ZZ
    D. 0TC63ZZ

    REFERENCE: AHA I-10 Coding Handbook, p 269

153. Reattachment severed left ear
    A. 09WJXZZ
    B. 09Q1XZZ
    C. 09M1XZZ
    D. 09S1XZZ

    REFERENCE: AHA I-10 Coding Handbook, pp 96, 97

154. Transuretheral cystoscopy with removal of right ureteral calculus
    A. 0TB68ZZ
    B. 0TJ98ZZ
    C. 0T68ZZ
    D. 0TC68ZZ

    REFERENCE: AHA I-10 Coding Handbook, p 269

155. Open reduction fracture left tibia
    A. 0QSH0ZZ
    B. 0QSH04Z
    C. 0QWH04Z
    D. 0QQH0ZZ

    REFERENCE: AHA I-10 Coding Handbook, pp 96, 97, 489, 490

156. Percutaneous insertion Greenfield IVC filer
    A. 06H03DZ
    B. 06L03DZ
    C. 06Q03ZZ
    D. 06V03DZ

    REFERENCE: AHA I-10 Coding Handbook, p 99

157. Incision and drainage external perianal abscess
    A. 0D9Q30Z
    B. 0D9RX0Z
    C. 0D9QXZZ
    D. 0D9QX0Z

    REFERENCE: AHA I-10 Coding Handbook, p 95

158. Removal FB left cornea
    A. 08B8XZZ
    B. 0858XZZ
    C. 08D8XZZ
    D. 08C9XZZ

    REFERENCE: AHA I-10 Coding Handbook, p 95

159. Percutaneous transposition left radial nerve
    A. 01X40ZZ
    B. 01S63ZZ
    C. 01Q63ZZ
    D. 01860ZZ

    REFERENCE: AHA I-10 Coding Handbook, pp 96, 97

160. Right TRAM pedicle flap reconstruction status post mastectomy, muscle only open
    A. 0KXK0Z
    B. 0KXF0ZZ
    C. 0KXK0Z6
    D. 0KXK0ZZ

    REFERENCE: AHA I-10 Coding Handbook, pp 276, 277

161. Laparotomy with exploration and adhesiolysis of the left ureter
    A. 0TN74ZZ
    B. 0TN70ZZ
    C. 0TN70ZZ
    D. 0T8N0ZZ

    REFERENCE: AHA I-10 Coding Handbook, p 96

162. Thoracentesis right pleural effusion
    A. 0W930ZZ
    B. 0W9C3ZZ
    C. 0W993ZZ
    D. 0W9C30Z

    REFERENCE: AHA I-10 Coding Handbook, p 236

163. Percutaneous radiofrequency ablation of the left vocal cord
    A. 0CBV3ZZ
    B. 0CPS30Z
    C. 0C5V3ZZ
    D. 0CYV0ZZ

    REFERENCE: AHA I-10 Coding Handbook, p 94

164. Excision malignant lesion upper lip
    A. 0CC00ZZ
    B. 0CQ00ZZ
    C. 0CT00ZZ
    D. 0CB0XZZ

    REFERENCE: AHA I-10 Coding Handbook, p 289

165. Laparoscopic appendectomy
     A. 0DBJ4ZZ
     B. 0DTJ4ZZ
     C. 0DNJ4ZZ
     D. 0DT8ZZ

     REFERENCE: AHA I-10 Coding Handbook, p 93

166. Nonexcisional debridement left heel ulcer
     A. 0HDNXZZ
     B. 0HBNXZZ
     C. 0HQNXZZ
     D. 0H5LXZZ

     REFERENCE: AHA I-10 Coding Handbook, p 94

167. Transurethral cystoscopy with fragmentation of bladder neck stones
     A. 0TBC8ZZ
     B. 0TFC8ZZ
     C. 0TFC8ZZ
     D. 0TPB8ZZ

     REFERENCE: AHA I-10 Coding Handbook, pp 95, 268

168. Laparoscopy with bilateral occlusion fallopian tubes using external clips
     A. 0UH843Z
     B. 0U774DZ
     C. 0UL74CZ
     D. 0UW84DZ

     REFERENCE: AHA I-10 Coding Handbook, pp 98, 436

169. Incision scar contracture right knee
     A. 0H8KXZZ
     B. 0HBKXZZ
     C. 0HNKXZZ
     D. 0HQKXZZ

     REFERENCE: AHA I-10 Coding Handbook, p 96

170. Colonoscopy with sigmoid colon polypectomy
     A. 0DFN8ZZ
     B. 0DBN8ZZ
     C. 0DCM8ZZ
     D. 0D5N8ZZ

     REFERENCE: AHA I-10 Coding Handbook, pp 92, 93

171. A percutaneous fascia transfer to cover defect of the anterior neck
     A. 0JX53ZZ
     B. 0JX43ZZ
     C. 0JR43ZZ
     D. 0JQ43ZZ

     REFERENCE: AHA I-10 Coding Handbook, pp 96, 97

172. Percutaneous embolization left uterine artery using coils
    A. 04VF3DZ
    B. 04QF3ZZ
    C. 04LF3DU
    D. 04LF3CZ

    REFERENCE: AHA I-10 Coding Handbook, pp 98, 436

173. Endoscopic retrograde cholangiopancreatography with lithotripsy of the pancreas
    A. 0FCD8ZZ
    B. 0FJD8ZZ
    C. 0FFD8ZZ
    D. 0FJD8ZZ

    REFERENCE: AHA I-10 Coding Handbook, pp 250, 251

174. Open left neck total lymphadenectomy
    A. 07T20ZZ
    B. 07B20ZZ
    C. 07520ZZ
    D. 07C20ZZ

    REFERENCE: AHA I-10 Coding Handbook, p 93

175. Percutaneous chest tube placement left pneumothorax
    A. 0W9B30Z
    B. 0W9D30Z
    C. 0W9B3ZZ
    D. 0W9D3ZZ

    REFERENCE: AHA I-10 Coding Handbook, p 95

176. Laparoscopy with excision old sutures from the peritoneum
    A. 0DBW4ZZ
    B. 0DNW4ZZ
    C. 0DCW4ZZ
    D. 0DPW4ZZ

    REFERENCE: AHA I-10 Coding Handbook, p 95

177. Closed reduction with percutaneous internal fixation left femoral neck fracture
    A. 0QSC34Z
    B. 0QS734Z
    C. 0QS934Z
    D. 0QS7X4Z

    REFERENCE: AHA I-10 Coding Handbook, pp 96, 97

178. Laparotomy and drain placement left lobe liver abscess
    A. 0F900ZZ
    B. 0F900ZZ
    C. 0F9030Z
    D. 0F9200Z

    REFERENCE: AHA I-10 Coding Handbook, p 95

179. Hysteroscopy with D&C, diagnostic
    A. 0UDB82X
    B. 0UDN82X
    C. 0U898ZZ
    D. 0U798ZZ

    REFERENCE: AHA I-10 Coding Handbook, p 94

180. Laparoscopy with destruction of endometriosis left ovary
    A. 0UB14ZZ
    B. 0UT14ZZ
    C. 0UP340Z
    D. 0U514ZZ

    REFERENCE: AHA I-10 Coding Handbook, p 94

181. DIP joint amputation left thumb
    A. 0X6M0Z3
    B. 0XGM022
    C. 0XGM021
    D. 0XGM020

    REFERENCE: AHA I-10 Coding Handbook, pp 86, 495

182. Removal right index fingernail
    A. 0HDQXZZ
    B. 0HPRXZZ
    C. 0HNQXZZ
    D. 0HTQXZZ

    REFERENCE: AHA I-10 Coding Handbook, p 94

183. Percutaneous drainage abdominal ascites
    A. 0W9G3ZZ
    B. 0W9G3ZZ
    C. 0W930Z
    D. 0W9H3ZZ

    REFERENCE: AHA I-10 Coding Handbook, p 95

184. Transurethral endoscopic ablation right hepatic duct
    A. 0F558ZZ
    B. 0FB58ZZ
    C. 0FT04ZZ
    D. 0FP040Z

    REFERENCE: AHA I-10 Coding Handbook, p 94

185. ERCP with balloon dilation cystic duct
    A. 0F784DZ
    B. 0F788ZZ
    C. 0F783DZ
    D. 0FT83ZZ

    REFERENCE: AHA I-10 Coding Handbook, p 98

186. Control of postoperative tonsillectomy is coded to which root operation?
   A. Revision
   B. Repair
   C. Control
   D. Change

   REFERENCE: AHA I-10 Coding Handbook, p 102

187. In the Medical Surgical Section, the third character position represents?
   A. Body System
   B. Approach
   C. Root Operation
   D. Qualifier

   REFERENCE: AHA I-10 Coding Handbook, p 72

188. In the Medical Surgical Section, the second character position represents?
   A. Body System
   B. Body Part
   C. Qualifier
   D. Approach

   REFERENCE: AHA I-10 Coding Handbook, p 70

189. In the Medical Surgical Section, the seventh character position represents?
   A. Qualifier
   B. Device
   C. Body System
   D. Approach

   REFERENCE: AHA I-10 Coding Handbook, p 80

190 In the Medical Surgical Section, the fourth character position represents?
   A. Section
   B. Body Part
   C. Body System
   D. Approach

   REFERENCE: AHA I-10 Coding Handbook, p 73

191. A complete redo of a knee replacement requiring a new prosthesis is coded to which root operation?
   A. Revision
   B. Replacement
   C. Change
   D. Insertion

   REFERENCE: AHA I-10 Coding Handbook, pp 99–100, 301

192. Reposition of a malfunctioning pacemaker lead is coded to which root operation?
   A. Change
   B. Revision
   C. Replacement
   D. Reposition

   REFERENCE: AHA I-10 Coding Handbook, pp 99–100, 416

193. Dilation of the ureter with insertion of a stent is coded to which root operation?
   A. Insertion
   B. Dilation
   C. Supplemental
   D. Inspection

   REFERENCE: AHA I-10 Coding Handbook, p 98

194. ERCP with biopsy of the common bile duct. Identify the approach.
   A. External
   B. Percutaneous Endoscopic Open
   C. Percutaneous
   D. Open

   REFERENCE: AHA I-10 Coding Handbook, p 75

195. Percutaneous insertion nephrostomy tube. Identify the approach.
    A. External
    B. Open
    C. Percutaneous
    D. Percutaneous Endoscopic

    REFERENCE: AHA I-10 Coding Handbook, p 75

196. Fulguration of anal warts. Identify the approach.
    A. Percutaneous
    B. External Endoscopic
    C. Percutaneous
    D. Open

    REFERENCE: AHA I-10 Coding Handbook, p 75

197. Percutaneous placement of pacemaker lead. Identify the approach.
    A. External
    B. Via natural or Artificial opening
    C. Percutaneous Endoscopic
    D. Percutaneous

    REFERENCE: AHA I-10 Coding Handbook, p 75

198. ESWL left ureter. Identify the approach.
    A. Percutaneous
    B. Via natural or Artificial opening
    C. External
    D. Open

    REFERENCE: AHA I-10 Coding Handbook, p 75

199. Laparoscopy with destruction of endometriosis. Identify the approach.
    A. Percutaneous
    B. Via natural/artificial opening
    C. Percutaneous Endoscopic
    D. External

    REFERENCE: AHA I-10 Coding Handbook, p 75

200. Colonoscopy. Identify the approach.
    A. Percutaneous
    B. Via natural or Artificial opening
    C. Percutaneous Endoscopic
    D. External

    REFERENCE: AHA I-10 Coding Handbook, p 75

Use this information to answer questions, pp 201–203.

Present on admission (POA) guidelines were established to identify and report diagnoses that are present at the time of a patient's admission. The reporting options for each ICD-9-CM code are

A. Y = Yes
B. N = No
C. U = Unknown
D. W = clinically undetermined
E. Unreported/Not Used (Exempt from POA) reporting

201. The physician explicitly documents that a condition is not present at the time of admission.
A. Y = Yes
B. N = No
C. U = Unknown
D. W = clinically undetermined
E. Unreported/Not Used (Exempt from POA) reporting

REFERENCE: AHA I-10 Coding Handbook, pp 571–574

202. The physician documents that the patient has diabetes that was diagnosed prior to admission.
A. Y = Yes
B. N = No
C. U = Unknown
D. W = clinically undetermined
E. Unreported/Not Used (Exempt from POA) reporting

REFERENCE: AHA I-10 Coding Handbook, pp 571–574

203. The medical record documentation is unclear as to whether the condition was present on admission.
A. Y = Yes
B. N = No
C. U = Unknown
D. W = clinically undetermined
E. Unreported/Not Used (Exempt from POA) reporting

REFERENCE: AHA I-10 Coding Handbook, pp 571–574

Answer Key for ICD-10-CM Coding

1.	D	52.	A	103.	C	155.	A
2.	B	53.	C	104.	B	156.	A
3.	A	54.	B	105.	A	157.	C
4.	C	55.	A	106.	C	158.	D
5.	D	56.	C	107.	D	159.	B
6.	C	57.	D	108.	C	160.	A
7.	D	58.	A	109.	D	161.	B
8.	C	59.	C	110.	A	162.	C
9.	A	60.	A	111.	A	163.	C
10.	B	61.	A	112.	B	164.	D
11.	C	62.	C	113.	D	165	B
12.	B	63.	B	114.	C	166.	A
13.	A	64.	D	115.	B	167.	C
14.	D	65.	B	116.	A	168.	C
15.	B	66.	D	117.	A	169.	C
16.	A	67.	B	118.	D	170.	B
17.	C	68.	D	119.	D	171.	B
18.	B	69.	A	120.	D	172.	C
19.	D	70.	B	121.	A	173.	C
20.	B	71.	A	122.	B	174.	A
21.	A	72.	C	123.	D	175.	A
22.	D	73.	B	125.	D	176.	C
23.	B	74.	D	126.	A	177.	A
24.	D	75.	C	127.	A	178.	D
25.	D	76.	D	128.	C	179.	A
26.	B	77.	C	129.	A	180.	D
27.	A	78.	B	130.	C	181.	A
28.	C	79.	C	131.	B	182.	A
29.	B	80.	D	132.	C	183.	A
30.	D	81.	B	133.	D	184.	A
31.	C	82.	C	134.	A	185.	B
32.	B	83.	A	135.	B	186.	C
33.	A	84.	B	136.	C	187.	C
34.	C	85.	D	137.	A	188.	A
35.	B	86.	A	138.	C	189.	A
36.	D	87.	A	139.	A	190.	B
37.	D	88.	D	140.	C	191.	A
38.	C	89.	C	141.	A	192.	B
39.	D	90.	A	142.	C	193.	B
40.	A	91.	C	143.	A	194.	B
41.	B	92.	B	144.	A	195.	C
42.	A	93.	A	145.	B	196.	B
43.	D	94.	C	146.	A	197.	D
44.	A	95.	D	147.	D	198.	C
45.	B	96.	C	148.	A	199.	C
46.	A	97.	B	149.	A	200.	B
47.	C	98.	A	150.	D	201.	B
48.	B	99.	D	151.	A	202.	A
49.	A	100.	C	152.	A	203.	C
50.	D	101.	A	153.	C		
51.	C	102.	D	154.	D		

REFERENCES

AHA ICD-10-CM and ICD-10-PCS Coding Handbook 2014

ICD-10-CM/PCS Chapter Competencies

Question	RHIA Domain	RHIT Domain
1–203	1	2

VII. CPT Coding

Lisa M. Delhomme, MHA, RHIA

Evaluation and Management

1. Patient is admitted to the hospital with acute abdominal pain. The attending medical physician requests a surgical consult. The consultant agrees to see the patient and conducts a comprehensive history and physical examination. The physician ordered lab work to rule out pancreatitis, along with an ultrasound of the gallbladder and abdominal x-ray. Due to the various diagnosis possibilities and the tests reviewed, a moderate medical decision was made.
    A. 99244
    B. 99222
    C. 99254
    D. 99204

    REFERENCE: AMA (7th ed.), pp 49, 54–55
    Green, pp 435–438
    Johnson and Linker, pp 153–154
    Smith, pp 213, 215–216

2. An established patient returns to the physician's office for follow-up on his hypertension and diabetes. The physician takes the blood pressure and references the patient's last three glucose tests. The patient is still running above normal glucose levels, so the physician decides to adjust the patient's insulin. An expanded history was taken and a physical examination was performed.
    A. 99213
    B. 99232
    C. 99202
    D. 99214

    REFERENCE: AMA (7th ed.), p 48
    Green, pp 428–429
    Johnson and Linker, p 149
    Smith, p 214

3. Patient arrives in the emergency room via a medical helicopter. The patient has sustained multiple life-threatening injuries due to a multiple car accident. The patient goes into cardiac arrest 10 minutes after arrival. An hour and 30 minutes of critical care time is spent trying to stabilize the patient.
    A. 99285; 99288; 99291
    B. 99291; 99292
    C. 99291; 99292; 99285
    D. 99282

    REFERENCE: AMA (7th ed.), pp 57–58
    Green, pp 439–441
    Johnson and Linker, pp 155–157
    Smith, pp 216–217

4. The physician provided services to a new patient who was in a rest home for an ulcerative sore on the hip. A problem-focused history and physical examination were performed and a straightforward medical decision was made.
    A. 99304
    B. 99325
    C. 99324
    D. 99334

    REFERENCE: AMA (7th ed.), p 55
    Green, pp 443–444
    Johnson and Linker, pp 158–159
    Smith, p 218

5. A doctor provides critical care services in the emergency department for a patient in respiratory failure. He initiates ventilator management and spends an hour and 10 minutes providing critical care for this patient.
   A. 99281, 99291, 99292, 94002
   B. 99291, 99292, 94002
   C. 99291, 94002
   D. 99291

REFERENCE: AMA (7th ed.), pp 57–58
            Green, pp 439–441
            Johnson and Linker, pp 155–157
            Smith, pp 216–217

6. Services were provided to a patient in the emergency room after the patient twisted her ankle stepping down from a curb. The emergency room physician ordered x-rays of the ankle, which came back negative for a fracture. A problem-focused history and physical examination were performed and ankle strapping was applied. A prescription for pain was given to the patient. Code the emergency room visit only.
   A. 99201   C. 99281
   B. 99282   D. 99211

REFERENCE: AMA (7th ed.), pp 47–48
            Green, pp 438–439
            Johnson and Linker, pp 155–157
            Smith, p 216

7. An established patient was seen in her primary physician's office. The patient fell at home and came to the physician's office for an examination. Due to a possible concussion, the patient was sent to the hospital to be admitted as an observation patient. A detailed history and physical examination were performed and the medical decision was low complexity. The patient stayed overnight and was discharged the next afternoon.
   A. 99214; 99234   C. 99218
   B. 99214; 99218; 99217   D. 99218; 99217

REFERENCE: AMA, 2014
            AMA (7th ed.), pp 48–49
            Green, pp 431–435
            Johnson and Linker, p 155
            Smith, pp 214–215

8. An out-of-town patient presents to a walk-in clinic to have a prescription refilled for a nonsteroidal anti-inflammatory drug. The physician performs a problem-focused history and physical examination with a straightforward decision.
    A. 99211
    B. 99201
    C. 99212
    D. 99202

REFERENCE: AMA (7th ed.), pp 39, 48
              Frisch, pp 49–51
              Green, pp 411–412
              Johnson and Linker, p 149
              Smith, pp 195–196

9. An office consultation is performed for a postmenopausal woman who is complaining of spotting in the past 6 months with right lower quadrant tenderness. A detailed history and physical examination were performed with a low-complexity medical decision.
    A. 99242
    B. 99243
    C. 99253
    D. 99254

REFERENCE: AMA (7th ed.), pp 39–40
              Green, pp 435–438
              Johnson and Linker, pp 153–154
              Smith, pp 215–216

Anesthesia

10. Code anesthesia for upper abdominal ventral hernia repair.
    A. 00832
    B. 00750
    C. 00752
    D. 00830

REFERENCE: AMA (7th ed.), pp 82–83
              Green, pp 483–485
              Johnson and Linker, p 175
              Smith, pp 249–252

11. Code anesthesia for total hip replacement.
    A. 01210
    B. 01402
    C. 01230
    D. 01214

REFERENCE: AMA (7th ed.), pp 82–83
              Green, p 487
              Smith, pp 249–252

12. Code anesthesia for vaginal hysterectomy.
    A. 00846
    B. 00944
    C. 00840
    D. 01963

REFERENCE: AMA (7th ed.), pp 82–83
              Green, pp 484–485
              Smith, pp 249–252

13. Code anesthesia for placement of vascular shunt in forearm.
    A. 01844
    B. 01850
    C. 00532
    D. 01840

REFERENCE: AMA (7th ed.), pp 82–83
              Green, p 487
              Smith, pp 249–252

14. Code anesthesia for decortication of left lung.
    A. 01638
    B. 00542
    C. 00546
    D. 00500

REFERENCE: AMA (7th ed.), pp 82–83
              Green, p 483
              Smith, pp 249–252

15. Code anesthesia for total shoulder replacement.
    A. 01760
    B. 01630
    C. 01402
    D. 01638

REFERENCE: AMA (7th ed.), pp 82–83
              Green, p 487
              Smith, pp 249–252

16. Code anesthesia for cesarean section.
    A. 00840
    B. 01961
    C. 00940
    D. 01960

REFERENCE: AMA (7th ed.), pp 82–83
              Green, p 489
              Smith, pp 249–252

17. Code anesthesia for procedures on bony pelvis.
    A. 00400
    B. 01170
    C. 01120
    D. 01190

REFERENCE: AMA (7th ed.), pp 82–83
              Green, p 487
              Smith, pp 249–252

18. Code anesthesia for corneal transplant.
    A. 00144
    B. 00140
    C. 00147
    D. 00190

REFERENCE: AMA (7th ed.), pp 82–83
              Green, p 481
              Smith, pp 249–252

Surgery—Integumentary System

19. Patient presents to the hospital for skin grafts due to previous third-degree burns. The burn eschar of the back was removed. Once the eschar was removed, the defect size measured 10 cm x 10 cm. A skin graft from a donor bank was placed onto the defect and sewn into place as a temporary wound closure.
    A. 15002, 15130
    B. 15002, 15271, 15272, 15272, 15272
    C. 15002, 15200
    D. 15002, 15273

REFERENCE: AMA, 2014

20. Patient presents to the operating room for excision of a 4.5 cm malignant melanoma of the left forearm. A 6 cm x 6 cm rotation flap was created for closure.
    A. 14021
    B. 11606; 14020
    C. 14301
    D. 11606; 15100

REFERENCE: AMA, 2014
            AMA (7th ed.), pp 103–104, 107
            Green, pp 517–521
            Smith, pp 72–73
            Smith (2), pp 26–27

21. Female patient has a percutaneous needle biopsy of the left breast lesion in the lower outer quadrant. Following the biopsy frozen section results, the physician followed this with an excisional removal of the same lesion.
    A. 19100; 19125
    B. 19100; 19120-LT
    C. 19120-LT
    D. 19100; 19120; 19120

REFERENCE: AMA (7th ed.), p 115
            Green, pp 535–536
            Smith, p 79
            Smith (2), p 30

22. Patient presents to the emergency room with lacerations of right lower leg that involved the fascia. Lacerations measured 5 cm and 2.7 cm.
    A. 11406; 11403
    B. 12034
    C. 12032; 12031
    D. 12032

REFERENCE: AMA (7th ed.), p 107
            Smith, pp 66–68
            Smith (2), p 21

23. Ten-square-centimeters epidermal autograft to the face from the back.
    A. 15110
    B. 15115
    C. 15110, 15115
    D. 15120

REFERENCE: AMA, 2014
            AMA (7th ed.), pp 109–110
            Smith (2), p 27

24. Nonhuman graft for temporary wound closure. Patient has a 5 cm defect on the scalp.
   - A. 15275, 15276
   - B. 15271
   - C. 15275
   - D. 15271, 15272

REFERENCE: AMA, 2014

25. Patient is admitted for a blepharoplasty of the left lower eyelid and a repair for a tarsal strip of the left upper lid.
   - A. 67917-E1; 15822-E2
   - B. 67917-E1; 15820-E2
   - C. 67917-E1
   - D. 67917-E1; 15823-E2

REFERENCE: AMA (7th ed.), pp 252–253
              CPT Assistant, January 2005, p 46
              Smith (2), p 165

26. Patient presents to the emergency room with lacerations sustained in an automobile accident. Repairs of the 3.3 cm skin laceration of the left leg that involved the fascia, 2.5 cm and 3 cm lacerations of the left arm involving the fascia, and 2.7 cm of the left foot, which required simple sutures, were performed. Sterile dressings were applied.
   - A. 12032; 12032-59; 12031-59; 12002-59
   - B. 12002, 12002-59
   - C. 12034, 12002-59
   - D. 13151; 12032-59, 12032-59, 12001-59

REFERENCE: AMA (7th ed.), pp 106–108
              Green, pp 524–526
              Smith, pp 66–68
              Smith (2), p 24

27. Patient presents to the operating room for excision of three lesions. The 1.5 cm and 2 cm lesions of the back were excised with one excision. The 0.5 cm lesion of the hand was excised. The pathology report identified both back lesions as squamous cell carcinoma. The hand lesion was identified as seborrheic keratosis.
   - A. 11604; 11420
   - B. 11402; 11420; 11403
   - C. 11403; 11642; 11642
   - D. 11602; 11402

REFERENCE: AMA (7th ed.), pp 101–104
              CPT Assistant, November 2002, pp 5–6, 8
              Green, pp 517–521
              Smith, pp 61–62
              Smith (2), pp 21–22

28. Patient presents to the radiology department where a fine-needle aspiration of the breast is performed utilizing computed tomography.
   - A. 19085; 77012
   - B. 19100
   - C. 19125
   - D. 10022, 77012

REFERENCE: AMA (7th ed.), pp 270, 330–331
              CPT Assistant, November 2002, pp 2–3
              Green, p 535
              Smith (2), p 29

29. Patient presents to the operating room where a 3.2 cm malignant lesion of the shoulder was excised and repaired with simple sutures. A 2 cm benign lesion of the cheek was excised and was repaired with a rotation skin graft.

 A. 11604, 11442; 14040; 12001
 B. 14040, 11604
 C. 15002, 15120
 D. 17264, 17000; 12001

REFERENCE: AMA (7th ed.), pp 101–107
CPT Assistant, July 1999, pp 3–4
CPT Assistant, August 2002, p 5
CPT Assistant, November 2002, pp 5–8
Green, pp 517–520, 526–527
Smith, pp 61–62, 73–75
Smith (2), pp 26–27

30. Patient was admitted to the hospital for removal of excessive tissue due to massive weight loss. Liposuction of the abdomen and bilateral thighs was performed.

 A. 15830
 B. 15830; 15833; 15833
 C. 15877; 15879-50
 D. 15839

REFERENCE: AMA, 2014

Surgery—Musculoskeletal

31. Patient presents to the hospital with ulcer of the right foot. Patient is taken to the operating room where a revision of the right metatarsal head is performed.

 A. 28104-RT
 B. 28111-RT
 C. 28288-RT
 D. 28899-RT

REFERENCE: AMA, 2014

32. Patient presents to the emergency room following a fall. X-rays were ordered for the lower leg and results showed a fracture of the proximal left tibia. The emergency room physician performed a closed manipulation of the fracture with skeletal traction.

 A. 27532-LT
 B. 27536-LT
 C. 27530-LT
 D. 27524-LT

REFERENCE: Green, pp 565–568
Smith, pp 84–85
Smith (2), pp 42–44

33. Trauma patient was rushed to the operating room with multiple injuries. Open reduction with internal fixation of intertrochanteric femoral fracture; open reduction of the tibial and fibula shaft with internal fixation was performed.

 A. 27245; 27759
 B. 20690
 C. 27248; 27756
 D. 27244; 27758

REFERENCE: Green, pp 565–568
Smith, pp 84–85
Smith (2), pp 42–44

34. Open I&D of a deep abscess of the cervical spine.

 A. 22010
 B. 22015
 C. 10060
 D. 10140

REFERENCE: AMA, 2014

35. Patient presents to the emergency room following an assault. Examination of the patient reveals blunt trauma to the face. Radiology reports that the patient suffers from a fracture to the frontal skull and a blow-out fracture of the orbital floor. Patient is admitted and taken to the operating room where a periorbital approach to the orbital fracture is employed and an implant is inserted.
   A. 21407; 21275
   B. 21387; 61330
   C. 21390
   D. 61340; 21401

REFERENCE: Smith, pp 84–85
              Smith (2), pp 42–44

36. Patient presents with a traumatic partial amputation of the second, third, and fourth fingers on the right hand. Patient was taken to the operating room where completion of the amputation of three fingers was performed with direct closure.
   A. 26910-F6; 26910-F7; 26910-F8
   B. 26843-RT
   C. 26951-F6; 26951-F7; 26951-F8
   D. 26550-RT

REFERENCE: AMA, 2014

37. Patient is brought to the emergency room following a shark attack. The paramedics have the patient's amputated foot. The patient is taken directly to the operating room to reattach the patient's foot.
   A. 28800
   B. 28200; 28208
   C. 28110
   D. 20838

REFERENCE: AMA, 2014

38. Patient presents to the hospital with a right index trigger finger. Release of the trigger finger was performed.
   A. 26060-F7
   B. 26055-F6
   C. 26170-F6
   D. 26110

REFERENCE: AMA, 2014

39. Patient had been diagnosed with a bunion. Patient was taken to the operating room where a simple resection of the base of the proximal phalanx along with the medial eminence was performed. Kirschner wire was placed to hold the joint in place.
   A. 28292
   B. 28290
   C. 28293
   D. 28294

REFERENCE: AMA, 2014
              AMA (7th ed.), pp 93–94, 132–135
              CPT Assistant, December 1995, pp 5–7
              Smith (2), pp 47–49

Surgery—Respiratory

40. Patient has a bronchoscopy with endobronchial biopsies of three sites.
   A. 31625; 31625; 31625
   B. 31625
   C. 31622; 31625
   D. 31622; 31625; 31625; 31625

REFERENCE: AMA (7th ed.), pp 139–141
              CPT Assistant, June 2004, p 11
              Green, pp 576–577
              Smith, pp 99–100
              Smith (2), p 61

41. Patient presents to the surgical unit and undergoes unilateral nasal endoscopy, partial ethmoidectomy, and maxillary antrostomy.
    A. 31254; 31256-51   C. 31290; 31267-51
    B. 31201; 31225-51   D. 31233; 31231-51

REFERENCE: AMA (7th ed.), pp 137–138
               CPT Assistant, January 1997, pp 4–6
               Green, pp 573–574
               Smith, p 93
               Smith (2), p 59

42. Patient has been diagnosed with metastatic laryngeal carcinoma. Patient underwent subtotal supraglottic laryngectomy with radical neck dissection.
    A. 31540   C. 31365
    B. 31367   D. 31368

REFERENCE: Green, pp 574–575

43. Patient was involved in an accident and has been sent to the hospital. During transport the patient develops breathing problems and, upon arrival at the hospital, an emergency transtracheal tracheostomy was performed. Following various x-rays, the patient was diagnosed with traumatic pneumothorax and a thoracentesis with insertion of tube was performed.
    A. 31603; 31612   C. 31603; 32555
    B. 31610; 32555   D. 31603; 32555

REFERENCE: AMA, 2014

44. Patient with laryngeal cancer has a tracheoesophageal fistula created and has a voicebox inserted.
    A. 31611   C. 31395
    B. 31580   D. 31502

REFERENCE: AMA, 2014

45. Upper lobectomy of the right lung with repair of the bronchus.
    A. 32480   C. 32320
    B. 32486   D. 32480, 32501

REFERENCE: AMA (7th ed.), pp 140–141
               Green, pp 578–579
               Smith (2), pp 61–62

46. Patient with a deviated nasal septum that was repaired by septoplasty.
    A. 30400   C. 30520
    B. 30620   D. 30630

REFERENCE: AMA, 2014

47. Lye burn of the larynx repaired by laryngoplasty.
    A. 31588   C. 31360
    B. 16020   D. 31540

REFERENCE: AMA, 2014

48. Bronchoscopy with multiple transbronchial right upper and right lower lobe lung biopsy with fluoroscopic guidance.
    A. 31628-RT; 76000-RT   C. 32405-RT
    B. 31717-RT; 31632-RT   D. 31628-RT; 31632-RT

REFERENCE: AMA (7th ed.), pp 139–140
               CPT Assistant, March 1999, p 3
               Green, pp 576–577
               Smith, pp 99–100
               Smith (2), p 61

49. Patient has recurrent spontaneous pneumothorax which has resulted in a chemical pleurodesis by thoracoscopy.
    A. 32650   C. 32601
    B. 32310; 32601   D. 32960

REFERENCE: AMA, 2014

50. Laryngoscopic stripping of vocal cords for leukoplakia of the vocal cords.
    A. 31535   C. 31541
    B. 31540   D. 31570

REFERENCE: AMA (7th ed.), pp 137–138
               Green, pp 574–575
               Smith, p 97

Surgery—Cardiovascular System

51. Patient returns to the operating room following open-heart bypass for exploration of blood vessel to control postoperative bleeding in the chest.
    A. 35820   C. 35761
    B. 20101   D. 35905

REFERENCE: AMA, 2014

52. Patient undergoes construction of apical aortic conduit with an insertion of a single-ventricle ventricular assist device.
    A. 33400   C. 33977
    B. 33975   D. 33975; 33404

REFERENCE: CPT Assistant, January 2004, p 28

53. Patient presents to the operating room where a CABG x 3 is performed using the mammary artery and two sections of the saphenous vein.
    A. 33534; 33511   C. 33535
    B. 33534; 33518; 33511   D. 33533; 33518

REFERENCE: AMA (7th ed.), pp 155–158
               Green, pp 599–600
               Smith, p 108
               Smith (2), pp 74–75

54. Patient complains of recurrent syncope following carotid thromboendarterectomy. Patient returns 2 weeks after initial surgery and undergoes repeat carotid thromboendarterectomy.
    A. 33510
    B. 35301
    C. 35201
    D. 35301; 35390

REFERENCE: CPT Assistant, Winter 1993, p 3
              Smith (2), pp 78–79

55. Patient is admitted with alcohol cirrhosis and has a TIPS procedure performed.
    A. 35476; 36011; 36481
    B. 37183
    C. 37182
    D. 37140

REFERENCE: CPT Assistant, December 2003, pp 1–3

56. Eighty-year-old patient has carcinoma and presents to the operating room for placement of a tunneled implantable centrally inserted venous access port.
    A. 36558
    B. 36571
    C. 36561
    D. 36481

REFERENCE: CPT Assistant, February 1999, pp 1–5
              CPT Assistant, November 1999, pp 19–20
              Green, pp 615–618
              Smith, pp 111–112
              Smith (2), pp 79–80

57. Patient presents to the operating room and undergoes an endovascular repair of an infrarenal abdominal aortic aneurysm utilizing a unibody bifurcated prosthesis.
    A. 34800; 34813
    B. 34802
    C. 34804
    D. 35081

REFERENCE: AMA (7th ed.), pp 159–161
              CPT Assistant, September 2002, p 4
              CPT Assistant, February 2003, pp 2–4, 16
              Green, p 620
              Smith (2), pp 76–77

58. The physician punctures the left common femoral to examine the right common iliac.
    A. 36245
    B. 36246
    C. 36247
    D. 36140

REFERENCE: AMA, 2014
              AMA (7th ed.), pp 283–285

59. Patient has a history of PVD for many years and experiences chest pains. The patient underwent Doppler evaluation, which showed a common femoral DVT. Patient is now admitted for thromboendarterectomy.
    A. 35371
    B. 35372
    C. 37224
    D. 35256

REFERENCE: AMA, 2014
              Smith (2), pp 78–79

60. Patient undergoes percutaneous transluminal iliac artery balloon angioplasty.
    A. 37228
    B. 37220
    C. 37222
    D. 37224

REFERENCE: AMA, 2014
              Smith, p 114

Surgery—Hemic and Lymphatic Systems, Mediastinum, and Diaphragm

61. Patient has breast carcinoma and is now undergoing sentinel node biopsy. Patient was injected for sentinel node identification and two deep axillary lymph nodes showed up intensely. These two lymph nodes were completely excised. Path report was positive for metastatic carcinoma.
    A. 38525; 38790
    B. 38589
    C. 38308; 38790
    D. 38525; 38792

REFERENCE: CPT Assistant, November 1998, pp 15–16
              CPT Assistant, July 1999, pp 6–12
              Green, p 624

62. Patient has a history of hiatal hernia for many years, which has progressively gotten worse. The decision to repair the hernia was made and the patient was sent to the operating room where the repair took place via the thorax and abdomen.
    A. 39545
    B. 43336
    C. 43332
    D. 39503

REFERENCE: AMA, 2014

63. Patient has a bone marrow aspiration of the iliac crest and of the tibia.
    A. 38220, 38220-59
    B. 38221
    C. 38230
    D. 38220

REFERENCE: AMA (7th ed.), pp 323–324
              CPT Assistant, January 2004, p 26
              Green, pp 623–624

64. Trauma patient is rushed to the operating room with multiple injuries. The patient had his spleen removed due to massive rupture with repair of lacerated diaphragm.
    A. 38115; 39501
    B. 38120; 39599
    C. 38102; 39540
    D. 38100; 39501

REFERENCE: AMA, 2014

65. Laparoscopic retroperitoneal lymph node biopsy.
    A. 38570
    B. 38780
    C. 49323
    D. 38589

REFERENCE: AMA, 2014

66. Excision of mediastinal cyst.
    A. 11400
    B. 39200
    C. 17000
    D. 39400

REFERENCE: AMA, 2014

67. Patient diagnosed with cystic hygroma of the axilla, which was excised.
    A. 38555   C. 38550
    B. 11400   D. 38300

REFERENCE: AMA, 2014

68. Laparoscopy with multiple biopsies of retroperitoneal lymph nodes.
    A. 38570   C. 38570-22
    B. 38571   D. 38572

REFERENCE: AMA, 2014

69. Cannulation of the thoracic duct.
    A. 38794   C. 36260
    B. 36810   D. 38999

REFERENCE: AMA, 2014

70. Patient has been on the bone marrow transplant recipient list for 3 months. A perfect match was made and the patient came in and received peripheral stem cell transplant.
    A. 38242   C. 38241
    B. 38230   D. 38240

REFERENCE: Green, pp 623–624

Surgery—Digestive System

71. Laparoscopic gastric banding.
    A. 43842   C. 43770
    B. 43843   D. 43771

REFERENCE: AMA, 2014

72. Patient presents with a history of upper abdominal pain. Cholangiogram was negative and patient was sent to the hospital for ERCP. During the procedure the sphincter was incised and a stent was placed for drainage.
    A. 43260; 43262; 43264   C. 43275
    B. 43262   D. 43274

REFERENCE: CPT Assistant, Spring 1994, pp 5–7
              Smith (2), pp 92–93

73. Patient presents to the emergency room with right lower abdominal pains. Emergency room physician suspects possible appendicitis. Patient was taken to the operating room where a laparoscopic appendectomy was performed. Pathology report was negative for appendicitis.
    A. 44950   C. 44970
    B. 44950; 49320   D. 44979

REFERENCE: AMA, 2014
              AMA (7th ed.), p 176
              Smith (2), p 97

74. Morbidly obese patient comes in for vertical banding of the stomach.
    A. 43848   C. 43842
    B. 43659   D. 43999

REFERENCE: CPT Assistant, May 1998, pp 5–6

75. Patient underwent anoscopy followed by colonoscopy. The physician examined the colon to 60 cm.
    A. 46600; 45378
    B. 46600; 45378-59
    C. 45378
    D. 45999

REFERENCE: Green, pp 650–652
               Smith, pp 120–121
               Smith (2), p 93

76. Injection snoreplasty for treatment of palatal snoring.
    A. 42299
    B. 42145
    C. 42999
    D. 40899

REFERENCE: CPT Assistant, December 2004, p 19

77. Patient arrives to the hospital and has a Nissen fundoplasty done laparoscopically.
    A. 43410
    B. 43415
    C. 43502
    D. 43280

REFERENCE: AMA, 2014
               Smith (2), p 97

78. Young child presents with cleft lip and cleft palate. This is the first attempt of repair, which includes major revision of the cleft palate and unilateral cleft lip repair.
    A. 42200; 40701
    B. 42225; 40700
    C. 42220; 40720
    D. 42215; 40700

REFERENCE: AMA, 2014

79. Patient has a history of chronic alcohol abuse with portal hypertension. Patient has been vomiting blood for the past 3 days and presented to his physician's office. Patient was sent to the hospital for evaluation and an EGD was performed. Biopsy findings showed gastritis, esophagitis, and bleeding esophageal varices, which were injected with sclerosing solution.
    A. 43235; 43244; 43204
    B. 43239; 43244
    C. 43239; 43243
    D. 43239; 43243; 43204

REFERENCE: AMA (7th ed.), pp 179–180
               Green, pp 641–645
               Smith, p 118
               Smith (2), p 92

Surgery—Urinary System

80. Patient is admitted for contact laser vaporization of the prostate. The physician performed a TURP and transurethral resection of the bladder neck at the same time.
    A. 52648
    B. 52648; 52450; 52500
    C. 52450; 53500
    D. 52648; 52450

REFERENCE: AMA (7th ed.), pp 197–198
               CPT Assistant, July 2005, p 15
               Smith (2), p 122

81. Patient comes to the hospital with a history of right flank pain. Urine tests are negative. Radiology examination reveals that the patient has renal cysts. Patient is now admitted for laparoscopic ablation of the cysts.
    A. 50541   C. 50280
    B. 50390   D. 50920

REFERENCE: AMA (7th ed.), p 192
               CPT Assistant, November 1999, p 25
               CPT Assistant, May 2000, p 4
               CPT Assistant, October 2001, p 8
               CPT Assistant, January 2003, p 19

82. Patient has extensive bladder cancer. She underwent a complete cystectomy with bilateral pelvic lymphadenectomy and creation of ureteroileal conduit.
    A. 51575; 50820   C. 51595
    B. 50825; 51570; 38770   D. 51550; 38770

REFERENCE: AMA, 2014

83. Patient presents to the hospital with right ureteral calculus. Patient is taken to the operating room where a cystoscopy with ureteroscopy is performed to remove the calculus.
    A. 52353   C. 51065
    B. 52310   D. 52352

REFERENCE: Green, pp 664–665
               Smith, p 134
               Smith (2), pp 111–112

84. Female with 6 months of stress incontinence. Outpatient therapies are not working and the patient decides to have the problem fixed. Laparoscopic urethral suspension was completed.
    A. 51992   C. 51840
    B. 51990   D. 51845

REFERENCE: CPT Assistant, November 1999, p 26
               CPT Assistant, May 2000, p 4
               CPT Changes: An Insider's View, 2000

85. Patient has ovarian vein syndrome and has ureterolysis performed.
    A. 58679   C. 52351
    B. 58660   D. 50722

REFERENCE: AMA, 2014

86. Male patient has been diagnosed with benign prostatic hypertrophy and undergoes a transurethral destruction of the prostate by radiofrequency thermotherapy.
    A. 52648   C. 52601
    B. 53852   D. 53850

REFERENCE: AMA (7th ed.), pp 197–198
               CPT Assistant, November 1997, p 20
               CPT Assistant, April 2001, p 4

87. Nephrectomy with resection of half of the ureter.
    A. 50220   C. 50230; 50650
    B. 50234   D. 50546

REFERENCE: AMA (7th ed.), p 192
              Green, pp 659–660

88. Male with urinary incontinence. Sling procedure was performed 6 months ago and now the patient has returned for a revision of the sling procedure.
    A. 53449   C. 53440
    B. 53442   D. 53431

REFERENCE: AMA, 2014

89. Excision of 2.5 cm bladder tumor with cystoscopy.
    A. 51550   C. 52235
    B. 51530   D. 51060

REFERENCE: AMA (7th ed.), pp 194–195
              Green, pp 644–645
              Smith, p 131

90. Closure of ureterocutaneous fistula.
    A. 50930   C. 57310
    B. 50920   D. 50520

REFERENCE: AMA, 2014

Surgery—Male Genital System

91. Removal of nephrostomy tube with fluoroscopic guidance.
    A. 50387   C. 99212
    B. 50389   D. 99213

REFERENCE: AMA, 2014
              AMA (7th ed.), p 196

92. Patient has been diagnosed with prostate cancer. Patient arrived in the operating room where a therapeutic orchiectomy is performed.
    A. 54560   C. 55899
    B. 54530   D. 54520

REFERENCE: CPT Assistant, October 2001, p 8
              Smith (2), p 122

93. Patient undergoes laparoscopic orchiopexy for intra-abdominal testes.
    A. 54650   C. 54692
    B. 54699   D. 55899

REFERENCE: CPT Assistant, November 1999, p 27
              CPT Assistant, May 2000, p 4
              CPT Assistant, October 2001, p 8
              Smith (2), p 122

94. Scrotal wall abscess drainage.
    A. 55100
    B. 55150
    C. 54700
    D. 55110

REFERENCE: AMA, 2014

95. Hydrocelectomy of spermatic cord.
    A. 55500
    B. 55000
    C. 55041
    D. 55520

REFERENCE: CPT Assistant, October 2001, p 8

96. Patient has been followed by his primary care physician for elevated PSA. Patient underwent prostate needle biopsy in the physician office 2 weeks ago and final pathology was positive for carcinoma. Patient is admitted for prostatectomy. Frozen section of the prostate and one lymph node is positive for prostate cancer with metastatic disease to the lymph node. Prostatectomy became a radical perineal with bilateral pelvic lymphadenectomy.
    A. 55845
    B. 55815
    C. 55815; 38562
    D. 38770

REFERENCE: Green, p 665
              Smith (2), p 122

97. Male presented to operating room for sterilization by bilateral vasectomy.
    A. 55200
    B. 55400
    C. 55250
    D. 55450

REFERENCE: CPT Assistant, June 1998, p 10
              CPT Assistant, July 1998, p 10

98. Laser destruction of penile condylomas.
    A. 54057
    B. 17106
    C. 17270
    D. 54055

REFERENCE: AMA, 2014
              Smith, p 139

99. First-stage repair for hypospadias with skin flaps.
    A. 54300
    B. 54308; 14040
    C. 54322
    D. 54304

REFERENCE: AMA, 2014

100. Priapism operation with spongiosum shunt.
    A. 54450
    B. 54352
    C. 54430
    D. 55899

REFERENCE: AMA, 2014

Surgery—Female Genital System

101. Patient was admitted to the hospital with sharp pelvic pains. A pelvic ultrasound was ordered and the results showed a possible ovarian cyst. The patient was taken to the operating room where a laparoscopic destruction of two corpus luteum cysts was performed.
    A. 49321
    B. 58925
    C. 58561
    D. 58662

REFERENCE: AMA, 2014
               Smith (2), p 534

102. Patient was admitted with a cystocele and rectocele. An anterior colporrhaphy was performed.
    A. 57250
    B. 57260
    C. 57240
    D. 57110

REFERENCE: AMA, 2014

103. Patient has a Bartholin's gland cyst that was marsupialized.
    A. 54640
    B. 10060
    C. 58999
    D. 56440

REFERENCE: AMA, 2014

104. Patient is at a fertility clinic and undergoes intrauterine embryo transplant.
    A. 58679
    B. 58322
    C. 58323
    D. 58974

REFERENCE: AMA, 2014

105. Patient has been diagnosed with carcinoma of the vagina, and she has a radical vaginectomy with complete removal of the vaginal wall.
    A. 57107
    B. 57110
    C. 58150
    D. 57111

REFERENCE: AMA, 2014
               Smith (2), p 133

106. Patient has been diagnosed with uterine fibroids and undergoes a total abdominal hysterectomy with bilateral salpingo-oophorectomy.
    A. 58200
    B. 58150
    C. 58262
    D. 58150; 58720

REFERENCE: AMA (7th ed.), pp 202–203
               Green, pp 682–685
               Johnson and Linker, p 380
               Smith, pp 145–146
               Smith (2), p 133

107. Hysteroscopy with D&C and polypectomy.
   A. 58563
   B. 58558
   C. 58120; 58100; 58555
   D. 58558; 58120

REFERENCE: AMA (7th ed.), pp 203–205
              Green, pp 682–685
              Smith, p 145
              Smith (2), p 132

108. Laparoscopic tubal ligation utilizing Endoloop.
   A. 58670
   B. 58615
   C. 58671
   D. 58611

REFERENCE: AMA (7th ed.), p 204
              Green, p 685

109. Laser destruction extensive herpetic lesions of the vulva.
   A. 17106
   B. 17004
   C. 56515
   D. 56501

REFERENCE: AMA, 2014
              Smith (2), p 131

110. Patient undergoes hysteroscopy with excision uterine fibroids.
   A. 58545
   B. 58140
   C. 58561
   D. 58140; 49320

REFERENCE: AMA (7th ed.), pp 203–204
              Green, pp 683–685
              Smith, p 145
              Smith (2), p 132

Surgery—Maternity Care and Delivery

111. Attempted vaginal delivery in a previous cesarean section patient, which resulted in a repeat cesarean section.
   A. 59409
   B. 59612
   C. 59620
   D. 59514

REFERENCE: AMA (7th ed.), p 208
              Green, pp 686–690
              Smith, p 146

112. Patient is admitted to the hospital following an ultrasound at 25 weeks, which revealed fetal pleural effusion. A fetal thoracentesis was performed.
   A. 59074
   B. 32554
   C. 32555
   D. 76815

REFERENCE: AMA (7th ed.), p 206
              CPT Assistant, May 2004, pp 3–4

113. Patient in late stages of labor arrives at the hospital. Her OB physician is not able to make the delivery and the house physician delivers the baby vaginally. Primary care physician resumes care after delivery. Code the delivery.
   A. 59409   C. 59620
   B. 59612   D. 59400

REFERENCE: AMA (7th ed.), pp 208–209
              Green, pp 686–690
              Smith, p 143

114. Patient is 24 weeks pregnant and arrives in the emergency room following an automobile accident. No fetal movement or heartbeat noted. Patient is taken to the OB ward where prostaglandin is given to induce abortion.
   A. 59200   C. 59821
   B. 59855   D. 59410

REFERENCE: Green, pp 686–690

115. Patient is 6 weeks pregnant and complains of left-sided abdominal pains. Patient is suspected of having an ectopic pregnancy. Patient has a laparoscopic salpingectomy with removal of the ectopic tubal pregnancy.
   A. 59120   C. 59121
   B. 59200   D. 59151

REFERENCE: AMA, 2014
              AMA (7th ed.), p 206

116. Cesarean delivery with antepartum and postpartum care.
   A. 59610   C. 59400
   B. 59514   D. 59510

REFERENCE: AMA (7th ed.), pp 208–209
              Green, pp 686–690
              Smith, p 146

117. A pregnant patient has an incompetent cervix, which was repaired using a vaginal cerclage.
   A. 57700   C. 59320
   B. 57531   D. 59325

REFERENCE: AMA, 2014
              AMA (7th ed.), p 207

118. A D&C is performed for postpartum hemorrhage.
   A. 59160   C. 58558
   B. 58120   D. 58578

REFERENCE: AMA, 2014

119. Hysterotomy for hydatidifom mole and tubal ligation.
   A. 58285; 58600   C. 51900; 58605
   B. 58150; 58605   D. 59100; 58611

REFERENCE: AMA, 2014

120. D&C performed for patient with a diagnosis of incomplete abortion at 8 weeks.
    A. 59812
    B. 59820
    C. 58120
    D. 59160

REFERENCE: Green, p 690

Surgery—Endocrine System

121. Patient comes in for a percutaneous needle biopsy of the thyroid gland.
    A. 60000
    B. 60270
    C. 60699
    D. 60100

REFERENCE: CPT Assistant, June 1997, p 5

122. Laparoscopic adrenalectomy, complete.
    A. 60650
    B. 60650-50
    C. 60659
    D. 60540

REFERENCE: AMA, 2014

123. Left carotid artery excision for tumor of carotid body.
    A. 60650
    B. 60600
    C. 60605
    D. 60699

REFERENCE: AMA, 2014

124. Patient undergoes total thyroidectomy with parathyroid autotransplantation.
    A. 60240; 60512
    B. 60520; 60500
    C. 60260; 60512
    D. 60650; 60500

REFERENCE: Green, p 692

125. Unilateral partial thyroidectomy.
    A. 60252
    B. 60210
    C. 60220
    D. 60520

REFERENCE: Green, p 692

Surgery—Nervous System

126. Patient comes in through the emergency room with a wound that was caused by an electric saw. Patient is taken to the operating room where two ulna nerves are sutured.
    A. 64837
    B. 64892; 69990
    C. 64836; 64837
    D. 64856; 64859

REFERENCE: AMA, 2014
                Smith (2), p 153

127. Laminectomy and excision of intradural lumbar lesion.
    A. 63272
    B. 63267
    C. 63282
    D. 63252

REFERENCE: AMA, 2014
                Smith (2) p 149

128. Patient comes in for steroid injection for lumbar herniated disk. Marcaine and Aristocort were injected into the L2-L3 space.
    A. 64520
    B. 64483
    C. 62311
    D. 64714

REFERENCE: CPT Assistant, September 1997, p 10
              Smith, p 153
              Smith (2), p 148

129. Patient with Parkinson's disease is admitted for insertion of a brain neurostimulator pulse generator with one electrode array.
    A. 61885
    B. 61850; 61863
    C. 61888
    D. 61867; 61870

REFERENCE: AMA (7th ed.), pp 222–224
              CPT Assistant, April 2001, pp 8–9
              CPT Assistant, June 2000, pp 4, 12
              Smith (2), p 145

130. Patient has rhinorrhea, which requires repair of the CSF leak with craniotomy.
    A. 63707
    B. 63709
    C. 62100
    D. 62010

REFERENCE: AMA, 2014
              Smith (2), pp 143–144

131. Patient has metastatic brain lesions. Patient undergoes stereotactic radiosurgery gamma knife of two lesions.
    A. 61533
    B. 61500
    C. 61796; 61797
    D. 61796

REFERENCE: AMA, 2014
              AMA (7th ed.), pp 221–222

132. Patient has right sacroiliac joint dysfunction and requires a right S2-S3 paravertebral facet joint anesthetic nerve block with image guidance.
    A. 62311
    B. 64493
    C. 64490
    D. 64520

REFERENCE: AMA, 2014
              Smith (2), pp 152–153

133. Patient requires repair of a 6 cm meningocele.
    A. 63700
    B. 63709
    C. 63180
    D. 63702

REFERENCE: AMA, 2014
              Smith (2), pp 151–152

134. Patient comes in through the emergency room with a laceration of the posterior tibial nerve. Patient is taken to the operating room where the nerve requires transposition and suture.
    A. 64856
    B. 64831; 64832; 64876
    C. 64840; 64874
    D. 64834; 64859; 64872

REFERENCE: AMA, 2014
             Smith (2), p 153

Surgery—Eye and Ocular Adnexa

135. Patient returns to the physician's office complaining of obscured vision. Patient has had cataract surgery 6 months prior. Patient requires laser discission of secondary cataract.
    A. 66821
    B. 66940
    C. 67835
    D. 66830

REFERENCE: AMA (7th ed.), p 297
             Smith, pp 157–158
             Smith (2), pp 162–163

136. Patient undergoes enucleation of left eye and muscles were reattached to an implant.
    A. 65135-LT
    B. 65105-LT
    C. 65730-LT
    D. 65103-LT

REFERENCE: AMA, 2014
             Smith (2), p 161

137. Patient suffers from strabismus and requires surgery. Recession of the lateral rectus (horizontal) muscle with adjustable sutures was performed.
    A. 67340; 67500
    B. 67314; 67320
    C. 67332; 67334
    D. 67311; 67335

REFERENCE: AMA, 2014
             AMA (7th ed.), p 253
             CPT Assistant, Summer 1993, p 20
             CPT Assistant, March 1997, p 5
             CPT Assistant, November 1998, p 1
             CPT Assistant, September 2002, p 10
             Smith, p 160
             Smith (2), p 165

138. Radial keratotomy.
    A. 92071
    B. 65855
    C. 65767
    D. 65771

REFERENCE: Green, pp 706–711
             Smith (2), pp 162–163

139. Correction of trichiasis by incision of lid margin.
    A. 67840
    B. 67830
    C. 67835
    D. 67850

REFERENCE: AMA, 2014
             Smith (2), p 165

140. Patient undergoes ocular resurfacing construction utilizing stem cell allograft from a cadaver.
   A. 67320
   B. 66999
   C. 68371
   D. 65781

REFERENCE: CPT Assistant, May 2004, pp 9–11
              Smith (2), pp 162–163

141. Aphakia penetrating corneal transplant.
   A. 65755
   B. 65730
   C. 65750
   D. 65765

REFERENCE: AMA, 2014
              AMA (7th ed.), pp 247–248
              Smith (2), pp 162–163

142. Lagophthalmos correction with implantation using gold weight.
   A. 67912
   B. 67911
   C. 67901
   D. 67121

REFERENCE: CPT Assistant, May 2004, p 12
              Smith (2), p 165

143. Lacrimal fistula closure.
   A. 68760
   B. 68761
   C. 68700
   D. 68770

REFERENCE: AMA, 2014
              AMA (7th ed.), pp 255–256
              Smith (2), pp 165–166

Surgery—Auditory

144. Patient comes into the office for removal of impacted earwax.
   A. 69210
   B. 69200
   C. 69222
   D. 69000

REFERENCE: AMA (7th ed.), p 257
              Green, pp 712–713
              Smith (2), p 120

145. Patient with a traumatic rupture of the eardrum. Repaired with tympanoplasty with incision of the mastoid. Repair of ossicular chain not required.
   A. 69641
   B. 69646
   C. 69642
   D. 69635

REFERENCE: AMA, 2014
              AMA (7th ed.), pp 258–259
              Smith (2), p 173

146. Patient came in for excision of a middle ear lesion.
   A. 11440
   B. 69540
   C. 69552
   D. 69535

REFERENCE: AMA, 2014
              Smith (2), p 173

147. Patient with chronic otitis media requiring eustachian tube catheterization.
    A. 69400
    B. 69424
    C. 69421
    D. 69405

REFERENCE: AMA, 2014
              AMA (7th ed.), p 258
              Smith (2), p 173

148. Modified radical mastoidectomy.
    A. 69511
    B. 69505
    C. 69635
    D. 69641

REFERENCE: AMA, 2014
              Smith (2), p 173

149. Decompression internal auditory canal.
    A. 69979
    B. 69915
    C. 69970
    D. 69960

REFERENCE: AMA, 2014
              Smith (2), pp 172–173

150. Myringoplasty.
    A. 69620
    B. 69635
    C. 69610
    D. 69420

REFERENCE: AMA (7th ed.), p 258
              CPT Assistant, March 2001, p 10

151. Insertion of cochlear device inner ear.
    A. 69711
    B. 69949
    C. 69930
    D. 69960; 69990

REFERENCE: AMA, 2014
              AMA (7th ed.), p 259
              Smith (2), p 173

152. Patient with Bell's palsy requiring a total facial nerve decompression.
    A. 64742
    B. 64771
    C. 69955
    D. 64864

REFERENCE: AMA, 2014
              Smith (2), p 173

153. Drainage of simple external ear abscess.
    A. 69000
    B. 69100
    C. 10060
    D. 69020

REFERENCE: CPT Assistant, October 1997, p 11
              CPT Assistant, October 1999, p 10
              Smith (2), p 173

Radiology

154. Administration of initial oral radionuclide therapy for hyperthyroidism.
    A. 78015
    B. 77402
    C. 78099
    D. 79005

REFERENCE: Green, pp 753–761

155. Patient comes into the outpatient department at the local hospital for an MRI of the cervical spine with contrast. Patient status post automobile accident.
    A. 72156
    B. 72142
    C. 72149
    D. 72126

REFERENCE: AMA (7th ed.), pp 277–278
                Smith, pp 175–176

156. Obstetric patient comes in for a pelvimetry with placental placement.
    A. 74710
    B. 76946
    C. 76805
    D. 76825

REFERENCE: AMA, 2014

157. Patient comes into his physician's office complaining of wrist pain. Physician gives the patient an injection and sends the patient to the hospital for an arthrography. Code the complete procedure.
    A. 73115
    B. 73100
    C. 73110
    D. 25246; 73115

REFERENCE: AMA, 2014
                AMA (7th ed.), pp 278–279

158. Patient has carcinoma of the breast and undergoes proton beam delivery of radiation to the breast with a single port.
    A. 77523
    B. 77432
    C. 77520
    D. 77402

REFERENCE: AMA (7th ed.), p 299
                Green, pp 753–761
                Smith, pp 178–180

159. CT scan of the head with contrast.
    A. 70460
    B. 70542
    C. 70551
    D. 70470

REFERENCE: AMA (7th ed.), p 274
                Smith, pp 175–176

160. Patient undergoes x-ray of the foot with three views.
    A. 73620
    B. 73610
    C. 73630
    D. 27648; 73615

REFERENCE: Smith, pp 175–176

161. Unilateral mammogram with computer-aided detection with further physician review and interpretation.
    A. 77055, 77032
    B. 77055-22
    C. 77056-52, 77051
    D. 77055, 77051

REFERENCE: AMA, 2014
              AMA (7th ed.), pp 291–292
              Green, pp 751–752

162. Pregnant female comes in for a complete fetal and maternal evaluation via ultrasound.
    A. 76856
    B. 76805
    C. 76811
    D. 76810

REFERENCE: AMA (7th ed.), pp 286–287
              Green, p 750

163. Ultrasonic guidance for the needle biopsy of the liver. Code the complete procedure.
    A. 47000; 76942
    B. 47000; 76937
    C. 47000; 76999
    D. 47000; 77002

REFERENCE: AMA (7th ed.), p 281
              Green, p 750

Pathology and Laboratory

164. What code is used for a culture of embryos less than 4 days?
    A. 89251
    B. 89272
    C. 89268
    D. 89250

REFERENCE: AMA (7th ed.), p 336
              CPT Assistant, April 2004, p 2
              CPT Assistant, May 2004, p 16
              CPT Assistant, June 2004, p 9
              Green, pp 790–791

165. Basic metabolic panel (calcium, total) and total bilirubin.
    A. 80048; 82247
    B. 80053
    C. 80100
    D. 82239; 80400; 80051

REFERENCE: AMA (7th ed.), p 309
              Green, p 778
              Smith, p 188

166. Huhner test and semen analysis.
    A. 89325
    B. 89258
    C. 89310
    D. 89300

REFERENCE: CPT Assistant, November 1997, p 36
              CPT Assistant, July 1998, p 10
              CPT Assistant, October 1998, p 1
              CPT Assistant, April 2004, p 3

167. Chlamydia culture.
    A. 87110   C. 87118
    B. 87106   D. 87109; 87168

REFERENCE: Green, pp 785–786

168. Partial thromboplastin time utilizing whole blood.
    A. 85732   C. 85245
    B. 85730   D. 85246

REFERENCE: AMA (7th ed.), p 323
               Smith, p 190

169. Pathologist bills for gross and microscopic examination of medial meniscus.
    A. 88300   C. 88325
    B. 88302; 88311   D. 88304

REFERENCE: AMA (7th ed.), p 334
               Green, pp 789–790
               Smith, p 190

170. Cytopathology of cervical Pap smear with automated thin-layer preparation utilizing computer screening and manual rescreening under physician supervision.
    A. 88175   C. 88160; 88141
    B. 88148   D. 88161

REFERENCE: AMA (7th ed.), p 329
               CPT Assistant, July 2003, p 9
               CPT Assistant, March 2004, p 4
               Green, pp 786–787

171. Pathologist performs a postmortem examination including brain of an adult. Tissue is being sent to the lab for microscopic examination.
    A. 88309   C. 88099
    B. 88025   D. 88028

REFERENCE: Green, p 486
               Smith, p 190

172. Clotting factor VII.
    A. 85220   C. 85362
    B. 85240   D. 85230

REFERENCE: Smith, p 190

Medicine Section

173. IV push of one antineoplastic drug.
    A. 96401   C. 96411
    B. 96409   D. 96413

REFERENCE: AMA (7th ed.), pp 418–419
               Green, pp 825–828
               Smith, pp 240–242

174. One-half hour of IV chemotherapy by infusion followed by IV push of a different drug.
     A. 96413   C. 96413; 96409
     B. 96413; 96411   D. 96409; 96411

REFERENCE: AMA (7th ed.), pp 417–418
               Green, pp 825–828
               Smith, pp 240–242

175. Caloric vestibular test using air.
     A. 92543; 92700   C. 92700
     B. 92543; 92543   D. 92543

REFERENCE: AMA (7th ed.), p 361
               CPT Assistant, November 2004, p 10

176. Patient presents to the emergency room with chest pains. The patient is admitted as a 23-hour observation. The cardiologist orders cardiac workup and the patient undergoes left heart catheterization via the left femoral artery with visualization of the coronary arteries and left ventriculography. The physician interprets the report. Code the heart catheterization.
     A. 93452; 93455
     B. 93452; 93458
     C. 93458
     D. 93459

REFERENCE: AMA, 2014

177. Patient with hematochromatosis had a therapeutic phlebotomy performed on an outpatient basis.
     A. 99195   C. 36514
     B. 36522   D. 99199

REFERENCE: AMA (7th ed.), p 307
               CPT Assistant, June 1996, p 10

178. A physician performs a PTCA with drug-eluting stent placement in the left anterior descending artery and angioplasty only in the right coronary artery.
     A. 92928-LD; 92929-RC   C. 92928-LD; 92920-RC
     B. 92928-LD; 92920-RC   D. 92920-RC; 92929-LD

REFERENCE: AMA (7th ed.), pp 366–367
               CPT Assistant, April 2005, p 14
               Smith, pp 231–234

179. Transesophageal echocardiography (TEE) with probe placement, image, and interpretation and report.
     A. 93307   C. 93312; 93313; 93314
     B. 93303; 93325   D. 93312

REFERENCE: AMA (7th ed.), pp 374–375
               CPT Assistant, December 1997, p 5
               CPT Assistant, January 2000, p 10

180. Which code listed below would be used to report an esophageal electrogram during an EPS?
    A. 93600
    B. 93615
    C. 93612
    D. 93616

REFERENCE: CPT Assistant, April 2004, p 9
                Smith, p 237

181. Cardioversion of cardiac arrhythmia by external forces.
    A. 92961
    B. 92950
    C. 92960
    D. 92970

REFERENCE: CPT Assistant, Summer 1993, p 13
                CPT Assistant, November 1999, p 49
                CPT Assistant, June 2000, p 5
                CPT Assistant, November 2000, p 9
                CPT Assistant, July 2001, p 11

182. Osteopathic manipulative treatment to three body regions.
    A. 98926
    B. 98941
    C. 97110
    D. 97012

REFERENCE: Green, p 830

183. Patient presents to the Respiratory Therapy Department and undergoes a pulmonary stress test. CO_2 production with O_2 uptake with recordings was also performed.
    A. 94450
    B. 94620
    C. 94002
    D. 94621

REFERENCE: CPT Assistant, November 1998, p 35
                CPT Assistant, January 1999, p 8
                CPT Assistant, August 2002, p 10

For the following questions, you will be utilizing the codes provided for the scenarios. You will need to code appropriate CPT-4 codes only.

184. Patient presents to the hospital for debridement of a diabetic ulcer of the left ankle. The patient has a history of recurrent ulcers. Medication taken by the patient includes Diabeta and the patient was covered in the hospital with insulin sliding scales. The decubitus ulcer was debrided down to the bone.

11043	Debridement, muscle and/or fascia (includes epidermis, dermis, and subcutaneous tissue, if performed); first 20 cm^2 or less
11044	Debridement, bone (includes epidermis, dermis, subcutaneous tissue, muscle and/or fascia, if performed); first 20 cm^2 or less
+11046	each additional 20 cm^2 thereof (List separately in addition to code for primary procedure.) (Use 11046 in conjunction with 11043.)
+11047	each additional 20 cm^2, or part thereof (List separately in addition to code for primary procedure.) (Use 11047 in conjunction with 11047.)

A. 11043, +11047

B. 11043, +11046

C. 11044

D. 11044, +11047

REFERENCE: AMA, 2014

185. Patient presents to the emergency room following a fall from a tree. X-rays were ordered for the left upper arm, which showed a fracture of the humerus shaft. The emergency room physician performed a closed reduction of the fracture and placed the patient in a long arm spica cast. Code the diagnoses and procedures, excluding the x-ray.

24500	Closed treatment of humeral shaft fracture; without manipulation
24505	Closed treatment of humeral shaft fracture; with manipulation, with or without skeletal traction
24515	Open treatment of humeral shaft fracture with plate/screws, with or without cerclage
29065	Application, cast; shoulder to hand (long arm)
LT	Left side

A. 24505-LT

B. 24515-LT

C. 24505-LT, 29065

D. 24500-LT

REFERENCE: AMA (7th ed.), pp 115, 134–135
Green, p 563
Smith, pp 84–85

186. Patient was admitted with hemoptysis and underwent a bronchoscopy with transbronchial lung biopsy. Following the bronchoscopy the patient was taken to the operating room where a left lower lobe lobectomy was performed without complications. Pathology reported large cell carcinoma of the left lower lobe.

31625	Bronchoscopy with bronchial or endobronchial biopsy, with or without fluoroscopic guidance
31628	Bronchoscopy with transbronchial lung biopsy, with or without fluoroscopic guidance
32405	Biopsy, lung or mediastinum, percutaneous needle
32440	Removal of lung, total pneumonectomy
32480	Removal of lung, other than total pneumonectomy, single lobe (lobectomy)
32484	Removal of lung, other than total pneumonectomy, single segment (segmentectomy)

A. 31625
B. 31628, 32480

C. 32405, 32484
D. 32440

REFERENCE: AMA (7th ed.), pp 140–141
CPT Assistant, June 2001, p 10
CPT Assistant, June 2002, p 10
CPT Assistant, September 2004, p 9
Green, pp 576–580
Smith, p 100

187. Patient was admitted for right upper quadrant pain. Workup included various x-rays that showed cholelithiasis. Patient was taken to the operating room where a laparoscopic cholecystectomy was performed. During the procedure, the physician was unable to visualize through the ports and an open cholecystectomy was elected to be performed. Intraoperative cholangiogram was performed. Pathology report states acute and chronic cholecystitis with cholelithiasis.

47605	Cholecystectomy with cholangiography
47563	Laparoscopy, surgical; cholecystectomy with cholangiography

A. 47563
B. 47563, 47605
C. 47605

REFERENCE: AMA (7th ed.), p 187
Green, p 654

188. Patient presents to the emergency room complaining of right forearm/elbow pain after racquetball last night. Patient states that he did not fall, but overworked his arm. Past medical history is negative and the physical examination reveals the patient is unable to supinate. A four-view x-ray of the right elbow is performed and is negative. The physician signs the patient out with right elbow sprain. Prescription of Motrin is given to the patient.

73040	X-ray of shoulder, arthrography radiological supervision and interpretation
73070	X-ray of elbow, two views
73080	X-ray of elbow, complete, minimum of three views
99281	E/M visit to emergency room—problem-focused history, problem-focused exam, straightforward medical decision
99282	E/M visit to emergency room—expanded problem-focused history, expanded problem-focused exam, and medical decision of low complexity
-25	Significant, separately identifiable evaluation and management service by the same physician on the same day of the procedure or other service

   A. 73080
   B. 99281, 73070
   C. 73080, 99282, 73040
   D. 99281-25, 73080

REFERENCE: AMA, 2014
               AMA (7th ed.), pp 56–57, 275, 276
               Smith, pp 175–176, 216

189. A physician orders a lipid panel on a 54-year-old male with hypercholesterolemia, hypertension, and a family history of heart disease. The lab employee in his office performs and reports the total cholesterol and HDL cholesterol only.

80061	Lipid panel; this panel must include the following: Cholesterol, serum, total (82465); Lipoprotein, direct measurement, high density cholesterol (HDL cholesterol) (83718); Triglycerides (84478)
82465	Cholesterol, serum or whole blood, total
83718	Lipoprotein, direct measurement; high density cholesterol (HDL cholesterol)
84478	Triglycerides
52	Reduced services

   A. 80061
   B. 80061-52
   C. 82465, 83718
   D. 82465, 84478

REFERENCE: AMA (7th ed.), p 308
               Green, p 788
               Smith, pp 188–189

190. Chronic nontraumatic rotator cuff tear. Arthroscopic subacromial decompression with coracoacromial ligament release, and open rotator cuff repair.

23410	Repair of ruptured musculotendinous cuff (e.g., rotator cuff); open, acute
23412	Repair of ruptured musculotendinous cuff (e.g., rotator cuff) open; chronic
29821	Arthroscopy, shoulder, surgical; synovectomy, complete
29823	Arthroscopy, shoulder, surgical; debridement, extensive
+29826	Arthroscopy, shoulder, surgical; decompression of subacromial space with partial acromioplasty, with coracoacromial ligament release (List separately in addition to code from primary procedure.)
29827	Arthroscopy, shoulder, surgical; with rotator cuff repair
-59	Distinct procedural service

A. 29823
B. 23412, 29826-59

C. 29826, 29821
D. 23410

REFERENCE: AMA (7th ed.), pp 135, 498
                          Smith, p 88

191. The patient is on vacation and presents to a physician's office with a lacerated finger. The physician repairs the laceration and gives a prescription for pain control and has the patient follow up with his primary physician when he returns home. The physician fills out the superbill as a problem-focused history and physical examination with straightforward medical decision making. Also checked is a laceration repair for a 1.5 cm finger wound.

99201	New patient office visit with a problem-focused history, problem-focused examination and straightforward medical decision making
99212	Established patient office visit with a problem-focused history, problem-focused examination and straightforward medical decision making
12001	Simple repair of superficial wounds of scalp, neck, axillae, external genitalia, trunk and/or extremities (including hands and feet); 2.5 cm or less
13131	Repair, complex, forehead, cheeks, chin, mouth, neck, axillae, genitalia, hands and/or feet; 1.1 cm to 2.5 cm

A. 99212; 13131
B. 12001

C. 99212; 12001
D. 99201; 12001

REFERENCE: AMA (7th ed.), pp 107, 447–448
                          Green, pp 428–429, 524–526
                          Smith, pp 66–68, 195–196

192. A 69-year-old established female patient presents to the office with chronic obstructive lung disease, congestive heart failure, and hypertension. The physician conducts a comprehensive history and physical examination and makes a medical decision of moderate complexity. Physician admits the patient from the office to the hospital for acute exacerbation of CHF.

99212	Established office visit for problem-focused history and exam, straightforward medical decision making
99214	Established office visit for a detailed history and physical exam, moderate medical decision making
99222	Initial hospital care for comprehensive history and physical exam, moderate medical decision making
99223	Initial hospital care for comprehensive history and physical exam, high medical decision making

A. 402.91; 496; 99214
B. 428.0; 496; 401.1; 99223
C. 428.0; 496; 401.9; 99222
D. 402.91; 496; 401.1; 99212

REFERENCE: AMA (7th ed.), p 48
Green, pp 432–435
Smith, pp 214–215

193. Established 42-year-old patient comes into your office to obtain vaccines required for his trip to Sri Lanka. The nurse injects intramuscularly the following vaccines: hepatitis A and B vaccines, cholera vaccine, and yellow fever vaccine. As the coding specialist, what would you report on the CMS 1500 form?
A. office visit, hepatitis A and B vaccine, cholera vaccine and yellow fever vaccine
B. office visit, intramuscular injection; HCPCS Level II codes
C. office visit; administration of two or more single vaccines; vaccine products for hepatitis A and B, cholera, and yellow fever
D. administration of two or more single vaccines; vaccine products for hepatitis A and B, cholera, and yellow fever

REFERENCE: Green, pp 802–804
Smith, p 226

194. Patient presents to the operating room where the physician performed, using imaging guidance, a percutaneous breast biopsy utilizing a rotating biopsy device.

19000	Puncture aspiration of cyst of breast
19103	Biopsy, breast, with placement of breast localization device(s), when performed, and imaging of the biopsy specimen, when performed, percutaneous; first lesion, including stereotactic guidance
19120	Excision of cyst, fibroadenoma, or other benign or malignant tumor, aberrant breast tissue, duct lesion, nipple or areolar lesion (except 19300), open, male or female, one or more lesions
19125	Excision of breast lesion identified by preoperative placement of radiological marker, open; single lesion
19283	Placement of breast localization device(s) (ed clip, metallic pellet, wire/needle, radioactive seeds), percutaneous; first lesion, including stereotactic guidance

A. 19081
B. 19125; 19283

C. 19120
D. 19000

REFERENCE: AMA (7th ed.), p 115
CPT Assistant, January 2001, pp 10–11
Green, pp 835–837
Smith, pp 79–80

195. Facelift utilizing the superficial musculoaponeurotic system (SMAS) flap technique.

15788	Chemical peel, facial; epidermal
15825	Rhytidectomy; neck with platysmal tightening (platysmal flap, P-flap)
15828	Rhytidectomy; cheek, chin, and neck
15829	Rhytidectomy; SMAS flap

A. 15825
B. 15788

C. 15829
D. 15828

REFERENCE: AMA, 2014
Green, pp 531–532

196. Tracheostoma revision with flap rotation.

31613	Tracheostoma revision; simple, without flap rotation
31614	Tracheostoma revision; complex, with flap rotation
31750	Tracheoplasty; cervical
31830	Revision of tracheostomy scar

A. 31830
B. 31750

C. 31614
D. 31613

REFERENCE: AMA, 2014

197. Blood transfusion of three units of packed red blood cells.

36430	Transfusion, blood or blood components
36455	Exchange transfusion; blood, other than newborn
36460	Transfusion, intrauterine, fetal

A. 36430
B. 36430; 36430; 36430

C. 36460
D. 36455

REFERENCE: AMA, 2014

198. Two-year-old patient returns to the hospital for cleft palate repair where a secondary lengthening procedure takes place.

40720	Plastic repair of cleft lip/nasal deformity; secondary, by re-creation of defect and reclosure
42145	Palatopharyngoplasty
42220	Palatoplasty for cleft palate; secondary lengthening procedure
42226	Lengthening of palate and pharyngeal flap

A. 40720
B. 42220

C. 42226
D. 42145

REFERENCE: AMA, 2014

199. Tonsillectomy on a 14-year-old.

42820	Tonsillectomy and adenoidectomy; under age 12
42821	Tonsillectomy and adenoidectomy; age 12 or over
42825	Tonsillectomy, primary or secondary; under age 12
42826	Tonsillectomy, primary or secondary; age 12 or over

A. 42820
B. 42821

C. 42825
D. 42826

REFERENCE: Green, p 640

200. Laparoscopic repair of umbilical hernia.

49580	Repair umbilical hernia, under age 5 years, reducible
49585	Repair umbilical hernia, age 5 years or over, reducible
49652	Laparoscopy, surgical, repair, ventral, umbilical, spigelian or epigastric hernia (includes mesh insertion when performed); reducible
49654	Laparoscopy, surgical, repair, incisional hernia (includes mesh insertion when performed); reducible

A. 49580
B. 49654

C. 49585
D. 49652

REFERENCE: AMA, 2014
                      AMA (7th ed.), p 189

201. Ureterolithotomy completed laparoscopically.

50600	Ureterotomy with exploration or drainage (separate procedure)
50945	Laparoscopy, surgical ureterolithotomy
52325	Cystourethroscopy; with fragmentation of ureteral calculus
52352	Cystourethroscopy, with urethroscopy and/or pyeloscopy; with removal or manipulation of calculus (ureteral catheterization is included)

    A. 52352   C. 50600
    B. 52325   D. 50945

REFERENCE: CPT Assistant, November 1999, p 26
                    CPT Assistant, May 2000, p 4
                    CPT Assistant, October 2001, p 8

202. Patient undergoes partial nephrectomy for carcinoma of the kidney.

50220	Nephrectomy, including partial ureterectomy, any open approach including rib resection
50234	Nephrectomy with total ureterectomy and bladder cuff; through same incision
50240	Nephrectomy, partial
50340	Recipient nephrectomy (separate procedure)

    A. 50234   C. 50340
    B. 50220   D. 50240

REFERENCE: AMA (7th ed.), p 193
                    Green, pp 659–660

203. Patient presents to the operating room for fulguration of bladder tumors. The cystoscope was inserted and entered the urethra, which was normal. Bladder tumors measuring approximately 1.5 cm were removed.

50957	Ureteral endoscopy through established ureterostomy, with or without irrigation, instillation, or ureteropyelography, exclusive of radiologic service; with fulguration and/or incision, with or without biopsy
51530	Cystotomy; for excision of bladder tumor
52214	Cystourethroscopy, with fulguration of trigone, bladder neck, prostatic fossa, urethra, or periurethral glands
52234	Cystourethroscopy, with fulguration (including cryosurgery or laser surgery) and/or resection of small bladder tumor(s) (0.5 up to 2.0 cm)

    A. 52234   C. 52214
    B. 50957   D. 51530

REFERENCE: AMA (7th ed.), pp 193–194
                    Green, pp 664–665
                    Smith, p 134

204. Excision of Cowper's gland.

53220	Excision or fulguration of carcinoma of urethra
53250	Excision of bulbourethral gland (Cowper's gland)
53260	Excision or fulguration; urethral polyp(s), distal urethra
53450	Urethromeatoplasty, with mucosal advancement

A. 53250 C. 53260
B. 53450 D. 53220

REFERENCE: AMA, 2014

205. Placement of double-J stent.

52320	Cystourethroscopy (including ureteral catheterization); with removal of ureteral calculus
52330	Cystourethroscopy; with manipulation, without removal of ureteral calculus
52332	Cystourethroscopy with insertion of indwelling ureteral stent (e.g., Gibbons or double-J type)
52341	Cystourethroscopy, with treatment of ureteral stricture (e.g., balloon dilation, laser electrocautery, and incision)

A. 52341 C. 52330; 52332
B. 52320 D. 52332

REFERENCE: AMA (7th ed.), pp 193–195
Green, pp 664–665
Smith, p 134

206. Litholapaxy, 3 cm calculus.

50590	Lithotripsy, extracorporeal shock wave
52317	Litholapaxy, simple or small (< 2.5 cm)
52318	Litholapaxy, complicated or large (over 2.5 cm)
52353	Cystourethroscopy, with ureteroscopy and/or pyeloscopy; with lithotripsy

A. 52353 C. 52318
B. 50590 D. 52317

REFERENCE: AMA, 2014

207. Patient presented to the operating room where an incision was made in the epigastric region for a repair of ureterovisceral fistula.

50520	Closure of nephrocutaneous or pyelocutaneous fistula
50525	Closure of nephrovisceral fistula, including visceral repair; abdominal approach
50526	Closure of nephrovisceral fistula, including visceral repair; thoracic approach
50930	Closure of ureterovisceral fistula (including visceral repair)

A. 50526 C. 50520
B. 50930 D. 50525

REFERENCE: AMA, 2014

208. Amniocentesis.

57530	Trachelectomy, amputation of cervix (separate procedure)
57550	Excision of cervical stump, vaginal approach
59000	Amniocentesis, diagnostic
59200	Insertion of cervical dilator (separate procedure)

A. 59000
B. 59200
C. 57550
D. 57530

REFERENCE: AMA, 2014
AMA (7th ed.), p 206

209. Patient is admitted to the hospital with facial droop and left-sided paralysis. CT scan of the brain shows subdural hematoma. Burr holes were performed to evacuate the hematoma.

61150	Burr hole(s) or trephine; with drainage of brain abscess or cyst
61154	Burr hole(s) with evacuation and/or drainage of hematoma, extradural or subdural
61156	Burr hole(s); with aspiration of hematoma or cyst, intracerebral
61314	Craniectomy or craniotomy for evacuation of hematoma, infratentorial; extradural or subdural

A. 61156
B. 61314
C. 61154
D. 61150

REFERENCE: Green, p 695

210. Spinal tap.

62268	Percutaneous aspiration, spinal cord cyst or syrinx
62270	Spinal puncture, lumbar diagnostic
62272	Spinal puncture, therapeutic, for drainage of cerebrospinal fluid (by needle or catheter)
64999	Unlisted procedure, nervous system

A. 62272
B. 64999
C. 62268
D. 62270

REFERENCE: AMA, 2014
AMA (7th ed.), p 445

211. Injection of anesthesia for nerve block of the brachial plexus.

64413	Injection, anesthetic agent; cervical plexus
64415	Injection, anesthetic agent; brachial plexus, single
64510	Injection, anesthetic agent; stellate ganglion (cervical sympathetic)
64530	Injection, anesthetic agent; celiac plexus, with or without radiologic monitoring

A. 64415
B. 64413
C. 64530
D. 64510

REFERENCE: AMA (7th ed.), p 448
Green, p 703

212. SPECT bone imaging.

77080	Dual energy x-ray absorptiometry (DXA), bone density study, one or more sites; axial skeleton (e.g., hips, pelvis, spine)
76977	Ultrasound bone density measurement and interpretation, peripheral site(s), any method
78300	Bone and/or joint imaging; limited area
78320	Bone and/or joint imaging; tomographic (SPECT)

A. 76977   C. 77080
B. 78320   D. 76977

REFERENCE: AMA, 2014
               AMA (7th ed.), pp 303–304
               CPT Assistant, June 2003, p 11

213. Vitamin B_{12}.

82180	Ascorbic acid (vitamin C), blood
82607	Cyanocobalamin (vitamin B_{12})
84590	Vitamin A
84591	Vitamin, not otherwise specified

A. 84590   C. 84591
B. 82180   D. 82607

REFERENCE: AMA (2014)
               Green, p 782
               Smith, p 190

214. Hepatitis C antibody.

86803	Hepatitis C antibody
86804	Hepatitis C antibody; confirmatory test (e.g., immunoblot)
87520	Infectious agent detection by nucleic acid (DNA or RNA); hepatitis C, direct probe technique
87522	Infectious agent detection by nucleic acid (DNA or RNA); hepatitis C, quantification

A. 86804   C. 87522
B. 86803   D. 87520

REFERENCE: AMA (2014)
               Green, p 784

215. Creatinine clearance.

82550	Creatine kinase (CK), (CPK); total
82565	Creatinine; blood
82575	Creatinine; clearance
82585	Cryofibrinogen

A. 82550   C. 82575
B. 82565   D. 82585

REFERENCE: Green, p 782
               Smith, p 190

216. Comprehensive electrophysiologic evaluation (EPS) with induction of arrhythmia.

93618	Induction of arrhythmia by electrical pacing
93619	Comprehensive electrophysiologic evaluation with right atrial pacing and recording, right ventricular pacing and recording, His bundle recording, including insertion and repositioning of multiple electrode catheters, without induction or attempted induction of arrhythmia
93620	Comprehensive electrophysiologic evaluation including insertion and repositioning of multiple electrode catheters with induction or attempted induction of arrhythmia; with right atrial pacing and recording, right ventricular pacing and recording, His bundle recording
+93623	Programmed stimulation and pacing after intravenous drug infusion (list separately in addition to code for primary procedure)
93640	Electrophysiologic evaluation of single- or dual-chamber pacing cardioverter-defibrillator leads including defibrillation threshold evaluation (induction of arrhythmia, evaluation of sensing and pacing for arrhythmia termination) at time of initial implantation or replacement

A. 93618; 93620   C. 93640; 93623
B. 93620   D. 93619; 93620

REFERENCE: AMA (7th ed.), p 149
               CPT Assistant, Summer 1994, p 12
               CPT Assistant, August 1997, p 9
               CPT Assistant, October 1997, p 10
               CPT Assistant, July 1998, p 10

217. Patient presents to the hospital for a two-view chest x-ray for a cough. The radiology report comes back negative. What would be the correct codes to report to the insurance company?

71010	Radiologic examination, chest; single view, frontal
71020	Radiologic examination, chest, two views, frontal and lateral
71035	Radiologic examination, chest, special views

A. 71010
B. 71020
C. 71035

REFERENCE: AMA, 2014
               Schraffenberger, pp 338–339

Answer Key for CPT-4 Coding

1.	C		43.	C	
2.	A		44.	A	
3.	B		45.	D	
4.	C		46.	C	
5.	D		47.	A	
6.	C		48.	D	
7.	D		49.	A	
8.	B		50.	B	
9.	B		51.	A	
10.	C		52.	B	
11.	D		53.	D	
12.	B		54.	B	
13.	A		55.	C	
14.	B		56.	C	
15.	D		57.	C	
16.	B		58.	A	
17.	C		59.	A	
18.	A		60.	B	
19.	D	The supply of skin substitutes graft(s) should be reported separately.	61.	D	
			62.	B	
			63.	A	
20.	C		64.	D	
21.	C		65.	A	
22.	B		66.	B	
23.	B		67.	C	
24.	C	The supply of skin substitutes graft(s) should be reported separately.	68.	A	
			69.	A	
			70.	D	
25.	B		71.	C	
26.	C		72.	D	Radiology codes would be used for the supervision and interpretation.
27.	A	See Principles of CPT Coding 7th edition, pages 103–104. If two lesions are removed with one excision, only one excision code would be reported			
			73.	C	
			74.	C	
			75.	C	
28.	D		76.	A	
29.	B		77.	D	
30.	C		78.	D	
31.	D		79.	C	
32.	A		80.	A	
33.	D		81.	A	
34.	A	Codes 10060 and 10140 are used for I&Ds of superficial abscesses.	82.	C	
			83.	D	
35.	C		84.	B	
36.	C		85.	D	
37.	D		86.	B	
38.	B		87.	A	
39.	A		88.	B	
40.	B		89.	C	
41.	A		90.	B	
42.	D		91.	B	

Answer Key for CPT-4 Coding

92.	D		137.	D	
93.	C		138.	D	
94.	A		139.	B	
95.	A		140.	D	
96.	B		141.	C	
97.	C		142.	A	
98.	A		143.	D	
99.	D		144.	A	
100.	C		145.	D	
101.	D		146.	B	
102.	C		147.	D	
103.	D		148.	B	
104.	D		149.	D	
105.	D		150.	A	
106.	B		151.	C	
107.	B		152.	C	
108.	C		153.	A	
109.	C		154.	D	
110.	C		155.	B	
111.	C		156.	A	
112.	A		157.	D	
113.	A		158.	C	
114.	B		159.	A	
115.	D		160.	C	
116.	D		161.	D	
117.	C		162.	C	
118.	A		163.	A	
119.	D	When tubal ligation is performed at the same time as hysterotomy, use 58611 in addition to 59100	164.	D	
			165.	A	
			166.	D	
			167.	A	
120.	A		168.	B	
121.	D		169.	D	
122.	A		170.	A	
123.	C		171.	B	
124.	A		172.	D	
125.	B		173.	B	
126.	C		174.	B	
127.	A		175.	C	Code 92543 is for use when an irrigation substance is used.
128.	C				
129.	A		176.	C	
130.	C		177.	A	
131.	C		178.	B	
132.	B		179.	D	
133.	D		180.	B	
134.	C		181.	C	
135.	A		182	A	
136.	B				

Answer Key for CPT-4 Coding

183.	D	
184.	C	
185.	A	Casting is included in the surgical procedure.
186.	B	
187.	C	
188.	D	
189.	C	In order to use the code for the panel, every test must have been performed.
190.	B	Code both the arthroscopic procedure and the open procedure. Both need to be reported because there were two separate procedures. Modifier -59 must be added to code 29826 because it is a component of the comprehensive procedure 23412. That is allowed if an appropriate modifier is used per NCCI edits.
191.	D	
192.	C	According to CPT guidelines, when a patient is admitted to the hospital on the same day as an office visit, the office visit is not billable. Code rules do not allow the use of 402.91 because the scenario given does not state that the patient has hypertensive heart disease.

193.	D	According to the CPT coding guidelines for vaccines, only a separate identifiable Evaluation and Management code may be billed in addition to the vaccine. In this scenario, the patient was seen only for his vaccines. This guideline immediately eliminates all the other answers.
194.	A	
195.	C	
196.	C	
197.	A	Report this code only once no matter how many units were given.
198.	B	
199.	D	
200.	D	
201.	D	
202.	D	
203.	A	
204.	A	
205.	D	
206.	C	
207.	B	
208.	A	
209.	C	
210.	D	
211.	A	
212.	B	
213.	D	
214.	B	
215.	C	
216.	B	
217.	B	

REFERENCES

American Medical Association (AMA). *CPT assistant*. Chicago: Author.

American Medical Association (AMA). (2013). *Principles of CPT coding* (7th ed.). Chicago: Author.

American Medical Association (AMA). (2013). *Physician's current procedural terminology (CPT) 2014, Professional Edition*. Chicago: Author.

Green, M. (2014). *3-2-1 Code It!* (4th ed.). Clifton Park, NY: Delmar Cengage Learning.

Hazelwood, A., & Venable, C. (2013). *ICD-9-CM and ICD-10-CM coding and reimbursement for physician services*. Chicago: American Health Information Management Association (AHIMA).

Johnson, S. L., & Linker, R. (2013). *Understanding medical coding: A comprehensive guide* (3rd ed.). Clifton Park, NY: Delmar Cengage Learning.

Smith, G. (2012). *Basic current procedural terminology and HCPCS coding, 2013 edition*. Chicago: American Health Information Management Association (AHIMA).

Smith, G. (2) (2011). *Coding surgical procedures: Beyond the basics*. Clifton Park, NY. Delmar Cengage Learning.

ICD-10-CM/PCS Competencies

Question	CCA Domain
1–203	1

VIII. Medical Billing and Reimbursement Systems

Toni Cade, MBA, RHIA, CCS, FAHIMA

1. The case-mix management system that utilizes information from the Minimum Data Set (MDS) in long-term care settings is called
   A. Medicare Severity Diagnosis Related Groups (MS-DRGs).
   B. Resource Based Relative Value System (RBRVS).
   C. Resource Utilization Groups (RUGs).
   D. Ambulatory Patient Classifications (APCs).

REFERENCE: Green, p 862

2. The prospective payment system used to reimburse home health agencies for patients with Medicare utilizes data from the:
   A. MDS (Minimum Data Set).
   B. OASIS (Outcome and Assessment Information Set).
   C. UHDDS (Uniform Hospital Discharge Data Set).
   D. UACDS (Uniform Ambulatory Core Data Set).

REFERENCE: Green, p 863
                Schraffenberger and Kuehn, p 140

3. Under APCs, the payment status indicator "N" means that the payment
   A. is for ancillary services.
   B. is for a clinic or an emergency visit.
   C. is discounted at 50%.
   D. is packaged into the payment for other services.

REFERENCE: Sayles, pp 275–276

4. All of the following items are "packaged" under the Medicare outpatient prospective payment system, EXCEPT for
   A. recovery room.   C. anesthesia.
   B. medical supplies.   D. medical visits.

REFERENCE: LaTour, Eichenwald-Maki, and Oachs, p 393
              Sayles, p 330

5. Under the RBRVS, each HCPCS/CPT code contains three components, each having assigned relative value units. These three components are
   A. geographic index, wage index, and cost of living index.
   B. fee-for-service, per diem payment, and capitation.
   C. conversion factor, CMS weight, and hospital-specific rate.
   D. physician work, practice expense, and malpractice insurance expense.

REFERENCE: Green, p 867

6. The prospective payment system used to reimburse hospitals for Medicare hospital outpatients is called
   A. APGs.   C. APCs.
   B. RBRVS.   D. MS-DRGs.

REFERENCE: Green, p 863
                Schraffenberger and Kuehn, p 196

7. A Medicare patient was seen by Dr. Zachary, who is a nonparticipating physician. The charge for the office visit was $125. The Medicare beneficiary had already met his deductible. The Medicare Fee Schedule amount is $100. Dr. Zachary does not accept assignment. The office manager will apply a practice termed as "balance billing," which means that the patient is
   A. financially liable for the Medicare Fee Schedule amount.
   B. financially liable for charges in excess of the Medicare Fee Schedule, up to a limit.
   C. not financially liable for any amount.
   D. financially liable for only the deductible.

REFERENCE: Sayles, pp 295–297

8. The prospective payment system based on resource utilization groups (RUGs) is used for reimbursement to _____ for patients with Medicare.
   A. freestanding ambulatory surgery centers
   B. hospital-based outpatients
   C. intermediate care facilities
   D. skilled nursing facilities

REFERENCE: Schraffenberger and Kuehn, p 212

9. The _____ is a statement sent to the provider to explain payments made by third-party payers.
   A. remittance advice   C. attestation statement
   B. advance beneficiary notice   D. acknowledgment notice

REFERENCE: Green, p 886
                Green and Rowell, p 768

10. How many major diagnostic categories are there in the MS-DRG system?
    A. 100   C. 80
    B. 2,000   D. 25

REFERENCE: Scott, p 37

11. The computer-to-computer transfer of data between providers and third-party payers in a data format agreed upon by both parties is called
    A. HIPAA (Health Insurance Portability and Accountability Act).
    B. electronic data interchange (EDI).
    C. health information exchange (HIE).
    D. health data exchange (HDE).

REFERENCE: Green and Rowell, pp 76, 751

12. A computer software program that assigns appropriate MS-DRGs according to the information provided for each episode of care is called a(n)
    A. encoder.
    C. grouper.
    B. case-mix analyzer.
    D. scrubber.

REFERENCE: Casto and Forrestal, p 134

13. The standard claim form used by hospitals to request reimbursement for inpatient and outpatient procedures performed or services provided is called the
    A. UB-04.
    C. CMS-1491.
    B. CMS-1500.
    D. CMS-1600.

REFERENCE: Brown and Tyler, p 37
                      Green and Rowell, p 771
                      Scott, p 76

14. Under ASCs, when multiple procedures are performed during the same surgical session, a payment reduction is applied. The procedure in the highest level group is reimbursed at _____ and all remaining procedures are reimbursed at _____.
    A. 50%, 25%
    C. 100%, 25%
    B. 100%, 50%
    D. 100%, 75%

REFERENCE: Casto and Forrestal, p 192

15. The _____ refers to a statement sent to the patient to show how much the provider billed, how much Medicare reimbursed the provider, and what the patient must pay the provider.
    A. Medicare summary notice
    C. advance beneficiary notice
    B. remittance advice
    D. coordination of benefits

REFERENCE: Green and Rowell, p 762
                      LaTour, Eichenwald-Maki, and Oachs, p 445
                      Sayles, pp 289–290

16. Currently, which prospective payment system is used to determine the payment to the "physician" for physician services covered under Medicare Part B, such as outpatient surgery performed on a Medicare patient?
    A. MS-DRGs
    C. RBRVS
    B. APCs
    D. ASCs

REFERENCE: Green, p 867
                      Schraffenberger and Kuehn, p 210

17. Which of the following best describes the situation of a provider who agrees to accept assignment for Medicare Part B services?
    A. The provider is reimbursed at 15% above the allowed charge.
    B. The provider is paid according to the Medicare Physician Fee Schedule (MPFS) plus 10%.
    C. The provider cannot bill the patients for the balance between the MPFS amount and the total charges.
    D. The provider is a nonparticipating provider.

REFERENCE: Green and Rowell, p 536

18. When the MS-DRG payment received by the hospital is lower than the actual charges for providing the inpatient services for a patient with Medicare, then the hospital
    A. makes a profit.
    B. can bill the patient for the difference.
    C. absorbs the loss.
    D. can bill Medicare for the difference.

REFERENCE: LaTour, Eichenwald-Maki, and Oachs, p 432

19. Under ASCs, bilateral procedures are reimbursed at _____ of the payment rate for their group.
    A. 50%   C. 200%
    B. 100%   D. 150%

REFERENCE: Casto and Forrestal, p 192

Use the following table to answer questions 20 through 23.

Plantation Hospital's TOP 10 MS-DRGs

MS-DRG	Description	Number of Patients	CMS Relative Weight
470	Major joint replacement or reattachment of lower extremity w/o MCC	2,750	1.9871
392	Esophagitis, gastroent & misc. digestive disorders w/o MCC	2,200	0.7121
194	Simple pneumonia & pleurisy w CC	1,150	1.0235
247	Perc cardiovasc proc 2 drug-eluting stent w/o MCC	900	2.1255
293	Heart failure & shock w/o CC/MCC	850	0.8765
313	Chest pain	650	0.5489
292	Heart failure & shock w CC	550	1.0134
690	Kidney & urinary tract infections w/o MCC	400	0.8000
192	Chronic obstructive pulmonary disease w/o CC/MCC	300	0.8145
871	Septicemia w/o MV 96+ hours w MCC	250	1.7484

20. The case-mix index (CMI) for the top 10 MS-DRGs above is
    A. 1.164.   C. 0.782.
    B. 1.278.   D. 1.097.

REFERENCE: Abdelhak, Grostick, and Hanken, p 671
              Casto and Forrestal, p 127
              Sayles, p 269

21. Which individual MS-DRGs has the highest reimbursement?
    A. 247   C. 871
    B. 470   D. 293
REFERENCE: Casto and Forrestal, p 127
                  Sayles, p 269

22. Based on this patient volume, during this time period, the MS-DRG that brings in the highest "total" reimbursement to the hospital is
    A. 470.   C. 392.
    B. 247.   D. 871.
REFERENCE: Casto and Forrestal, p 127
                  Sayles, p 296

23. Based on this patient volume, the MS-DRG that brings in the highest total profit to the hospital is
    A. 470.   C. 392.
    B. 247.   D. It cannot be determined from this information.
REFERENCE: Casto and Forrestal, p 127
                  Sayles, p 269

24. The Health Insurance Portability and Accountability Act (HIPAA) requires the retention of health insurance claims and accounting records for a minimum of ____ years, unless state law specifies a longer period.
    A. six
    B. five
    C. seven
    D. ten
REFERENCE: Green and Rowell, p 114

25. ____ is knowingly making false statements or representation of material facts to obtain a benefit or payment for which no entitlement would otherwise exist.
    A. Fraud
    B. Whistle-blowing
    C. Abuse
    D. Assault
REFERENCE: Abdelhak, Gorstick, and Hanken, p 672

26. These are assigned to every HCPCS/CPT code under the Medicare hospital outpatient prospective payment system to identify how the service or procedure described by the code would be paid.
    A. geographic practice cost indices   C. minimum data set
    B. major diagnostic categories   D. payment status indicator
REFERENCE: Casto and Forrestal, p 177

27. The term used to indicate that the service or procedure is reasonable and necessary for the diagnosis or treatment of illness or injury consistent with generally accepted standards of care is
    A. appropriateness.   C. benchmarking.
    B. evidence-based medicine.   D. medical necessity.
REFERENCE: Green and Rowell, pp 4, 146

28. This law prohibits a physician from referring Medicare patients to clinical laboratory services where the doctor or a member of his family has a financial interest.
    A. the False Claims Act
    B. the Civil Monetary Penalties Act
    C. the Federal Antikickback Statute
    D. the Stark I Law

REFERENCE: Green, p 884
               Green and Bowie, p 325

29. ____ are errors in medical care that are clearly identifiable, preventable, and serious in their consequences for patients.
    A. Sentinel events
    B. Adverse preventable events
    C. Never events
    D. Potential compensable events

REFERENCE: Green and Bowie, p 326

30. When a provider, knowingly or unknowingly, uses practices that are inconsistent with accepted medical practice and that directly or indirectly result in unnecessary costs to the Medicare program, this is called
    A. fraud.
    B. abuse.
    C. unbundling.
    D. hypercoding.

REFERENCE: Abdelhak, Gostick, and Hanken, p 672

31. What prospective payment system reimburses the provider according to prospectively determined rates for a 60-day episode of care?
    A. home health resource groups
    B. inpatient rehabilitation facility
    C. long-term care Medicare severity diagnosis-related groups
    D. the skilled nursing facility prospective payment system

REFERENCE: Green and Bowie, p 313

32. If the Medicare non-PAR approved payment amount is $128.00 for a proctoscopy, what is the total Medicare approved payment amount for a doctor who does not accept assignment, applying the limiting charge for this procedure?
    A. $140.80   C. $192.00
    B. $143.00   D. $147.20

REFERENCE: Green and Rowell, pp 64–65

33. Under the inpatient prospective payment system (IPPS), there is a 3-day payment window (formerly referred to as the 72-hour rule). This rule requires that outpatient preadmission services that are provided by a hospital up to three calendar days prior to a patient's inpatient admission be covered by the IPPS MS-DRG payment for
    A. diagnostic services.
    B. therapeutic (or nondiagnostic) services whereby the inpatient principal diagnosis code (ICD-9-CM) exactly matches the code used for preadmission services.
    C. therapeutic (or nondiagnostic) services whereby the inpatient principal diagnosis code (ICD-9-CM) does not match the code used for preadmission services.
    D. both A and B.

REFERENCE: Green, pp 858–859
               Green and Bowie, p 313
               Green and Rowell, pp 371–372

34. This initiative was instituted by the government to eliminate fraud and abuse and recover overpayments, and involves the use of _____. Charts are audited to identify Medicare overpayments and underpayments. These entities are paid based on a percentage of money they identify and collect on behalf of the government.
    A. Clinical Data Abstraction Centers (CDAC)
    B. Quality Improvement Organizations (QIO)
    C. Medicare Code Editors (MCE)
    D. Recovery Audit Contractors (RAC)

REFERENCE: Green, p 850
               Scott, p 119

35. When a patient is discharged from the inpatient rehabilitation facility and returns within three calendar days (prior to midnight on the third day) this is called a(n)
    A. interrupted stay.   C. per diem.
    B. transfer.   D. qualified discharge.

REFERENCE: Casto and Forrestal, pp 233–234
               Scott, pp 68–69

36. In a global payment methodology, which is sometimes applied to radiological and similar types of procedures that involve professional and technical components, all of the following are part of the "technical" components EXCEPT
    A. radiological equipment.   C. radiological supplies.
    B. physician services.   D. radiologic technicians

REFERENCE: Green and Rowell, p 320
               LaTour, Eichenwald-Maki, and Oachs, p 430
               Sayles, pp 263–264

37. Changes in case-mix index (CMI) may be attributed to all of the following factors EXCEPT
    A. changes in medical staff composition.
    B. changes in coding rules.
    C. changes in services offered.
    D. changes in coding productivity.

REFERENCE: Schraffenberger and Kuehn, pp 484–485

38. This prospective payment system replaced the Medicare physician payment system of "customary, prevailing, and reasonable (CPR)" charges whereby physicians were reimbursed according to their historical record of the charge for the provision of each service.
    A. Medicare Physician Fee Schedule (MPFS)
    B. Medicare Severity-Diagnosis Related Groups (MS-DRGs)
    C. Global payment
    D. Capitation

REFERENCE: Green, p 867
               Green and Rowell, pp 379–380

39. CMS-identified "Hospital-Acquired Conditions" mean that when a particular diagnosis is not "present on admission," CMS determines it to be
    A. medically necessary.
    B. reasonably preventable.
    C. a valid comorbidity.
    D. the principal diagnosis.

REFERENCE: LaTour, Eichenwald-Maki, and Oachs, pp 433–434

40. This process involves the gathering of charge documents from all departments within the facility that have provided services to patients. The purpose is to make certain that all charges are coded and entered into the billing system.
    A. precertification
    B. insurance verification
    C. charge capturing
    D. revenue cycle

REFERENCE: Diamond, p 9

41. The Correct Coding Initiative (CCI) edits contain a listing of codes under two columns titled "comprehensive codes" and "component codes." According to the CCI edits, when a provider bills Medicare for a procedure that appears in both columns for the same beneficiary on the same date of service
    A. code only the component code.
    B. do not code either one.
    C. code only the comprehensive code.
    D. code both the comprehensive code and the component code.

REFERENCE: Green, pp 395–398
               Green and Rowell, p 333

42. The following type of hospital is considered excluded when it applies for and receives a waiver from CMS. This means that the hospital does not participate in the inpatient prospective payment system (IPPS)
    A. rehabilitation hospital
    B. long-term care hospital
    C. psychiatric hospital
    D. cancer hospital

REFERENCE: Green, p 858

43. These are financial protections to ensure that certain types of facilities (e.g., children's hospitals) recoup all of their losses due to the differences in their APC payments and the pre-APC payments.
    A. limiting charge
    B. indemnity insurance
    C. hold harmless
    D. pass through

REFERENCE: Casto and Forrestal, p 176

44. LCDs and NCDs are review policies that describe the circumstances of coverage for various types of medical treatment. They advise physicians which services Medicare considers reasonable and necessary and may indicate the need for an advance beneficiary notice. They are developed by the Centers for Medicare and Medicaid Services (CMS) and Medicare Administrative Contractors. LCD and NCD are acronyms that stand for
    A. local covered determinations and noncovered determinations.
    B. local coverage determinations and national coverage determinations.
    C. list of covered decisions and noncovered decisions.
    D. local contractor's decisions and national contractor's decisions.

REFERENCE: Green, p 775
               Green and Rowell, pp 418–419

Use the following table to answer questions 45 through 50.

EXAMPLE OF A CHARGE DESCRIPTION MASTER (CDM) FILE LAYOUT

Charge Service Code	Item Service Description	General Ledger Key	HCPCS Code		Charge	Revenue Code	Activity Date
			Medicare	Medicaid			
49683105	CT scan; head; w/out contrast	3	70450	70450	500.00	0351	1/1/2013
49683106	CT scan; head; with contrast	3	70460	70460	675.00	0351	1/1/2013

45. This information is printed on the UB-04 claim form to represent the cost center (e.g., lab, radiology, cardiology, respiratory, etc.) for the department in which the item is provided. It is used for Medicare billing.
    A. HCPCS
    B. revenue code
    C. charge/service code
    D. general ledger key

REFERENCE: Green, pp 870–871
               Green and Rowell, pp 386–388
               Schraffenberger and Kuehn, pp 225–226

46. This information is used because it provides a uniform system of identifying procedures, services, or supplies. Multiple columns can be available for various financial classes.
    A. HCPCS code
    B. revenue code
    C. general ledger key
    D. charge/service code

REFERENCE: Green, pp 780–781
               Green and Rowell, pp 386–388
               Schraffenberger and Kuehn, pp 226–227

47. This information provides a narrative name of the services provided. This information should be presented in a clear and concise manner. When possible, the narratives from the HCPCS/CPT book should be utilized.
    A. general ledger key
    B. HCPCS
    C. item/service description
    D. revenue code

REFERENCE: Green, pp 870–871
                Green and Rowell, pp 386–388
                Schraffenberger and Kuehn, p 225

48. This information is the numerical identification of the service or supply. Each item has a unique number with a prefix that indicates the department number (the number assigned to a specific ancillary department) and an item number (the number assigned by the accounting department or the business office) for a specific procedure or service represented on the chargemaster.
    A. charge/service code
    B. HCPCS code
    C. revenue code
    D. general ledger key

REFERENCE: Green, pp 870–871
                Green and Rowell, pp 386–388
                Schraffenberger and Kuehn, p 225

49. This information is used to assign each item to a particular section of the general ledger in a particular facility's accounting section. Reports can be generated from this information to include statistics related to volume in terms of numbers, dollars, and payer types.
    A. general ledger key
    B. charge/service code
    C. revenue code
    D. HCPCS code

REFERENCE: Green, pp 870–871
                Schraffenberger and Kuehn, p 225

50. Under APCs, the patient is responsible for paying the coinsurance amount based upon ____ of the national median charge for the services rendered.
    A. 50%
    B. 15%
    C. 20%
    D. 80%

REFERENCE: Green and Bowie, p 314

51. ____ is a joint federal and state program that provides health care coverage to low-income populations and certain aged and disabled individuals.
    A. TRICARE
    B. Medicare Part A
    C. Medicaid
    D. Medicare Part B

REFERENCE: Green, p 851

52. The DNFB report includes all patients who have been discharged from the facility but for whom, for one reason or another, the billing process is not complete. DNFB is an acronym for

    _____.
    A. diagnosis not finally balanced
    B. days not fiscally balanced
    C. dollars not fully billed
    D. discharged not final billed

REFERENCE: Schraffenberger and Kuehn, p 461

53. The limiting charge is a percentage limit on fees specified by legislation that the nonparticipating physician may bill Medicare beneficiaries above the non-PAR fee schedule amount. The limiting charge is
   A. 10%.
   B. 15%.
   C. 20%.
   D. 50%.

REFERENCE: Green and Rowell, pp 380–383

Use the following case scenario to answer questions 54 through 58.

A patient with Medicare is seen in the physician's office.
The total charge for this office visit is $250.00.
The patient has previously paid his deductible under Medicare Part B.
The PAR Medicare Fee Schedule amount for this service is $200.00.
The non-PAR Medicare Fee Schedule amount for this service is $190.00.

54. The patient is financially liable for the coinsurance amount, which is
   A. 80%.
   B. 100%.
   C. 20%.
   D. 15%.

REFERENCE: Green and Rowell, pp 380–383

55. If this physician is a participating physician who accepts assignment for this claim, the total amount the physician will receive is
   A. $200.00.
   B. $250.00.
   C. $218.50.
   D. $190.00.

REFERENCE: Green and Rowell, pp 380–383

56. If this physician is a nonparticipating physician who does NOT accept assignment for this claim, the total amount the physician will receive is
   A. $250.00.
   B. $200.00.
   C. $218.50.
   D. $190.00.

REFERENCE: Green and Rowell, pp 380–383

57. If this physician is a participating physician who accepts assignment for this claim, the total amount of the patient's financial liability (out-of-pocket expense) is
   A. $200.00.
   B. $40.00.
   C. $160.00.
   D. $30.00.

REFERENCE: Green and Rowell, pp 380–383

58. If this physician is a nonparticipating physician who does NOT accept assignment for this claim, the total amount of the patient's financial liability (out-of-pocket expense) is
   A. $66.50.
   B. $38.00.
   C. $190.00.
   D. $152.00.

REFERENCE: Green and Rowell, pp 380–383

59. A fiscal year is a yearly accounting period. It is the 12-month period on which a budget is planned. The federal fiscal year is
   A. October 1st through September 30 of the next year.
   B. January 1st through December 31.
   C. July 1st through the June 30 of the next year.
   D. April 1st through March 31 of the next year.

REFERENCE: Casto and Forrestal, p 309

60. There are times when documentation is incomplete or insufficient to support the diagnoses found in the chart. The most common way of communicating with the physician for answers is by
    A. e-mailing physicians.
    B. using physician query forms.
    C. calling the physician's office.
    D. leaving notes in the chart.

REFERENCE: Green, pp 15–17
               Scott, pp 189–199

61. Under APCs, payment status indicator "X" means
    A. ancillary services.
    B. clinic or emergency department visit (medical visits).
    C. significant procedure, multiple procedure reduction applies.
    D. significant procedure, not discounted when multiple.

REFERENCE: Casto and Forrestal, p 177
               Diamond, p 337
               LaTour, Eichenwald-Maki, and Oachs, p 436

62. Under APCs, payment status indicator "V" means
    A. ancillary services.
    B. clinic or emergency department visit (medical visits).
    C. inpatient procedure.
    D. significant procedure, not discounted when multiple.

REFERENCE: Casto and Forrestal, p 177
               Diamond, p 337
               LaTour, Eichenwald-Maki, and Oachs, p 436

63. Under APCs, payment status indicator "S" means
    A. ancillary services.
    B. clinic or emergency department visit (medical visits).
    C. significant procedure, multiple procedure reduction applies.
    D. significant procedure, multiple procedure reduction does not apply.

REFERENCE: Casto and Forrestal, p 177
               Diamond, p 337
               Green and Rowell, pp 373–374
               LaTour, Eichenwald-Maki, and Oachs, p 436

64. Under APCs, payment status indicator "T" means
    A. ancillary services.
    B. clinic or emergency department visit (medical visits).
    C. significant procedure, multiple procedure reduction applies.
    D. significant procedure, not discounted when multiple.

REFERENCE: Casto and Forrestal, p 177
               Diamond, p 337
               Green, pp 863–864
               LaTour, Eichenwald-Maki, and Oachs, p 436

65. Under APCs, payment status indicator "C" means
    A. ancillary services.
    B. inpatient procedures/services.
    C. significant procedure, multiple procedure reduction applies.
    D. significant procedure, not discounted when multiple.

REFERENCE: Casto and Forrestal, p 177
               Diamond, p 337
               LaTour, Eichenwald-Maki, and Oachs, p 436

66. This is a 10-digit, intelligence-free, numeric identifier designed to replace all previous provider legacy numbers. This number identifies the physician universally to all payers. This number is issued to all HIPAA-covered entities. It is mandatory on the CMS-1500 and UB-04 claim forms.
    A. National Practitioner Databank (NPD)
    B. Universal Physician Number (UPN)
    C. Master Patient Index (MPI)
    D. National Provider Identifier (NPI)

REFERENCE: Green and Rowell, pp 29, 126
               Rimmer, p 30

67. In the managed care industry, there are specific reimbursement concepts, such as "capitation." All of the following statements are true in regard to the concept of "capitation," EXCEPT
    A. each service is paid based on the actual charges.
    B. the volume of services and their expense do not affect reimbursement.
    C. capitation means paying a fixed amount per member per month.
    D. capitation involves a group of physicians or an individual physician.

REFERENCE: Green and Rowell, p 45

68. Which of the following statements is FALSE regarding the use of modifiers with the CPT codes?
    A. All modifiers will alter (increase or decrease) the reimbursement of the procedure.
    B. Some procedures may require more than one modifier.
    C. Modifiers are appended to the end of the CPT code.
    D. Not all procedures need a modifier.

REFERENCE: Richards, p 147

69. This document is published by the Office of Inspector General (OIG) every year. It details the OIG's focus for Medicare fraud and abuse for that year. It gives health care providers an indication of general and specific areas that are targeted for review. It can be found on the Internet on CMS' Web site.
    A. the OIG's Evaluation and Management Documentation Guidelines
    B. the OIG's Model Compliance Plan
    C. the Federal Register
    D. the OIG's Workplan

REFERENCE: Sayles, p 305

70. Accounts Receivable (A/R) refers to
    A. cases that have not yet been paid.
    B. the amount the hospital was paid.
    C. cases that have been paid.
    D. denials that have been returned to the hospital.

REFERENCE: Schraffenberger and Kuehn, p 458

71. The following coding system(s) is/are utilized in the MS-DRG prospective payment methodology for assignment and proper reimbursement.
    A. HCPCS/CPT codes
    B. ICD-9-CM codes
    C. both HCPCS/CPT codes and ICD-9-CM codes
    D. none of the above

REFERENCE: Green, p 862
               Sayles, p 267

72. The following coding system(s) is/are utilized in the Inpatient Psychiatric Facilities (IPFs) prospective payment methodology for assignment and proper reimbursement.
    A. HCPCS/CPT codes
    B. ICD-9-CM codes
    C. both HCPCS/CPT codes and ICD-9-CM codes
    D. none of the above

REFERENCE: Green, p 865
               Sayles, p 285

73. An Advance Beneficiary Notice (ABN) is a document signed by the
    A. utilization review coordinator indicating that the patient stay is not medically necessary.
    B. physician advisor indicating that the patient's stay is denied.
    C. patient indicating whether he/she wants to receive services that Medicare probably will not pay for.
    D. provider indicating that Medicare will not pay for certain services.

REFERENCE: Green, p 358
               LaTour, Eichenwald-Maki, and Oachs, pp 449–450

74. CMS identified Hospital-Acquired Conditions (HACs). Some of these HACs include foreign objects retained after surgery, blood incompatibility, and catheter-associated urinary tract infection. The importance of the HAC payment provision is that the hospital
    A. will receive additional payment for these conditions when they are not present on admission.
    B. will not receive additional payment for these conditions when they are not present on admission.
    C. will receive additional payment for these conditions whether they are present on admission or not.
    D. will not receive additional payment for these conditions when they are present on admission.

REFERENCE: LaTour, Eichenwald-Maki, and Oachs, pp 433–434

75. Under Medicare Part B, all of the following statements are true and are applicable to nonparticipating physician providers, EXCEPT
    A. providers must file all Medicare claims.
    B. nonparticipating providers have a higher fee schedule than that for participating providers.
    C. fees are restricted to charging no more than the "limiting charge" on nonassigned claims.
    D. collections are restricted to only the deductible and coinsurance due at the time of service on an assigned claim.

REFERENCE: Green and Rowell, pp 380–383

76. Under Medicare, a beneficiary has lifetime reserve days. All of the following statements are true, EXCEPT
    A. the patient has a total of 60 lifetime reserve days.
    B. lifetime reserve days are usually reserved for use during the patient's final (terminal) hospital stay.
    C. lifetime reserve days are paid under Medicare Part B.
    D. lifetime reserve days are not renewable, meaning once a patient uses all of their lifetime reserve days, the patient is responsible for the total charges.

REFERENCE: Green and Rowell, pp 528–529

77. When a provider bills separately for procedures that are a part of the major procedure, this is called
    A. fraud.   C. unbundling.
    B. packaging.   D. discounting.

REFERENCE: Brown and Tyler, p 192

78. Once all data are posted to a patient's account, the claim can be reviewed for accuracy and completeness. Many facilities have internal auditing systems. The auditing systems run each claim through a set of edits specifically designed for the various third-party payers. The auditing system identifies data that have failed edits and flags the claim for correction. These "internal" auditing systems are called
    A. scrubbers.   C. groupers.
    B. pricers.   D. encoders.

REFERENCE: Casto and Forrestal, p 262

79. To compute the reimbursement to a particular hospital for a particular MS-DRG, multiply the hospital's base payment rate by the
    A. conversion factor.   C. geographic practice cost index.
    B. case-mix index.   D. relative weight for the MS-DRG.

REFERENCE: Casto and Forrestal, p 134

80. Under the APC methodology, discounted payments occur when
    A. there are two or more (multiple) procedures that are assigned to status indicator "T."
    B. there are two or more (multiple) procedures that are assigned to status indicator "S."
    C. modifier-73 is used to indicate a procedure is terminated after the patient is prepared but before anesthesia is started.
    D. both A and C.

REFERENCE: Green and Rowell, pp 373–374
               Schraffenberger and Kuehn, pp 207–209

81. This prospective payment system is for _____ and utilizes a Patient Assessment Instrument (PAI) to classify patients into case-mix groups (CMGs).
    A. skilled nursing facilities
    B. inpatient rehabilitation facilities
    C. home health agencies
    D. long-term acute care hospitals

REFERENCE: Green and Rowell, p 377
              Schraffenberger and Kuehn, p 213

82. Home Health Agencies (HHAs) utilize a data entry software system developed by the Centers for Medicare and Medicaid Services (CMS). This software is available to HHAs at no cost through the CMS Web site or on a CD-ROM.
    A. PACE (Patient Assessment and Comprehensive Evaluation)
    B. HAVEN (Home Assessment Validation and Entry)
    C. HHASS (Home Health Agency Software System)
    D. PEPP (Payment Error Prevention Program)

REFERENCE: Green and Rowell, p 367
              LaTour, Eichenwald-Maki, and Oachs, p 438
              Sayles, p 278

83. This information is published by the Medicare Administrative Contractors (MACs) to describe when and under what circumstances Medicare will cover a service. The ICD-9-CM and CPT/HCPCS codes are listed in the memoranda.
    A. LCD (Local Coverage Determinations)
    B. SI/IS (Severity of Ilness/Intensity of Service Criteria)
    C. OSHA (Occupational Safety and Health Administration)
    D. PEPP (Payment Error Prevention Program)

REFERENCE: Green and Rowell, pp 418–419

84. The term "hard coding" refers to
    A. HCPCS/CPT codes that are coded by the coders.
    B. HPCS/CPT codes that appear in the hospital's chargemaster and will be included automatically on the patient's bill.
    C. ICD-9-CM codes that are coded by the coders.
    D. ICD-9-CM codes that appear in the hospital's chargemaster and that are automatically included on the patient's bill.

REFERENCE: Schraffenberger and Kuehn, pp 228–229

85. This is the amount collected by the facility for the services it bills.
    A. costs
    B. charges
    C. reimbursement
    D. contractual allowance

REFERENCE: Schraffenberger and Kuehn, pp 433–434

86. Assume the patient has already met his or her deductible and that the physician is a Medicare participating (PAR) provider. The physician's standard fee for the services provided is $120.00. Medicare's PAR fee is $60.00. How much reimbursement will the physician receive from Medicare?
    A. $120.00
    B. $ 60.00
    C. $ 48.00
    D. $ 96.00

REFERENCE: Green and Rowell, pp 380–383

87. This accounting method attributes a dollar figure to every input required to provide a service.
    A. cost accounting
    B. charge accounting
    C. reimbursement
    D. contractual allowance

REFERENCE: Schraffenberger and Kuehn, p 433

88. This is the amount the facility actually bills for the services it provides.
    A. costs
    B. charges
    C. reimbursement
    D. contractual allowance

REFERENCE: Schraffenberger and Kuehn, p 433

89. This is the difference between what is charged and what is paid.
    A. costs
    B. customary
    C. reimbursement
    D. contractual allowance

REFERENCE: Schraffenberger and Kuehn, p 433

90. When appropriate, under the outpatient PPS, a hospital can use this CPT code in place of, but not in addition to, a code for a medical visit or emergency department service.
    A. CPT Code 99291 (critical care)
    B. CPT Code 99358 (prolonged evaluation and management service)
    C. CPT Code 35001 (direct repair of aneurysm)
    D. CPT Code 50300 (donor nephrectomy)

REFERENCE: Kirchoff, p 42

91. To monitor timely claims processing in a hospital, a summary report of "patient receivables" is generated frequently. Aged receivables can negatively affect a facility's cash flow; therefore, to maintain the facility's fiscal integrity, the HIM manager must routinely analyze this report. Though this report has no standard title, it is often called the
    A. remittance advice.
    B. periodic interim payments.
    C. DNFB (discharged, no final bill).
    D. chargemaster.

REFERENCE: LaTour, Eichenwald-Maki, and Oachs, p 470

92. Assume the patient has already met his or her deductible and that the physician is a nonparticipating Medicare provider but does accept assignment. The standard fee for the services provided is $120.00. Medicare's PAR fee is $60.00 and Medicare's non-PAR fee is $57.00. How much reimbursement will the physician receive from Medicare?
    A. $120.00
    B. $60.00
    C. $57.00
    D. $45.60

REFERENCE: Green and Rowell, pp 380–383

93. CMS assigns one _____ to each APC and each _____ code.
    A. payment status indicator, HCPCS
    B. CPT code, HCPCS
    C. MS-DRG, CPT
    D. payment status indicator, ICD-9-CM

REFERENCE: Kirchoff, p 11

94. All of the following statements are true of MS-DRGs, EXCEPT
    A. a patient claim may have multiple MS-DRGs.
    B. the MS-DRG payment received by the hospital may be lower than the actual cost of providing the services.
    C. special circumstances can result in a cost outlier payment to the hospital.
    D. there are several types of hospitals that are excluded from the Medicare inpatient PPS.

REFERENCE: Green and Rowell, pp 367–370
               Johns, pp 321–324
               LaTour, Eichenwald-Maki, and Oachs, pp 431–433
               Sayles, pp 266–270

95. This program, formerly called CHAMPUS (Civilian Health and Medical Program—Uniformed Services), is a health care program for active members of the military and other qualified family members.
    A. TRICARE   C. Indian Health Service
    B. CHAMPVA   D. workers' compensation

REFERENCE: Green and Rowell, p 602
               Richards, pp 116–118, 300
               Sayles, p 251

96. When health care providers are found guilty under any of the civil false claims statutes, the Office of Inspector General is responsible for negotiating these settlements and the provider is placed under a
    A. Fraud Prevention Memorandum of Understanding.
    B. Noncompliance Agreement.
    C. Corporate Integrity Agreement.
    D. Recovery Audit Contract.

REFERENCE: Brown and Tyler, p 267

97. Regarding hospital emergency department and hospital outpatient evaluation and management CPT code assignment, which statement is true?
    A. Each facility is accountable for developing and implementing its own methodology.
    B. The level of service codes reported by the facility must match those reported by the physician.
    C. Each facility must use the same methodology used by physician coders based on the history, examination, and medical decision-making components.
    D. Each facility must use acuity sheets with acuity levels and assign points for each service performed.

REFERENCE: Diamond, pp 285–287

98. CMS adjusts the Medicare Severity DRGs and the reimbursement rates every
    A. calendar year beginning January 1.
    B. quarter.
    C. month.
    D. fiscal year beginning October 1.

REFERENCE: Sayles, p 268

99. In calculating the fee for a physician's reimbursement, the three relative value units are each multiplied by the
    A. geographic practice cost indices.
    B. national conversion factor.
    C. usual and customary fees for the service.
    D. cost of living index for the particular region.

REFERENCE: Green, p 867
               Green and Rowell, pp 379–380

100. If a participating provider's usual fee for a service is $700.00 and Medicare's allowed amount is $450.00, what amount is written off by the physician?
    A. none of it is written off   C. $340.00
    B. $250.00   D. $391.00

REFERENCE: Green and Rowell, pp 380–383

101. Health plans that use _____ reimbursement methods issue lump-sum payments to providers to compensate them for all the health care services delivered to a patient for a specific illness and/or over a specific period of time.
    A. episode-of-care (EOC)   C. fee-for-service
    B. capitation   D. bundled

REFERENCE: Sayles, p 262

102. _____ offers voluntary, supplemental medical insurance to help pay for physician's services, outpatient hospital services, medical services, and medical-surgical supplies not covered by the hospitalization plan.
    A. Medicare Part A
    B. Medicare Part B
    C. Medicare Part C
    D. Medicare Part D

REFERENCE: Kirchoff, p 296

103. Commercial insurance plans usually reimburse health care providers under some type of _____ payment system, whereas the federal Medicare program uses some type of _____ payment system.
    A. prospective, retrospective   C. retrospective, prospective
    B. retrospective, concurrent   D. prospective, concurrent

REFERENCE: Green and Rowell, pp 360–361
               Sayles, pp 260–261

104. When the third-party payer refuses to grant payment to the provider, this is called a
    A. denied claim.
    B. clean claim.
    C. rejected claim.
    D. unprocessed claim.

REFERENCE: Rimmer, p 62

105. Some services are performed by a nonphysician practitioner (such as a Physician Assistant). These services are an integral yet incidental component of a physician's treatment. A physician must have personally performed an initial visit and must remain actively involved in the continuing care. Medicare requires direct supervision for these services to be billed. This is called
    A. "Technical component" billing.
    B. "Assignment" billing.
    C. "Incident to" billing.
    D. "Assistant" billing.

REFERENCE: Green and Rowell, p 385

106. When payments can be made to the provider by EFT, this means that the reimbursement is
    A. sent to the provider by check.
    B. sent to the patient, who then pays the provider.
    C. combined with all other payments from the third party payer.
    D. directly deposited into the provider's bank account.

REFERENCE: Richards, p 175

107. The following services are excluded under the Hospital Outpatient Prospective Payment System (OPPS) Ambulatory Payment Classification (APC) methodology.
    A. surgical procedures
    B. clinical lab services
    C. clinic/emergency visits
    D. radiology/radiation therapy

REFERENCE: Diamond, p 333

108. A HIPPS (Health Insurance Prospective Payment System) code is a five-character alphanumeric code. A HIPPS code is used by
    A. ambulatory surgery centers (ASC).
    B. home health agencies (HHA).
    C. inpatient rehabilitation facilities (IRF).
    D. B and C.

REFERENCE: Casto and Forrestal, p 310

109. The Centers for Medicare and Medicaid Services (CMS) will make an adjustment to the MS-DRG payment for certain conditions that the patient was not admitted with, but were acquired during the hospital stay. Therefore, hospitals are required to report an indicator for each diagnosis. This indicator is referred to as
    A. a sentinel event.
    B. a payment status indicator.
    C. a hospital acquired condition.
    D. present on admission.

REFERENCE: Casto and Forrestal, pp 293–294

110. A patient is admitted for a diagnostic workup for cachexia. The final diagnosis is malignant neoplasm of lung with metastasis. The present on admission (POA) indicator is
    A. Y = Present at the time of inpatient admission.
    B. N = Not present at the time of inpatient admission.
    C. U = Documentation is insufficient to determine if condition was present at the time of admission.
    D. W = Provider is unable to clinically determine if condition was present at the time of admission.

REFERENCE: Green, p 861
              LaTour, Eichenwald-Maki, and Oachs, pp 433–434

111. A patient undergoes outpatient surgery. During the recovery period, the patient develops atrial fibrillation and is subsequently admitted to the hospital as an inpatient. The present on admission (POA) indicator is
    A. Y = Present at the time of inpatient admission.
    B. N = Not present at the time of inpatient admission.
    C. U = Documentation is insufficient to determine if condition was present at the time of admission.
    D. W = Provider is unable to clinically determine if condition was present at the time of admission.

REFERENCE: Green, p 861
              LaTour, Eichenwald-Maki, and Oachs, pp 433–434

112. A patient is admitted to the hospital for a coronary artery bypass surgery. Postoperatively, he develops a pulmonary embolism. The present on admission (POA) indicator is
    A. Y = Present at the time of inpatient admission.
    B. N = Not present at the time of inpatient admission.
    C. U = Documentation is insufficient to determine if condition was present at the time of admission.
    D. W = Provider is unable to clinically determine if condition was present at the time of admission.

REFERENCE: Green, p 861
              LaTour, Eichenwald-Maki, and Oachs, pp 433–434

113. The nursing initial assessment upon admission documents the presence of a decubitus ulcer. There is no mention of the decubitus ulcer in the physician documentation until several days after admission. The present on admission (POA) indicator is
    A. Y = Present at the time of inpatient admission.
    B. N = Not present at the time of inpatient admission.
    C. U = Documentation is insufficient to determine if condition was present at the time of admission.
    D. W = Provider is unable to clinically determine if condition was present at the time of admission.

REFERENCE: Green, p 861
              LaTour, Eichenwald-Maki, and Oachs, pp 433–434

114. The present on admission (POA) indicator is required to be assigned to the _____ diagnosis(es) for _____ claims on _____ admissions.
    A. principal and secondary, Medicare, inpatient
    B. principal, all, inpatient
    C. principal and secondary, all, inpatient and outpatient
    D. principal, Medicare, inpatient and outpatient

REFERENCE: Green, p 861
              LaTour, Eichenwald-Maki, and Oachs, pp 433–434

Answer Key for Medical Billing and Reimbursement Systems

	ANSWER	EXPLANATION
1.	C	
2.	B	
3.	A	
4.	D	
5.	D	
6.	C	
7.	B	
8.	D	
9.	A	
10.	D	
11.	B	
12.	C	
13.	A	The UB-04 is used by hospitals. The CMS-1500 is used by physicians and other noninstitutional providers and suppliers. The CMS-1491 is used by ambulance services.
14.	B	
15.	A	
16.	C	The prospective payment system used to reimburse the "hospital" for outpatient surgery is APCs. The prospective payment used to reimburse a "free-standing surgery center" for outpatient surgery is ASCs. The prospective payment system used to reimburse the "physician" for outpatient surgery is RBRVS.
17.	C	Since the provider accepts assignment, he will accept the Medicare Physician Fee Schedule (MPFS) payment as payment in full.
18.	C	
19.	D	
20.	B	12781.730/10,000 = 1.278

MS-DRG	Description	Number of Patients	CMS Relative Weight	Total CMS Relative Weight
470	Major joint replacement or reattachment of lower extremity w/o MCC	2,750	1.9871	5464.525
392	Esophagitis, gastroent & misc. digestive disorders w/o MCC	2,200	0.7121	1566.620
194	Simple pneumonia & pleurisy w CC	1,150	1.0235	1177.025
247	Perc cardiovasc proc 2 drug-eluting stent w/o MCC	900	2.1255	1912.950
293	Heart failure & shock w/o CC/MCC	850	0.8765	745.025
313	Chest pain	650	0.5489	356.785
292	Heart failure & shock w CC	550	1.0134	557.350
690	Kidney & urinary tract infections w/o MCC	400	0.8000	320.000
192	Chronic obstructive pulmonary disease w/o CC/MCC	300	0.8145	244.350
871	Septicemia w/o MV 96+ hours w MCC	250	1.7484	437.100
	Total	10,000		12781.730
	Case-Mix Index Total CMS Relative Weights (12781.730) divided by (10,000) patients			1.278

Answer Key for Medical Billing and Reimbursement Systems

ANSWER   EXPLANATION

21.   A   (See table on answer key under question 20.)
22.   A   (See table on answer key under question 20.)
23.   D   Total profit cannot be determined from this information alone. A comparison of the total charges on the bills and the PPS amount (reimbursement amount) that the hospital would receive for each MS-DRG could identify the total profit.
24.   A
25.   A
26.   D
27.   D
28.   D
29.   C
30.   B
31.   A
32.   D   The limiting charge is 15% above Medicare's approved payment amount for doctors who do NOT accept assignment ($128.00 × 1.15 = $147.20).
33.   D
34.   D
35.   A
36.   B
37.   D   Coding productivity will not directly affect CMI. Inaccuracy or poor coding quality can affect CMI.
38.   A   The Medicare Physician Fee Schedule (MPFS) reimburses providers according to predetermined rates assigned to services.
39.   B
40.   C
41.   C
42.   D   Cancer hospitals can apply for and receive waivers from the Centers for Medicare and Medicaid Services (CMS) and are therefore excluded from the inpatient prospective payment system (MS-DRGs). Rehabilitation hospitals are reimbursed under the Inpatient Rehabilitation Prospective Payment System (IRF PPS). Long-term care hospitals are reimbursed under the Long-Term Care Hospital Prospective Payment System (LTCH PPS). Skilled nursing facilities are reimbursed under the Skilled Nursing Facility Prospective Payment System (SNF PPS).
43.   C
44.   B
45.   B
46.   A
47.   C
48.   A
49.   A
50.   C
51.   C
52.   D
53.   B
54.   C

Answer Key for Medical Billing and Reimbursement Systems

ANSWER   EXPLANATION

55.   A   If a physician is a participating physician who accepts assignment, he will receive the lesser of "the total charges" or "the PAR Medicare Fee Schedule amount." In this case, the Medicare Fee Schedule amount is less; therefore, the total received by the physician is $200.00.

56.   C   If a physician is a nonparticipating physician who does not accept assignment, he can collect a maximum of 15% (the limiting charge) over the non-PAR Medicare Fee Schedule amount. In this case, the non-PAR Medicare Fee Schedule amount is $190.00 and 15% over this amount is $28.50; therefore, the total that he can collect is $218.50.

57.   B   The PAR Medicare Fee Schedule amount is $200.00. The patient has already met the deductible. Of the $200.00, the patient is responsible for 20% ($40.00). Medicare will pay 80% ($160.00). Therefore, the total financial liability for the patient is $40.00.

58.   A   If a physician is a nonparticipating physician who does not accept assignment, he may collect a maximum of 15% (the limiting charge) over the non-PAR Medicare Fee Schedule amount.

$190.00 = non-PAR Medicare Fee Schedule amount

$190.00 × 0.20 = $38.00 = patient liable for 20% coinsurance (patient previously met the deductible)

$190.00 × 0.80 = $152.00 = Medicare pays 80%

$190.00 × 0.15 = $28.50 = 15% (limiting charge) over non-PAR Medicare Fee Schedule amount

Physician can balance bill and collect from the patient the difference between the non-PAR Medicare Fee Schedule amount and the total charge amount. Therefore, the patient's financial liability is $38.00 (coinsurance) + 28.50 (limiting charge) = $66.50.

59.   A

60.   B

61.   A   Under the APC system, there exists a list of status indicators (also called service indicators, payment status indicators, or payment indicators). This indicator is provided for every HCPCS/CPT code and identifies how the service or procedure would be paid (if covered) by Medicare for hospital outpatient visits.

62.   B   Under the APC system, there exists a list of status indicators (also called service indicators, payment status indicators, or payment indicators). This indicator is provided for every HCPCS/CPT code and identifies how the service or procedure would be paid (if covered) by Medicare for hospital outpatient visits.

63.   D   Under the APC system, there exists a list of status indicators (also called service indicators, payment status indicators, or payment indicators). This indicator is provided for every HCPCS/CPT code and identifies how the service or procedure would be paid (if covered) by Medicare for hospital outpatient visits. Payment Status Indicator (PSI) "S" means that if a patient has more than one CPT code with this PSI, none of the procedures will be discounted or reduced. They will all be paid at 100%.

64.   C   Under the APC system, there exists a list of status indicators (also called service indicators, payment status indicators, or payment indicators). This indicator is provided for every HCPCS/CPT code and identifies how the service or procedure would be paid (if covered) by Medicare for hospital outpatient visits. Payment Status Indicator (PSI) "T" means that if a patient has more than one CPT code with this PSI, the procedure with the highest weight will be paid at 100% and all others will be reduced or discounted and paid at 50%.

Answer Key for Medical Billing and Reimbursement Systems

ANSWER   EXPLANATION

65.   B   Under the APC system, there exists a list of status indicators (also called service indicators, payment status indicators, or payment indicators). This indicator is provided for every HCPCS/CPT code and identifies how the service or procedure would be paid (if covered) by Medicare for hospital outpatient visits.

66.   D

67.   A

68.   A

69.   D

70.   A

71.   B

72.   B

73.   C

74.   B   When these conditions are not present on admission, it is assumed that it was hospital acquired and therefore, the hospital may not receive additional payment.

75.   B   Under Medicare Part B, Congress has mandated special incentives to increase the number of health care providers signing PAR (participating) agreements with Medicare. One of those incentives includes a 5% higher fee schedule for PAR providers than for non-PAR (nonparticipating) providers.

76.   C   Lifetime reserve days are applicable for hospital inpatient stays that are payable under Medicare Part A, not Medicare Part B.

77.   C

78.   A

79.   D   The relative weight is a number assigned to each MS-DRG published in the Federal Register, and it is used as a multiplier to determine reimbursement. Each hospital's prospective payment system (PPS) rate is a dollar amount based on that hospital's costs of operating as determined by several blended factors. This base payment rate is multiplied by the MS-DRG's (relative) weight to calculate that hospital's reimbursement for a given MS-DRG. Additional payments are made if applicable (such as disproportionate share, teaching hospital, cost outlier, etc.). The prospective payment system used to reimburse the "hospital" for outpatient surgery is APCs. The prospective payment used to reimburse a "free-standing surgery center" for outpatient surgery is ASCs. The prospective payment system used to reimburse the "physician" for outpatient surgery is RBRVS.

80.   D   Discounts are applied to those multiple procedures identified by CPT codes with status indicator "T" and also those CPT codes assigned with the modifier-73.

81.   B

82.   B

83.   A   Local Coverage Determinations (LCDs) were formerly called local medical review policies (LMRPs).

84.   B

85.   C

86.   C   If the physician is a participating physician (PAR) who accepts the assignment, he will receive the lesser of the "total charges" or the "PAR amount" (on the Medicare Physician Fee Schedule). Since the PAR amount is lower, the physician collects 80% of the PAR amount ($60.00) x .80 =$48.00, from Medicare. The remaining 20% ($60.00 x .20 = $12.00) of the PAR amount is paid by the patient to the physician. Therefore, the physician will receive $48.00 directly from Medicare.

Answer Key for Medical Billing and Reimbursement Systems

ANSWER   EXPLANATION

87. A

88. B

89. D

90. A When a patient meets the definition of critical care, the hospital must use CPT Code 99291 to bill for outpatient encounters in which critical care services are furnished. This code is used instead of another E&M code.

91. C DNFB stands for "Discharged, Not Final Billed"

92. D Since the physician is a nonparticipating physician, he will receive the non-PAR fee.
The Medicare non-PAR fee is $57.00.
Medicare will pay 80% of the non-PAR fee ($57.00 x 0.80 = $45.60).
The patient will pay 20% of the non-PAR fee ($57.00 x 0.20 = $11.40).
Since the physician is accepting assignment on this claim, he cannot charge the patient any more than the 20% copayment. Therefore, the physician will receive $45.60 directly from Medicare.

93. A

94. A Only one MS-DRG is assigned per inpatient hospitalization.

95. A

96. C

97. A

98. D

99. A The three relative value units are physician work, practice expense, and malpractice expense. These are adjusted by multiplying them by the geographical practice cost indices. Then, this total is multiplied by the national conversion factor.

100. B The participating physician agrees to accept Medicare's fee as payment in full; therefore, the physician would write off the difference between $700.00 and $450.00, which is 250.00.

101. A

102. B

103. C

104. A

105. C

106. A

107. B

108. D Inpatient Rehabilitation Facilities (IRF) reports the HIPPS (Health Insurance Prospective Payment System) code on the claim. The HIPPS code is a five-digit CMG (Case Mix Group). Therefore, the HIPPS code for a patient with tier 1 comorbidity and a CMG of 0109 is B0109. Home Health Agencies (HHA) report the HIPPS code on the claim. The HIPPS code is a five-character alphanumeric code. The first character is the letter "H." The second, third, and fourth characters represent the HHRG (Home Health Resource Group). The fifth character represents what elements are computed or derived. Therefore, the HIPPS code for the HHRG C0F0S0 would be HAEJ1.

109. D

110. A The malignant neoplasm was clearly present on admission, although it was not diagnosed until after the admission occurred.

111. A The atrial fibrillation developed prior to a written order for inpatient admission; therefore, it was present at the time of inpatient admission.

Answer Key for Medical Billing and Reimbursement Systems

ANSWER   EXPLANATION

112.   B   The pulmonary embolism is an acute condition that was not present on admission because it developed after the patient was admitted and after the patient had surgery.

113.   C   Query the physician as to whether the decubitus ulcer was present on admission or developed after admission.

114.   A

REFERENCES

Abdelhak, M., Grostick, S., and Hanken, M. (2012). *Health information management: management of a strategic resource* (4th ed.). St. Louis, MO: Elsevier Saunders.

Brown, S. and Tyler, L. (2014). *Guide to advanced medical billing: a reimbursement approach* (3rd ed.). Upper Saddle River, NJ: Pearson Education, Inc.

Casto, A. B., & Forrestal, E. (2013). *Principles of healthcare reimbursement* (4th ed.). Chicago: American Health Information Management Association (AHIMA).

CMS Web site: http://www.cms.hhs.gov/home/Medicare.asp (This Web site provides links to pages containing official informational materials on all of the Medicare Fee-For-Service Payment Systems.)

Diamond, M. S. (2012). *Understanding hospital coding and billing: A worktext* (2nd ed.).Clifton Park, NY: Delmar Cengage Learning.

Green, M. A. (2014). *3-2-1-Code It!* (4th ed.). Clifton Park, NY: Delmar Cengage Learning.

Green, M. A., & Rowell, J. C. (2013). *Understanding health insurance: A guide to billing and reimbursement* (11th ed.). Clifton Park, NY: Delmar Cengage Learning.

Green, M. A., & Bowie, M. J. (2011). *Essentials of health information management: Principles and practices* (2nd ed.). Clifton Park, NY: Delmar Cengage Learning.

Kirchoff, S. (2009). *Coding and reimbursement for hospital outpatient services.* Chicago: American Health Information Management Association (AHIMA).

LaTour, K., Eichenwald-Maki, S. and Oachs, P. (2013). *Health information management: Concepts, principles, and practice* (4th ed.). Chicago: American Health Information Management Association (AHIMA).

Richards, C. (2010). *Medical billing and reimbursement fundamentals.* Clifton Park, NY: Delmar Cengage Learning.

Rimmer, M. (2010). *Understanding medical collections.* Clifton Park, NY: Delmar Cengage Learning.

Sayles, N. (2013). *Health information management technology: An applied approach* (4th ed.). Chicago: American Health Information Management Association (AHIMA).

Schraffenberger, L. A., & Kuehn, L. (2011). *Effective management of coding services* (4th ed.). Chicago: American Health Information Management Association (AHIMA).

Scott, K. (2011). *Coding and reimbursement for hospital inpatient services* (3rd ed.). Chicago: American Health Information Management Association (AHIMA).

Medical Billing and Reimbursement Systems Competencies

Question	RHIA Domain	RHIT Domain
1–114	1	7

IX. CCA Mock Quiz

CCA Quiz

1. Chronic otitis media with bilateral myringotomy and tube insertion using local anesthesia. (Code ICD-10-CM for diagnoses and CPT for procedures.)

H65.193	Acute nonsuppurative otitis media, unspecified
H65.113	Acute allergic mucoid otitis media
H66.93	Unspecified otitis media
69400	Eustachian tube inflation, transnasal; with catheterization
69405	Eustachian tube catheterization, transtympanic
69420	Myringotomy including aspiration and/or eustachian tube inflation
69433	Tympanostomy (requiring insertion of ventilating tube), local or topical anesthesia
-50	Bilateral Procedure

A. H66.93, 69420-50
B. H66.93, 69433-50
C. H65.113, 69405-50
D. H65.193, 69400-50

2. A coworker complained of the sudden onset of chest pain and was admitted. A myocardial infarction was ruled out. You would code
   A. the myocardial infarction as if it were an established condition.
   B. both the infarction and the chest pain and sequence the infarction first.
   C. as an impending myocardial infarction.
   D. only the chest pain.

3. A 32-year-old female, known to be HIV positive, was admitted with lesions of the anterior trunk. Excisional diagnostic biopsies of the skin lesions were positive for Kaposi's sarcoma. Further examination revealed thrush. (Choose the correct ICD-10-CM diagnoses.)

B20	Human immunodeficiency virus (HIV) disease
Z21	Nonspecific serological evidence of HIV
C46.0	Kaposi's sarcoma, skin
L08.0	Pyoderma, unspecified
L08.0	Candidiasis of mouth
K13.79	Other and unspecified diseases of the oral soft tissues

A. B20, L08.0, L08.0
B. B20, C46.0, L08.0
C. Z21, C46.0, K13.79
D. Z21, L08.0, K13.79

4. An 89-year-old male is admitted to a nursing home with confusion, hypotension, a temperature of 103.5, and obvious dehydration. Blood cultures were negative; however, urine culture was positive for *Escherichia coli*. The physician documents final diagnosis as septicemia, septic shock, UTI due to *E. coli*, and dehydration. (Code the ICD-10-CM diagnoses.)

A41.9	Septicemia, unspecified
A49.8	*E. coli*
E86.0	Dehydration
F29	Psychosis, unspecified
I95.9	Hypotension, unspecified
N39.0	UTI, site not specified
R50.9	Fever, unspecified
R65.21	Septic shock
R65.21	Severe sepsis

A. N39.0, I95.9, A49.8, R50.9, E86.0, F29
B. A41.9, R65.21, R65.21, N39.0, A49.8, E86.0, F29
C. N39.0, A41.9, A49.8, E86.0, R65.21, F29
D. A41.9, E86.0, A49.8, R50.9, R65.21, F29

Current Procedural Terminology © 2013 American Medical Association. All Rights Reserved.

5. Mary is 6 weeks postmastectomy for carcinoma of the breast. She is admitted for chemotherapy. What is the correct sequencing of the codes? (Code the ICD-10-CM diagnoses.)

C50.911	Malignant neoplasm of the female breast, unspecified site
Z85.3	Personal history of malignant neoplasm of the breast
Z51.11	Encounter for antineoplastic chemotherapy
Z08	Follow-up examination following surgery, unspecified

A. Z51.11, C50.911
B. Z51.11, Z85.3
C. Z08, Z51.11
D. Z85.3

6. Chip is 35 years old and has been previously diagnosed with lung cancer. He has been receiving chemotherapy and radiation. He develops seizures and is admitted. Workup revealed metastasis of the lung cancer to the brain.

Z85.118	Personal history of malignant neoplasm of the bronchus and lung
Z85.841	Personal history of malignant neoplasm of the brain
C43.90	Malignant neoplasm of the bronchus/lung, unspecified site
C71.9	Malignant neoplasm of the brain, unspecified
C71.9	Secondary malignant neoplasm of lung
C79.31	Secondary malignant neoplasm of brain and spinal cord
R56.9	Other convulsions (seizures, not otherwise specified)

A. R56.9, C43.90, C71.9, Z85.118
B. R56.9, C79.31, C43.90
C. R56.9, Z85.118, Z85.841
D. C79.31, C43.90

7. Which of the following is coded as an adverse effect in ICD-10-CM?
A. tinnitus due to allergic reaction after administration of ear drops
B. mental retardation due to intracranial abscess
C. rejection of transplanted kidney
D. nonfunctioning pacemaker due to defective soldering

8. Mitch was diagnosed by his physician as having dehydration. Mitch has had gastroenteritis for several days, which has resulted in dehydration and requires intravenous hydration. Mitch also has chronic kidney disease and is at high risk for acute on chronic kidney failure. Two days following admission, Mitch develops acute renal failure. Mitch also has hypertension. (Code the ICD-10-CM diagnoses.)

E86.0	Dehydration
I10	Essential hypertension, unspecified benign or malignant
I12.9	Hypertensive chronic kidney disease stage I through stage IV, or unspecified, unspecified benign, or malignant
I12.0	Hypertensive chronic kidney disease stage V or end-stage renal disease, unspecified benign, or malignant
N17.9	Acute kidney failure, unspecified
N18.9	Chronic kidney disease, unspecified
N19	Renal failure, unspecified

A. N17.9, I12.9, E86.0
B. E86.0, N17.9, N18.9, I12.9
C. I12.0, E86.0
D. E86.0, N19, N17.9, I10

9. Aunt Elsie is brought to the emergency room for increased confusion. She is subsequently diagnosed with Alzheimer's disease with dementia and cerebral atherosclerosis. She is also treated for hypertension and hypothyroidism. (Code the ICD-10-CM diagnoses.)

E03.9	Unspecified acquired hypothyroidism
E30.90	Dementia in conditions classified elsewhere without behavioral disturbance (manifestation)
E03.91	Dementia in conditions classified elsewhere with behavioral disturbance (manifestation)
J30.9	Alzheimer's disease
I10	Essential hypertension, unspecified benign or malignant
I67.2	Cerebral atherosclerosis

A. I67.2, E30.90, E03.9, I10
B. E30.90, I10, E03.9
C. J30.9, E03.9, I10, E03.91
D. J30.9, E30.90, I67.2, E03.9, I10

10. The patient presented to his physician's office due to increasingly severe pain in his right arm, shoulder, and neck for the past 6 weeks. MRI tests showed herniation of the C5–C6 disc. Patient was admitted and underwent an open cervical laminotomy and diskectomy of the C5–C6 disk. The patient is currently being treated for COPD and CAD with a history of PTCA. (Code the ICD-10-CM diagnoses and the procedures using ICD-10-PCS.)

M50.22	Displacement of cervical intervertebral disc without myelopathy
M50.02	Intervertebral disc disorder with myelopathy, cervical region
J43.9	Other emphysema
J44.9	Chronic airway obstruction, not elsewhere classified
I25.10	Coronary atherosclerosis of native coronary artery
Z98.61	Percutaneous transluminal coronary angioplasty status
0RB30ZZ	Excision of intervertebral disc
0RB30ZZ	Other exploration and decompression of spinal canal (Decompression, laminotomy)

A. M50.22, J43.9, I25.10, Z98.61, 0RB30ZZ
B. M50.02, J44.9, I25.10, Z98.61, 0RB30ZZ
C. M50.02, J43.9, 0RB30ZZ
D. M50.22, J44.9, I25.10, Z98.61, 0RB30ZZ

11. Tom visits his physician because he has been feeling acute chest pain. Final diagnoses listed include acute pulmonary edema with congestive heart failure, subendocardial anterior wall myocardial infarction, hypertensive heart disease, and chronic obstructive pulmonary disease. (Code the ICD-10-CM diagnoses.)

I21.09	Acute myocardial infarction, of other anterior wall, initial episode of care
I21.4	Acute subendocardial infarction, initial episode of care
I11.9	Hypertensive heart disease, without heart failure, unspecified benign or malignant
I11.0	Hypertensive heart disease, with heart failure, unspecified benign or malignant
I50.9	Congestive heart failure, unspecified
I50.1	Left heart failure
J44.9	Chronic airway obstruction, not elsewhere classified
J81.0	Acute edema of lung, unspecified

A. I21.4, I11.0, J44.9, I50.9
B. I21.09, I50.9. J81.0, I11.0, J44.9, I50.1
C. I21.4, I21.09, I11.0, J81.0, J44.9, I50.9
D. I21.09, I50.9. I11.9, J81.0, J44.9, I50.1

12. Patient was admitted from the nursing home with acute respiratory failure due to congestive heart failure. Chest x-rays also showed acute pulmonary edema. Patient was intubated and placed on mechanical ventilation for less than 24 hours and expired the day after admission.

I50.9	Congestive heart failure, unspecified
I50.1	Left heart failure
J81.0	Acute edema of lung, unspecified
J96.00	Acute respiratory failure
J96.20	Acute and chronic respiratory failure
0BH17EZ	Insertion of endotrachial tube
5A1935Z	Continuous invasive mechanical ventilation for less than 96 consecutive hours

   A. I50.9, J96.20, J81.0, 0BH17EZ, 5A1935Z
   B. I50.9, I50.9, J96.00, J81.0, 0BH17EZ, 5A1935Z
   C. J96.00, I50.9, 5A1935Z, 0BH17EZ
   D. I50.9, J81.0, 0BH17EZ, 5A1935Z

13. Diverticulitis large bowel with ascending colon abscess was the diagnosis for a patient who presented with abdominal pain. Right hemicolectomy with colostomy performed. (Code the ICD-10-CM diagnoses and procedures using ICD-10-PCS.)

K57.90	Diverticulosis of colon (without mention of hemorrhage)
K57.92	Diverticulitis of colon (without mention of hemorrhage)
K62.0	Abscess of intestine
0DTK0ZZ	Open and other right hemicolectomy
0DTL0ZZ	Open and other resection of transverse colon
0D1K0Z4	Exteriorization of large intestine (loop colostomy)

   A. K57.90, 0DTL0ZZ, 0D1K0Z4
   B. K57.92, 0DTK0ZZ, 0D1K0Z4
   C. K57.92, K62.0, 0DTK0ZZ
   D. K57.92, K62.0, 0DTL0ZZ

14. Patient has bilateral inguinal hernias; the left is indirect and the right is direct. He has repairs of both hernias with mesh prosthesis. (Code the ICD-10-CM diagnoses and procedures using ICD-10-PCS.)

K40.90	Inguinal hernia, without mention of obstruction or gangrene, unilateral or unspecified (not specified as recurrent)
K40.91	Inguinal hernia, without mention of obstruction or gangrene, unilateral or unspecified, recurrent
K40.20	Inguinal hernia, without mention of obstruction or gangrene, bilateral (not specified as recurrent)
0YQ50ZZ	Other and open unilateral repair of direct inguinal hernia
0YQ60ZZ	Other and open unilateral repair of indirect inguinal hernia
0YUA0KZ	Other and open bilateral repair of inguinal hernia, one direct and one indirect, with graft or prosthesis

   A. K40.91, K40.20, 0YUA0KZ
   B. K40.90, 0YQ50ZZ, 0YQ60ZZ
   C. K40.20, 0YUA0KZ
   D. K40.20, 0YQ50ZZ, 0YQ60ZZ

15. Vaginal delivery of a full-term liveborn infant. Patient undergoes episiotomy with repair and postdelivery elective tubal ligation.

O80	Normal delivery
VZ30.2	Encounter for contraceptive management, sterilization
Z37.0	Single liveborn
0UL70ZZ	Other bilateral ligation and division of fallopian tubes
10E0XZZ	Other manually assisted delivery
0W8NXZZ	Episiotomy (with subsequent repair)

A. O80, VZ30.2, Z37.0, 0UL70ZZ, 0W8NXZZ
B. Z37.0, 0W8NXZZ, 0UL70ZZ
C. O80, Z37.0, 0UL70ZZ
D. O80, Z37.0, 10E0XZZ, 0UL70ZZ

16. Incomplete abortion complicated by excessive hemorrhage; dilation and curettage performed. (Code the ICD-10-CM diagnoses and procedures using ICD-10-PCS.)

D62	Acute blood-loss anemia
O03.1	Spontaneous abortion complicated by delayed or excessive hemorrhage, incomplete
O03.6	Spontaneous abortion complicated by delayed or excessive hemorrhage, complete
O03.4	Spontaneous abortion without complication, incomplete
10D17ZZ	Dilation and curettage following delivery or abortion
0UDB7ZZ	Other dilation and curettage

A. O03.1, 0UDB7ZZ
B. O03.1, D62, 0UDB7ZZ
C. O03.1, 10D17ZZ
D. O03.4, 10D17ZZ

17. John has chronic ulcers of the right calf and back. Both ulcers are excisionally debrided, and the ulcer of the back has a split-thickness skin graft, autologous. (Code the ICD-10-CM diagnoses and procedures using ICD-10-PCS.)

L97.219	Ulcer of calf
L98.429	Chronic ulcer of other specified sites
0HBKXZZ	Excisional debridement of wound, infection, or burn
0HB6XZZ	Excisional debridement of wound, infection, or burn
0HRKX74	Skin graft

A. L97.219, L98.429, 0HBKXZZ, 0HB6XZZ, 0HRKX74
B. L97.219, L98.429, 0HBKXZZ
C. L98.429, 0HB6XZZ, 0HRKX74
D. L98.429, 0HBKXZZ, 0HB6XZZ, 0HRKX74

18. The physician has documented the final diagnoses as acute myocardial infarction, COPD, CHF, hypertension, atrial fibrillation, and status postcholecystectomy. The following conditions should be reported. (Code the ICD-10CM diagnoses.)

I10	Essential hypertension, benign
I10	Essential hypertension, unspecified
I11.0	Hypertensive heart disease, unspecified as to malignant or benign, with heart failure
I21.3	Acute myocardial infarction, unspecified site, initial episode of care
I48.91	Atrial fibrillation
I50.39	Congestive heart failure, unspecified
J44.9	Chronic obstructive pulmonary disease
Z90.89	Acquired absence of organ

   A. I21.3, J44.9, I11.0, I48.91, Z90.89
   B. I21.3, J44.9, I50.39, I10, I48.91
   C. I21.3, J44.9, I50.39, I10, I48.91, Z90.89
   D. I21.3, J44.9, I50.39, I10, I48.91

19. Which of the following is the term describing a woman who has delivered one child?
   A. primipara
   B. primigravida
   C. nulligravida
   D. paragravida

20. HPV or human papillomavirus is
   A. caused by the spirochete *Treponema pallidum*.
   B. a vaginal inflammation that is caused by a protozoan parasite.
   C. also known as genital warts.
   D. characterized by painful urination and an abnormal discharge.

21. A marked loss of bone density and increase in bone porosity is
   A. lumbago.
   B. osteoarthritis.
   C. spondylitis.
   D. osteoporosis.

22. The blood disorder in which red blood cells lack the normal ability to produce hemoglobin is called
   A. aplastic anemia.
   B. hemolytic anemia.
   C. pernicious anemia.
   D. thalassemia.

23. Which diagnostic technique records the patient's heart rates and rhythms over a 24-hour period?
   A. echocardiography
   B. electrocardiography
   C. Holter monitor
   D. angiocardiography

24. The physician's office note states: "Counseling visit, 15 minutes counseling in follow-up with a patient newly diagnosed with diabetes." If the physician reports code 99214, which piece of documentation is missing to substantiate this code?
   A. chief complaint
   B. history
   C. exam
   D. total length of visit

25. A patient initially consulted with Dr. Vasseur at the request of Dr. Meche, the patient's primary care physician. Dr. Vasseur examined the patient, prescribed medication, and ordered tests. Additional visits to Dr. Vasseur's office for continuing care would be assigned from which E/M section?
   A. Office and other outpatient services, new patient
   B. Office and other outpatient services, established patient
   C. Office or other outpatient consultations, new or established patient
   D. Confirmatory consultations, new or established patient

26. In order to correctly code a hernia repair, the coder needs to know all of the following EXCEPT
 A. the type of hernia.
 B. whether the hernia is strangulated or incarcerated.
 C. the age of the patient.
 D. whether the patient is obese or not.

27. According to CPT, a biopsy of the breast that involves removal of only a portion of the lesion for pathologic examination is
 A. percutaneous.
 B. incisional.
 C. excisional.
 D. punch.

28. A patient is seen in the emergency room following an accident. The physician documents that the wound required multiple layers and extensive undermining. According to CPT definitions, this type of repair would be classified as
 A. complex.
 B. intermediate.
 C. simple.
 D. advancement flap.

29. The emergency room discharge diagnosis for this ER encounter is "rule out myocardial infarction." The coder would assign
 A. a code for a myocardial infarction.
 B. a code for the patient's symptoms.
 C. a code for an impending myocardial infarction.
 D. no code for this condition.

30. _____ is a defect characterized by four anatomical abnormalities within the heart that results in poorly oxygenated blood being pumped to the body.
 A. Atrial septal defect
 B. Patent ductus arteriosus
 C. Tetralogy of Fallot
 D. Coarctation of the aorta

31. Urinary frequency, urgency, nocturia, incontinence, and hesitancy are all symptoms of
 A. BPH.
 B. end-stage kidney disease.
 C. salpingitis.
 D. genital prolapse.

32. Down's syndrome, Edwards' syndrome, and Patau syndrome are all examples of _____ defects.
 A. musculoskeletal
 B. chromosomal
 C. genitourinary tract
 D. digestive system

33. The type of anemia caused by a failure of the bone marrow to produce red blood cells is
 A. acute blood-loss anemia.
 B. sickle cell anemia.
 C. iron-deficiency anemia.
 D. aplastic anemia.

34. A patient has major surgery and sees the surgeon 10 days later for an unrelated E/M service. Indicate the modifier that should be attached to the E/M code for the service provided.
 A. -24
 B. -25
 C. -59
 D. -79

35. Patient presents to the hospital for a three-view x-ray of the right shoulder. The diagnosis is shoulder pain and the radiology report states the patient has a dislocated shoulder. What would be the correct codes to report to the insurance company?

M25.511	Right shoulder pain
S43.004A	Closed dislocation shoulder, unspecified, initial
S43014A	Closed dislocation shoulder, anterior, initial
73020	Radiologic examination, shoulder; one view
73030	Radiologic examination, shoulder; complete, minimum of two views
73060	Radiologic examination; humerus, minimum of two views
RT	Right side

 A. S43.004A; 73060-RT
 B. M25.511; 73020-RT
 C. S43.004A; 73030-RT
 D. S43014A; 73030-RT

Current Procedural Terminology © 2013 American Medical Association. All Rights Reserved.

CCA QUIZ Answer Key

ANSWER   EXPLANATION

1. B   CPT notes immediately following code 69433 instruct the coder to report 69433 with modifier -50 for a procedure performed bilaterally.

REFERENCE: AHA, p 219
             Green, pp 713–714

2. D

REFERENCE: AHA, pp 38, 58

3. B   The medical term for thrush is candidiasis.

REFERENCE: AHA, pp 156–158

4. B

REFERENCE: AHA, pp 150–152

5. A   The cancer is coded as a current condition as long as the patient is receiving adjunct therapy.

REFERENCE: AHA, pp 439, 452, 456–457, 459, 461

6. D   Additional conditions that may not be routinely associated with a disease process should be coded when present. Seizures are not routinely associated with cancer; therefore, it is coded.

REFERENCE: AHA, pp 206, 439–465

7. A

REFERENCE: AHA, pp 513–518, 521–522

8. B

REFERENCE: AHA, pp 263–265, 458

9. D

REFERENCE: AHA, pp 173, 206

10. D   When a patient has no known history of CABG and is diagnosed with coronary artery disease (CAD) with no mention of a specific vessel, it is appropriate to assign code I25.10 (coronary atherosclerosis of native coronary artery) since there is no history of prior bypass surgery.

REFERENCE: AHA, pp 229–231, 294, 296–297, 392

11. A   Subendocardial MI takes precedence over anatomical site unless there were two separate acute MIs. Acute pulmonary edema is included in the code for congestive heart failure (CHF).

REFERENCE: AHA, pp 229–231, 325–326, 386–389, 394–395, 403–405

12. C   Acute pulmonary edema is included in the code for congestive heart failure (CHF).

REFERENCE: AHA, pp 233–235, 238–240, 385, 395

13. C

REFERENCE: AHA, pp 243–244, 247–248

CCA QUIZ Answer Key

ANSWER EXPLANATION

14. C

REFERENCE: AHA, p 253

15. A

REFERENCE: AHA, pp 316, 319, 336, 338

16. C

REFERENCE: AHA, pp 192, 346–347, 352

17. A

REFERENCE: AHA, pp 286–287, 290

18. B Category Z90.89, acquired absence of organ, is intended to be used for patient care where the absence of an organ affects treatment.

REFERENCE: AHA, pp 34–36

      Frisch, pp 139, 146–148

19. A

REFERENCE: Jones, p 808

20. C

REFERENCE: Jones, p 716
      Neighbors and Tannehill-Jones, p 370
      Scott and Fong, p 470
      Sormunen, pp 511, 515

21. D

REFERENCE: Neighbors and Tannehill-Jones, p 100
      Scott and Fong, pp 113–114
      Sormunen, p 154

22. D

REFERENCE: Jones, p 335
      Neighbors and Tannehill-Jones, p 138
      Scott and Fong, pp 250–251

23. C

REFERENCE: Scott and Fong, p 270
      Sormunen, p 221

24. D In order to use time as a factor in determining the appropriate E/M code, the total time spent with the patient, as well as the amount of time spent in counseling, must be recorded.

REFERENCE: Johnson and Linker, pp 141–143

CCA QUIZ Answer Key

    ANSWER   EXPLANATION

25. B Consultation codes can no longer be coded when the physician has taken an active part in the continued care of the patient.

REFERENCE: Frisch, pp 77–82
                       Johnson and Linker, pp 153–154

26. D

REFERENCE: AHA, p 253

27. B

REFERENCE: Johnson and Linker, pp 218–219

28. A

REFERENCE: Johnson and Linker, pp 224–225

29. B When a diagnosis is preceded by the phrase "rule out" in the outpatient setting, code condition(s) to the highest degree of certainty for that encounter/visit, such as symptoms, signs, abnormal test results, or other reasons for the visit.

REFERENCE: AHA, pp 57–58

30. C

REFERENCE: Jones, p 409
                       Neighbors and Tannehill-Jones, p 444

31. A

REFERENCE: Bowie and Schaffer (2012), pp 243–245
                       Neighbors and Tannehill-Jones, p 376

32. B

REFERENCE: Bowie and Schaffer (2012), p 405
                       Scott and Fong, p 483

33. D

REFERENCE: AHA, pp 194–195

34. A

REFERENCE: AMA (2014), p 645
                       Frisch, pp 386–395
                       Green, p 364
                       Johnson and McHugh, p 115
                       Smith, p 210

35. D

REFERENCE: AHA, pp 30–31
                       AMA CPT (2014)

REFERENCES

Abdelhak, M., Grostick, S., Hanken, M. A., & Jacobs, E. (Eds.). (2012). *Health information: Management of a strategic resource* (5th ed.). St. Louis, MO: Saunders Elsevier.

American Hospital Association (AHA). (2013). *ICD-10-CM and ICD-10-PCS coding handbook 2014 (with Answers)*. Chicago: Nelly Leon-Chisen, RHIA Central Office on ICD-10-CM and ICD-10-PCS of the American Hospital Association (AHA).

American Medical Association (AMA). *CPT assistant.* Chicago: Author.

American Medical Association (AMA). (2014). *Current procedural terminology (CPT) 2014 professional edition.* Chicago: Author.

Bowie, M., & Schaffer, L. (2013). *Understanding procedural coding: A worktext.* Clifton Park, NY: Delmar Cengage Learning.

Frisch, B. (2007). *Correct coding for Medicare compliance and reimbursement.* Clifton Park, NY: Delmar Cengage Learning.

Green, M. A. (2014). *3-2-1 code it!* (4th ed.). Clifton Park, NY: Delmar Cengage Learning.

Green, M., & Bowie, M. J. (2011). *Essentials of health information management: Principles and practices* (2nd ed.). Clifton Park, NY: Delmar Cengage Learning.

Green, M. A., & Rowell, J. C. (2011). *Understanding health insurance: A guide to billing and reimbursement* (10th ed.). Clifton Park, NY: Delmar Cengage Learning.

Johnson, S. L., & Linker, R. (2013). *Understanding medical coding: A comprehensive guide* (3rd ed.). Clifton Park, NY: Delmar Cengage Learning.

Jones, B. D. (2011). *Comprehensive medical terminology* (4th ed.). Clifton Park, NY: Delmar Cengage Learning.

LaTour, K., Eichenwald-Maki, S., and Oachs, P. (2013). *Health information management concepts: Principles and practice* (4th ed.). Chicago: American Health Information Management Association (AHIMA).

Neighbors, M., & Tannehill-Jones, R. (2010). *Human diseases* (3rd ed.). Clifton Park, NY: Delmar Cengage Learning.

OptumInsight. (2013). *ICD-10-CM for hospitals: The complete official draft code set.* Salt Lake City, UT: Author.

Rimmer, M. (2008). *Medical billing 101.* Clifton Park, NY: Delmar Cengage Learning.

Sayles, N. B. (2013). *Health information technology: An applied approach* (4th ed.). Chicago: American Health Information Management Association (AHIMA).

Scott, A. S., & Fong, P. E. (2009). *Body structures and functions* (11th ed.). Clifton Park, NY: Delmar Cengage Learning.

Smith, G. (2013). *Basic current procedure terminology and HCPCS coding.* Chicago: American Health Information Management Association (AHIMA).

Sormunen, C. (2013). *Terminology for allied health professionals* (7th ed.). Clifton Park, NY: Delmar Cengage Learning.

Competencies for the CCA Quiz	
Question	CCA Domain
1–35	1

X. CCA Mock Examination

CCA Mock Examination

1. Your organization is sending confidential patient information across the Internet using technology that will transform the original data into unintelligible code that can be re-created by authorized users. This technique is called
   A. a firewall.
   B. validity processing.
   C. a call-back process.
   D. data encryption.

2. As part of a concurrent record review, you need to locate the initial plan of action based on the attending physician's initial assessment of the patient. You can expect to find this documentation either within the body of the history and physical or in the
   A. doctor's admitting progress note.
   B. nurse's admit note.
   C. review of systems.
   D. discharge summary.

3. Employing the SOAP style of progress notes, choose the "assessment" statement from the following:
   A. Patient states low back pain with sciatica is as severe as it was on admission.
   B. Patient moving about very cautiously and appears to be in pain.
   C. Adjust pain medication; begin physical therapy tomorrow.
   D. Sciatica unimproved with hot pack therapy.

4. You have been hired to work with a computer-assisted coding initiative. The technology that you will be working with is
   A. electronic data interchange.
   B. intraoperability.
   C. message standards.
   D. natural language processing.

5. A final progress note is appropriate as a discharge summary for a hospitalization in which the patient
   A. dies within 24 hours of admission.
   B. has no comorbidities or complications during this episode of care.
   C. was admitted within 30 days with the same diagnosis.
   D. was an obstetric admission with a normal delivery and no complications.

6. In reviewing a medical record for coding purposes, the coder notes that the discharge summary has not yet been transcribed. In its absence, the best place to look for the patient's response to treatment and documentation of any complications that may have developed during this episode of care is in the
   A. doctors' progress note section.
   B. operative report.
   C. history and physical.
   D. doctors' orders.

7. You would expect to find documentation regarding the assessment of an obstetric patient's lochia, fundus, and perineum on the
   A. prenatal record.
   B. labor record.
   C. delivery room record.
   D. postpartum record.

8. A patient is admitted through the emergency department with diabetes mellitus. Three days after admission, the physician documents uncontrolled diabetes mellitus. What is the "present on admission" (POA) indicator for uncontrolled diabetes mellitus?

A. Y
B. U
C. W
D. N

SAMPLE MS-DRG REPORT		
MS-DRG IDENTIFIER	RELATIVE WEIGHT	NUMBER OF PATIENTS WITH THIS MS-DRG
A	1.234	12
B	3.122	10
C	2.165	19
D	5.118	16

9. Based on the preceding sample MS-DRG report, what is the case-mix index for this facility?

A. 42.26275
B. 2.965807
C. 11.639
D. 2.90975

10. The special form that plays the central role in planning and providing care at nursing, psychiatric, and rehabilitation facilities is the

A. interdisciplinary patient care plan.
B. medical history and review of systems.
C. interval summary.
D. problem list.

11. What legal term is used in describing sexual harassment in reference to unwelcome sexual advances, the request for sexual favors, and verbal or physical conduct of a sexual nature made in return for job benefits?

A. res ipsa loquitur
B. qui tam
C. quid pro quo
D. respondeat superior

12. Your facility would like to improve physician documentation in order to allow improved coding. As coding supervisor, you have found it very effective to provide the physicians with

A. a copy of the facility coding guidelines, along with written information on improved documentation.
B. the UHDDS and information on where each data element is collected and/or verified in your facility.
C. regular in-service presentations on documentation, including its importance and tips for improvement.
D. feedback on specific instances when improved documentation would improve coding.

EMPLOYEE NUMBER	INPATIENT	OUTPATIENT PROCEDURE	OUTPATIENT OBSERVATION OR EMERGENCY RECORDS
425	120	35	16
426	48	89	95
427	80	92	4
428	65	109	16

WATERSIDE HOSPITAL CODING PRODUCTIVITY WEEK ENDING JANUARY 2, 2012

13. The performance standard for coders is 28–33 workload units per day. Workload units are calculated as follows:

Inpatient records = 1 workload unit
Outpatient surgical procedure records = 0.75 workload units
Outpatient observation/Emergency records = 0.50 workload units

One week's productivity information is shown in the preceding table. What percentage of the coders is meeting the productivity standards?
A. 100%
B. 75%
C. 50%
D. 25%

14. Which of the following diagnoses or procedures would prevent the normal delivery code, O80, from being assigned?
A. occiput presentation
B. single liveborn
C. episiotomy
D. low forceps

15. Which of the following are considered late effects (sequelae) regardless of time?
A. congenital defect
B. nonunion
C. nonhealing fracture
D. poisoning

16. Patient is admitted for elective cholecystectomy for treatment of chronic cholecystitis with cholelithiasis. Prior to administration of general anesthesia, patient suffers cerebral thrombosis. Surgery is subsequently canceled. Code and sequence the coding from the following codes.

I66.90 Cerebral thrombosis without cerebral infarction
K80.10 Calculus of gallbladder with other cholecystitis without mention of obstruction
Z53.09 Surgical or other procedure not carried out because of contraindication
I97.821 Iatrogenic cerebrovascular infarction or hemorrhage
0FT40ZZ Cholecystectomy (open)

A. I97.821, K80.10, 0FT40ZZ
B. K80.10, 434.00, Z53.09
C. I97.821, I66.9, Z53.09
D. I66.9, Z53.09

17. Some ICD-9-CM codes are exempt from POA reporting because they
    A. represent circumstances regarding the health care encounter or factors influencing health status that do not represent a current disease or injury.
    B. are always present on admission.
    C. are both A and B.
    D. represent V codes and E codes.

18. Which of these conditions are always considered "present on admission" (POA)?
    A. congenital conditions
    B. E codes
    C. acute conditions
    D. possible, probable, or suspected conditions

19. When coding multiple wound repairs in CPT,
    A. only the most complex repair is reported.
    B. only the least complex repair is reported.
    C. up to nine individual repair codes may be reported.
    D. all wound repairs are coded, with the most complex reported first.

20. Which of the following is vital for determining why the reimbursement from an insurance company is less than that which was expected?
    A. a CPT codebook
    B. the remittance advice
    C. talking to the patient
    D. knowledge of the individual insurance company's policies

21. Four people were seen in your Emergency Department yesterday. Which one will be coded as a poisoning?

    Robert: diagnosed with digitalis intoxication
    Gary: had an allergic reaction to a dye administered for a pyelogram
    David: developed syncope after taking Contac pills with a double scotch
    Brian: had an idiosyncratic reaction between two properly administered prescription drugs

    A. Robert   C. David
    B. Gary   D. Brian

22. Present on Admission (POA) indicators apply to
    A. inpatient reporting of diagnosis codes.
    B. outpatient reporting of procedure codes.
    C. inpatient reporting of diagnosis and procedure codes.
    D. outpatient reporting of diagnosis and procedure codes.

23. Using the ICD-10-CM code structure, which of the following would be used for "right upper quadrant abdominal tenderness"?
    A. 108.11   C. R10.811
    B. R10811.11   D. 1.0811

24. Which of the following scenarios identifies a pathologic fracture?
    A. greenstick fracture secondary to fall from a bed
    B. compression fracture of the skull after being hit with a baseball bat
    C. vertebral fracture with cord compression following a car accident
    D. compression fracture of the vertebrae as a result of bone metastasis

25. All of the following signs/symptoms suggest gram-negative pneumonia EXCEPT
    A. fever.
    B. patchy infiltrate.
    C. purulent sputum.
    D. decreased leukocyte count.

26. During her hospitalization for her third delivery, Janet had a sterilization procedure performed. When the record is coded, the code for sterilization, Z30.2, is
    A. not used.
    B. used and sequenced as the principal diagnosis.
    C. used and sequenced as a secondary diagnosis.
    D. the only code used.

27. Ensuring that data have been modified or accessed only by individuals who are authorized to do so is a function of data
    A. accuracy.
    B. validity.
    C. integrity.
    D. quality.

28. Which of the following statements is true?
    A. A surgical procedure may include one or more surgical operations.
    B. The terms *surgical operation* and *surgical procedure* are synonymous.
    C. A surgical operation may include one or more surgical procedures.
    D. The term *surgical procedure* is an incorrect term and should not be used.

29. Security devices that form barriers between routers of a public network and a private network to protect access by unauthorized users are called
    A. data translators.
    B. passwords.
    C. data manipulation engines.
    D. firewalls.

30. The Joint Commission requires that all medical records be completed within _____ following patient discharge
    A. 30 days
    B. 14 days
    C. 7 days
    D. 90 days

31. You are conducting an educational session on benchmarking. You tell your audience that the key to benchmarking is to use the comparison to
    A. implement your QI process.
    B. make recommendations for improvement to the other department or organization.
    C. improve your department's processes.
    D. compare your department with another.

32. Which of the following procedures can be identified as "destruction" of lesions in CPT coding?
    A. removal of skin tags
    B. shaving of skin lesion
    C. laser removal of condylomata
    D. paring of hyperkeratotic lesion

33. A _____ is a collection of information or data that is organized in such a way that its contents can be queried and relationships created.
    A. database
    B. field
    C. record
    D. table

34. Staging
    A. refers to the monitoring of incidence and trends associated with a disease.
    B. is continued medical surveillance of a case.
    C. is a system for documenting the extent or spread of cancer.
    D. designates the degree of differentiation of cells.

35. Which diagnosis should be listed first when sequencing inpatient codes using the UHDDS?
    A. primary diagnosis   C. significant diagnosis
    B. principal diagnosis   D. admitting diagnosis

36. Which of the following would NOT require HCPCS/CPT codes?
    A. hospital ambulatory surgery visit   C. clinic visit
    B. hospital outpatient visit   D. hospital inpatient procedure

37. Patient was seen in the emergency department with lacerations on the left arm. Two lacerations, one 7 cm and one 9 cm, were closed with layered sutures.

12002	Simple repair of superficial wounds of scalp, neck, axillae, external genitalia, trunk and/or extremities (including hands and feet); 2.6 cm to 7.5 cm
12004	Simple repair of superficial wounds of scalp, neck, axillae, external genitalia, trunk, and/or extremities (including hands and feet); 7.6 cm to 12.5 cm
12035	Layer closure of wounds of scalp, axillae, trunk, and/or extremities (excluding hands and feet); 12.6 cm to 20 cm
12045	Layer closure of wounds of neck, hands, feet, and/or external genitalia; 12.6 cm to 20 cm

    A. 12045   C. 12002, 12004
    B. 12035   D. 12004

38. Patient was seen for excision of two interdigital neuromas from the left foot.

28080	Excision, interdigital (Morton's) neuroma, single, each
64774	Excision of neuroma; cutaneous nerve, surgically identifiable
64776	Excision of neuroma; digital nerve, one or both, same digit

    A. 64774   C. 28080
    B. 64776   D. 28080, 28080

39. Patient was seen today for regular hemodialysis. No problems reported; patient tolerated procedure well.

> 90935   Hemodialysis procedure with single physician evaluation
>
> 90937   Hemodialysis procedure requiring repeated evaluation(s) with or without substantial revision of dialysis prescription
>
> 90945   Dialysis procedure other than hemodialysis (e.g., peritoneal dialysis, hemofiltration, or other continuous renal replacement therapies), with single physician evaluation
>
> +99354   Prolonged service in the office or other outpatient setting requiring direct (face-to-face) contact beyond the usual service, first hour (List separately in addition to code for office or other outpatient Evaluation and Management service.)

A. 90937   C. 90945
B. 99354   D. 90935

40. Office visit for 43-year-old male, new patient, with no complaints. Patient is applying for life insurance and requests a physical examination. A detailed health and family history was obtained, and a basic physical was done. Physician completed life insurance physical form at patient's request. Blood and urine were collected.

> 99381   Initial comprehensive preventive medicine evaluation and management of an individual including an age and gender appropriate history, examination, counseling/anticipatory guidance/risk factor reduction interventions, and the ordering of appropriate laboratory/diagnostic procedures, new patient; infant (age under 1 year)
>
> 99386   Initial comprehensive preventive medicine evaluation and management of an individual including an age and gender appropriate history examination, counseling/anticipatory guidance/risk factor reduction interventions, and the ordering of appropriate laboratory/diagnostic procedures, new patient; 40–64 years
>
> 99396   Periodic comprehensive preventive medicine reevaluation and management of an individual including an age and gender appropriate history, examination, counseling/anticipatory guidance/risk factor reduction interventions, and the ordering of appropriate laboratory/diagnostic procedures, established patient; 40–64 years
>
> 99450   Basic life and/or disability examination that includes completion of a medical history following a life insurance pro forma

A. 99450   C. 99396
B. 99386   D. 99381

41. Provide the CPT code for a quantitative drug assay that was performed for a patient to determine digoxin level.

> 80050   General health panel
>
> 80101   Drug screen, qualitative; single drug class method (e.g., immunoassay, enzyme assay), each drug class
>
> 80162   Digoxin (therapeutic drug assay, quantitative examination)
>
> 80166   Doxepin (therapeutic drug assay, quantitative examination)

A. 80101   C. 80166
B. 80050   D. 80162

42. Provide the CPT code for anesthesia services for the transvenous insertion of a pacemaker.

> 00530 Anesthesia for permanent transvenous pacemaker insertion
> 00560 Anesthesia for procedures on heart, pericardial sac, and great vessels of chest; without pump oxygenator
> 33202 Insertion of epicardial electrode(s); by open incision
> 33206 Insertion of new or replacement of permanent pacemaker with transvenous electrode(s); atrial

A. 00560
B. 33202, 00530

C. 00530
D. 33206, 00560

43. A 4-year-old had a repair of an incarcerated inguinal hernia. This is the first time this child has been treated for this condition.

> 49496 Repair initial inguinal hernia full-term infant, under age 6 months, or preterm infant over 50 weeks postconception age and under 6 months at the time of surgery with or without hydrocelectomy; incarcerated or strangulated
> 49501 Repair initial inguinal hernia, age 6 months to under 5 years, with or without hydrocelectomy; incarcerated or strangulated
> 49521 Repair recurrent inguinal hernia, any age; incarcerated or strangulated
> 49553 Repair initial femoral hernia, any age; incarcerated or strangulated

A. 49553
B. 49496

C. 49521
D. 49501

44. The patient had a thrombectomy, without catheter, of the peroneal artery, by leg incision.

> 34203 Embolectomy or thrombectomy, with or without catheter; popliteal-tibio-peroneal artery, by leg incision
> 35226 Repair blood vessel, direct; lower extremity
> 35302 Thromboendarterectomy, including patch graft, if performed, superficial femoral artery
> 37799 Unlisted procedure, vascular surgery

A. 34203
B. 37799

C. 35302
D. 35226

45. A patient with lung cancer and bone metastasis is seen for complex treatment planning by a radiation oncologist.

> 77263 Therapeutic radiology treatment planning, complex
> 77290 Therapeutic radiology simulation-aided field setting; complex
> 77315 Teletherapy, isodose plan (whether hand or computer calculated); complex (mantle or inverted Y, tangential ports, the use of wedges, compensators, complex blocking, rotational beam, or special beam considerations)
> 77334 Treatment devices, design and construction; complex (irregular blocks, special shields, compensators, wedges, molds, or casts)

A. 77315
B. 77263

C. 77290
D. 77334

46. An established patient was seen by physician in her office for DTaP vaccine and Hib.

90471	Immunization administration (includes percutaneous, intradermal, subcutaneous, or intramuscular injections); one vaccine (single or combination vaccine/toxoid)
90700	Diphtheria, tetanus toxoids, and acellular pertussis vaccine (DTaP), when administered to individuals younger than 7 years, for intramuscular use
90720	Diphtheria, tetanus toxoids, and whole cell pertussis vaccine and Hemophilus influenza B vaccine (DTP-Hib), for intramuscular use
90721	Diphtheria, tetanus toxoids, and acellular pertussis vaccine and Hemophilus influenza B vaccine (DTaP-Hib), for intramuscular use
90748	Hepatitis B and Hemophilus influenza B vaccine (Hep B-Hib), for intramuscular use
99211	Office or other outpatient visit for the evaluation and management of an established patient, which may not require the presence of a physician. Usually, the presenting problem(s) are minimal. Typically, 5 minutes are spent performing or supervising these services

A. 90721
B. 90720, 90471
C. 90700, 90748, 99211
D. 90471, 90721

47. Which of the following procedures would NOT be coded to "resection" when using ICD-10-PCS?
A. resection of the upper right lobe
B. partial resection of upper left lobe
C. excision of gallbladder
D. excision of the sigmoid colon

48. If the same condition is described as both acute and chronic and separate subentries exist in the ICD-9-CM alphabetic index at the same indentation level,
A. they should both be coded, acute sequenced first.
B. they should both be coded, chronic sequenced first.
C. only the acute condition should be coded.
D. only the chronic condition should be coded.

49. A patient was sent to the surgeon's office as requested by the patient because the insurance company requires a second opinion regarding surgery. The patient has been complaining of lower back pain for over a year due to a herniated disk. The patient presents to the surgeon's office where a detailed history and physical examination was performed. Medical records from the primary care physician and the physical therapist were reviewed along with the tests performed in the office. Low medical decision making was made. A copy of the surgeon's reports was sent to the insurance company.
A. 99242–32
B. 99243
C. 99253–32
D. 99203–32

50. Patient arrives in the emergency room via a medical helicopter. The patient has sustained multiple life-threatening injuries due to a multiple car accident. The patient goes into cardiac arrest upon arrival. An hour and 30 minutes of critical care time is spent trying to stabilize the patient.

99282   Emergency department visit for the evaluation and management of a patient, which requires these three key components:
- An expanded problem focused history;
- An expanded problem focused examination; and
- Medical decision making of low complexity.

Counseling and/or coordination of care with other providers or agencies are provided consistent with the nature of the problem(s) and the patient's and/or family's needs.
Usually, the presenting problem(s) are of low to moderate severity.

99285   Emergency department visit for the evaluation and management of a patient, which requires these three key components within the constraints imposed by the urgency clinical condition and/or mental status:
- A comprehensive history;
- A comprehensive examination; and
- Medical decision making of high complexity.

Counseling and/or coordination of care with other providers or agencies are provided consistent with the nature of the problem(s) and the patient's and/or family's needs.
Usually, the presenting problem(s) are of high severity and pose an immediate significant threat to life or physiologic function.

99288   Physician direction of emergency medical systems (EMS) emergency care, advanced life support

99291   Critical care, evaluation and management of the critically ill or critically injured patient; first 30–74 minutes

+99292 Each additional 30 minutes (list separately in addition to code for primary service)

A. 99285, 99288, 99291
B. 99291, 99292

C. 99291, 99292, 99285
D. 99282

51. Patient presents with a diabetic ulcer that needs to be debrided. The patient was taken to the operating room where debridement of the muscle took place.

> 11011   Debridement including removal of foreign material associated with open fracture(s) and, or dislocation(s); skin, subcutaneous tissue, muscle fascia, and muscle
>
> 11043   Debridement, muscle, and/or fascia (includes epidermis, dermis, and subcutaneous tissue, if performed); first 20 sq cm or less
>
> 11400   Excision, benign lesion including margins, except skin tag (unless listed elsewhere), trunk, arms or legs; excised diameter 0.5 cm or less
>
> 15999   Unlisted procedure, excision pressure ulcer (for free skin graft to close ulcer or donor site, see 15002 et seq)

A. 15999   C. 11011
B. 11400   D. 11043

52. Excision 2 cm subcutaneous soft tissue lipoma of the back. (Code for diagnoses using ICD-10-CM. Code for procedure using CPT.)

> D17.30   Lipoma of other skin and subcutaneous tissue
>
> D23.5   Benign neoplasm of the skin of the trunk except scrotum
>
> D23.9   Benign neoplasm of the skin, site unspecified
>
> 11600   Excision, malignant lesion, trunk, arms, or legs, lesion diameter 0.5 cm or less
>
> 21556   Excision, tumor, soft tissue of neck or anterior thorax; subfascial (e.g., intramuscular); less than 5 cm
>
> 21925   Biopsy, soft tissue of back or flank; deep
>
> 21930   Excision, tumor, soft tissue of back or flank, subcutaneous; less than 3 cm

A. D23.5, 11600   C. D23.9, 21556
B. D17.30, 21925   D. D17.30, 21930

53. Patient undergoes a posterior L1-L5 spinal fusion for scoliosis with placement of a Harrington rod. Code using CPT.

> 22612   Arthrodesis, posterior or posteriorlateral technique, single level; lumbar (with lateral transverse technique, when performed
>
> 22800   Arthrodesis, posterior, for spinal deformity, with or without cast; up to 6 vertebral segments.
>
> +22840   Posterior nonsegmental instrumentation (e.g., Harrington rod technique, pedicle fixation across one interspace, atlantoaxial transarticular screw fixation, sublaminar wiring at C1, facet screw fixation) (list separately in addition to code for primary procedure)
>
> +22841   Internal spinal fixation by wiring spinous processes (list separately in addition to code for primary procedure)
>
> +22842   Posterior segmental instrumentation (e.g., pedicle fixation, dual rods with multiple hooks and sublaminar wires); 3–6 vertebral segments (list separately in addition to code for primary procedure)
>
> +22846   Anterior instrumentation; 4–7 vertebral segments (list separately in addition to code for primary procedure)

A. 22800, 22846   C. 22800, 22840
B. 22800, 22842   D. 22612, 22800, 22841

54. Patient has tear of the medial meniscus with loose bodies in the medial compartment of the left knee that was repaired by arthroscopic medial meniscectomy, shaving and trimming of meniscal rim, resection of synovium, and removal of the loose bodies. (Code using CPT procedure codes.)

27331	Arthrotomy, knee; including joint exploration, biopsy, or removal of loose or foreign bodies
27333	Arthrotomy, knee; medial and lateral
29800	Arthroscopy, temporomandibular joint, diagnostic, with or without synovial biopsy (separate procedure)
29804	Arthroscopy, temporomandibular joint, surgical; (for open procedures, use 21010)
29819	Arthroscopy, shoulder, surgical; with removal of loose body or foreign body (for open procedure, see 23040–23044, 23107)
29874	Arthroscopy, knee, surgical; for removal of loose body or foreign body (e.g., osteocondritis dissecans fragmentation, chondral fragmentation)
29881	Arthroscopy, knee, surgical; with meniscectomy (medial OR lateral, including any meniscal shaving)
LT	Left side

A. 29804
B. 27333-LT, 27331-LT
C. 29800-LT, 29819-LT
D. 29881-LT

55. Single lung transplant without cardiopulmonary bypass. (Code for physician using CPT procedure codes only.)

32652	Thoracoscopy, surgical; with total pulmonary decortication, including intrapleural pneumonolysis
32850	Donor pneunomectomy(s) (including cold preservation), from cadaver donor
32851	Lung transplant, single; without cardiopulmonary bypass
32852	Lung transplant, single; with cardiopulmonary bypass

A. 32850
B. 32652
C. 32852
D. 32851

56. Patient has a year history of mitral valve regurgitation and now presents for a mitral valve replacement with bypass. (Code for physician using CPT procedure codes only.)

33425	Valvuloplasty, mitral valve, with cardiopulmonary bypass
33430	Replacement, mitral valve, with cardiopulmonary bypass
33460	Valvectomy, tricuspid valve, with cardiopulmonary bypass
35231	Repair blood vessel with vein graft; neck

A. 33430
B. 33460
C. 33425
D. 35231

57. Patient has breast carcinoma and is now undergoing complete axillary lymphadenectomy. (Code for physician using CPT procedure codes only.)

38525	Biopsy or excision of lymph nodes; open, deep axillary node(s)
38562	Limited lymphadenectomy for staging (separate procedure); pelvic and para-aortic
38740	Axillary lymphadenectomy; superficial
38745	Axillary lymphadenectomy; complete

    A. 38525   C. 38562

    B. 38740   D. 38745

58. Patient presents to the GI lab for a colonoscopy. During the colonoscopy, polyps were discovered in the ascending colon and in the transverse colon. Polyps in the ascending colon were removed via hot biopsy forceps, and the polyps in the transverse colon were removed by snare technique.

D12.2	Benign neoplasm of ascending colon
44392	Colonoscopy through stoma; with removal of polyps, hot biopsy forceps
44394	Colonoscopy through stoma; with removal of polyps, snare technique
45355	Colonoscopy, transabdominal via colotomy
45383	Colonoscopy, with ablation of polyps, not by hot biopsy forceps or snare technique
45384	Colonoscopy with removal of polyps, hot biopsy forceps
45385	Colonoscopy with removal of polyps, snare technique
-59	Distinct procedural service

    A. D12.2, 45355   C. D12.2, 44392, 44394–59

    B. D12.2, 45384, 45385–59   D. D12.23, 45355, 45383–59

59. Patient came to the hospital ambulatory surgical center for repair of incisional hernia. This is the second time the patient has developed this problem. The hernia was repaired with a Gore-Tex graft. Choose the appropriate ICD-9-CM and CPT codes.

K30.40	Inguinal hernia, with obstruction, without gangrene, unilateral or unspecified
K43.9	Ventral hernia, unspecified without obstruction or gangrene
K40.90	Incisional hernia, without obstruction or gangrene
49520	Repair recurrent inguinal hernia, any age, reducible
49560	Repair initial incisional or ventral hernia, reducible
49565	Repair recurrent incisional or ventral hernia, reducible
+49568	Implantation of mesh or other prosthesis for incisional or ventral hernia repair or mesh for closure of debridement for necrotizing soft tissue infection. (List separately in addition to code for the incisional or ventral hernia repair.)

    A. K40.90, 49565, 49568

    B. K43.9, K40.90, 49520, 49568

    C. K30.40, 49565

    D. K30.40, K43.9, 49560, 49568

60. Female with 6 months of stress incontinence. Laparoscopic urethral suspension was completed. Choose the appropriate ICD-9-CM and CPT codes.

> N39.3 Urinary stress incontinence female
> R32 Urinary incontinence, unspecified
> 788.32 Urinary stress incontinence male
> 51840 Anterior vesicourethropexy or urethropexy (e.g., Marshall-Marchetti-Krantz, Burch); simple
> 51845 Abdominovaginal vesical neck suspension with or without endoscopic control
> 51990 Laparoscopy, surgical; urethral suspension for stress incontinence
> 51992 Laparoscopy, surgical; sling operation for stress incontinence

    A. R32, 51992   C. N39.3, 51840
    B. N39.3, 51990   D. R32, 51845

61. A patient is diagnosed with psychogenic paroxysmal tachycardia.
    A. I47.9   C. I47.8, F54
    B. F54   D. I47.9, F54

62. A patient is diagnosed with Alzheimer's disease with dementia.
    A. G30.8, F02.81, Z91.83   C. G30.0, F02.81, Z91.83
    B. F02.81, G30.0, Z91.73   D. G30.0, Z91.73

63. A patient has end-stage kidney disease, which resulted from malignant hypertension.
    A. I12.0, N18.6   C. I13.11, N18.6
    B. I10, N18.6   D. I15.1, N18.6

64. A patient presents with dermatitis due to a prescription topical antibiotic cream used as directed by a physician.
    A. L08.89, T49.0x5   C. L02.91, T49.0x5
    B. L25.1, T49.0x5A   D. T49.0x5, L25.1

65. A patient presents with cervical spina bifida with hydrocephalus.
    A. Q76.0   C. Q05.0
    B. Q05   D. Q05.5

66. An infant has hypoglycemia and a mother with diabetes.
    A. P70.0   C. P70.1
    B. P70.2   D. P70.4

67. A woman has a Pap smear that detected cervical high-risk human papillomavirus (HPV). The DNA test was positive.
    A. R87.810   C. R87.820
    B. R87.811   D. R87.811

68. A patient suffered dizziness as a result of taking prescribed phenobarbital. The patient took his medication with beer.
    A. R42, T42.4x1A   C. T42.4x2A, R42
    B. R42, T42.3x5A   D. T42.4x1A, R42

69. The patient presents for a screening examination for lung cancer.
    A. Z03.89
    B. C78.00
    C. Z12.2
    D. C34.90

70. The diagnosis is as follows: "Carcinoma of axillary lymph nodes and lungs, metastatic from breast." Given this, which is (are) the primary cancer site(s)?
    A. axillary lymph nodes
    B. lungs
    C. breast
    D. both A and B

71. Robert Thompson was admitted with a chronic cough and the physician records "rule out lung cancer." What should be coded as the patient's diagnosis?
    A. chronic cough
    B. observation and evaluation without need for further medical care
    C. diagnosis of unknown etiology
    D. lung cancer

72. A patient who is taking the drug Antivert may have a diagnosis of
    A. dizziness.
    B. urinary tract infection.
    C. arthritis.
    D. congestive heart failure.

73. The use of radioactive sources placed into a tumor-bearing area to generate high-intensity radiation is termed
    A. stereotactic radiation treatment.
    B. proton beam treatment.
    C. brachytherapy.
    D. external beam radiation.

74. A patient has a total abdominal hysterectomy with bilateral salpingectomy. The coder selected the following codes:

58150	Total abdominal hysterectomy (corpus and cervix), with or without removal of tube(s) with or without removal of ovary(s)
58700	Salpingectomy, complete or partial unilateral or bilateral (separate procedure)

This type of coding is referred to as
    A. upcoding.
    B. unbundling.
    C. maximizing.
    D. optimization.

75. Which of the following is classified as a poisoning in ICD-10-CM?
    A. syncope due to Contac pills and a three-martini lunch
    B. digitalis intoxication
    C. reaction to dye administered for pyelogram
    D. idiosyncratic reaction between various drugs

76. CPT codes for a laparoscopic removal and replacement of both a gastric band and the subcutaneous port components.
    A. 43774, 43659
    B. 43659
    C. 43773
    D. 43848

77. CPT code(s) for a laryngoscopic submucosal removal of nonneoplastic lesion of the vocal cord with graft reconstruction. An operating microscope was used.
    A. 31546, 69990
    B. 31546, 20926
    C. 31546
    D. 31546, 20926-51

78. CPT code(s) for a laparoscopic takedown of the splenic flexure and a partial colectomy with anastomosis.
    A. 44140, 44213   C. 44213
    B. 44204   D. 44204, 44213

79. CPT code for a laparoscopic gastric restrictive procedure and placement of an adjustable gastric band.
    A. 43770   C. 43845
    B. 43800   D. 43846

80. CPT code for a high-energy ESW of the lateral humeral epicondyle using general anesthesia.
    A. 0019T   C. 0102T
    B. 0101T   D. 28890

81. A 32-year-old patient has a colonoscopy with removal of three polyps by snare. Moderate sedation was used and provided by the physician. The intraservice time was 30 minutes. (CPT coding)
    A. 45385, 45385-51, 45385-51   C. 45385
    B. 45385, 99144   D. 45385, 45385-51, 45385-51, 99144

82. Male patient has been diagnosed with benign prostatic hypertrophy and undergoes a transurethral destruction of the prostate by radiofrequency thermotherapy. (Code ICD-10-CM for diagnoses and CPT for procedures.)

N40.0	Hypertrophy (benign of prostate) without urinary obstruction and other lower urinary tract symptoms (LUTS)
52601	Transurethral electrosurgical resection of prostate including control of postoperative bleeding, complete (vasectomy, meatotomy, cystourethroscopy, urethral calibration and/or dilation, and internal urethrotomy are included)
52648	Laser vaporization of prostate, including control of postoperative bleeding, complete (vasectomy, meatotomy, cystourethroscopy, urethral calibration and/or dilation, internal urethrotomy, and transurethral transection of the prostate are included if performed)
53850	Transurethral destruction of prostate tissue; by microwave thermotherapy
53852	Transurethral destruction of prostate tissue; by radiofrequency thermotherapy

    A. N40.0, 52648   C. N40.0, 52601
    B. N40.0, 53852   D. N04.0, 53850

83. Hysteroscopy with D&C and polypectomy. (Code CPT for procedures.)

58100	Endometrial sampling (biopsy) with or without endocervical sampling (biopsy), without cervical dilation, any method (separate procedure)
58120	Dilation and curettage, diagnostic and/or therapeutic (nonobstetrical)
58555	Hysteroscopy, diagnostic (separate procedure)
58558	Hysteroscopy, surgical; with sampling (biopsy) of endometrium and/or polypectomy, with or without D&C
58563	Hysteroscopy, surgical; with endometrial ablation (e.g., endometrial resection, electrosurgical ablation, thermoablation)

    A. 58563   C. 58120, 58100, 58555
    B. 58558   D. 58558, 58120

84. Cesarean delivery with antepartum and postpartum care. (Code CPT for procedures.)

59400	Routine obstetric care, including antepartum care, vaginal delivery (with or without episiotomy and/or forceps), and postpartum care
59510	Routine obstetric care including antepartum care, cesarean delivery, and postpartum care
59514	Cesarean delivery only
59610	Routine obstetric care including antepartum care, vaginal delivery (with or without episiotomy and/or forceps) and postpartum care, after previous cesarean delivery

A. 59610
B. 59514

C. 59400
D. 59510

85. D&C for missed abortion, first trimester. (Code CPT for procedures.)

59820	Treatment of missed abortion, completed surgically; first trimester
59840	Induced abortion, by dilation and curettage
59850	Induced abortion, by one or more intra-amniotic injections (amniocentesis injections) including hospital admission and visits, delivery of fetus and secundines
59855	Induced abortion, by one or more vaginal suppositories (e.g., prostaglandin), with or without cervical dilation (e.g., laminaria), including hospital admission and visits, delivery of fetus and secundines

A. 59840
B. 59850

C. 59855
D. 59820

86. Total transcervical thymectomy. (Code CPT for procedures.)

60200	Excision of cyst or adenoma of thyroid, or transection of isthmus
60240	Thyroidectomy, total or complete
60520	Thymectomy, partial or total; transcervical approach (separate procedure)
60540	Adrenalectomy, partial or complete, or exploration of adrenal gland with or without biopsy, transabdominal, lumbar or dorsal (separate procedure)

A. 60520
B. 60540

C. 60240
D. 60200

87. Patient with carpal tunnel comes in for an open carpal tunnel release. (Code ICD-9-CM for diagnoses and CPT for procedures.)

G650.0	Carpal tunnel syndrome
64721	Neuroplasty and/or transposition; median nerve at carpal tunnel
64892	Nerve graft (includes obtaining graft), single strand, arm or leg; up to 4 cm length
64905	Nerve pedicle transfer; first stage
64999	Unlisted procedure, nervous system

A. 354.0, 64999
B. 354.0, 64721

C. 354.0, 64905
D. 354.0, 64892

88. Lumbar laminectomy (one segment) for decompression of spinal cord. (Code CPT for procedures.)

62263	Percutaneous lysis of epidural adhesions using solution injection (e.g., hypertonic saline, enzyme) or mechanical means (e.g., catheter) including radiologic localization (includes contrast when administered), multiple adhesiolysis sessions; 2 or more days
63005	Laminectomy, with exploration and/or decompression of spinal cord and/or cauda equina, without facetectomy, foraminotomy, or diskectomy (e.g., spinal stenosis), one or two vertebral segments; lumbar except for spondylolisthesis
63030	Laminotomy (hemilaminectomy), with decompression of nerve root(s), including partial facetectomy, foraminotomy, and/or excision of herniated intervertebral disk; one interspace, lumbar
63170	Laminectomy with myelotomy (e.g., Bischof or DREZ type), cervical, thoracic, or thoracolumbar

A. 63005
B. 62263
C. 63170
D. 63030

89. Phacoemulsification of left cataract with IOL implant and subconjunctival injection. (Code ICD-9-CM for diagnosis and CPT for procedures.)

H26.9	Unspecified cataract
66940	Removal of lens material; extracapsular
66983	Intracapsular cataract extraction with insertion of intraocular lens prosthesis (one-stage procedure)
66984	Extracapsular cataract removal with insertion of intraocular lens prosthesis (one-stage procedure) manual or mechanical technique (e.g., irrigation and aspiration or phacoemulsification)
68200	Subconjunctival injection

A. 366.9, 66940-LT
B. 366.9, 66983, 68200
C. 366.9, 66984-LT
D. 366.9, 66984-LT, 68200-LT

90. When a patient is admitted because of a primary neoplasm with metastasis and treatment is directed toward the secondary neoplasm only,
   A. code only the primary neoplasm as the principal diagnosis.
   B. the primary neoplasm is coded as the principal diagnosis and the secondary neoplasm is coded as an additional diagnosis.
   C. the secondary neoplasm is coded as the principal diagnosis, and the primary neoplasm is coded as an additional diagnosis.
   D. code only the secondary neoplasm as the principal diagnosis.

91. A document that acknowledges patient responsibility for payment if Medicare denies the claim is a(n)
   A. explanation of benefits.
   B. remittance advice.
   C. advance beneficiary notice.
   D. CMS-1500 claim form.

92. The patient sees a participating (PAR) provider and has a procedure performed after meeting the annual deductible. If the Medicare-approved amount is $200, how much is the patient's out-of-pocket expense?
   A. $0
   B. $20
   C. $40
   D. $100

93. The purpose of the Correct Coding Initiative is to
   A. increase fines and penalties for bundling services into comprehensive CPT codes.
   B. restrict Medicare reimbursement to hospitals for ancillary services.
   C. teach coders how to unbundle codes.
   D. detect and prevent payment for improperly coded services.

94. CMS delegates its daily operations of the Medicare and Medicaid programs to
   A. the office of the Inspector General.
   B. the PRO in each state.
   C. the National Center for Vital and Health Statistics.
   D. the Medicare administrative contractor (MAC).

95. The _____ are the organizations that contract with Medicare to perform reviews of medical records with the corresponding Medicare claims to detect and correct improper payments.
   A. Atlas Systems
   B. medical outcomes study
   C. recovery audit contractors (RACs)
   D. adjusted clinical groups (ACGs) system

96. Which of the following could influence a facility's case mix?
   A. changes in DRG weights
   B. changes in the services offered by a facility
   C. accuracy of coding
   D. all of the above

97. The chargemaster relieves the coders from coding repetitive services that require little, if any, formal documentation analysis. This is called
   A. grouping.   C. soft coding.
   B. hard coding.   D. mapping.

98. The practice of using a code that results in a higher payment to the provider than the code that more accurately reflects the service provided is known as
   A. unbundling.   C. optimizing.
   B. upcoding.   D. downcoding.

99. The APC payment system is based on what coding system(s)?
   A. AMA's CPT codes
   B. CPT and ICD-9-CM diagnosis and procedure codes
   C. ICD-9-CM diagnosis and procedure codes
   D. CPT/HCPCS codes

100. Which of the following contains a list of coding edits developed by CMS in an effort to promote correct coding nationwide and to prevent the inappropriate unbundling of related services?
   A. National Coverage Determination (NCD)
   B. National Correct Coding Initiative (NCCI)
   C. CPT Assistant
   D. Healthcare Common Procedure Coding System (HCPCS)

CCA MOCK Exam Answer Key

ANSWER EXPLANATION

1. D

REFERENCE: LaTour, Eichenwald-Maki, and Oachs, pp 99–100
      Sayles, p 1042

2. A A clinical impression and an intended course of action are either entered in the physical examination or provided in the admission note. The admission note provides an overview of the patient and adds any relevant information that is not included in the history and physical examination.

REFERENCE: LaTour, Eichenwald-Maki, and Oachs, p 248
      Sayles, pp 83, 1240

3. D Progress note elements written in the acronym "SOAP" style are:
    S—subjective, records what the patient states is the problem
    O—objective, records what the practitioner identifies through the history, physical examination, and diagnostic tests
    A—assessment, combines the subjective and objective into a conclusion
    P—plan, what approach is going to be taken to resolve the problem

REFERENCE: Abdelhak, pp 118–119
      Sayles, p 126

4. D

REFERENCE: LaTour, Eichenwald-Maki, and Oachs, pp 444–445, 904
      Sayles, pp 217–219, 223, 318, 395, 413, 1194

5. D A final note may substitute for a discharge summary for patients admitted for less than 48 hours with minor problems, uncomplicated deliveries, and for normal neonates.

REFERENCE: Abdelhak, p 113
      LaTour, Eichenwald-Maki, and Oachs, p 251

6. A The physician releasing the patient should write a final note of summary of the patient's course of treatment, stating the patient's condition at discharge, and instructions for the patient's activity, diet, and medications as well as any follow-up appointments or instructions. If a patient expires, the final notes describe the circumstances regarding the death, the findings, the cause of death, and whether or not an autopsy was performed.

REFERENCE: LaTour, Eichenwald-Maki, and Oachs, pp 248, 251
      Sayles, pp 83, 93–95

7. D The postpartum record contains information about the condition of the mother after delivery and includes an assessment of the lochia and conditions of the breasts, fundus, and perineum.

REFERENCE: Abdelhak, p 114
      Green and Bowie, pp 182, 184
      LaTour, Eichenwald-Maki, and Oachs, p 252
      Sayles, p 98

CCA MOCK Exam Answer Key

ANSWER   EXPLANATION

8. D Not all of the components of the combination code for diabetes mellitus, uncontrolled, were present on admission. The diabetes mellitus was present on admission, but it was not "uncontrolled" until 3 days after admission.
    A. Y = yes, present on admission
    B. U = no information in the record
    C. W = clinically undetermined
    D. N = no, not present on admission

REFERENCE: AHA, pp 571–574

9. B   CALCULATION:

Step 1: Multiply each row (relative weight × number of patients).

Step 2: Sum the totals of each row (169.051).

Step 3: Divide the total relative weight sums (169.051) by the total number of patients (57)

$$\frac{169.051 \text{ total relative weight}}{57 \text{ total patients seen}} = 2.965807$$

REFERENCE: AHA, pp 565–566
                 LaTour, Eichenwald-Maki, and Oachs, p 433
                 Sayles, p 499

10. A The interdisciplinary care plan is the foundation around which patient care is organized. It contains input from the unique perspective of each discipline involved. It includes an assessment, statement of goals, identification of specific activities, or strategies to achieve those goals and periodic assessments of goal attainment.

REFERENCE: Abdelhak, p 107
                 LaTour, Eichenwald-Maki, and Oachs, p 254
                 Sayles, pp 111, 114, 696

11. C

REFERENCE: McWay, pp 369, 519

12. D

REFERENCE: Abdelhak, pp 197–199
                 LaTour, Eichenwald-Maki, and Oachs, pp 243, 442, 470
                 Sayles, pp 121, 292–293, 306–307

CCA MOCK Exam Answer Key

ANSWER   EXPLANATION

13. A employee number 425: $120 + (35 \times 0.75) + (16 \times 0.5) = 154.25$

          $154.25/5 = 30.85$ average work units per day

        Employee number 426: $48 + (89 \times 0.75) + (95 \times 0.5) = 162.25$

          $162.25/5 = 32.45$ average work units per day

        Employee number 427: $80 + (92 \times 0.75) + (4 \times 0.5) = 151$

          $151/5 = 30.2$ average work units per day

        Employee number 428: $65 + (109 \times 0.75) + (16 \times 0.5) = 154.75$

          $154.75/5 = 30.95$ average work units per day

REFERENCE: Abdelhak, pp 19, 621–622

14. D

REFERENCE: AHA, pp 320–321

15. B

REFERENCE: AHA, pp 15, 60–62, 303, 484–485, 499

16. B

REFERENCE: AHA, pp 126, 249, 398–401

17. C

REFERENCE: AHA, pp 571–574

18. A

REFERENCE: AHA, pp 571–574

19. D

REFERENCE: Johnson and Linker, pp 442–443

20. B

REFERENCE: Frisch, pp 189–192
                 Green and Rowell, pp 6, 69, 70–71
                 Johnson and Linker, pp 539–540
                 Rimmer, pp 94–95

21. C The condition should be coded as a poisoning when there is an interaction of an over-the-counter drug and alcohol. Answers A, B, and D are adverse effects of a correctly administered prescription drug.

REFERENCE: AHA, pp 513–518

22. A

REFERENCE: AHA, pp 571–574

CCA MOCK Exam Answer Key

ANSWER   EXPLANATION

23. C All ICD-10-CM codes start with an alphabetic character. The basic code structure consists of three digits and then a decimal point. Most codes contain a maximum of six characters, with a few chapters having a seventh character.

REFERENCE: AHA, pp 7–8

24. D

REFERENCE: AHA, pp 299–300, 489

25. D

REFERENCE: AHA, pp 224–226

26. C

REFERENCE: AHA, pp 337–340

27. C

REFERENCE: LaTour, Eichenwald-Maki, and Oachs, pp 229, 353, 728, 907
                    Sayles, pp 391, 885, 1056

28. C A surgical operation is one or more surgical procedures performed at one time for one patient using a common approach or for a common purpose.

REFERENCE: Koch, p 180

29. D

REFERENCE: LaTour, Eichenwald-Maki, and Oachs, pp 100–101
                    Sayles, pp 1042, 1208

30. A

REFERENCE: LaTour, Eichenwald-Maki, and Oachs, p 266

31. C Benchmarking involves comparing your department to other departments or organizations known to be excellent in one or more areas. The success of benchmarking involves finding out how the other department functions and then incorporating their ideas into your department.

REFERENCE: LaTour, Eichenwald-Maki, and Oachs, p 499
                    Sayles, p 497

32. C

REFERENCE: Johnson and Linker, pp 216–217

33. A

REFERENCE: McWay, pp 261–263, 505

CCA MOCK Exam Answer Key

ANSWER   EXPLANATION

34. C *Staging* is a term used to refer for the progression of cancer. In accessing most types of cancer, a method (staging) is used to determine how far the cancer has progressed. The cancer is described in terms of how large the main tumor is, the degree to which it has invaded surrounding tissue, and the extent to which it has spread to lymph glands or other areas of the body. Staging not only helps to assess outlook but also the most appropriate treatment.

REFERENCE: Abdelhak, pp 488–489
                  LaTour, Eichenwald-Maki, and Oachs, pp 371, 949
                  Sayles, p 439

35. B According to the UHDDS, the principal diagnosis is to be sequenced first.

REFERENCE: AHA, pp 30–33

36. D The hospital inpatient procedure would not be coded using HCPCS/CPT codes. Hospital inpatient visit diagnoses and procedures are coded using ICD-9-CM codes.

REFERENCE: Green, p 372
                  Johnson and Linker, pp 11–12
                  LaTour, Eichenwald-Maki, and Oachs, pp 389–394
                  Sayles, pp 182–183, 190–193 199–205, 275, 665, 1198
                  Smith, p 1

37. B The sizes of the layered wound repairs of the same body area are added together in order to select the correct CPT code.

REFERENCE: Green, pp 524–525
                  Johnson and Linker, pp 120–122
                  Smith, pp 66–68

38. D Look up in CPT code book under foot, neuroma.

REFERENCE: AMA CPT (2014)

39. D *Dialysis* is the main term to be referenced in the CPT manual index.

REFERENCE: Bowie and Schaffer (2013), pp 429–431
                  Green, pp 808–810
                  Johnson and Linker, pp 432–433
                  Smith, p 229

40. A The codes in this subsection are used to report evaluations for life or disability insurance baseline information.

REFERENCE: AMA CPT (2014), p 40
                  Bowie and Schaffer (2013), pp 77–79
                  Green, p 448
                  Johnson and Linker, pp 161–165

CCA MOCK Exam Answer Key

ANSWER   EXPLANATION

41. D

REFERENCE: Bowie and Schaffer (2013), p 419
Green, p 779
Johnson and Linker, p 418

42. C

REFERENCE: Bowie and Schaffer (2013), pp 188–195
Green, pp 482–484
Johnson and Linker, pp 175–178

43. D

REFERENCE: Bowie and Schaffer (2013), pp 274–275
Green, pp 655–656
Johnson and Linker, pp 192–193
Smith, pp 126–128

44. A

REFERENCE: Bowie and Schaffer (2013), p 212
Green, p 606
Johnson and Linker, p 17

45. B

REFERENCE: AMA CPT (2014), pp 420–421
Bowie and Schaffer (2013), pp 404–408
Green, pp 753–756
Johnson and Linker, p 403
Smith, pp 179–180

46. D If immunization is the only service that the patient receives, then two codes are used to report the service: the immunization administration code is first, and then the code for the vaccine/toxoid.

REFERENCE: AMA CPT (2014), pp 522–527
Green, pp 802–804
Johnson and Linker, p 429
Smith, pp 226–227

47. B

REFERENCE: AHA, p 93

48. A

REFERENCE: AHA, pp 58–59

CCA MOCK Exam Answer Key

| ANSWER | EXPLANATION |

49. D

REFERENCE: AMA CPT (2014), pp 18–20
Frisch, pp 16, 49–53
Green, pp 439–441
Johnson and Linker, pp 149–154
Smith, pp 216–217

50. B

REFERENCE: AMA CPT (2014), pp 23–25
Bowie and Schaffer (2013), pp 63–65
Frisch, pp 27–32
Green, pp 439–441
Johnson and Linker, pp 155–157
Smith, pp 216–217

51. D

REFERENCE: Bowie and Schaffer (2013), p 113
Johnson and Linker, p 218

52. D Excision of lipomas code to excision of soft tissue.

REFERENCE: AHA, pp 440–441
Green, p 557
Smith, p 63

53. C

REFERENCE: AMA CPT (2014), pp 117–118
Bowie and Schaffer (2013), p 145
Green, p 562
Johnson and Linker, pp 275–276

54. D If debridement or shaving of articular cartilage and a menisectomy are performed in the same compartment of the knee, then code only 29881.

REFERENCE: Bowie and Schaffer (2013), pp 163–164
CPT Assistant, April 2001, pp 5–7, 12
CPT Assistant, April 2003, pp 12, 14
Green, pp 568–569
Johnson and Linker, pp 268–271

55. D

REFERENCE: Bowie and Schaffer (2013), pp 163–164
CPT Assistant, Winter 1993, p 2
Green, pp 579–580

56. A Valvuloplasty is a plastic repair of a valve.

REFERENCE: Bowie and Schaffer (2013), p 206
Green, p 599
Johnson and Linker, p 315

CCA MOCK Exam Answer Key

ANSWER   EXPLANATION

57. D

REFERENCE: Bowie and Schaffer (2013), p 35
                 Green, p 624
                 Johnson and Linker, p 85

58. B According to CPT Assistant, when a colonoscopy with polypectomy is performed by two different techniques, both techniques are coded.

REFERENCE: Bowie and Schaffer (2013), pp 269–270
                 Green, pp 651–652
                 Johnson and Linker, p 188
                 Smith, pp 121–122

59. A The mesh is reported as an additional code. The hernia is considered recurrent because this documentation states this is the second hernia.

REFERENCE: AHA, p 253
                 AMA (2014), pp 288–289
                 Bowie and Schaffer (2013), pp 274–275
                 Green, pp 655–656
                 Johnson and Linker, pp 192–193
                 Smith, pp 126–127

60. B

REFERENCE: AHA, p 262
                 Bowie and Schaffer (2013), p 94
                 Johnson and Linker, pp 194–195

61. D

REFERENCE: AHA, p 179

62. C

REFERENCE: AHA, pp 173, 206

63. A

REFERENCE: AHA, pp 263, 264

64. B

REFERENCE: AHA, p 284

65. C

REFERENCE: AHA, p 359

66. C

REFERENCE: AHA, p 373

67. A

REFERENCE: AHA, pp 140, 141

CCA MOCK Exam Answer Key

ANSWER   EXPLANATION

68. B

REFERENCE: AHA, p 518

69. D

REFERENCE: AHA, p 132

70. C

REFERENCE: AHA, pp 447–449

71. D

REFERENCE: AHA, p 58

72. A Antivert is used for the management of nausea and dizziness associated with motion sickness and in vertigo associated with diseases affecting the vestibular system.

REFERENCE: Nobles, p 543

73. C

REFERENCE: Bowie and Shaffer (2013), p 407
              Johnson and Linker, p 404
              Smith, pp 178–179

74. B

REFERENCE: Bowie and Schaffer (2013), pp 109–110
              Frisch, pp 235–240, 341
              Johnson and Linker, p 628
              Smith, pp 56–57

75. A A reaction due to mixing drugs and alcohol is coded as a poisoning.

REFERENCE: AHA, pp 514–518

76. B

REFERENCE: CPT Assistant, June 2006, p 16

77. C

REFERENCE: CPT Assistant, May 2006, pp 16–17

78. D

REFERENCE: CPT Assistant, April 2006, p 19

79. A

REFERENCE: CPT Assistant, April 2006, p 2

80. C

CCA MOCK Exam Answer Key

    ANSWER   EXPLANATION

81. C CPT designates certain procedures as including moderate sedation; therefore, moderate sedation is included in the code for the removal of polyps.

REFERENCE: AMA CPT (2014)
              CPT Assistant, February 2006, pp 9–10

82. B

REFERENCE: AHA, pp 270–271
              Bowie and Schaffer (2013), p 296
              Green, pp 676–679

83. B

REFERENCE: Bowie and Schaffer (2013), p 322
              Green, pp 683–685
              Johnson and Linker, pp 380–381

84. D

REFERENCE: Bowie and Schaffer (2013), p 333
              Green, pp 686–690
              Johnson and Linker, pp 346–348

85. D

REFERENCE: Bowie and Schaffer (2013), pp 335–336
              Green, pp 690–691
              Johnson and Linker, pp 353–354

86. A

REFERENCE: Bowie and Schaffer (2013), pp 344–345
              Green, p 692

87. B

REFERENCE: AHA, p 213
              Green, p 704

88. A

REFERENCE: Green, pp 701–702
              Johnson and Linker, pp 275–276

89. C Subconjunctival injections are included in 66984.

REFERENCE: AHA, pp 163, 216
              AMA, pp 297, 302
              CPT Assistant, Fall 1992, pp 5, 8
              CPT Assistant, February 2001, p 7
              CPT Assistant, November 2003, p 11
              Green, pp 708–709
              Johnson and Linker, pp 200–201

CCA MOCK Exam Answer Key

ANSWER EXPLANATION

90. C

REFERENCE: AHA, p 457

91. C

REFERENCE: Frisch, pp 90, 169–177
Green and Rowell, pp 16, 69–71, 73

92. C Medicare pays 80%, or $160, and the patient pays 20%, or $40.

REFERENCE: Green and Rowell, pp 401–402

93. D

REFERENCE: Frisch, pp 235–240
Johnson and Linker, pp 624–626

94. D Medicare administrative contractor is the new name for the previously termed carriers and fiscal intermediaries.

REFERENCE: Green, pp 812–813

95. C

REFERENCE: Sayles, pp 855–856, 944

96. D

REFERENCE: Sayles, pp 471–472

97. B

REFERENCE: Sayles, pp 299, 1210

98. B

REFERENCE: Sayles, pp 303, 1255

99. D

REFERENCE: Sayles, pp 274–275, 1080

100. B

REFERENCE: LaTour, Eichenwald-Maki, and Oachs, pp 447, 932
Sayles, p 289

REFERENCES

Abdelhak, M., Grostick, S., Hanken, M. A., & Jacobs, E. (Eds.). (2012). *Health information: Management of a strategic resource* (5th ed.). St. Louis, MO: Saunders Elsevier.

American Hospital Association (AHA). (2013). *ICD-10-CM and ICD-10-PCS coding handbook 2014 (with Answers)*. Chicago: Nelly Leon-Chisen, RHIA Central Office on ICD-10-CM and ICD-10-PCS of the American Hospital Association (AHA).

American Medical Association (AMA). *CPT assistant*. Chicago: Author.

American Medical Association (AMA). (2013). *Physicians' current procedural terminology (CPT) 2014 professional edition*. Chicago: Author.

Bowie, M., & Schaffer, L. (2013). *Understanding procedural coding: A worktext*. Clifton Park, NY: Delmar Cengage Learning.

Frisch, B. (2007). *Correct coding for Medicare, compliance, and reimbursement*. Clifton Park, NY: Delmar Cengage Learning.

Green, M. (2014). *3-2-1 Code it!* (4th ed.). Clifton Park, NY: Delmar Cengage Learning.

Green, M. A., & Bowie, M. J. (2011). *Essentials of health information management: Principles and practices*. Clifton Park, NY: Delmar Cengage Learning.

Green, M., & Rowell, J. C. (2011). *Understanding health insurance: A guide to billing and reimbursement* (10th ed.). Clifton Park, NY: Delmar Cengage Learning.

Johnson, S. L., & Linker, R. (2013). *Understanding medical coding: A comprehensive guide* (3rd ed.). Clifton Park, NY: Delmar Cengage Learning.

Jones, B. D. (2011). *Comprehensive medical terminology* (4th ed.). Clifton Park, NY: Delmar Cengage Learning.

Koch, G. (2008). *Basic allied health statistics and analysis* (3rd ed.). Clifton Park, NY: Delmar Cengage Learning.

LaTour, K., Eichenwald-Maki, S., and Oachs, P. (2013). *Health information management concepts: Principles and practice* (4th ed.). Chicago: American Health Information Management Association (AHIMA).

McWay, D. C. (2014). *Today's health information management: An integrated approach* (2nd ed.). Clifton Park, NY: Delmar Cengage Learning.

Neighbors, M., & Tannehill-Jones, R. (2010). *Human diseases* (3rd ed.). Clifton Park, NY: Delmar Cengage Learning.

OptumInsight. (2013). *ICD-10-CM for hospitals: The complete official draft code set.* Salt Lake City, UT: Author.

Rimmer, M. (2008). *Medical billing 101*. Clifton Park, NY: Delmar Cengage Learning.

Sayles, N. B. (2013). *Health information technology: An applied approach* (4th ed.). Chicago: American Health Information Management Association (AHIMA).

Smith, G. (2013). *Basic current procedure terminology and HCPCS coding*. Chicago: American Health Information Management Association (AHIMA).

Sormunen, C. (2013). *Terminology for allied health professionals* (7th ed.). Clifton Park, NY: Delmar Cengage Learning.

Competencies for the CCA Mock Examination

Question	CCA Domain					
	1	2	3	4	5	6
1					X	
2			X			
3			X			
4					X	
5			X			
6			X			
7			X			
8	X					
9		X				
10			X			
11						X
12		X				
13			X			
14	X					
15	X					
16	X					
17	X					
18	X					
19	X					
20		X				
21	X					
22	X					
23	X					
24	X					
25	X					
26	X					
27						X
28	X					
29					X	
30			X			
31			X			
32	X					
33					X	
34	X					
35		X				

Competencies for the CCA Mock Examination

Question	CCA Domain					
	1	2	3	4	5	6
36	X					
37	X					
38	X					
39	X					
40	X					
41	X					
42	X					
43	X					
44	X					
45	X					
46	X					
47	X					
48	X					
49	X					
50	X					
51	X					
52	X					
53	X					
54	X					
55	X					
56	X					
57	X					
58	X					
59	X					
60	X					
61	X					
62	X					
63	X					
64	X					
65	X					
66	X					
67	X					
68	X					
69	X					
70	X					

Competencies for the CCA Mock Examination

Question	CCA Domain					
	1	2	3	4	5	6
71	X					
72	X					
73	X					
74	X					
75	X					
76	X					
77	X					
78	X					
79	X					
80	X					
81	X					
82	X					
83	X					
84	X					
85	X					
86	X					
87	X					
88	X					
89	X					
90	X					
91		X				
92		X				
93				X		
94				X		
95		X				
96		X				
97					X	
98		X				
99		X				
100		X				

APPENDIX A
PHARMACOLOGY

The most common prescription drugs with examples of diagnoses

Analgesics

acetaminophen w/codeine (Tylenol #2, #3, #4) mild to moderate pain
Advil (ibuprofen) mild to moderate pain
aspirin, enteric coated (salicylate) reduces fever, relieves mild to moderate pain
Dilaudid (hydromorphine HCl) moderate to severe pain
Feldene (piroxicam) NSAID
hydrocodone w/APAP (Lortab 2.5) pain, moderate to severe; antitussives/expectorants, back pain
ibuprofen (Advil, Motrin) NSAID, arthritis, osteoarthritis; rheumatoid arthritis, dysmenorrhea; mild to moderate pain, fever; gout
Lortab (hydrocodone w/APAP) moderate to severe pain, expectorant
Motrin (ibuprofen) mild to moderate pain
oxycodone pain
piroxicam (Feldene) NSAID
tramadol (Ultram) moderate to severe pain
Tylenol #2, #3, #4 (acetaminophen w/codeine) mild to moderate pain
Ultram (tramadol) short-term pain

Antibacterial

amoxicillin (AMOXIL) antibiotic; broad-spectrum antibacterial drug, urinary tract infections, strep throat
Amoxil (amoxicillin) antibiotic; broad-spectrum antibacterial drug
Augmentin (amoxicilln with clavulanate potassium) treats certain bacterial infections of the ears, lungs, sinus, skin, and urinary tract
Avelox (moxifloxacin hydrochloride) for susceptible strains of designated microorganisms
Bactroban (mupirocin) topical antibiotic
cephalexin, USP (Keflex) antibiotic–antibacterial
ciprofloxacin (Cipro) antibacterial (drug-resistant bacteria)
Cipro (ciprofloxacin) antibacterial (drug-resistant bacteria)
clindamycin (Cleocin) antibacterial
doxycycline hyclate (Vibra-Tabs) antibacterial (drug-resistant bacteria)
erythromycin (Ery-Tab, Erythrocin) macrolide antibiotic
Flagyl (metronidazole) trichomoniasis
Keflex (cephalexin, USP) antibacterial antibiotic
levofloxacin (Levaquin) antibacterial (drug-resistant bacteria)
Levaquin (levofloxacin) antibacterial (drug-resistant bacteria), acute bacterial sinusitis
metronidazole tabs (Fagyl) trichomoniasis
minocycline (Solodyn) used to treat moderate to severe acne
mupirocin (Bactroban) topical antibiotic
Omnicef (cefdinir) drug-resistant bacteria
Penicillin VK infections
Solodyn (minocycline HCl) used to treat moderate to severe acne
tetracycline HCl (Sumycin, Panmycin) antibiotic
Vibra-Tabs (doxycycline hyclate, USP) antibacterial (drug-resistant bacteria)

Anti-inflammatory

Anaprox (naproxen) relieves pain and swelling

Asacol (mesalamine) GI anti-inflammatory (5-aminosalicylic acid derivate)

Celebrex (celecoxib) osteoarthritis, rheumatoid arthritis

celecoxib (Celebrex) osteoarthritis and rheumatoid arthritis, adenomatous colorectal polyps

diclofenac (Voltaren) osteoarthritis, rheumatoid arthritis

Indocin (indomethacin) relieves pain, swelling, and joint stiffness

Lidoderm (lidocaine-transdermal) topical analgesic

Lortab (hydrocodone bitartrate and acetaminophen) relieves moderate to moderately severe pain

Medrol (methylprednisolone) reduces swelling and redness

methylprednisolone (Medrol) inflammatory disorders

Mobic (meloxicam) osteoarthritis and rheumatoid arthritis

Motrin (ibuprofen) relieves pain and swelling

Nalfon (fenoprofen calcium) reduces pain, swelling, and joint stiffness from arthritis

naproxen (Anaprox) NSAID, mild to moderate pain, osteoarthritis, rheumatoid arthritis, dysmenorrhea, gout, ankylosing spondylitis, fever

prednisone (Deltasone) inflammatory disorders, adrenal insufficiency, MS relapsing, pneumocystic pneumonia, asthma, inflammatory bowel disease

Ultram (tramadol hydrochloride) juvenile rheumatoid arthritis, rheumatoid arthritis, chronic fatigue syndrome

Voltaren (diclofenac) osteoarthritis, rheumatoid arthritis

Antifungal

Nystatin (Nystatin oral) antifungal agent

Nystatin (Nystop) topical antifungal cream

Antineoplastic

Arimidex (anastrozole) treats breast cancer

anastrozole (Arimidex) treats breast cancer

Gleevec (imatinib mesylate) treats certain types of cancer (e.g., chronic myeloid leukemia, gastrointestinal stromal tumors, and myelodysplastic/myeloproliferative diseases). Stops or slows growth of cancer cells (tumors); causes cancer cells to die

imatinib (Gleevec) treats certain types of cancer (e.g., chronic myeloid leukemia, gastrointestinal stromal tumors, and myelodysplastic/myeloproliferative diseases). Stops or slows growth of cancer cells (tumors); causes cancer cells to die

Nolvadet (tamoxifen citrate) antineoplastic agent, SERM, estrogen receptor antagonist

tamoxifen citrate (Nolvadet) antineoplastic agent, SERM, estrogen receptor antagonist

Antiviral

acyclovir (Zovirax) decreases pain and speed healing of sores or blisters from varicella (chickenpox), herpes zoster (shingles), and outbreaks of genital herpes

Atripla (evavirenz/emtricitabine/tenofovir disoproxil fumarate) HIV in adults

Reyataz (atazanavir) HIV protease inhibitors

Tamiflu (oseltamivir phosphate) antiviral

Truvada (emtricitabine and tenofovir) HIV treatment

Cardiovascular

Accupril (quinapril) hypertension (HTN)

Aldomet (methyldopa) HTN

Altace (ramipril) reduces risk of MI, stroke, HTN

Amodarone (cordarone, pacerone) antiarrhythmic

amlodipidine (Norvasc) angina, essential HTN (calcium channel blocker)

Atacand (candesartan cilexetil) antihypertensive

atenolol (Tenomin) angina pectoris, essential HTN, myocardial infarction

atorvastatin (Lipitor) hypercholesterolemia, hyperlipidemia; dysbetalipoproteinemia

Avalide (irbesartan-hydrochlorothiazide) HTN

Avapro (irbesartan) HTN

benazepril (Lotensin) HTN, congestive heart failure (CHF)

Benicar (olmesartan medoxomil) HTN

Caduet (amlodipine besylate with atorvastatin) antihypertensive

Cardura (doxazosin) HTN

Catapres (clonidine HCl) HTN

Clonidine high blood pressure

clopidogrel bisulfate (Plavix) reduction of atherothrombotic events

Coreg (carvedilol) congestive heart failure

Coumadin (warfarin sodium) anticoagulant venous thrombosis, pulmonary embolism

Cozaar (losartan potassium) HTN

Crestor (rosuvastatin calcium) cholesterol

Digoxin (lanoxin) heart failure, irregular heartbeat (chronic atrial fibrillation)

Digitek heart failure

Diovan (valsartan) hypertension, heart failure, postmyocardial infarction

doxazosin (Cardura) HTN, BPH

Dyazide (triamterene/HCTZ) diuretic, HTN

Enalapril maleate (Vasotec) hypertension

enalapril (Vasotec) HTN, CHF, acute MI, nephropathy, asymptomatic left ventricular dysfunction

furosemide (Lasix) diuretic, peripheral and pulmonary edema, hypercalcemia, kidney failure

Gemfibrozil high serum triglyceride

Hyzaar (losartan potassium-hydrochlorithiazide) HTN

Imdur (isosorbide mononitrate) angina

Inderal (propranolol HCl) beta-blocker, antihypertensive

isosorbide mononitrate (Imdur, ISMO) angina

ISMO (isosorbide mononitrate) angina

lanoxin (Digoxin) CHF, atrial fibrillation/flutter, paroxysmal atrial tachycardia

Lasix (furosemide) CHF, HTN, diuretic

Lipitor (atorvastatin) high cholesterol

lisinopril (Prinivil, Zestril) HTN, CHF, acute MI

Lopressor (metoprolol) HTN

Lotensin (benazepril) HTN

Lotrel (amlodipine besylate and benazepril HCl) HTN

Lovaza (omega-3-acid ethyl esters) antihyperlipidemic

metoprolol tartrate (Lopressor, Toprol XL) HTN, CHF, acute MI, angina

Mevacor (lovastatin) cholesterol-lowering agent

Miscardis HCT (telmisartan with hydrochlorothiazide)

Minipress (prazosin HCl) HTN

nifedipine ER (Procardia, Adalat) angina

Nitrostat (nitroglycerin) angina pectoris due to coronary artery disease

Norvasc (amlodipine besylate) HTN

Cardiovascular (continued)

Plavix (clopidogrel bisulfate) reduces risk of atherothrombotic events, heart attack, stroke, peripheral vascular disease

Pravachol (pravastatin sodium) hypercholesterolemia, hyperlipidemia, dysbetalipoproteinemia

Prinivil (lisinopril) HTN

quinapril (Accupril) hypertension, CHF

ramipril (Altace) reduces risk of MI, stroke, hypertension

simvastatin (Zocor) hypercholesterolemia, hypertriglyceridemia, dysbetalipoproteinemia

Toprol XL (metoprolol) HTN

triamterene/HCTZ (Dyazide) diuretic, hypertension, peripheral edema

Tricor (penofibrate) hypercholesterolemia

Trizac (diltiazem hydrochloride) hypertension

valsartan (Diovan) HTN

Vasotec (enalapril) HTN

verapamil angina, hypertension, supraventricular arrhythmia, atrial fibrillation/flutter, migraine prophylaxis

Vytorin (ezetimibe with simvastatin) cholesterol

warfarin (Coumadin) anticoagulation

Zestril (lisinopril) HTN

Zetia (ezetimibe) primary hypercholesterolemia

Zocor (simvastatin) high cholesterol

Electrolytes

K-Dur (potassium chloride) hypokalemia, prevention of hypokalemia

Klor-Con (potassium chloride) hypokalemia, prevention of hypokalemia

potassium chloride (K-Dur, Klor-Con) hypokalemia, prevention of hypokalemia

Endocrinology

Actos (pioglitazone hydrochloride) DM type 2

Aldactone (spironolactone) hyperaldosteronism

allopurinol (Zyloprim) gout

Byetta (exenatide) antidiabetic (incretin mimetic)

DiaBeta (glyburide) DM type 2

Estrace (estrogen) reduces menopausal symptoms

glipizide (Glucotrol XL) DM type 2

Glucophage XR (metformin hydrochloride) diabetes

Glucotrol XL (glipizide) DM type 2

glyburide (DiaBeta, Micronase) DM type 2

Humalog (insulin lispro, rDNA origin) diabetes

Januvia (sitagliptin) DM type 2

Lantus (insulin glargine [rDNA origin] injection) DM type 1

Levothroid (levothyroxine) hypothyroidism

levothyroxine (Levoxyl, Synthroid, Levothroid) hypothyroidism, myxedema coma, thyroid cancer

Levoxyl (levothyroxine sodium) hypothyroidism, pituitary TSH suppression

metformin (Glucophage) DM type 2

methylprednisolone endocrine disorders, rheumatic disorders

Micronase (glyburide) DM type 2

NovoLog (insulin) antidiabetic

Synthroid (levothyroxine) hypothyroidism

Gastrointestinal
Aciphex (rabeprazole sodium) erosive or ulcerative GERD
esomeprazole magnesium (Nexium) GERD
Humira (adalimumab) injection, Crohn's disease
Lomotil (diphenoxylate) diarrhea
metoclopramide (Reglan) GERD
Nexium (esomeprazole magnesium) GERD
omeprazole (Prilosec) GERD, erosive esophagitis, gastric/duodenal ulcer, *H. pylori*
pantoprazole sodium (Protonix) GERD
Pepcid (famotidine) GERD, duodenal ulcer
Prevacid (lansoprazole) GERD
Prilosec (omeprazole) GERD
Protonix (pantoprazole sodium) GERD, stomach ulcers, heartburn
Xantac (ranitidine HCl) duodenal ulcer, gastric ulcer

Genitourinary
allopurinol (Zyloprim) prophylaxis for gout, urate nephropathy, calcium oxalate calculi
Aviane contraceptive
Avodart (dutasteride) prostate anti-inflammatory
azithromycin (Zithromax) chlamydia
Cialis (tadalifil) erectile dysfunction
conjugated estrogens (Premarin, Prempro) antineoplastics; cancer of breast and prostate, menopause; osteoporosis prevention; ovarian failure; primary atrophic vaginitis
Detrol (tolterodine tartrate) overactive bladder, urinary incontinence
Diflucan (fluconazole) vaginal yeast infections
Ditropan (oxybutynin chloride) urinary antispasmodic agent
Estrace (estradiol) reduces menopausal symptoms
estradiol (Estrace) vasomotor symptoms, atrophic vaginitis, osteoporosis prevention, palliative treatment for breast cancer and prostate cancer
Flomax (tamsulosin hydrochloride) benign prostatic hyperplasia
fluconazole (Diflucan) vaginal candidiasis, oropharyngeal and esophageal candidiasis, cryptococcal meningitis
Demadex (torsemide) loop diuretic
Levitra (vardenafil HCl) erectile dysfunction
medroxyprogesterone (Provera) HRT, amenorrhea, dysfunctional uterine bleeding
norgestimate/ethinyl estradiol (Ortho Tri-Cyclen) oral contraceptive
Nuvaring (etonogestrel/ethinyl estradiol vaginal ring) contraceptive
Ortho Evra (norelgestromin/ethinyl estradiol) contraceptive
Ortho Tri-Cyclen (norgestimate/ethinyl estradiol) contraceptive
Premarin (conjugated estrogens) vasomotor symptoms and vaginal atrophy due to menopause, breast cancer, prostate cancer
Prempro (conjugated estrogens/medroxyprogesterone) reduces menopausal symptoms
Provera (medroxyprogesterone) restores normal menstrual periods
Pyridium (phenazopyridine HCl) urinary tract analgesic
Septra (trimethoprim/sulfametoxazole) antibacterial bladder infections
sildenafil citrate (Viagra) erectile dysfunction
trimethoprim/sulfametoxazole (Septra) antibacterial bladder infections
Trisprintec (Ortho Tri-Cyclen) (norgestimate/ethinyl estradiol) contraceptive
Valtrex (valacyclovir hydrochloride) herpes zoster, genital herpes
Vesicare (solifenacin succinate) anticholinergic agent (urinary bladder modifier)
Viagra (sildenafil citrate) erectile dysfunction
Yasmin (drospirenone and ethinyl estradiol) contraceptive
Zithromax (azithromycin) treat STD (chlamydia)
Zyloprim (allopurinol) gout, kidney stones

Immunology and Allergy

Adrenalin (epinephrine) allergies
Allegra (fexofenadine hydrochloride) allergies, hay fever
Astelin (azelastine hydrochloride) allergic rhinitis
CellCept (mycophenolate mofetil) lowers body's immune system, used to prevent body rejecting a kidney, liver, or heart transplant
Cetirizine (Zyrtec) allergies
Chlor-Trimeton (chlorapheneramine maleate) allergies
Clarinex (desloratadine) seasonal allergic rhinitis
Dimetane (brompheniramine maleate) allergies
fexofenadine (Allegra) allergic rhinitis, chronic urticaria
Flonase (fluticasone propionate) allergic rhinitis, sleep apnea
fluticasone proprionate (Flonase) allergic rhinitis, sleep apnea
Humira Pen (aldalimumab injection) reduces pain and swelling due to arthritis, psoriasis, blocks a protein tumor necrosis factor (TNF)
momentasone nasal (Nasonex) seasonal and year-round allergy symptoms of the nose
mycophenolate mofetil (CellCept) lowers body's immune system, used to prevent body rejecting a kidney, liver, or heart transplant
Nasacort (triamcinolone acetonide, USP) seasonal and perennial allergic rhinitis
Nasonex (mometasone nasal) seasonal and year-round allergy symptoms of the nose
Rhinocort Aqua (budesonide nasal spray) antiallergy
Prograf (tacrolimus) lowers immune system to prevent rejection of transplanted organ
promethazine (Phenergan) allergic symptoms, nausea, motion sickness
Singular (montelukast sodium) allergic rhinitis
tacrolimus (Prograf) lowers immune system to prevent rejection of transplanted organ
Tussionex (chlorpheniramine with hydrocodone) antihistamine/antitussive
Zyrtec (cetirizine) allergic rhinitis, chronic urticaria

Musculoskeletal

Actonel (risedronate sodium) osteoporosis
alendronate (Fosamax) osteoporosis, Paget's disease
Baclofen (lioresal, kemstro) skeletal muscle relaxant
Boniva (ibandronate sodium) osteoporosis in postmenopausal women
carisoprodol (Soma) muscle spasm
cyclobenzaprine (Flexeril) muscle spasm
Evista (raloxifene hydrochloride) osteoporosis
Flexeril (cyclobenzaprine) muscle spasm, sciatica
Fosamax (alendronate sodium) osteoporosis
Skelaxin (metaxalone) acute, painful musculoskeletal conditions
Soma (carisoprodol) treats pain and discomfort from muscle injuries

Neurological

Aricept (donepezil hydrochloride) mild to moderate dementias of the Alzheimer's type
benztropine mesylate (Cogentin) treats tremors, symptoms of Parkinson's disease
clonazepam (Klonopin) neuralgia, absence seizures, epilepsy, panic attacks
Depakote (divalproex) seizure disorders, psychiatric conditions, prevents migraines
Dilantin (phenytoin sodium) seizures
divalproex (Depakote) seizure disorder, mania, migraine prophylaxis
gabapentin (Neurontin) partial seizures, neuropathic pain, postherpetic neuralgia in adults, epilepsy
Imitrex (sumatriptan succinate) hemiplegic or basilar migraine
Keppra (levetiracetam) partial onset seizures due to epilepsy
Klonopin (clonazepam) seizure disorders and panic attacks
Lamictal (lamotrigine) epilepsy
Lyrica (pregablalin) neurolopathic pain, postherpetic neuralgia, partial onset seizures, fibromyalgia
Mirapex (pramipexol dihydrochloride) anti-Parkinson's agent–dopamine agonist
Namenda (memantine HCl) agent for Alzheimer's dementia (NMDA receptor antagonist)
Neurontin (gabapentin) controls seizures, nerve pain
Requip (ropinirole HCl) anti-Parkinson's agent–dopamine agonist
Trileptal (oxcarbazepin) antiepileptic
Topamax (topiramate) epilepsy

Optical

Alphagan-P (brimonidine tartrate) glaucoma
Cosopt (dorzolamide hydrochloride and timolol maleate) reduces intraocular pressure in ocular hypertension, glaucoma
Lumigan (bimatoprost) glaucoma
Patanol (olopatadine) allergic conjunctivitis
TobraDex (tobramycin and dexamethasone) antibiotic ophthalmic corticosteroid
Travatan (travoprost) antiglaucoma agent (ophthalmic prostaglandin)
Vigamox (moxifloxacin hydrochloride) bacterial conjunctivitis
Xalatan (latanoprost) reduces intraocular pressure, glaucoma

Psychiatric

Abilify (aripiprazole) schizophrenia
Adderall ADHD
alprazolam (Xanax) anxiety, panic disorder
Ambien (zolpidem tartrate) sleep disorders, insomnia
amitriptyline (Elavil, Endep) depression, chronic pain
Ativan (lorazepam) anxiety
bupropion HCl (Wellbutrin SR) major depressive disorder
Budisol (butabarbital sodium) sedative or hypnotic, insomnia
Celexa (citalopram) depression
Citalopram (Celexa) depression
Concerta (methylphenidate HCl extended release) ADHD
Cymbalta (duloxetine hydrochloride) suicidal tendencies and depression
Desyrel (trazodone) depression
diazepam (Valium) anxiety, alcohol withdrawal stress, muscle spasm, seizure disorder, status epilepticus
Effexor XR (venlafaxine hydrochloride) major depressive disorder
Elavil (amitriptyline) depression, fibromyalgia
Endep (amitriptyline) depression
escitapropram oxalate (Lexapro) antidepressant

Psychiatric (continued)

fluoxetine hydrochloride (Prozac) bulimia nervosa, depression, obsessive-compulsive disorder, social anxiety disorder

Focalin XR (dexmethylphenidate HCl) ADHD

Geodon (ziprasidone hydrochloride) antipsychotic schizophrenia, bipolar disorder

Haldol (haloperidol) treats mental/mood disorders

hydroxyzine (Atarax) anxiety, psychoneurosis

Lexapro (escitapropram oxalate) antidepressant, anxiety

lisdexamfetamine (Vyvanse) ADHD

lorazepam (Ativan) anxiety, panic attacks, depression

Lunesta (eszopiclone) non-BZD (nonbenzodiazepines drug) hypnotic

modafinil (Provigil) sleep disorders

nortriptyline (Pamelor) depression

Privigil (modafinil) sleep disorders

paroxetine (Paxil) anxiety, panic disorder, depression, obsessive-compulsive disorder

Paxil (paroxetine) panic attacks, depression, obsessive-compulsive disorder, post-traumatic stress disorder (PTSD)

Prozac (fluoxetine) depression, obsessive-compulsive disorder, panic attacks, bulimia, premenstrual syndrome

Restoril (temazepam) insomnia

Risperdal (risperidone) schizophrenia

Seroquel (quetiapine fumarate) treatment of bipolar mania

sertraline (Zoloft) anxiety, panic disorder, depression, obsessive-compulsive disorder

Strattera (atomoxetine HCl) ADHD

trazodone (Desyrel) depression

Valium (diazepam) anxiety

venlafaxine (Effexor EX) depression, anxiety

Vyvanse (lisdexamfetamine) ADHD

Wellbutrin SR (bupropion HCl) major depressive disorder

Xanax (alprazolam) anxiety and panic disorders

ziprasidone hydrochloride (Geodon) antipsychotic schizophrenia, bipolar disorder

Zoloft (sertraline hydrochloride) depression, panic attacks, post-traumatic stress disorder

zolpidem (Ambien) insomnia

Zyprexa (olanzapine) dementia-related psychosis

Respiratory

Advair Diskus (fluticasone propionate) treatment of asthma

albuterol (Proventil, Ventolin) asthma

budenoside (Plumicort) antiasthmatic

Combivent Flovent (fluticasone propionate) asthma

fluticasone propionate (Flovent) asthma

montelukast (Singular) asthma

Proair FHA (albuterol sulfate inhalation aerosol) asthma

Proventil (albuterol) asthma

Symbicort (budesonide and formoterol) prevents bronchospasm in patients with asthma or COPD

Singulair (montelukast) asthma

Spiriva (tiotropium bromide inhalation powder) bronchospasm associated with COPD

Tussionex (pennkinetic) cough and upper respiratory symptoms with allergy or cold

Ventolin (albuterol) asthma

Xopenex (levalbuterol HCl) antiasthmatic (beta 2 agonist)

Smoking Cessation

Chantix (varenicline) aid to smoking cessation

Common Abbreviations

Always use with caution! Abbreviations may have multiple meanings.

a	before	**IVPB**	IV piggyback (2nd line)
ac, a.c.	before meals	**K**	potassium
AD	right ear	**kg**	kilogram
ad lib	as desired	**L**	liter
alt dieb	alternate days	**Liq**	liquid
alt hr	alternate hours	**mcg**	microgram
alt noc	alternate nights	**mg**	milligram(s)
am, AM	morning	**ml, mL**	milliliter(s)
amt	amount	**mm**	millimeter
ante	before	**NaCl 0.9%**	normal saline
aq	aqueous (water)	**NKA**	no known allergy
AS	left ear	**NKDA**	no known drug allergy
AU	both ears	**noc, noct**	night
Ba	barium	**non rep**	do not repeat
bid, b.i.d.	two times a day	**NPO**	nothing by mouth
bin	two times a night	**NS**	normal saline
C	100	**NSAID**	nonsteroidal anti-inflammatory drug(s)
c, w/	with	**O**	pint
cap(s)	capsule(s)	**od**	once day/daily
cc	cubic centimeter	**OD**	right eye
CHF	congestive heart failure	**om**	every morning
d	day	**OTC**	over the counter
Dx	diagnosis	**Oz, oz**	ounce
D₅W	5% dextrose in water	**Pc, p.c.**	after meals
D/C, dc	discontinue	**PCA**	patient-controlled analgesia, patient-controlled administration
dil	dilute	**PCN**	penicillin
disp	dispense	**PDR**	Physician's Desk Reference
DM	diabetes mellitus	**per**	with
dr	dram	**PM, pm**	evening
elix	elixir	**PRN, prn**	as needed as necessary
emul	emulsion	**PO, po, p.o.**	by mouth
et	and	**pt**	pint, patient
ext	extract/external	**pulv**	powder
FDA	Food and Drug Administration	**Q, q**	every
Fe	iron	**q2h**	every 2 hours
Fl	fluid	**qAM**	every morning
G	gauge	**qd, q.d.**	every day
g, GM, gm, gr	gram(s)	**qh, q.h.**	every hour
gal	gallon	**qh.s.**	every bedtime
gt, gtt	drop(s)	**qid, q.i.d.**	four times a day
H	hour/hypodermic	**qns**	quantity not sufficient
HRT	hormone replacement therapy	**qPM**	every evening
Hs, h.s.	hour of sleep (bedtime)	**qs, q.s.**	as much as needed, sufficient quantity
HTN	hypertension	**Rx**	prescription
IM	intramuscular		
Inj	injection		
IU	international units		
IV	intravenous		

Note: D_5W = 5% dextrose in water

Common Abbreviations
(continued)

SC, sc, sq, subc, subq. Subcutaneous

Sig, sig........ let be labeled as follows, directions

SL .... sublingual

SOB ....shortness of breath

susp............................... suspension

T, tbsp .... tablespoon

tab .... tablet

tid, t.i.d................. three times a day

TO........................... telephone order

Top, top ....apply topically

tsp ....teaspoon

TX....................................treatment

ut, diet, UD .... as directed

wt.. weight

BE ALERT FOR SOUNDALIKES

Drug names may be similar in sound as well as spelling. It is important to be alert when referring to drugs. For example:

Celebrex..................... NSAID
> **vs**
Cerebyx........... anticonvulsant

DiaBeta ....oral hypoglycemic
> **vs**
Zebeta beta-adrenergic blocker

Paxil .... antidepressant
> **vs**
Taxol .... antineoplastic

REFERENCES FOR PHARMACOLOGY

Spratto, G. R. (2013). *Delmar health care drug handbook.* Clifton Park, NY: Delmar Cengage Learning.

Woodrow, R. (2011). *Essentials of pharmacology for health occupations* (6th ed.). Clifton Park, NY: Delmar Cengage Learning.

Web sites for Pharmacology: http://www.rxlist.com/script/main/hp.asp
http://www.epocrates.com/
http://www.fda.gov/drugs/
http://pdr.net/
http://mayoclinic.com/

HEMATOLOGY/COAGULATION

Complete Blood Count
Use: basic blood evaluation
AKA: CBC, CBC with differential
Note: usually includes Hct, Hgb, WBC counts and differential, platelet count, and often RBC count

Erythrocyte Count
AKA: RBC count (red blood cell)
High: acute hepatitis, acute MI, PID, rheumatoid arthritis
Low: anemias, leukemias, and following severe hemorrhage

Hematocrit
Use: determines the percent of whole blood composed of red blood cells
AKA: Hct, HCT, PVC
High: dehydration, Addison's disease, polycythemia due to dehydration, and shock
Low: anemia, severe hemorrhage

Hemoglobin
Use: measures Hgb in the blood
AKA: Hb, Hgb
High: dehydration, pernicious anemia, sickle cell anemia, thalassemia, polycythemia, obstructive pulmonary diseases, CHF
Low: excessive fluid intake, iron-deficiency anemia, pregnancy

Hemoglobin, Glycated
Use: monitors blood sugar control
AKA: HbA1C, GHb, DM control index
Note: Abnormal results over time indicate inadequate control

Leukocyte Count
AKA: WBC Count (white blood cell)
High: acute infections, leukemias, acute hemorrhage
Low: chemotherapy, shock, cachexia

Partial Thromboplastin Time
Use: measures intrinsic clotting time
AKA: APTT, activated
High: cirrhosis, leukemia, vitamin K deficiency, hemophilia

Low: extensive ca, early stages of disseminated intravascular coagulation

Platelet Count
Use: dx a bleeding disorder or bone marrow disease
High: iron-deficiency anemia, postop patients, malignancies, polycythemia
Low: acute leukemia, aplastic anemia, thrombocytopenic purpura

Prothrombin Time
Use: monitors blood-thinning medications used to prevent blood clots
AKA: PT, Pro Time
Prolonged: severe liver damage, heparin use, low vitamin K diet, colitis, chronic diarrhea

Reticulocyte Count
Use: measures percent of reticulocytes (slightly immature red blood cells)
High: need for RBCs, hemolytic anemias, acute or severe bleeding
Low: bone marrow failure (toxicity, tumor, fibrosis, infection), cirrhosis, iron deficiency, radiation therapy

Sedimentation Rate
Use: monitors inflammatory and malignant diseases and acute MI
AKA: erythrocyte sedimentation rate, sed rate, ESR
High: pregnancy, menstruation, infectious diseases, tissue damage

SERUM ELECTROLYTES

AKA: "Lytes"
Note: essential to normal metabolism, exists as acids, bases, and salts

Calcium, Total
Use: blood test to screen/monitor diseases of bone or calcium regulation (diseases of parathyroid and kidneys)
AKA: Ca^{+2}, Ca^{++}, serum calcium

SERUM ELECTROLYTES (continued)

High: metastatic ca of bone, lung, breast, Paget's disease, hyperparathyroidism, excess vitamin D
Low: severe pancreatitis, renal insufficiency, uremia, malabsorption, osteomalacia, hypoparathyroidism

Chloride
AKA: Cl
High: renal insufficiency, necrosis, dehydration, renal tubular acidosis, Cushing's syndrome, hyperventilation
Low: CHF, chronic renal failure, diabetic acidosis, diarrhea, excessive sweating, emphysema

Magnesium
AKA: Mg^{+2}
High: renal insufficiency, use of antacids with magnesium
Low: chronic alcoholism, chronic diarrhea, hepatic insufficiency

Phosphorus
AKA: PO4
High: renal insufficiency, healing fx, hypoparathyroidism, excess vitamin D
Low: chronic alcoholism, ketoacidosis, hyperalimentation, hyperparathyroidism

Potassium
AKA: K
High: renal insufficiency, adrenal insufficiency, Addison's disease, hypoventilation
Low: chronic diarrhea, vomiting or malabsorption syndrome, diabetic acidosis, chronic kidney disease, use of thiazide diuretics

Sodium
AKA: NA
High: (hypernatremia) excessive dietary intake, Cushing's disease, excessive sweating, diabetes insipidus
Low: (hyponatremia) ascites, CHF, insufficient intake, diarrhea, vomiting, SIADH (syndrome of inappropriate diuretic hormone), diuretic use, chronic renal insufficiency, excessive water intake, peripheral edema, pleural effusion

SERUM/URINE/STOOL

Acid Phosphatase
High: metastatic ca of bone, prostatic ca, some liver diseases, MI, pulmonary embolism, hepatobiliary diseases, hyperparathyroidism

Alanine Aminotransferase
Use: screens for liver disease
AKA: ALT, SGPT
High: acute hepatitis, liver necrosis

Albumin
Use: screens for liver or kidney disease or evaluates nutritional status
AKA: ALB
Note: Albumin is a protein
High: shock, dehydration, multiple myeloma
Low: malnutrition, malabsorption, acute or chronic glomerulonephritis, cancers, leukemia, hepatitis, cirrhosis, hepatocellular necrosis

Alkaline Phosphatase
Use: screens/monitors treatment for liver or bone disorders
AKA: ALP, alk phos
High: biliary duct obstruction, hyperparathyroidism, healing fx, rickets, osteomalacia, neoplastic bone disorders, liver diseases

Ammonia
AKA: NH^{4+}
Note: particularly toxic to the brain; can cause confusion and lethargy
High: CHF, liver failure, GI bleed, leukemia, pericarditis

Amylase
Use: blood test to diagnose/monitor pancreatic disease (blood)
Note: amylase is an enzyme that helps digest glycogen and starch
High: acute pancreatitis, ca of the pancreas, ovaries, or lungs, mumps, intestinal obstruction
Low: acute and chronic hepatitis, cirrhosis, toxemia of pregnancy

SERUM/URINE/STOOL (continued)

Anion Gap
Use: dx and tx of acidosis
High: lactic acidosis, diabetic ketoacidosis, alcoholic ketoacidosis, starvation, renal failure
Low: multiple myeloma, chronic vomiting, hyperaldosteronism

Arterial Blood Gases
AKA: ABGs
Abnormal Results: respiratory, metabolic or renal diseases, trauma

Aspartate Aminotransferase
Use: detects liver damage
AKA: AST, SGOT
High: acute MI, liver disease, diseases of skeletal muscles

Bilirubin, Total
Use: screens/monitors liver disorders
Note: bilirubin is a product of hemoglobin breakdown, causes jaundice
High: acute/chronic hepatitis, gallstones, toxic reaction to drugs/chemicals, infectious mononucleosis

Blood Urea Nitrogen
Use: evaluates kidney function and dialysis effectiveness
AKA: BUN
High: GI hemorrhage, dehydration, renal insufficiency
Low: hepatic failure, cachexia

Carbon Dioxide, Total
AKA: CO_2
High: respiratory diseases, vomiting, intestinal obstruction
Decreased: acidosis, nephritis, diarrhea

Carcinoembryonic Antigen
Use: dx cancer and monitor tx
AKA: CEA
High: colon, breast, lung, pancreatic, thyroid ca, also heavy smoking

Cholesterol, Total
Use: screens for heart disease
High: MI, uncontrolled DM, hypothyroidism, atherosclerosis, hypercholesterolemia, hyperlipidemia
Low: acute MI, pernicious anemia, malnutrition, liver disease, sepsis, malabsorption

Creatinine
Use: evaluates kidney function and tx
High: dehydration, diabetic nephropathy, kidney disease

Creatine (Phospho) Kinase
Use: evaluates muscle damage
AKA: CPK, CK
High: acute MI, muscular dystrophies, muscle injury, CNS trauma, stroke

Globulin
Use: protein evaluation
AKA: CPK, CK
High: hepatic disease, plasma cell neoplasms, lupus, malaria

Glucose
Use: diagnoses and manages DM
AKA: GTT glucose tolerance test
High: DM, IV therapy, hyperthyroidism, hyperpituitarism, liver diseases, nephritis
Low: hyperinsulinism, hyperthyroidism, Addison's disease

Iron
AKA: Fe
High: anemias, liver disease
Low: iron-deficiency anemia, excessive fluid intake, pregnancy

Lactose Dehydrogenase
AKA: LDH
High: acute MI, infectious hepatitis, malignant tumors and widespread ca, hemolytic and pernicious anemias, acute leukemias
Low: x-ray irradiation

Oxygen Saturation
AKA: oximetry, O_2
High: hyperventilation
Low: inadequate O_2 inspiration, hypoxic lung diseases, hypoxic cardiac diseases, severe hypoventilation

Prostate-Specific Antigen
AKA: PSA
High: BPH, prostate ca, prostatism

Stool Guaiac Test
Use: detects hidden blood in stool
AKA: hemoccult
Abnormal Results: NSAIDs, colon polyps, colon ca, GI tumors, esophagitis, gastritis, inflammatory bowel disease, peptic ulcer

Thyrotropin
AKA: THS
Abnormal Findings: hyperthyroidism, hypothyroidism, depression, acute starvation, pregnancy, old age

Thyroxine
AKA: T_4
High: Graves' disease, toxic thyroid adenoma, acute thyroiditis
Low: cretinism, myxedema, pituitary or iodine insufficiency, hypothalamic failure, renal failure, Cushing's disease, cirrhosis, advanced cancer

Triglycerides
AKA: TG
High: hyperlipidemias, hypothyroidism, poorly controlled DM, nephrotic syndrome, hypertension, alcoholic cirrhosis, pregnancy, MI
Low: malabsorption syndrome, malnutrition, hyperthyroidism

Uric Acid
High: gout, leukemia, renal insufficiency, polycythemia, pneumonia
Low: acute hepatitis

Viral Load
Use: severity of immune system damage, monitors HIV status and treatment
AKA: CD4 lymphocyte count
Low below 350 mL: herpes simplex, herpes zoster, TB
Low below 200 mL: pneumocystis carinii pneumonia
Low below 100 mL: AIDS dementia
Low below 50 mL: cytomegalovirus

COMMON ABBREVIATIONS

AKA ....also known as
ca, Ca ....cancer, calcium
CHF ....congestive heart failure
DM.........................diabetes mellitus
Dx ....diagnosis
fx ....fracture
GI................................. gastrointestinal
HIV..........human immunodeficiency virus
IV .... intravenous
MI .... myocardial infarction
NIDDM .... non–insulin-dependent DM
NSAID ..... nonsteroidal anti-inflammatory
tx ....treatment

REFERENCES FOR LAB TESTING

Daniels, R. (2010). *Delmar's manual of laboratory and diagnostic tests* (2nd ed.). Clifton Park, NY: Delmar Cengage Learning.

Estridge, B. H., & Reynolds, A. P. (2012). *Basic clinical laboratory techniques* (6th ed.). Clifton Park, NY: Delmar Cengage Learning.

Ridley, J. (2011). *Essentials of clinical laboratory science.* Clifton Park, NY: Delmar Cengage Learning.

ONLINE RESOURCES:
Lab Tests Online
        http://www.labtestsonline.org/

Labcorp (Laboratory Corporation of America)
        https://www.labcorp.com/wps/portal/provider/testmenu/

Laboratory testing
        http://www.thedoctorsdoctor.com/laboratory_testing.htm

MedlinePlus
        http://www.nlm.nih.gov/medlineplus/laboratorytests.html

Test Reference
        http://www.testreference.net/

APPENDIX C

ICD-10-CM Official Guidelines for Coding and Reporting
2014

Narrative changes appear in bold text
Items <u>underlined</u> have been moved within the guidelines since the 2013 version
Italics are used to indicate revisions to heading changes

The Centers for Medicare and Medicaid Services (CMS) and the National Center for Health Statistics (NCHS), two departments within the U.S. Federal Government's Department of Health and Human Services (DHHS) provide the following guidelines for coding and reporting using the International Classification of Diseases, 10th Revision, Clinical Modification (ICD-10-CM). These guidelines should be used as a companion document to the official version of the ICD-10-CM as published on the NCHS website. The ICD-10-CM is a morbidity classification published by the United States for classifying diagnoses and reason for visits in all health care settings. The ICD-10-CM is based on the ICD-10, the statistical classification of disease published by the World Health Organization (WHO).

These guidelines have been approved by the four organizations that make up the Cooperating Parties for the ICD-10-CM: the American Hospital Association (AHA), the American Health Information Management Association (AHIMA), CMS, and NCHS.

These guidelines are a set of rules that have been developed to accompany and complement the official conventions and instructions provided within the ICD-10-CM itself. The instructions and conventions of the classification take precedence over guidelines. These guidelines are based on the coding and sequencing instructions in the Tabular List and Alphabetic Index of ICD-10-CM, but provide additional instruction. Adherence to these guidelines when assigning ICD-10-CM diagnosis codes is required under the Health Insurance Portability and Accountability Act (HIPAA). The diagnosis codes (Tabular List and Alphabetic Index) have been adopted under HIPAA for all healthcare settings. A joint effort between the healthcare provider and the coder is essential to achieve complete and accurate documentation, code assignment, and reporting of diagnoses and procedures. These guidelines have been developed to assist both the healthcare provider and the coder in identifying those diagnoses that are to be reported. The importance of consistent, complete documentation in the medical record cannot be overemphasized. Without such documentation accurate coding cannot be achieved. The entire record should be reviewed to determine the specific reason for the encounter and the conditions treated.

The term encounter is used for all settings, including hospital admissions. In the context of these guidelines, the term provider is used throughout the guidelines to mean physician or any qualified health care practitioner who is legally accountable for establishing the patient's diagnosis. Only this set of guidelines, approved by the Cooperating Parties, is official.

The guidelines are organized into sections. Section I includes the structure and conventions of the classification and general guidelines that apply to the entire classification, and chapter-specific guidelines that correspond to the chapters as they are arranged in the classification. Section II includes guidelines for selection of principal diagnosis for non-outpatient settings. Section III includes guidelines for reporting additional diagnoses in non-outpatient settings. Section IV is for outpatient coding and reporting. It is necessary to review all sections of the guidelines to fully understand all of the rules and instructions needed to code properly.

Courtesy of the Centers for Disease Control and Prevention, www.cdc.gov

Courtesy of the Centers for Disease Control and Prevention, www.cdc.gov

Section I. Conventions, general coding guidelines and chapter specific guidelines

The conventions, general guidelines and chapter-specific guidelines are applicable to all health care settings unless otherwise indicated. The conventions and instructions of the classification take precedence over guidelines.

A. Conventions for the ICD-10-CM

The conventions for the ICD-10-CM are the general rules for use of the classification independent of the guidelines. These conventions are incorporated within the Alphabetic Index and Tabular List of the ICD-10-CM as instructional notes.

1. The Alphabetic Index and Tabular List

The ICD-10-CM is divided into the Alphabetic Index, an alphabetical list of terms and their corresponding code, and the Tabular List, a structured list of codes divided into chapters based on body system or condition. The Alphabetic Index consists of the following parts: the Index of Diseases and Injury, the Index of External Causes of Injury, the Table of Neoplasms and the Table of Drugs and Chemicals.

See Section I.C2. General guidelines
See Section I.C.19. Adverse effects, poisoning, underdosing and toxic effects

2. Format and Structure:

The ICD-10-CM Tabular List contains categories, subcategories and codes. Characters for categories, subcategories and codes may be either a letter or a number. All categories are 3 characters. A three-character category that has no further subdivision is equivalent to a code. Subcategories are either 4 or 5 characters. Codes may be 3, 4, 5, 6 or 7 characters. That is, each level of subdivision after a category is a subcategory. The final level of subdivision is a code. Codes that have applicable 7th characters are still referred to as codes, not subcategories. A code that has an applicable 7th character is considered invalid without the 7th character.

The ICD-10-CM uses an indented format for ease in reference.

3. Use of codes for reporting purposes

For reporting purposes only codes are permissible, not categories or subcategories, and any applicable 7th character is required.

4. Placeholder character

The ICD-10-CM utilizes a placeholder character "X". The "X" is used as a placeholder at certain codes to allow for future expansion. An example of this is at the poisoning, adverse effect and underdosing codes, categories T36-T50.

Where a placeholder exists, the X must be used in order for the code to be considered a valid code.

5. 7th Characters

Certain ICD-10-CM categories have applicable 7th characters. The applicable 7th character is required for all codes within the category, or as the notes in the Tabular List instruct. The 7th character must always be the 7th character in the data field. If a code that requires a 7th character is not 6 characters, a placeholder X must be used to fill in the empty characters.

6. Abbreviations

a. Alphabetic Index abbreviations

NEC   "Not elsewhere classifiable"
This abbreviation in the Alphabetic Index represents "other specified". When a specific code is not available for a condition, the Alphabetic Index directs the coder to the "other specified" code in the Tabular List.

NOS   "Not otherwise specified"
This abbreviation is the equivalent of unspecified.

b. Tabular List abbreviations

NEC   "Not elsewhere classifiable"
This abbreviation in the Tabular List represents "other specified". When a specific code is not available for a condition the Tabular List includes an NEC entry under a code to identify the code as the "other specified" code.

NOS   "Not otherwise specified"
This abbreviation is the equivalent of unspecified.

7. Punctuation

[ ]   Brackets are used in the Tabular List to enclose synonyms, alternative wording or explanatory phrases. Brackets are used in the Alphabetic Index to identify manifestation codes.

( )   Parentheses are used in both the Alphabetic Index and Tabular List to enclose supplementary words that may be present or absent in the statement of a disease or procedure without affecting the code number to which it is assigned. The terms within the parentheses are referred to as nonessential modifiers. **The nonessential modifiers in the Alphabetic Index to Diseases apply to subterms following a main term except when a nonessential modifier and a subentry are mutually exclusive, the subentry takes precedence. For example, in the ICD-10-CM**

Alphabetic Index under the main term Enteritis, "acute" is a nonessential modifier and "chronic" is a subentry. In this case, the nonessential modifier "acute" does not apply to the subentry "chronic".

:   Colons are used in the Tabular List after an incomplete term which needs one or more of the modifiers following the colon to make it assignable to a given category.

8. Use of "and".

See Section I.A.14. Use of the term "And"

9. Other and Unspecified codes

a. "Other" codes

Codes titled "other" or "other specified" are for use when the information in the medical record provides detail for which a specific code does not exist. Alphabetic Index entries with NEC in the line designate "other" codes in the Tabular List. These Alphabetic Index entries represent specific disease entities for which no specific code exists so the term is included within an "other" code.

b. "Unspecified" codes

Codes titled "unspecified" are for use when the information in the medical record is insufficient to assign a more specific code. For those categories for which an unspecified code is not provided, the "other specified" code may represent both other and unspecified.

See Section I.B.18 Use of Signs/Symptom/Unspecified Codes

10. Includes Notes

This note appears immediately under a three character code title to further define, or give examples of, the content of the category.

11. Inclusion terms

List of terms is included under some codes. These terms are the conditions for which that code is to be used. The terms may be synonyms of the code title, or, in the case of "other specified" codes, the terms are a list of the various conditions assigned to that code. The inclusion terms are not necessarily exhaustive. Additional terms found only in the Alphabetic Index may also be assigned to a code.

12.   Excludes Notes

The ICD-10-CM has two types of excludes notes. Each type of note has a different definition for use but they are all similar in that they indicate that codes excluded from each other are independent of each other.

a.   Excludes1

A type 1 Excludes note is a pure excludes note. It means "NOT CODED HERE!" An Excludes1 note indicates that the code excluded should never be used at the same time as the code above the Excludes1 note. An Excludes1 is used when two conditions cannot occur together, such as a congenital form versus an acquired form of the same condition.

b.   Excludes2

A type 2 Excludes note represents "Not included here". An excludes2 note indicates that the condition excluded is not part of the condition represented by the code, but a patient may have both conditions at the same time. When an Excludes2 note appears under a code, it is acceptable to use both the code and the excluded code together, when appropriate.

13.   Etiology/manifestation convention ("code first", "use additional code" and "in diseases classified elsewhere" notes)

Certain conditions have both an underlying etiology and multiple body system manifestations due to the underlying etiology. For such conditions, the ICD-10-CM has a coding convention that requires the underlying condition be sequenced first followed by the manifestation. Wherever such a combination exists, there is a "use additional code" note at the etiology code, and a "code first" note at the manifestation code. These instructional notes indicate the proper sequencing order of the codes, etiology followed by manifestation.

In most cases the manifestation codes will have in the code title, "in diseases classified elsewhere." Codes with this title are a component of the etiology/ manifestation convention. The code title indicates that it is a manifestation code. "In diseases classified elsewhere" codes are never permitted to be used as first-listed or principal diagnosis codes. They must be used in conjunction with an underlying condition code and they must be listed following the underlying condition. See category F02, Dementia in other diseases classified elsewhere, for an example of this convention.

There are manifestation codes that do not have "in diseases classified elsewhere" in the title. For such codes, there is a "use additional code" note at the etiology code and a "code first" note at the manifestation code and the rules for sequencing apply.

In addition to the notes in the Tabular List, these conditions also have a specific Alphabetic Index entry structure. In the Alphabetic Index both conditions are listed together with the etiology code first followed by the manifestation codes in brackets. The code in brackets is always to be sequenced second.

An example of the etiology/manifestation convention is dementia in Parkinson's disease. In the Alphabetic Index, code G20 is listed first, followed by code F02.80 or F02.81 in brackets. Code G20 represents the underlying etiology, Parkinson's disease, and must be sequenced first, whereas codes F02.80 and F02.81 represent the manifestation of dementia in diseases classified elsewhere, with or without behavioral disturbance.

"Code first" and "Use additional code" notes are also used as sequencing rules in the classification for certain codes that are not part of an etiology/ manifestation combination.

See Section I.B.7. Multiple coding for a single condition.

14.   "And"

The word "and" should be interpreted to mean either "and" or "or" when it appears in a title.

For example, cases of "tuberculosis of bones", "tuberculosis of joints" and "tuberculosis of bones and joints" are classified to subcategory A18.0, Tuberculosis of bones and joints.

15.   "With"

The word "with" should be interpreted to mean "associated with" or "due to" when it appears in a code title, the Alphabetic Index, or an instructional note in the Tabular List.

The word "with" in the Alphabetic Index is sequenced immediately following the main term, not in alphabetical order.

16.   "See" and "See Also"

The "see" instruction following a main term in the Alphabetic Index indicates that another term should be referenced. It is necessary to go to the main term referenced with the "see" note to locate the correct code.

A "see also" instruction following a main term in the Alphabetic Index instructs that there is another main term that may also be referenced that may provide additional Alphabetic Index entries that may be useful. It is not necessary to follow the "see also" note when the original main term provides the necessary code.

17.   **"Code also note"**

A "code also" note instructs that two codes may be required to fully describe a condition, but this note does not provide sequencing direction.

18.   **Default codes**

A code listed next to a main term in the ICD-10-CM Alphabetic Index is referred to as a default code. The default code represents that condition that is most commonly associated with the main term, or is the unspecified code for the condition. If a condition is documented in a medical record (for example, appendicitis) without any additional information, such as acute or chronic, the default code should be assigned.

B. General Coding Guidelines

1.   **Locating a code in the ICD-10-CM**

To select a code in the classification that corresponds to a diagnosis or reason for visit documented in a medical record, first locate the term in the Alphabetic Index, and then verify the code in the Tabular List. Read and be guided by instructional notations that appear in both the Alphabetic Index and the Tabular List.

It is essential to use both the Alphabetic Index and Tabular List when locating and assigning a code. The Alphabetic Index does not always provide the full code. Selection of the full code, including laterality and any applicable 7th character can only be done in the Tabular List. A dash (-) at the end of an Alphabetic Index entry indicates that additional characters are required. Even if a dash is not included at the Alphabetic Index entry, it is necessary to refer to the Tabular List to verify that no 7th character is required.

2.   **Level of Detail in Coding**

Diagnosis codes are to be used and reported at their highest number of characters available.

ICD-10-CM diagnosis codes are composed of codes with 3, 4, 5, 6 or 7 characters. Codes with three characters are included in ICD-10-CM as the heading of a category of codes that may be further subdivided by the use of fourth and/or fifth characters and/or sixth characters, which provide greater detail.

A three-character code is to be used only if it is not further subdivided. A code is invalid if it has not been coded to the full number of characters required for that code, including the 7th character, if applicable.

3. **Code or codes from A00.0 through T88.9, Z00-Z99.8**

    The appropriate code or codes from A00.0 through T88.9, Z00-Z99.8 must be used to identify diagnoses, symptoms, conditions, problems, complaints or other reason(s) for the encounter/visit.

4. **Signs and symptoms**

    Codes that describe symptoms and signs, as opposed to diagnoses, are acceptable for reporting purposes when a related definitive diagnosis has not been established (confirmed) by the provider. Chapter 18 of ICD-10-CM, Symptoms, Signs, and Abnormal Clinical and Laboratory Findings, Not Elsewhere Classified (codes R00.0 - R99) contains many, but not all codes for symptoms.

    See Section I.B.18 Use of Signs/Symptom/Unspecified Codes

5. **Conditions that are an integral part of a disease process**

    Signs and symptoms that are associated routinely with a disease process should not be assigned as additional codes, unless otherwise instructed by the classification.

6. **Conditions that are not an integral part of a disease process**

    Additional signs and symptoms that may not be associated routinely with a disease process should be coded when present.

7. **Multiple coding for a single condition**

    In addition to the etiology/manifestation convention that requires two codes to fully describe a single condition that affects multiple body systems, there are other single conditions that also require more than one code. "Use additional code" notes are found in the Tabular List at codes that are not part of an etiology/manifestation pair where a secondary code is useful to fully describe a condition. The sequencing rule is the same as the etiology/manifestation pair, "use additional code" indicates that a secondary code should be added.

    For example, for bacterial infections that are not included in chapter 1, a secondary code from category B95, Streptococcus, Staphylococcus, and Enterococcus, as the cause of diseases classified elsewhere, or B96, Other bacterial agents as the cause of diseases classified elsewhere, may be required to identify the bacterial organism causing the infection. A "use additional code" note will normally be found at the infectious disease code, indicating a need for the organism code to be added as a secondary code.

    "Code first" notes are also under certain codes that are not specifically manifestation codes but may be due to an underlying cause. When there is a "code first" note and an underlying condition is present, the underlying condition should be sequenced first.

ICD-10-CM Official Guidelines for Coding and Reporting
2014
Page 13 of 117
Courtesy of the Centers for Disease Control and Prevention, www.cdc.gov

"Code, if applicable, any causal condition first", notes indicate that this code may be assigned as a principal diagnosis when the causal condition is unknown or not applicable. If a causal condition is known, then the code for that condition should be sequenced as the principal or first-listed diagnosis.

Multiple codes may be needed for sequela, complication codes and obstetric codes to more fully describe a condition. See the specific guidelines for these conditions for further instruction.

8. Acute and Chronic Conditions

If the same condition is described as both acute (subacute) and chronic, and separate subentries exist in the Alphabetic Index at the same indentation level, code both and sequence the acute (subacute) code first.

9. Combination Code

A combination code is a single code used to classify:
Two diagnoses, or
A diagnosis with an associated secondary process (manifestation)
A diagnosis with an associated complication

Combination codes are identified by referring to subterm entries in the Alphabetic Index and by reading the inclusion and exclusion notes in the Tabular List.

Assign only the combination code when that code fully identifies the diagnostic conditions involved or when the Alphabetic Index so directs. Multiple coding should not be used when the classification provides a combination code that clearly identifies all of the elements documented in the diagnosis. When the combination code lacks necessary specificity in describing the manifestation or complication, an additional code should be used as a secondary code.

10. Sequela (Late Effects)

A sequela is the residual effect (condition produced) after the acute phase of an illness or injury has terminated. There is no time limit on when a sequela code can be used. The residual may be apparent early, such as in cerebral infarction, or it may occur months or years later, such as that due to a previous injury. Coding of sequela generally requires two codes sequenced in the following order: The condition or nature of the sequela is sequenced first. The sequela code is sequenced second.

An exception to the above guidelines are those instances where the code for the sequela is followed by a manifestation code identified in the Tabular List and title, or the sequela code has been expanded (at the fourth, fifth or sixth character levels) to include the manifestation(s). The code for the acute phase of an illness or injury that led to the sequela is never used with a code for the late effect.

See Section I.C.9. Sequelae of cerebrovascular disease
See Section I.C.15. Sequelae of complication of pregnancy, childbirth and the puerperium
See Section I.C.19. Application of 7th characters for Chapter 19

11. Impending or Threatened Condition

Code any condition described at the time of discharge as "impending" or "threatened" as follows:

If it did occur, code as confirmed diagnosis.

If it did not occur, reference the Alphabetic Index to determine if the condition has a subentry term for "impending" or "threatened" and also reference main term entries for "Impending" and for "Threatened."

If the subterms are listed, assign the given code.

If the subterms are not listed, code the existing underlying condition(s) and not the condition described as impending or threatened.

12. Reporting Same Diagnosis Code More than Once

Each unique ICD-10-CM diagnosis code may be reported only once for an encounter. This applies to bilateral conditions when there are no distinct codes identifying laterality or two different conditions classified to the same ICD-10-CM diagnosis code.

13. Laterality

Some ICD-10-CM codes indicate laterality, specifying whether the condition occurs on the left, right or is bilateral. If no bilateral code is provided and the condition is bilateral, assign separate codes for both the left and right side. If the side is not identified in the medical record, assign the code for the unspecified side.

14. Documentation for BMI, Non-pressure ulcers and Pressure Ulcer Stages

For the Body Mass Index (BMI), depth of non-pressure chronic ulcers and pressure ulcer stage codes, code assignment may be based on medical record documentation from clinicians who are not the patient's provider (i.e., physician or other qualified healthcare practitioner legally accountable for establishing the patient's diagnosis), since this information is typically documented by other clinicians involved in the care of the patient (e.g., a dietitian often documents the BMI and nurses often documents the pressure ulcer stages). However, the associated diagnosis (such as overweight, obesity, or pressure ulcer) must be documented by the patient's provider. If there is conflicting medical record documentation, either from the same clinician or different clinicians, the patient's attending provider should be queried for clarification.

The BMI codes should only be reported as secondary diagnoses. As with all other secondary diagnosis codes, the BMI codes should only be assigned when they meet the definition of a reportable additional diagnosis (see Section III, Reporting Additional Diagnoses).

15. Syndromes

Follow the Alphabetic Index guidance when coding syndromes. In the absence of Alphabetic Index guidance, assign codes for the documented manifestations of the syndrome. Additional codes for manifestations that are not an integral part of the disease process may also be assigned when the condition does not have a unique code.

16. Documentation of Complications of Care

Code assignment is based on the provider's documentation of the relationship between the condition and the care or procedure. The guideline extends to any complications of care, regardless of the chapter the code is located in. It is important to note that not all conditions that occur during or following medical care or surgery are classified as complications. There must be a cause-and-effect relationship between the care provided and the condition, and an indication in the documentation that it is a complication. Query the provider for clarification, if the complication is not clearly documented.

17. Borderline Diagnosis

If the provider documents a "borderline" diagnosis at the time of discharge, the diagnosis is coded as confirmed, unless the classification provides a specific entry (e.g., borderline diabetes). If a borderline condition has a specific index entry in ICD-10-CM, it should be coded as such. Since borderline conditions are not uncertain diagnoses, no distinction is made between the care setting (inpatient versus outpatient). Whenever the documentation is unclear regarding a borderline condition, coders are encouraged to query for clarification.

18. Use of Sign/Symptom/Unspecified Codes

Sign/symptom and "unspecified" codes have acceptable, even necessary, uses. While specific diagnosis codes should be reported when they are supported by the available medical record documentation and clinical knowledge of the patient's health condition, there are instances when signs/symptoms or unspecified codes are the best choices for accurately reflecting the healthcare encounter. Each healthcare encounter should be coded to the level of certainty known for that encounter.

If a definitive diagnosis has not been established by the end of the encounter, it is appropriate to report codes for sign(s) and/or symptom(s)

in lieu of a definitive diagnosis. When sufficient clinical information isn't known or available about a particular health condition to assign a more specific code, it is acceptable to report the appropriate "unspecified" code (e.g., a diagnosis of pneumonia has been determined, but not the specific type). Unspecified codes should be reported when they are the codes that most accurately reflects what is known about the patient's condition at the time of that particular encounter. It would be inappropriate to select a specific code that is not supported by the medical record documentation or conduct medically unnecessary diagnostic testing in order to determine a more specific code.

C. Chapter-Specific Coding Guidelines

In addition to general coding guidelines, there are guidelines for specific diagnoses and/or conditions in the classification. Unless otherwise indicated, these guidelines apply to all health care settings. Please refer to Section II for guidelines on the selection of principal diagnosis.

1. Chapter 1: Certain Infectious and Parasitic Diseases (A00-B99)

a. Human Immunodeficiency Virus (HIV) Infections

1) Code only confirmed cases

Code only confirmed cases of HIV infection/illness. This is an exception to the hospital inpatient guideline Section II, H.

In this context, "confirmation" does not require documentation of positive serology or culture for HIV; the provider's diagnostic statement that the patient is HIV positive, or has an HIV-related illness is sufficient.

2) Selection and sequencing of HIV codes

(a) Patient admitted for HIV-related condition

If a patient is admitted for an HIV-related condition, the principal diagnosis should be B20, Human immunodeficiency virus [HIV] disease followed by additional diagnosis codes for all reported HIV-related conditions.

(b) Patient with HIV disease admitted for unrelated condition

If a patient with HIV disease is admitted for an unrelated condition (such as a traumatic injury), the code for the unrelated condition (e.g., the nature of injury code) should be the principal diagnosis. Other diagnoses would be B20 followed by additional diagnosis codes for all reported HIV-related conditions.

(c) **Whether the patient is newly diagnosed**

Whether the patient is newly diagnosed or has had previous admissions/encounters for HIV conditions is irrelevant to the sequencing decision.

(d) **Asymptomatic human immunodeficiency virus**

Z21, Asymptomatic human immunodeficiency virus [HIV] infection status, is to be applied when the patient without any documentation of symptoms is listed as being "HIV positive," "known HIV," "HIV test positive," or similar terminology. Do not use this code if the term "AIDS" is used or if the patient is treated for any HIV-related illness or is described as having any condition(s) resulting from his/her HIV positive status; use B20 in these cases.

(e) **Patients with inconclusive HIV serology**

Patients with inconclusive HIV serology, but no definitive diagnosis or manifestations of the illness, may be assigned code R75, Inconclusive laboratory evidence of human immunodeficiency virus [HIV].

(f) **Previously diagnosed HIV-related illness**

Patients with any known prior diagnosis of an HIV-related illness should be coded to B20. Once a patient has developed an HIV-related illness, the patient should always be assigned code B20 on every subsequent admission/encounter. Patients previously diagnosed with any HIV illness (B20) should never be assigned to R75 or Z21, Asymptomatic human immunodeficiency virus [HIV] infection status.

(g) **HIV Infection in Pregnancy, Childbirth and the Puerperium**

During pregnancy, childbirth or the puerperium, a patient admitted (or presenting for a health care encounter) because of an HIV-related illness should receive a principal diagnosis code of O98.7-, Human immunodeficiency [HIV] disease complicating pregnancy, childbirth and the puerperium, followed by B20 and the code(s) for the HIV-related illness(es).

Codes from Chapter 15 always take sequencing priority.

Patients with asymptomatic HIV infection status admitted (or presenting for a health care encounter) during pregnancy, childbirth, or the puerperium should receive codes of O98.7- and Z21.

(h) **Encounters for testing for HIV**

If a patient is being seen to determine his/her HIV status, use code Z11.4, Encounter for screening for human immunodeficiency virus [HIV]. Use additional codes for any associated high risk behavior.

If a patient with signs or symptoms is being seen for HIV testing, code the signs and symptoms. An additional counseling code Z71.7, Human immunodeficiency virus [HIV] counseling, may be used if counseling is provided during the encounter for the test.

When a patient returns to be informed of his/her HIV test results and the test result is negative, use code Z71.7, Human immunodeficiency virus [HIV] counseling.

If the results are positive, see previous guidelines and assign codes as appropriate.

b. **Infectious agents as the cause of diseases classified to other chapters**

Certain infections are classified in chapters other than Chapter 1 and no organism is identified as part of the infection code. In these instances, it is necessary to use an additional code from Chapter 1 to identify the organism. A code from category B95, Streptococcus, Staphylococcus, and Enterococcus as the cause of diseases classified to other chapters, B96, Other bacterial agents as the cause of diseases classified to other chapters, or B97, Viral agents as the cause of diseases classified to other chapters, is to be used as an additional code to identify the organism. An instructional note will be found at the infection code advising that an additional organism code is required.

c. **Infections resistant to antibiotics**

Many bacterial infections are resistant to current antibiotics. It is necessary to identify all infections documented as antibiotic resistant. Assign a code from category Z16, Resistance to antimicrobial drugs, following the infection code only if the infection code does not identify drug resistance.

d. Sepsis, Severe Sepsis, and Septic Shock

1) Coding of Sepsis and Severe Sepsis

(a) Sepsis

For a diagnosis of sepsis, assign the appropriate code for the underlying systemic infection. If the type of infection or causal organism is not further specified, assign code A41.9, Sepsis, unspecified organism.

A code from subcategory R65.2, Severe sepsis, should not be assigned unless severe sepsis or an associated acute organ dysfunction is documented.

(i) Negative or inconclusive blood cultures and sepsis

Negative or inconclusive blood cultures do not preclude a diagnosis of sepsis in patients with clinical evidence of the condition, however, the provider should be queried.

(ii) Urosepsis

The term urosepsis is a nonspecific term. It is not to be considered synonymous with sepsis. It has no default code in the Alphabetic Index. Should a provider use this term, he/she must be queried for clarification.

(iii)   Sepsis with organ dysfunction

If a patient has sepsis and associated acute organ dysfunction or multiple organ dysfunction (MOD), follow the instructions for coding severe sepsis.

(iv)   Acute organ dysfunction that is not clearly associated with the sepsis

If a patient has sepsis and an acute organ dysfunction, but the medical record documentation indicates that the acute organ dysfunction is related to a medical condition other than the sepsis, do not assign a code from subcategory R65.2, Severe sepsis. An acute organ dysfunction must be associated with the sepsis in order to assign the severe sepsis code. If the documentation is not clear as to whether an acute organ dysfunction is related to the sepsis or another medical condition, query the provider.

(b)   **Severe sepsis**

The coding of severe sepsis requires a minimum of 2 codes: first a code for the underlying systemic infection, followed by a code from subcategory R65.2, Severe sepsis. If the causal organism is not documented, assign code A41.9, Sepsis, unspecified organism, for the infection. Additional code(s) for the associated acute organ dysfunction are also required.

Due to the complex nature of severe sepsis, some cases may require querying the provider prior to assignment of the codes.

2)   **Septic shock**

(a)   Septic shock generally refers to circulatory failure associated with severe sepsis, and therefore, it represents a type of acute organ dysfunction.

For cases of septic shock, the code for the systemic infection should be sequenced first, followed by code R65.21, Severe sepsis with septic shock or code T81.12, Postprocedural septic shock. Any additional codes for the other acute organ dysfunctions should also be assigned. As noted in the sequencing instructions in the Tabular List, the code for septic shock cannot be assigned as a principal diagnosis.

3) **Sequencing of severe sepsis**

If severe sepsis is present on admission, and meets the definition of principal diagnosis, the underlying systemic infection should be assigned as principal diagnosis followed by the appropriate code from subcategory R65.2 as required by the sequencing rules in the Tabular List. A code from subcategory R65.2 can never be assigned as a principal diagnosis.

When severe sepsis develops during an encounter (it was not present on admission) the underlying systemic infection and the appropriate code from subcategory R65.2 should be assigned as secondary diagnoses.

Severe sepsis may be present on admission but the diagnosis may not be confirmed until sometime after admission. If the documentation is not clear whether severe sepsis was present on admission, the provider should be queried.

4) **Sepsis and severe sepsis with a localized infection**

If the reason for admission is both sepsis or severe sepsis and a localized infection, such as pneumonia or cellulitis, a code(s) for the underlying systemic infection should be assigned first and the code for the localized infection should be assigned as a secondary diagnosis. If the patient has severe sepsis, a code from subcategory R65.2 should also be assigned as a secondary diagnosis. If the patient is admitted with a localized infection, such as pneumonia, and sepsis/severe sepsis doesn't develop until after admission, the localized infection should be assigned first, followed by the appropriate sepsis/severe sepsis codes.

5) **Sepsis due to a postprocedural infection**

(a) **Documentation of causal relationship**

As with all postprocedural complications, code assignment is based on the provider's documentation of the relationship between the infection and the procedure.

(b) **Sepsis due to a postprocedural infection**

For such cases, the postprocedural infection code, such as, T80.2, Infections following infusion, transfusion, and therapeutic injection, T81.4, Infection following a procedure, T88.0, Infection following immunization, or O86.0, Infection of obstetric surgical wound, should be coded first, followed by the code for the specific infection. If the patient has severe sepsis the appropriate code from subcategory R65.2 should also be assigned with the additional code(s) for any acute organ dysfunction.

(c) Postprocedural infection and postprocedural septic shock

In cases where a postprocedural infection has occurred and has resulted in severe sepsis and postprocedural septic shock, the code for the precipitating complication such as code T81.4, Infection following a procedure, or O86.0, Infection of obstetrical surgical wound should be coded first followed by code R65.21, Severe sepsis with septic shock and a code for the systemic infection.

6) Sepsis and severe sepsis associated with a noninfectious process (condition)

In some cases a noninfectious process (condition), such as trauma, may lead to an infection which can result in sepsis or severe sepsis. If sepsis or severe sepsis is documented as associated with a noninfectious condition, such as a burn or serious injury, and this condition meets the definition for principal diagnosis, the code for the noninfectious condition should be sequenced first, followed by the code for the resulting infection. If severe sepsis, is present a code from subcategory R65.2 should also be assigned with any associated organ dysfunction(s) codes. It is not necessary to assign a code from subcategory R65.1, Systemic inflammatory response syndrome (SIRS) of non-infectious origin, for these cases.

If the infection meets the definition of principal diagnosis it should be sequenced before the non-infectious condition. When both the associated non-infectious condition and the infection meet the definition of principal diagnosis either may be assigned as principal diagnosis.

Only one code from category R65, Symptoms and signs specifically associated with systemic inflammation and infection, should be assigned. Therefore, when a non-infectious condition leads to an infection resulting in severe sepsis, assign the appropriate code from subcategory R65.2, Severe sepsis. Do not additionally assign a code from subcategory R65.1, Systemic inflammatory response syndrome (SIRS) of non-infectious origin.

See Section I.C.18. SIRS due to non-infectious process

7) **Sepsis and septic shock complicating abortion, pregnancy, childbirth, and the puerperium**

See Section I.C.15. Sepsis and septic shock complicating abortion, pregnancy, childbirth and the puerperium

8) **Newborn sepsis**

See Section I.C.16. f. Bacterial sepsis of Newborn

e. Methicillin Resistant *Staphylococcus aureus* (MRSA) Conditions

1) Selection and sequencing of MRSA codes

(a) Combination codes for MRSA infection

When a patient is diagnosed with an infection that is due to methicillin resistant *Staphylococcus aureus* (MRSA), and that infection has a combination code that includes the causal organism (e.g., sepsis, pneumonia) assign the appropriate combination code for the condition (e.g., code A41.02, Sepsis due to Methicillin resistant Staphylococcus aureus or code J15.212, Pneumonia due to Methicillin resistant Staphylococcus aureus). Do not assign code B95.62, Methicillin resistant Staphylococcus aureus infection as the cause of diseases classified elsewhere, as an additional code because the combination code includes the type of infection and the MRSA organism. Do not assign a code from subcategory Z16.11, Resistance to penicillins, as an additional diagnosis.

See Section C.1. for instructions on coding and sequencing of sepsis and severe sepsis.

(b) Other codes for MRSA infection

When there is documentation of a current infection (e.g., wound infection, stitch abscess, urinary tract infection) due to MRSA, and that infection does not have a combination code that includes the causal organism, assign the appropriate code to identify the condition along with code B95.62, Methicillin resistant Staphylococcus aureus infection as the cause of diseases classified elsewhere for the MRSA infection. Do not assign a code from subcategory Z16.11, Resistance to penicillins.

(c)   **Methicillin susceptible Staphylococcus aureus (MSSA) and MRSA colonization**

The condition or state of being colonized or carrying MSSA or MRSA is called colonization or carriage, while an individual person is described as being colonized or being a carrier. Colonization means that MSSA or MSRA is present on or in the body without necessarily causing illness. A positive MRSA colonization test might be documented by the provider as "MRSA screen positive" or "MRSA nasal swab positive".

Assign code Z22.322, Carrier or suspected carrier of Methicillin resistant Staphylococcus aureus, for patients documented as having MRSA colonization. Assign code Z22.321, Carrier or suspected carrier of Methicillin susceptible Staphylococcus aureus, for patient documented as having MSSA colonization. Colonization is not necessarily indicative of a disease process or as the cause of a specific condition the patient may have unless documented as such by the provider.

(d)   **MRSA colonization and infection**

If a patient is documented as having both MRSA colonization and infection during a hospital admission, code Z22.322, Carrier or suspected carrier of Methicillin resistant Staphylococcus aureus, and a code for the MRSA infection may both be assigned.

2.   Chapter 2: Neoplasms (C00-D49)

General guidelines

Chapter 2 of the ICD-10-CM contains the codes for most benign and all malignant neoplasms. Certain benign neoplasms, such as prostatic adenomas, may be found in the specific body system chapters. To properly code a neoplasm it is necessary to determine from the record if the neoplasm is benign, in-situ, malignant, or of uncertain histologic behavior. If malignant, any secondary (metastatic) sites should also be determined.

Primary malignant neoplasms overlapping site boundaries

A primary malignant neoplasm that overlaps two or more contiguous (next to each other) sites should be classified to the subcategory/code .8 ('overlapping lesion'), unless the combination is specifically indexed elsewhere. For multiple neoplasms of the same site that are not contiguous such as tumors in different quadrants of the same breast, codes for each site should be assigned.

Malignant neoplasm of ectopic tissue

Malignant neoplasms of ectopic tissue are to be coded to the site of origin mentioned, e.g., ectopic pancreatic malignant neoplasms involving the stomach are coded to pancreas, unspecified (C25.9).

The neoplasm table in the Alphabetic Index should be referenced first. However, if the histological term is documented, that term should be referenced first, rather than going immediately to the Neoplasm Table, in order to determine which column in the Neoplasm Table is appropriate. For example, if the documentation indicates "adenoma," refer to the term in the Alphabetic Index to review the entries under this term and the instructional note to "see also neoplasm, by site, benign." The table provides the proper code based on the type of neoplasm and the site. It is important to select the proper column in the table that corresponds to the type of neoplasm. The Tabular List should then be referenced to verify that the correct code has been selected from the table and that a more specific site code does not exist. *See Section I.C.21. Factors influencing health status and contact with health services, Status, for information regarding Z15.0, codes for genetic susceptibility to cancer.*

a. Treatment directed at the malignancy

If the treatment is directed at the malignancy, designate the malignancy as the principal diagnosis.

The only exception to this guideline is if a patient admission/encounter is solely for the administration of chemotherapy, immunotherapy or radiation therapy, assign the appropriate Z51.-- code as the first-listed or principal diagnosis, and the diagnosis or problem for which the service is being performed as a secondary diagnosis.

b. Treatment of secondary site

When a patient is admitted because of a primary neoplasm with metastasis and treatment is directed toward the secondary site only, the secondary neoplasm is designated as the principal diagnosis even though the primary malignancy is still present.

c. Coding and sequencing of complications

Coding and sequencing of complications associated with the malignancies or with the therapy thereof are subject to the following guidelines:

1) Anemia associated with malignancy

When admission/encounter is for management of an anemia associated with the malignancy, and the treatment is only for anemia, the appropriate code for the malignancy is sequenced as the principal or first-listed diagnosis followed by the appropriate code for the anemia (such as code D63.0, Anemia in neoplastic disease).

2) **Anemia associated with chemotherapy, immunotherapy and radiation therapy**

When the admission/encounter is for management of an anemia associated with an adverse effect of the administration of chemotherapy or immunotherapy and the only treatment is for the anemia, the anemia code is sequenced first followed by the appropriate codes for the neoplasm and the adverse effect (T45.1X5, Adverse effect of antineoplastic and immunosuppressive drugs).

When the admission/encounter is for management of an anemia associated with an adverse effect of radiotherapy, the anemia code should be sequenced first, followed by the appropriate neoplasm code and code Y84.2, Radiological procedure and radiotherapy as the cause of abnormal reaction of the patient, or of later complication, without mention of misadventure at the time of the procedure.

3) **Management of dehydration due to the malignancy**

When the admission/encounter is for management of dehydration due to the malignancy and only the dehydration is being treated (intravenous rehydration), the dehydration is sequenced first, followed by the code(s) for the malignancy.

4) **Treatment of a complication resulting from a surgical procedure**

When the admission/encounter is for treatment of a complication resulting from a surgical procedure, designate the complication as the principal or first-listed diagnosis if treatment is directed at resolving the complication.

d. **Primary malignancy previously excised**

When a primary malignancy has been previously excised or eradicated from its site and there is no further treatment directed to that site and there is no evidence of any existing primary malignancy, a code from category Z85, Personal history of malignant neoplasm, should be used to indicate the former site of the malignancy. Any mention of extension, invasion, or metastasis to another site is coded as a secondary malignant neoplasm to that site. The secondary site may be the principal or first-listed with the Z85 code used as a secondary code.

e. **Admissions/Encounters involving chemotherapy, immunotherapy and radiation therapy**

1) **Episode of care involves surgical removal of neoplasm**

When an episode of care involves the surgical removal of a neoplasm, primary or secondary site, followed by adjunct chemotherapy or radiation treatment during the same episode of care, the code for the neoplasm should be assigned as principal or first-listed diagnosis.

2) **Patient admission/encounter solely for administration of chemotherapy, immunotherapy and radiation therapy**

If a patient admission/encounter is solely for the administration of chemotherapy, immunotherapy or radiation therapy assign code Z51.0, Encounter for antineoplastic radiation therapy, or Z51.11, Encounter for antineoplastic chemotherapy, or Z51.12, Encounter for antineoplastic immunotherapy as the first-listed or principal diagnosis. If a patient receives more than one of these therapies during the same admission more than one of these codes may be assigned, in any sequence.

The malignancy for which the therapy is being administered should be assigned as a secondary diagnosis.

3) **Patient admitted for radiation therapy, chemotherapy or immunotherapy and develops complications**

When a patient is admitted for the purpose of radiotherapy, immunotherapy or chemotherapy and develops complications such as uncontrolled nausea and vomiting or dehydration, the principal or first-listed diagnosis is Z51.0, Encounter for antineoplastic radiation therapy, or Z51.11, Encounter for antineoplastic chemotherapy, or Z51.12, Encounter for antineoplastic immunotherapy followed by any codes for the complications.

f. **Admission/encounter to determine extent of malignancy**

When the reason for admission/encounter is to determine the extent of the malignancy, or for a procedure such as paracentesis or thoracentesis, the primary malignancy or appropriate metastatic site is designated as the principal or first-listed diagnosis, even though chemotherapy or radiotherapy is administered.

g. **Symptoms, signs, and abnormal findings listed in Chapter 18 associated with neoplasms**

Symptoms, signs, and ill-defined conditions listed in Chapter 18 characteristic of, or associated with, an existing primary or secondary site malignancy cannot be used to replace the malignancy as principal or first-listed diagnosis, regardless of the number of admissions or encounters for treatment and care of the neoplasm.
See section I.C.21. Factors influencing health status and contact with health services, Encounter for prophylactic organ removal.

h. **Admission/encounter for pain control/management**

See Section I.C.6. for information on coding admission/encounter for pain control/management.

i. **Malignancy in two or more noncontiguous sites**

A patient may have more than one malignant tumor in the same organ. These tumors may represent different primaries or metastatic disease, depending on the site. Should the documentation be unclear, the provider should be queried as to the status of each tumor so that the correct codes can be assigned.

j. **Disseminated malignant neoplasm, unspecified**

Code C80.0, Disseminated malignant neoplasm, unspecified, is for use only in those cases where the patient has advanced metastatic disease and no known primary or secondary sites are specified. It should not be used in place of assigning codes for the primary site and all known secondary sites.

k. **Malignant neoplasm without specification of site**

Code C80.1, Malignant (primary) neoplasm, unspecified, equates to Cancer, unspecified. This code should only be used when no determination can be made as to the primary site of a malignancy. This code should rarely be used in the inpatient setting.

l. **Sequencing of neoplasm codes**

1) **Encounter for treatment of primary malignancy**

If the reason for the encounter is for treatment of a primary malignancy, assign the malignancy as the principal/first-listed diagnosis. The primary site is to be sequenced first, followed by any metastatic sites.

2) **Encounter for treatment of secondary malignancy**

When an encounter is for a primary malignancy with metastasis and treatment is directed toward the metastatic (secondary) site(s) only, the metastatic site(s) is designated as the principal/first-listed diagnosis. The primary malignancy is coded as an additional code.

3)   Malignant neoplasm in a pregnant patient

When a pregnant woman has a malignant neoplasm, a code from subcategory O9A.1-, Malignant neoplasm complicating pregnancy, childbirth, and the puerperium, should be sequenced first, followed by the appropriate code from Chapter 2 to indicate the type of neoplasm.

4)   Encounter for complication associated with a neoplasm

When an encounter is for management of a complication associated with a neoplasm, such as dehydration, and the treatment is only for the complication, the complication is coded first, followed by the appropriate code(s) for the neoplasm.

The exception to this guideline is anemia. When the admission/encounter is for management of an anemia associated with the malignancy, and the treatment is only for anemia, the appropriate code for the malignancy is sequenced as the principal or first-listed diagnosis followed by code D63.0, Anemia in neoplastic disease.

5)   Complication from surgical procedure for treatment of a neoplasm

When an encounter is for treatment of a complication resulting from a surgical procedure performed for the treatment of the neoplasm, designate the complication as the principal/first-listed diagnosis. See guideline regarding the coding of a current malignancy versus personal history to determine if the code for the neoplasm should also be assigned.

6)   Pathologic fracture due to a neoplasm

When an encounter is for a pathological fracture due to a neoplasm, and the focus of treatment is the fracture, a code from subcategory M84.5, Pathological fracture in neoplastic disease, should be sequenced first, followed by the code for the neoplasm.

If the focus of treatment is the neoplasm with an associated pathological fracture, the neoplasm code should be sequenced first, followed by a code from M84.5 for the pathological fracture.

m. **Current malignancy versus personal history of malignancy**

When a primary malignancy has been excised but further treatment, such as an additional surgery for the malignancy, radiation therapy or chemotherapy is directed to that site, the primary malignancy code should be used until treatment is completed.

When a primary malignancy has been previously excised or eradicated from its site, there is no further treatment (of the malignancy) directed to that site, and there is no evidence of any existing primary malignancy, a code from category Z85, Personal history of malignant neoplasm, should be used to indicate the former site of the malignancy.

See Section I.C.21. Factors influencing health status and contact with health services, History (of)

n. **Leukemia, Multiple Myeloma, and Malignant Plasma Cell Neoplasms in remission versus personal history**

The categories for leukemia, and category C90, Multiple myeloma and malignant plasma cell neoplasms, have codes indicating whether or not the leukemia has achieved remission. There are also codes Z85.6, Personal history of leukemia, and Z85.79, Personal history of other malignant neoplasms of lymphoid, hematopoietic and related tissues. If the documentation is unclear, as to whether the leukemia   has achieved remission, the provider should be queried.

See Section I.C.21. Factors influencing health status and contact with health services, History (of)

o. **Aftercare following surgery for neoplasm**

See Section I.C.21. Factors influencing health status and contact with health services, Aftercare

p. **Follow-up care for completed treatment of a malignancy**

See Section I.C.21. Factors influencing health status and contact with health services, Follow-up

q. **Prophylactic organ removal for prevention of malignancy**

See Section I.C. 21, Factors influencing health status and contact with health services, Prophylactic organ removal

r. **Malignant neoplasm associated with transplanted organ**

A malignant neoplasm of a transplanted organ should be coded as a transplant complication. Assign first the appropriate code from category T86.-, Complications of transplanted organs and tissue, followed by code C80.2, Malignant neoplasm associated with transplanted organ. Use an additional code for the specific malignancy.

3. **Chapter 3: Disease of the blood and blood-forming organs and certain disorders involving the immune mechanism (D50-D89)**

Reserved for future guideline expansion

4. **Chapter 4: Endocrine, Nutritional, and Metabolic Diseases (E00-E89)**

a. **Diabetes mellitus**

The diabetes mellitus codes are combination codes that include the type of diabetes mellitus, the body system affected, and the complications affecting that body system. As many codes within a particular category as are necessary to describe all of the complications of the disease may be used. They should be sequenced based on the reason for a particular encounter. Assign as many codes from categories E08 – E13 as needed to identify all of the associated conditions that the patient has.

1) **Type of diabetes**

The age of a patient is not the sole determining factor, though most type 1 diabetics develop the condition before reaching puberty. For this reason type 1 diabetes mellitus is also referred to as juvenile diabetes.

2) **Type of diabetes mellitus not documented**

If the type of diabetes mellitus is not documented in the medical record the default is E11.-, Type 2 diabetes mellitus.

3) **Diabetes mellitus and the use of insulin**

If the documentation in a medical record does not indicate the type of diabetes but does indicate that the patient uses insulin, code E11, Type 2 diabetes mellitus, should be assigned. Code Z79.4, Long-term (current) use of insulin, should also be assigned to indicate that the patient uses insulin. Code Z79.4 should not be assigned if insulin is given temporarily to bring a type 2 patient's blood sugar under control during an encounter.

4)   Diabetes mellitus in pregnancy and gestational diabetes

See Section I.C.15. Diabetes mellitus in pregnancy.
See Section I.C.15. Gestational (pregnancy induced) diabetes

5)   Complications due to insulin pump malfunction

(a)   **Underdose of insulin due to insulin pump failure**

An underdose of insulin due to an insulin pump failure should be assigned to a code from subcategory T85.6, Mechanical complication of other specified internal and external prosthetic devices, implants and grafts, that specifies the type of pump malfunction, as the principal or first-listed code, followed by code T38.3x6-, Underdosing of insulin and oral hypoglycemic [antidiabetic] drugs. Additional codes for the type of diabetes mellitus and any associated complications due to the underdosing should also be assigned.

(b)   **Overdose of insulin due to insulin pump failure**

The principal or first-listed code for an encounter due to an insulin pump malfunction resulting in an overdose of insulin, should also be T85.6-, Mechanical complication of other specified internal and external prosthetic devices, implants and grafts, followed by code T38.3x1-, Poisoning by insulin and oral hypoglycemic [antidiabetic] drugs, accidental (unintentional).

6)   Secondary diabetes mellitus

Codes under categories E08, Diabetes mellitus due to underlying condition, E09, Drug or chemical induced diabetes mellitus, and E13, Other specified diabetes mellitus, identify complications/manifestations associated with secondary diabetes mellitus. Secondary diabetes is always caused by another condition or event (e.g., cystic fibrosis, malignant neoplasm of pancreas, pancreatectomy, adverse effect of drug, or poisoning).

(a)   **Secondary diabetes mellitus and the use of insulin**

For patients who routinely use insulin, code Z79.4, Long-term (current) use of insulin, should also be assigned. Code Z79.4 should not be assigned if insulin is given temporarily to bring a patient's blood sugar under control during an encounter.

(b) **Assigning and sequencing secondary diabetes codes and its causes**

The sequencing of the secondary diabetes codes in relationship to codes for the cause of the diabetes is based on the Tabular List instructions for categories E08, E09 and E13.

(i) **Secondary diabetes mellitus due to pancreatectomy**

For postpancreatectomy diabetes mellitus (lack of insulin due to the surgical removal of all or part of the pancreas), assign code E89.1, Postprocedural hypoinsulinemia. Assign a code from category E13 and a code from subcategory Z90.41-, Acquired absence of pancreas, as additional codes.

(ii) **Secondary diabetes due to drugs**

Secondary diabetes may be caused by an adverse effect of correctly administered medications, poisoning or sequela of poisoning. *See section I.C.19.e for coding of adverse effects and poisoning, and section I.C.20 for external cause code reporting.*

5. Chapter 5: Mental, Behavioral and Neurodevelopmental disorders (F01 – F99)

a. Pain disorders related to psychological factors

Assign code F45.41, for pain that is exclusively related to psychological disorders. As indicated by the Excludes 1 note under category G89, a code from category G89 should not be assigned with code F45.41

Code F45.42, Pain disorders with related psychological factors, should be used with a code from category G89, Pain, not elsewhere classified, if there is documentation of a psychological component for a patient with acute or chronic pain.

See Section I.C.6. Pain

c.   **Mental and behavioral disorders due to psychoactive substance use**

1)   In Remission

Selection of codes for "in remission" for categories F10-F19, Mental and behavioral disorders due to psychoactive substance use (categories F10-F19 with -.21) requires the provider's clinical judgment. The appropriate codes for "in remission" are assigned only on the basis of provider documentation (as defined in the Official Guidelines for Coding and Reporting).

2)   Psychoactive Substance Use, Abuse And Dependence

When the provider documentation refers to use, abuse and dependence of the same substance (e.g. alcohol, opioid, cannabis, etc.), only one code should be assigned to identify the pattern of use based on the following hierarchy:
- If both use and abuse are documented, assign only the code for abuse
- If both abuse and dependence are documented, assign only the code for dependence
- If use, abuse and dependence are all documented, assign only the code for dependence
- If both use and dependence are documented, assign only the code for dependence.

3)   Psychoactive Substance Use

As with all other diagnoses, the codes for psychoactive substance use (F10.9-, F11.9-, F12.9-, F13.9-, F14.9-, F15.9-, F16.9-) should only be assigned based on provider documentation and when they meet the definition of a reportable diagnosis (see Section III, Reporting Additional Diagnoses). The codes are to be used only when the psychoactive substance use is associated with a mental or behavioral disorder, and such a relationship is documented by the provider.

6.   **Chapter 6: Diseases of the Nervous System (G00-G99)**

a.   **Dominant/nondominant side**

Codes from category G81, Hemiplegia and hemiparesis, and subcategories, G83.1, Monoplegia of lower limb, G83.2, Monoplegia of upper limb, and G83.3, Monoplegia, unspecified, identify whether the dominant or nondominant side is affected. Should the affected side be documented, but not specified as dominant or nondominant, and the classification system does not indicate a default, code selection is as follows:

- For ambidextrous patients, the default should be dominant.
- If the left side is affected, the default is non-dominant.
- If the right side is affected, the default is dominant.

b. Pain - Category G89

1) General coding information

Codes in category G89, Pain, not elsewhere classified, may be used in conjunction with codes from other categories and chapters to provide more detail about acute or chronic pain and neoplasm-related pain, unless otherwise indicated below.

If the pain is not specified as acute or chronic, post-thoracotomy, postprocedural, or neoplasm-related, do not assign codes from category G89.

A code from category G89 should not be assigned if the underlying (definitive) diagnosis is known, unless the reason for the encounter is pain control/ management and not management of the underlying condition.

When an admission or encounter is for a procedure aimed at treating the underlying condition (e.g., spinal fusion, kyphoplasty), a code for the underlying condition (e.g., vertebral fracture, spinal stenosis) should be assigned as the principal diagnosis. No code from category G89 should be assigned.

(a) Category G89 Codes as Principal or First-Listed Diagnosis

Category G89 codes are acceptable as principal diagnosis or the first-listed code:

- When pain control or pain management is the reason for the admission/encounter (e.g., a patient with displaced intervertebral disc, nerve impingement and severe back pain presents for injection of steroid into the spinal canal). The underlying cause of the pain should be reported as an additional diagnosis, if known.

- When a patient is admitted for the insertion of a neurostimulator for pain control, assign the appropriate pain code as the principal or first-listed diagnosis. When an admission or encounter is for a procedure aimed at treating the underlying condition and a neurostimulator is inserted for pain control during the same admission/encounter, a code for the underlying condition should be assigned as the principal diagnosis and the appropriate pain code should be assigned as a secondary diagnosis.

(b) **Use of Category G89 Codes in Conjunction with Site Specific Pain Codes**

(i) **Assigning Category G89 and Site-Specific Pain Codes**

Codes from category G89 may be used in conjunction with codes that identify the site of pain (including codes from chapter 18) if the category G89 code provides additional information. For example, if the code describes the site of the pain, but does not fully describe whether the pain is acute or chronic, then both codes should be assigned.

(ii) **Sequencing of Category G89 Codes with Site-Specific Pain Codes**

The sequencing of category G89 codes with site-specific pain codes (including chapter 18 codes), is dependent on the circumstances of the encounter/admission as follows:

- If the encounter is for pain control or pain management, assign the code from category G89 followed by the code identifying the specific site of pain (e.g., encounter for pain management for acute neck pain from trauma is assigned code G89.11, Acute pain due to trauma, followed by code M54.2, Cervicalgia, to identify the site of pain).

- If the encounter is for any other reason except pain control or pain management, and a related definitive diagnosis has not been established (confirmed) by the provider, assign the code for the specific site of pain first, followed by the appropriate code from category G89.

2) **Pain due to devices, implants and grafts**

See Section I.C.19. Pain due to medical devices

3) **Postoperative Pain**

The provider's documentation should be used to guide the coding of postoperative pain, as well as *Section III. Reporting Additional Diagnoses* and *Section IV. Diagnostic Coding and Reporting in the Outpatient Setting.*

The default for post-thoracotomy and other postoperative pain not specified as acute or chronic is the code for the acute form.

Routine or expected postoperative pain immediately after surgery should not be coded.

(a) **Postoperative pain not associated with specific postoperative complication**

Postoperative pain not associated with a specific postoperative complication is assigned to the appropriate postoperative pain code in category G89.

(b) **Postoperative pain associated with specific postoperative complication**

Postoperative pain associated with a specific postoperative complication (such as painful wire sutures) is assigned to the appropriate code(s) found in Chapter 19, Injury, poisoning, and certain other consequences of external causes. If appropriate, use additional code(s) from category G89 to identify acute or chronic pain (G89.18 or G89.28).

4) **Chronic pain**

Chronic pain is classified to subcategory G89.2. There is no time frame defining when pain becomes chronic pain. The provider's documentation should be used to guide use of these codes.

5) **Neoplasm Related Pain**

Code G89.3 is assigned to pain documented as being related, associated or due to cancer, primary or secondary malignancy, or tumor. This code is assigned regardless of whether the pain is acute or chronic.

This code may be assigned as the principal or first-listed code when the stated reason for the admission/encounter is documented as pain control/pain management. The underlying neoplasm should be reported as an additional diagnosis.

When the reason for the admission/encounter is management of the neoplasm and the pain associated with the neoplasm is also documented, code G89.3 may be assigned as an additional diagnosis. It is not necessary to assign an additional code for the site of the pain.

See Section I.C.2 for instructions on the sequencing of neoplasms for all other stated reasons for the admission/encounter (except for pain control/pain management).

6) **Chronic pain syndrome**

Central pain syndrome (G89.0) and chronic pain syndrome (G89.4) are different than the term "chronic pain," and therefore codes should only be used when the provider has specifically documented this condition.

See Section I.C.5. Pain disorders related to psychological factors

7. **Chapter 7: Diseases of the Eye and Adnexa (H00-H59)**

a. **Glaucoma**

1) **Assigning Glaucoma Codes**

Assign as many codes from category H40, Glaucoma, as needed to identify the type of glaucoma, the affected eye, and the glaucoma stage.

2) **Bilateral glaucoma with same type and stage**

When a patient has bilateral glaucoma and both eyes are documented as being the same type and stage, and there is a code for bilateral glaucoma, report only the code for the type of glaucoma, bilateral, with the seventh character for the stage.

When a patient has bilateral glaucoma and both eyes are documented as being the same type and stage, and the classification does not provide a code for bilateral glaucoma (i.e. subcategories H40.10, H40.11 and H40.20) report only one code for the type of glaucoma with the appropriate seventh character for the stage.

3) **Bilateral glaucoma stage with different types or stages**

When a patient has bilateral glaucoma and each eye is documented as having a different type or stage, and the classification distinguishes laterality, assign the appropriate code for each eye rather than the code for bilateral glaucoma.

When a patient has bilateral glaucoma and each eye is documented as having a different type, and the classification does not distinguish laterality (i.e. subcategories H40.10, H40.11 and H40.20), assign one code for each type of glaucoma with the appropriate seventh character for the stage.

When a patient has bilateral glaucoma and each eye is documented as having the same type, but different stage, and the classification does not distinguish laterality (i.e. subcategories H40.10, H40.11 and H40.20), assign a code for the type of glaucoma for each eye with the seventh character for the specific glaucoma stage documented for each eye.

4) **Patient admitted with glaucoma and stage evolves during the admission**

If a patient is admitted with glaucoma and the stage progresses during the admission, assign the code for highest stage documented.

5) **Indeterminate stage glaucoma**

Assignment of the seventh character "4" for "indeterminate stage" should be based on the clinical documentation. The seventh character "4" is used for glaucomas whose stage cannot be clinically determined. This seventh character should not be confused with the seventh character "0", unspecified, which should be assigned when there is no documentation regarding the stage of the glaucoma.

8. **Chapter 8: Diseases of the Ear and Mastoid Process (H60-H95)**

Reserved for future guideline expansion

9.   **Chapter 9: Diseases of the Circulatory System (I00-I99)**

    a.   **Hypertension**

        1)   **Hypertension with Heart Disease**

Heart conditions classified to I50.- or I51.4-I51.9, are assigned to, a code from category I11, Hypertensive heart disease, when a causal relationship is stated (due to hypertension) or implied (hypertensive). Use an additional code from category I50, Heart failure, to identify the type of heart failure in those patients with heart failure.

The same heart conditions (I50.-, I51.4-I51.9) with hypertension, but without a stated causal relationship, are coded separately. Sequence according to the circumstances of the admission/encounter.

        2)   **Hypertensive Chronic Kidney Disease**

Assign codes from category I12, Hypertensive chronic kidney disease, when both hypertension and a condition classifiable to category N18, Chronic kidney disease (CKD), are present. Unlike hypertension with heart disease, ICD-10-CM presumes a cause-and-effect relationship and classifies chronic kidney disease with hypertension as hypertensive chronic kidney disease.
The appropriate code from category N18 should be used as a secondary code with a code from category I12 to identify the stage of chronic kidney disease.

See Section I.C.14. Chronic kidney disease.

If a patient has hypertensive chronic kidney disease and acute renal failure, an additional code for the acute renal failure is required.

        3)   **Hypertensive Heart and Chronic Kidney Disease**

Assign codes from combination category I13, Hypertensive heart and chronic kidney disease, when both hypertensive kidney disease and hypertensive heart disease are stated in the diagnosis. Assume a relationship between the hypertension and the chronic kidney disease, whether or not the condition is so designated. If heart failure is present, assign an additional code from category I50 to identify the type of heart failure.

The appropriate code from category N18, Chronic kidney disease, should be used as a secondary code with a code from category I13 to identify the stage of chronic kidney disease.

See Section I.C.14. Chronic kidney disease.

The codes in category I13, Hypertensive heart and chronic kidney disease, are combination codes that include hypertension, heart disease and chronic kidney disease. The Includes note at I13 specifies that the conditions included at I11 and I12 are included together in I13. If a patient has hypertension, heart disease and chronic kidney disease then a code from I13 should be used, not individual codes for hypertension, heart disease and chronic kidney disease, or codes from I11 or I12.

For patients with both acute renal failure and chronic kidney disease an additional code for acute renal failure is required.

4) **Hypertensive Cerebrovascular Disease**

For hypertensive cerebrovascular disease, first assign the appropriate code from categories I60-I69, followed by the appropriate hypertension code.

5) **Hypertensive Retinopathy**

Subcategory H35.0, Background retinopathy and retinal vascular changes, should be used with a code from category I10 – I15, Hypertensive disease to include the systemic hypertension. The sequencing is based on the reason for the encounter.

6) **Hypertension, Secondary**

Secondary hypertension is due to an underlying condition. Two codes are required: one to identify the underlying etiology and one from category I15 to identify the hypertension. Sequencing of codes is determined by the reason for admission/encounter.

7) **Hypertension, Transient**

Assign code R03.0, Elevated blood pressure reading without diagnosis of hypertension, unless patient has an established diagnosis of hypertension. Assign code O13.-, Gestational [pregnancy-induced] hypertension without significant proteinuria, or O14.-, Pre-eclampsia, for transient hypertension of pregnancy.

8)   Hypertension, Controlled

This diagnostic statement usually refers to an existing state of hypertension under control by therapy. Assign the appropriate code from categories I10-I15, Hypertensive diseases.

9)   Hypertension, Uncontrolled

Uncontrolled hypertension may refer to untreated hypertension or hypertension not responding to current therapeutic regimen. In either case, assign the appropriate code from categories I10-I15, Hypertensive diseases.

b.   Atherosclerotic Coronary Artery Disease and Angina

ICD-10-CM has combination codes for atherosclerotic heart disease with angina pectoris. The subcategories for these codes are I25.11, Atherosclerotic heart disease of native coronary artery with angina pectoris and I25.7, Atherosclerosis of coronary artery bypass graft(s) and coronary artery of transplanted heart with angina pectoris.

When using one of these combination codes it is not necessary to use an additional code for angina pectoris. A causal relationship can be assumed in a patient with both atherosclerosis and angina pectoris, unless the documentation indicates the angina is due to something other than the atherosclerosis.

If a patient with coronary artery disease is admitted due to an acute myocardial infarction (AMI), the AMI should be sequenced before the coronary artery disease.

See Section I.C.9. Acute myocardial infarction (AMI)

c.   Intraoperative and Postprocedural Cerebrovascular Accident

Medical record documentation should clearly specify the cause- and-effect relationship between the medical intervention and the cerebrovascular accident in order to assign a code for intraoperative or postprocedural cerebrovascular accident.
Proper code assignment depends on whether it was an infarction or hemorrhage and whether it occurred intraoperatively or postoperatively. If it was a cerebral hemorrhage, code assignment depends on the type of procedure performed.

d.   Sequelae of Cerebrovascular Disease

1)   Category I69, Sequelae of Cerebrovascular disease

Category I69 is used to indicate conditions classifiable to categories I60-I67 as the causes of sequela (neurologic deficits), themselves classified elsewhere. These "late effects" include neurologic deficits that persist after initial onset of conditions classifiable to categories I60-I67. The neurologic deficits caused by cerebrovascular disease may be present from the onset or may arise at any time after the onset of the condition classifiable to categories I60-I67.

Codes from category I69, Sequelae of cerebrovascular disease, that specify hemiplegia, hemiparesis and monoplegia identify whether the dominant or nondominant side is affected. Should the affected side be documented, but not specified as dominant or nondominant, and the classification system does not indicate a default, code selection is as follows:

- For ambidextrous patients, the default should be dominant.
- If the left side is affected, the default is non-dominant.
- If the right side is affected, the default is dominant.

2)   Codes from category I69 with codes from I60-I67

Codes from category I69 may be assigned on a health care record with codes from I60-I67, if the patient has a current cerebrovascular disease and deficits from an old cerebrovascular disease.

3)   Codes from category I69 and Personal history of transient ischemic attack (TIA) and cerebral infarction (Z86.73)

Codes from category I69 should not be assigned if the patient does not have neurologic deficits.

See Section I.C.21. 4. History (of) for use of personal history codes

e.   Acute myocardial infarction (AMI)

1)   ST elevation myocardial infarction (STEMI) and non ST elevation myocardial infarction (NSTEMI)

The ICD-10-CM codes for acute myocardial infarction (AMI) identify the site, such as anterolateral wall or true posterior wall. Subcategories I21.0-I21.2 and code I21.3 are used for ST elevation myocardial infarction (STEMI). Code I21.4, Non-ST elevation (NSTEMI) myocardial infarction, is used for non ST elevation myocardial infarction (NSTEMI) and nontransmural MIs.

If NSTEMI evolves to STEMI, assign the STEMI code. If STEMI converts to NSTEMI due to thrombolytic therapy, it is still coded as STEMI.

For encounters occurring while the myocardial infarction is equal to, or less than, four weeks old, including transfers to another acute setting or a postacute setting, and the patient requires continued care for the myocardial infarction, codes from category I21 may continue to be reported. For encounters after the 4 week time frame and the patient is still receiving care related to the myocardial infarction, the appropriate aftercare code should be assigned, rather than a code from category I21. For old or healed myocardial infarctions not requiring further care, code I25.2, Old myocardial infarction, may be assigned.

2)   Acute myocardial infarction, unspecified

Code I21.3, ST elevation (STEMI) myocardial infarction of unspecified site, is the default for unspecified acute myocardial infarction. If only STEMI or transmural MI without the site is documented, assign code I21.3.

3)   AMI documented as nontransmural or subendocardial but site provided

If an AMI is documented as nontransmural or subendocardial, but the site is provided, it is still coded as a subendocardial AMI.

See Section I.C.21.3 for information on coding status post administration of tPA in a different facility within the last 24 hours.

4) **Subsequent acute myocardial infarction**

A code from category I22, Subsequent ST elevation (STEMI) and non ST elevation (NSTEMI) myocardial infarction, is to be used when a patient who has suffered an AMI has a new AMI within the 4 week time frame of the initial AMI. A code from category I22 must be used in conjunction with a code from category I21. The sequencing of the I22 and I21 codes depends on the circumstances of the encounter.

10. Chapter 10: Diseases of the Respiratory System (J00-J99)

a. Chronic Obstructive Pulmonary Disease [COPD] and Asthma

1) **Acute exacerbation of chronic obstructive bronchitis and asthma**

The codes in categories J44 and J45 distinguish between uncomplicated cases and those in acute exacerbation. An acute exacerbation is a worsening or a decompensation of a chronic condition. An acute exacerbation is not equivalent to an infection superimposed on a chronic condition, though an exacerbation may be triggered by an infection.

b. Acute Respiratory Failure

1) **Acute respiratory failure as principal diagnosis**

A code from subcategory J96.0, Acute respiratory failure, or subcategory J96.2, Acute and chronic respiratory failure, may be assigned as a principal diagnosis when it is the condition established after study to be chiefly responsible for occasioning the admission to the hospital, and the selection is supported by the Alphabetic Index and Tabular List. However, chapter-specific coding guidelines (such as obstetrics, poisoning, HIV, newborn) that provide sequencing direction take precedence.

2) **Acute respiratory failure as secondary diagnosis**

Respiratory failure may be listed as a secondary diagnosis if it occurs after admission, or if it is present on admission, but does not meet the definition of principal diagnosis.

3) **Sequencing of acute respiratory failure and another acute condition**

When a patient is admitted with respiratory failure and another acute condition, (e.g., myocardial infarction, cerebrovascular accident, aspiration pneumonia), the principal diagnosis will not be the same in every situation. This applies whether the other acute condition is a respiratory or nonrespiratory condition. Selection of the principal diagnosis will be dependent on the circumstances of admission. If both the respiratory failure and the other acute condition are equally responsible for occasioning the admission to the hospital, and there are no chapter-specific sequencing rules, the guideline regarding two or more diagnoses that equally meet the definition for principal diagnosis *(Section II, C.)* may be applied in these situations.

If the documentation is not clear as to whether acute respiratory failure and another condition are equally responsible for occasioning the admission, query the provider for clarification.

c. Influenza due to certain identified influenza viruses

Code only confirmed cases of influenza due to certain identified influenza viruses (category J09), and due to other identified influenza virus (category J10). This is an exception to the hospital inpatient guideline Section II, H. (Uncertain Diagnosis).

In this context, "confirmation" does not require documentation of positive laboratory testing specific for avian or other novel influenza A or other identified influenza virus. However, coding should be based on the provider's diagnostic statement that the patient has avian influenza, or other novel influenza A, for category J09, or has another particular identified strain of influenza, such as H1N1 or H3N2, but not identified as novel or variant, for category J10.

If the provider records "suspected" or "possible" or "probable" avian influenza, or novel influenza, or other identified influenza, then the appropriate influenza code from category J11, Influenza due to unidentified influenza virus, should be assigned. A code from category J09, Influenza due to certain identified influenza viruses, should not be assigned nor should a code from category J10, Influenza due to other identified influenza virus.

d. Ventilator associated Pneumonia

1) Documentation of Ventilator associated Pneumonia

As with all procedural or postprocedural complications, code assignment is based on the provider's documentation of the relationship between the condition and the procedure.

Code J95.851, Ventilator associated pneumonia, should be assigned only when the provider has documented ventilator associated pneumonia (VAP). An additional code to identify the organism (e.g., Pseudomonas aeruginosa, code B96.5) should also be assigned. Do not assign an additional code from categories J12-J18 to identify the type of pneumonia.

Code J95.851 should not be assigned for cases where the patient has pneumonia and is on a mechanical ventilator and the provider has not specifically stated that the pneumonia is ventilator-associated pneumonia. If the documentation is unclear as to whether the patient has a pneumonia that is a complication attributable to the mechanical ventilator, query the provider.

2) Ventilator associated Pneumonia Develops after Admission

A patient may be admitted with one type of pneumonia (e.g., code J13, Pneumonia due to Streptococcus pneumonia) and subsequently develop VAP. In this instance, the principal diagnosis would be the appropriate code from categories J12-J18 for the pneumonia diagnosed at the time of admission. Code J95.851, Ventilator associated pneumonia, would be assigned as an additional diagnosis when the provider has also documented the presence of ventilator associated pneumonia.

11. Chapter 11: Diseases of the Digestive System (K00-K95)

Reserved for future guideline expansion

12. Chapter 12: Diseases of the Skin and Subcutaneous Tissue (L00-L99)

a. Pressure ulcer stage codes

1) Pressure ulcer stages

Codes from category L89, Pressure ulcer, are combination codes that identify the site of the pressure ulcer as well as the stage of the ulcer.

The ICD-10-CM classifies pressure ulcer stages based on severity, which is designated by stages 1-4, unspecified stage and unstageable.

Assign as many codes from category L89 as needed to identify all the pressure ulcers the patient has, if applicable.

2) Unstageable pressure ulcers

Assignment of the code for unstageable pressure ulcer (L89.--0) should be based on the clinical documentation. These codes are used for pressure ulcers whose stage cannot be clinically determined (e.g., the ulcer is covered by eschar or has been treated with a skin or muscle graft) and pressure ulcers that are documented as deep tissue injury but not documented as due to trauma. This code should not be confused with the codes for unspecified stage (L89.--9). When there is no documentation regarding the stage of the pressure ulcer, assign the appropriate code for unspecified stage (L89.--9).

3) Documented pressure ulcer stage

Assignment of the pressure ulcer stage code should be guided by clinical documentation of the stage or documentation of the terms found in the Alphabetic Index. For clinical terms describing the stage that are not found in the Alphabetic Index, and there is no documentation of the stage, the provider should be queried.

4) Patients admitted with pressure ulcers documented as healed

No code is assigned if the documentation states that the pressure ulcer is completely healed.

5) Patients admitted with pressure ulcers documented as healing

Pressure ulcers described as healing should be assigned the appropriate pressure ulcer stage code based on the documentation in the medical record. If the documentation does not provide information about the stage of the healing pressure ulcer, assign the appropriate code for unspecified stage.

If the documentation is unclear as to whether the patient has a current (new) pressure ulcer or if the patient is being treated for a healing pressure ulcer, query the provider.

6) Patient admitted with pressure ulcer evolving into another stage during the admission

If a patient is admitted with a pressure ulcer at one stage and it progresses to a higher stage, assign the code for the highest stage reported for that site.

13. Chapter 13: Diseases of the Musculoskeletal System and Connective Tissue (M00-M99)

a. Site and laterality

Most of the codes within Chapter 13 have site and laterality designations. The site represents the bone, joint or the muscle involved. For some conditions where more than one bone, joint or muscle is usually involved, such as osteoarthritis, there is a "multiple sites" code available. For categories where no multiple site code is provided and more than one bone, joint or muscle is involved, multiple codes should be used to indicate the different sites involved.

1) Bone versus joint

For certain conditions, the bone may be affected at the upper or lower end, (e.g., avascular necrosis of bone, M87, Osteoporosis, M80, M81). Though the portion of the bone affected may be at the joint, the site designation will be the bone, not the joint.

b. Acute traumatic versus chronic or recurrent musculoskeletal conditions

Many musculoskeletal conditions are a result of previous injury or trauma to a site, or are recurrent conditions. Bone, joint or muscle conditions that are the result of a healed injury are usually found in chapter 13. Recurrent bone, joint or muscle conditions are also usually found in chapter 13. Any current, acute injury should be coded to the appropriate injury code from chapter 19. Chronic or recurrent conditions should generally be coded with a code from chapter 13. If it is difficult to determine from the documentation in the record which code is best to describe a condition, query the provider.

c. Coding of Pathologic Fractures

7th character A is for use as long as the patient is receiving active treatment for the fracture. Examples of active treatment are: surgical treatment, emergency department encounter, evaluation and treatment by a new physician. 7th character, D is to be used for encounters after the patient has completed active treatment. The other 7th characters, listed under each subcategory in the Tabular List, are to be used for subsequent encounters for treatment of problems associated with the healing, such as malunions, nonunions, and sequelae.
Care for complications of surgical treatment for fracture repairs during the healing or recovery phase should be coded with the appropriate complication codes.

See Section I.C.19. Coding of traumatic fractures.

d. Osteoporosis

Osteoporosis is a systemic condition, meaning that all bones of the musculoskeletal system are affected. Therefore, site is not a component of the codes under category M81, Osteoporosis without current pathological fracture. The site codes under category M80, Osteoporosis with current pathological fracture, identify the site of the fracture, not the osteoporosis.

1) Osteoporosis without pathological fracture

Category M81, Osteoporosis without current pathological fracture, is for use for patients with osteoporosis who do not currently have a pathologic fracture due to the osteoporosis, even if they have had a fracture in the past. For patients with a history of osteoporosis fractures, status code Z87.310, Personal history of (healed) osteoporosis fracture, should follow the code from M81.

2) Osteoporosis with current pathological fracture

Category M80, Osteoporosis with current pathological fracture, is for patients who have a current pathologic fracture at the time of an encounter. The codes under M80 identify the site of the fracture. A code from category M80, not a traumatic fracture code, should be used for any patient with known osteoporosis who suffers a fracture, even if the patient had a minor fall or trauma, if that fall or trauma would not usually break a normal, healthy bone.

14. Chapter 14: Diseases of Genitourinary System (N00-N99)

a. Chronic kidney disease

1) Stages of chronic kidney disease (CKD)

The ICD-10-CM classifies CKD based on severity. The severity of CKD is designated by stages 1-5. Stage 2, code N18.2, equates to mild CKD; stage 3, code N18.3, equates to moderate CKD; and stage 4, code N18.4, equates to severe CKD. Code N18.6, End stage renal disease (ESRD), is assigned when the provider has documented end-stage-renal disease (ESRD).

If both a stage of CKD and ESRD are documented, assign code N18.6 only.

2) Chronic kidney disease and kidney transplant status

Patients who have undergone kidney transplant may still have some form of chronic kidney disease (CKD) because the kidney transplant may not fully restore kidney function. Therefore, the presence of CKD alone does not constitute a transplant complication. Assign the appropriate N18 code for the patient's stage of CKD and code Z94.0, Kidney transplant status. If a transplant complication such as failure or rejection or other transplant complication is documented, see section I.C.19.g for information on coding complications of a kidney transplant. If the documentation is unclear as to whether the patient has a complication of the transplant, query the provider.

3) Chronic kidney disease with other conditions

Patients with CKD may also suffer from other serious conditions, most commonly diabetes mellitus and hypertension. The sequencing of the CKD code in relationship to codes for other contributing conditions is based on the conventions in the Tabular List.

See I.C.9. Hypertensive chronic kidney disease.
See I.C.19. Chronic kidney disease and kidney transplant complications.

15. Chapter 15: Pregnancy, Childbirth, and the Puerperium (O00-O9A)

a. General Rules for Obstetric Cases

1) Codes from chapter 15 and sequencing priority

Obstetric cases require codes from chapter 15, codes in the range O00-O9A, Pregnancy, Childbirth, and the Puerperium. Chapter 15 codes have sequencing priority over codes from other chapters. Additional codes from other chapters may be used in conjunction with chapter 15 codes to further specify conditions. Should the provider document that the pregnancy is incidental to the encounter, then code Z33.1, Pregnant state, incidental, should be used in place of any chapter 15 codes. It is the provider's responsibility to state that the condition being treated is not affecting the pregnancy.

2) Chapter 15 codes used only on the maternal record

Chapter 15 codes are to be used only on the maternal record, never on the record of the newborn.

3) Final character for trimester

The majority of codes in Chapter 15 have a final character indicating the trimester of pregnancy. The timeframes for the trimesters are indicated at the beginning of the chapter. If trimester is not a component of a code it is because the condition always occurs in a specific trimester, or the concept of trimester of pregnancy is not applicable. Certain codes have characters for only certain trimesters because the condition does not occur in all trimesters, but it may occur in more than just one.

Assignment of the final character for trimester should be based on the provider's documentation of the trimester (or number of weeks) for the current admission/encounter. This applies to the assignment of trimester for pre-existing conditions as well as those that develop during or are due to the pregnancy. The provider's documentation of the number of weeks may be used to assign the appropriate code identifying the trimester.

Whenever delivery occurs during the current admission, and there is an "in childbirth" option for the obstetric complication being coded, the "in childbirth" code should be assigned.

4)   **Selection of trimester for inpatient admissions that encompass more than one trimester**

In instances when a patient is admitted to a hospital for complications of pregnancy during one trimester and remains in the hospital into a subsequent trimester, the trimester character for the antepartum complication code should be assigned on the basis of the trimester when the complication developed, not the trimester of the discharge. If the condition developed prior to the current admission/encounter or represents a pre-existing condition, the trimester character for the trimester at the time of the admission/encounter should be assigned.

5)   **Unspecified trimester**

Each category that includes codes for trimester has a code for "unspecified trimester." The "unspecified trimester" code should rarely be used, such as when the documentation in the record is insufficient to determine the trimester and it is not possible to obtain clarification.

6)   **7th character for Fetus Identification**

Where applicable, a 7th character is to be assigned for certain categories (O31, O32, O33.3 - O33.6, O35, O36, O40, O41, O60.1, O60.2, O64, and O69) to identify the fetus for which the complication code applies.

Assign 7th character "0":
- For single gestations
- When the documentation in the record is insufficient to determine the fetus affected and it is not possible to obtain clarification.
- When it is not possible to clinically determine which fetus is affected.

b. Selection of OB Principal or First-listed Diagnosis

1) Routine outpatient prenatal visits

For routine outpatient prenatal visits when no complications are present, a code from category Z34, Encounter for supervision of normal pregnancy, should be used as the first-listed diagnosis. These codes should not be used in conjunction with chapter 15 codes.

2) Prenatal outpatient visits for high-risk patients

For routine prenatal outpatient visits for patients with high-risk pregnancies, a code from category O09, Supervision of high-risk pregnancy, should be used as the first-listed diagnosis. Secondary chapter 15 codes may be used in conjunction with these codes if appropriate.

3) Episodes when no delivery occurs

In episodes when no delivery occurs, the principal diagnosis should correspond to the principal complication of the pregnancy which necessitated the encounter. Should more than one complication exist, all of which are treated or monitored, any of the complications codes may be sequenced first.

4) When a delivery occurs

When a delivery occurs, the principal diagnosis should correspond to the main circumstances or complication of the delivery. In cases of cesarean delivery, the selection of the principal diagnosis should be the condition established after study that was responsible for the patient's admission. If the patient was admitted with a condition that resulted in the performance of a cesarean procedure, that condition should be selected as the principal diagnosis. If the reason for the admission/encounter was unrelated to the condition resulting in the cesarean delivery, the condition related to the reason for the admission/encounter should be selected as the principal diagnosis.

5) Outcome of delivery

A code from category Z37, Outcome of delivery, should be included on every maternal record when a delivery has occurred. These codes are not to be used on subsequent records or on the newborn record.

c. Pre-existing conditions versus conditions due to the pregnancy

Certain categories in Chapter 15 distinguish between conditions of the mother that existed prior to pregnancy (pre-existing) and those that are a direct result of pregnancy. When assigning codes from Chapter 15, it is important to assess if a condition was pre-existing prior to pregnancy or developed during or due to the pregnancy in order to assign the correct code.

Categories that do not distinguish between pre-existing and pregnancy-related conditions may be used for either. It is acceptable to use codes specifically for the puerperium with codes complicating pregnancy and childbirth if a condition arises postpartum during the delivery encounter.

d. Pre-existing hypertension in pregnancy

Category O10, Pre-existing hypertension complicating pregnancy, childbirth and the puerperium, includes codes for hypertensive heart and hypertensive chronic kidney disease. When assigning one of the O10 codes that includes hypertensive heart disease or hypertensive chronic kidney disease, it is necessary to add a secondary code from the appropriate hypertension category to specify the type of heart failure or chronic kidney disease.

See Section I.C.9. Hypertension.

e. Fetal Conditions Affecting the Management of the Mother

1) Codes from categories O35 and O36

Codes from categories O35, Maternal care for known or suspected fetal abnormality and damage, and O36, Maternal care for other fetal problems, are assigned only when the fetal condition is actually responsible for modifying the management of the mother, i.e., by requiring diagnostic studies, additional observation, special care, or termination of pregnancy. The fact that the fetal condition exists does not justify assigning a code from this series to the mother's record.

2) **In utero surgery**

In cases when surgery is performed on the fetus, a diagnosis code from category O35, Maternal care for known or suspected fetal abnormality and damage, should be assigned identifying the fetal condition. Assign the appropriate procedure code for the procedure performed.

No code from Chapter 16, the perinatal codes, should be used on the mother's record to identify fetal conditions. Surgery performed in utero on a fetus is still to be coded as an obstetric encounter.

f. **HIV Infection in Pregnancy, Childbirth and the Puerperium**

During pregnancy, childbirth or the puerperium, a patient admitted because of an HIV-related illness should receive a principal diagnosis from subcategory O98.7-, Human immunodeficiency [HIV] disease complicating pregnancy, childbirth and the puerperium, followed by the code(s) for the HIV-related illness(es).

Patients with asymptomatic HIV infection status admitted during pregnancy, childbirth, or the puerperium should receive codes of O98.7- and Z21, Asymptomatic human immunodeficiency virus [HIV] infection status.

g. **Diabetes mellitus in pregnancy**

Diabetes mellitus is a significant complicating factor in pregnancy. Pregnant women who are diabetic should be assigned a code from category O24, Diabetes mellitus in pregnancy, childbirth, and the puerperium, first, followed by the appropriate diabetes code(s) (E08-E13) from Chapter 4.

h. **Long term use of insulin**

Code Z79.4, Long-term (current) use of insulin, should also be assigned if the diabetes mellitus is being treated with insulin.

i. **Gestational (pregnancy induced) diabetes**

Gestational (pregnancy induced) diabetes can occur during the second and third trimester of pregnancy in women who were not diabetic prior to pregnancy. Gestational diabetes can cause complications in the pregnancy similar to those of pre-existing diabetes mellitus. It also puts the woman at greater risk of developing diabetes after the pregnancy. Codes for gestational diabetes are in subcategory O24.4, Gestational diabetes mellitus. No other code from category O24,

Diabetes mellitus in pregnancy, childbirth, and the puerperium, should be used with a code from O24.4

The codes under subcategory O24.4 include diet controlled and insulin controlled. If a patient with gestational diabetes is treated with both diet and insulin, only the code for insulin-controlled is required. Code Z79.4, Long-term (current) use of insulin, should not be assigned with codes from subcategory O24.4.

An abnormal glucose tolerance in pregnancy is assigned a code from subcategory O99.81, Abnormal glucose complicating pregnancy, childbirth, and the puerperium.

j.   Sepsis and septic shock complicating abortion, pregnancy, childbirth and the puerperium

When assigning a chapter 15 code for sepsis complicating abortion, pregnancy, childbirth, and the puerperium, a code for the specific type of infection should be assigned as an additional diagnosis. If severe sepsis is present, a code from subcategory R65.2, Severe sepsis, and code(s) for associated organ dysfunction(s) should also be assigned as additional diagnoses.

k.   Puerperal sepsis

Code O85, Puerperal sepsis, should be assigned with a secondary code to identify the causal organism (e.g., for a bacterial infection, assign a code from category B95-B96, Bacterial infections in conditions classified elsewhere). A code from category A40, Streptococcal sepsis, or A41, Other sepsis, should not be used for puerperal sepsis. If applicable, use additional codes to identify severe sepsis (R65.2-) and any associated acute organ dysfunction.

l.   Alcohol and tobacco use during pregnancy, childbirth and the puerperium

1)   Alcohol use during pregnancy, childbirth and the puerperium

Codes under subcategory O99.31, Alcohol use complicating pregnancy, childbirth, and the puerperium, should be assigned for any pregnancy case when a mother uses alcohol during the pregnancy or postpartum. A secondary code from category F10, Alcohol related disorders, should also be assigned to identify manifestations of the alcohol use.

2) Tobacco use during pregnancy, childbirth and the puerperium

Codes under subcategory O99.33, Smoking (tobacco) complicating pregnancy, childbirth, and the puerperium, should be assigned for any pregnancy case when a mother uses any type of tobacco product during the pregnancy or postpartum. A secondary code from category F17, Nicotine dependence, should also be assigned to identify the type of nicotine dependence.

m. Poisoning, toxic effects, adverse effects and underdosing in a pregnant patient

A code from subcategory O9A.2, Injury, poisoning and certain other consequences of external causes complicating pregnancy, childbirth, and the puerperium, should be sequenced first, followed by the appropriate injury, poisoning, toxic effect, adverse effect or underdosing code, and then the additional code(s) that specifies the condition caused by the poisoning, toxic effect, adverse effect or underdosing.

> See Section I.C.19. Adverse effects, poisoning, underdosing and toxic effects.

n. Normal Delivery, Code O80

1) Encounter for full term uncomplicated delivery

Code O80 should be assigned when a woman is admitted for a full-term normal delivery and delivers a single, healthy infant without any complications antepartum, during the delivery, or postpartum during the delivery episode. Code O80 is always a principal diagnosis. It is not to be used if any other code from chapter 15 is needed to describe a current complication of the antenatal, delivery, or perinatal period. Additional codes from other chapters may be used with code O80 if they are not related to or are in any way complicating the pregnancy.

2) Uncomplicated delivery with resolved antepartum complication

Code O80 may be used if the patient had a complication at some point during the pregnancy, but the complication is not present at the time of the admission for delivery.

3) Outcome of delivery for O80

Z37.0, Single live birth, is the only outcome of delivery code appropriate for use with O80.

o. **The Peripartum and Postpartum Periods**

1) **Peripartum and Postpartum periods**

The postpartum period begins immediately after delivery and continues for six weeks following delivery. The peripartum period is defined as the last month of pregnancy to five months postpartum.

2) **Peripartum and postpartum complication**

A postpartum complication is any complication occurring within the six-week period.

3) **Pregnancy-related complications after 6 week period**

Chapter 15 codes may also be used to describe pregnancy-related complications after the peripartum or postpartum period if the provider documents that a condition is pregnancy related.

4) **Admission for routine postpartum care following delivery outside hospital**

When the mother delivers outside the hospital prior to admission and is admitted for routine postpartum care and no complications are noted, code Z39.0, Encounter for care and examination of mother immediately after delivery, should be assigned as the principal diagnosis.

5) **Pregnancy associated cardiomyopathy**

Pregnancy associated cardiomyopathy, code O90.3, is unique in that it may be diagnosed in the third trimester of pregnancy but may continue to progress months after delivery. For this reason, it is referred to as peripartum cardiomyopathy. Code O90.3 is only for use when the cardiomyopathy develops as a result of pregnancy in a woman who did not have pre-existing heart disease.

p. **Code O94, Sequelae of complication of pregnancy, childbirth, and the puerperium**

1) **Code O94**

Code O94, Sequelae of complication of pregnancy, childbirth, and the puerperium, is for use in those cases when an initial complication of a pregnancy develops a sequelae requiring care or treatment at a future date.

2) After the initial postpartum period

This code may be used at any time after the initial postpartum period.

3) Sequencing of Code O94

This code, like all sequela codes, is to be sequenced following the code describing the sequelae of the complication.

q. *Termination of Pregnancy and Spontaneous abortions*

1) Abortion with Liveborn Fetus

When an attempted termination of pregnancy results in a liveborn fetus, assign code Z33.2, Encounter for elective termination of pregnancy and a code from category Z37, Outcome of Delivery.

2) Retained Products of Conception following an abortion

Subsequent encounters for retained products of conception following a spontaneous abortion or elective termination of pregnancy are assigned the appropriate code from category O03, Spontaneous abortion, or codes O07.4, Failed attempted termination of pregnancy without complication and Z33.2, Encounter for elective termination of pregnancy. This advice is appropriate even when the patient was discharged previously with a discharge diagnosis of complete abortion.

3) Complications leading to abortion

Codes from Chapter 15 may be used as additional codes to identify any documented complications of the pregnancy in conjunction with codes in categories in O07 and O08.

r. Abuse in a pregnant patient

For suspected or confirmed cases of abuse of a pregnant patient, a code(s) from subcategories O9A.3, Physical abuse complicating pregnancy, childbirth, and the puerperium, O9A.4, Sexual abuse complicating pregnancy, childbirth, and the puerperium, and O9A.5, Psychological abuse complicating pregnancy, childbirth, and the puerperium, should be sequenced first, followed by the appropriate codes (if applicable) to identify any associated current injury due to physical abuse, sexual abuse, and the perpetrator of abuse.

See Section I.C.19. Adult and child abuse, neglect and other maltreatment.

16. Chapter 16: Certain Conditions Originating in the Perinatal Period (P00-P96)

For coding and reporting purposes the perinatal period is defined as before birth through the 28th day following birth. The following guidelines are provided for reporting purposes

a. General Perinatal Rules

1) Use of Chapter 16 Codes

Codes in this chapter are <u>never</u> for use on the maternal record. Codes from Chapter 15, the obstetric chapter, are never permitted on the newborn record. Chapter 16 codes may be used throughout the life of the patient if the condition is still present.

2) Principal Diagnosis for Birth Record

When coding the birth episode in a newborn record, assign a code from category Z38, Liveborn infants according to place of birth and type of delivery, as the principal diagnosis. A code from category Z38 is assigned only once, to a newborn at the time of birth. If a newborn is transferred to another institution, a code from category Z38 should not be used at the receiving hospital.

A code from category Z38 is used only on the newborn record, not on the mother's record.

3) Use of Codes from other Chapters with Codes from Chapter 16

Codes from other chapters may be used with codes from chapter 16 if the codes from the other chapters provide more specific detail. Codes for signs and symptoms may be assigned when a definitive diagnosis has not been established. If the reason for the encounter is a perinatal condition, the code from chapter 16 should be sequenced first.

4) Use of Chapter 16 Codes after the Perinatal Period

Should a condition originate in the perinatal period, and continue throughout the life of the patient, the perinatal code should continue to be used regardless of the patient's age.

5) Birth process or community acquired conditions

If a newborn has a condition that may be either due to the birth process or community acquired and the documentation does not indicate which it is, the default is due to the birth process and the code from Chapter 16 should be used.   If the condition is community-acquired, a code from Chapter 16 should not be assigned.

6) Code all clinically significant conditions

All clinically significant conditions noted on routine newborn examination should be coded. A condition is clinically significant if it requires:

- clinical evaluation; or
- therapeutic treatment; or
- diagnostic procedures; or
- extended length of hospital stay; or
- increased nursing care and/or monitoring; or
- has implications for future health care needs

Note: The perinatal guidelines listed above are the same as the general coding guidelines for "additional diagnoses", except for the final point regarding implications for future health care needs. Codes should be assigned for conditions that have been specified by the provider as having implications for future health care needs.

b. Observation and Evaluation of Newborns for Suspected Conditions not Found

Reserved for future expansion

c. Coding Additional Perinatal Diagnoses

1) Assigning codes for conditions that require treatment

Assign codes for conditions that require treatment or further investigation, prolong the length of stay, or require resource utilization.

2) Codes for conditions specified as having implications for future health care needs

Assign codes for conditions that have been specified by the provider as having implications for future health care needs.

Note: This guideline should not be used for adult patients.

d. Prematurity and Fetal Growth Retardation

Providers utilize different criteria in determining prematurity. A code for prematurity should not be assigned unless it is documented. Assignment of codes in categories P05, Disorders of newborn related to slow fetal growth and fetal malnutrition, and P07, Disorders of newborn related to short gestation and low birth weight, not elsewhere classified, should be based on the recorded birth weight and estimated gestational age. Codes from category P05 should not be assigned with codes from category P07.

When both birth weight and gestational age are available, two codes from category P07 should be assigned, with the code for birth weight sequenced before the code for gestational age.

e. Low birth weight and immaturity status

Codes from category P07, Disorders of newborn related to short gestation and low birth weight, not elsewhere classified, are for use for a child or adult who was premature or had a low birth weight as a newborn and this is affecting the patient's current health status.

See Section I.C.21. Factors influencing health status and contact with health services, Status.

f. Bacterial Sepsis of Newborn

Category P36, Bacterial sepsis of newborn, includes congenital sepsis. If a perinate is documented as having sepsis without documentation of congenital or community acquired, the default is congenital and a code from category P36 should be assigned. If the P36 code includes the causal organism, an additional code from category B95, Streptococcus, Staphylococcus, and Enterococcus as the cause of diseases classified elsewhere, or B96, Other bacterial agents as the cause of diseases classified elsewhere, should not be assigned. If the P36 code does not include the causal organism, assign an additional code from category B96. If applicable, use additional codes to identify severe sepsis (R65.2-) and any associated acute organ dysfunction.

g. Stillbirth

Code P95, Stillbirth, is only for use in institutions that maintain separate records for stillbirths. No other code should be used with P95. Code P95 should not be used on the mother's record.

17. Chapter 17: Congenital malformations, deformations, and chromosomal abnormalities (Q00-Q99)

Assign an appropriate code(s) from categories Q00-Q99, Congenital malformations, deformations, and chromosomal abnormalities when a malformation/deformation or chromosomal abnormality is documented. A malformation/deformation/or chromosomal abnormality may be the principal/first-listed diagnosis on a record or a secondary diagnosis.

When a malformation/deformation/or chromosomal abnormality does not have a unique code assignment, assign additional code(s) for any manifestations that may be present.

When the code assignment specifically identifies the malformation/deformation/or chromosomal abnormality, manifestations that are an inherent component of the anomaly should not be coded separately. Additional codes should be assigned for manifestations that are not an inherent component.

Codes from Chapter 17 may be used throughout the life of the patient. If a congenital malformation or deformity has been corrected, a personal history code should be used to identify the history of the malformation or deformity. Although present at birth, malformation/deformation/or chromosomal abnormality may not be identified until later in life. Whenever the condition is diagnosed by the physician, it is appropriate to assign a code from codes Q00-Q99.For the birth admission, the appropriate code from category Z38, Liveborn infants, according to place of birth and type of delivery, should be sequenced as the principal diagnosis, followed by any congenital anomaly codes, Q00- Q99.

18.   **Chapter 18: Symptoms, signs, and abnormal clinical and laboratory findings, not elsewhere classified (R00-R99)**

Chapter 18 includes symptoms, signs, abnormal results of clinical or other investigative procedures, and ill-defined conditions regarding which no diagnosis classifiable elsewhere is recorded. Signs and symptoms that point to a specific diagnosis have been assigned to a category in other chapters of the classification.

a.   **Use of symptom codes**

Codes that describe symptoms and signs are acceptable for reporting purposes when a related definitive diagnosis has not been established (confirmed) by the provider.

b.   **Use of a symptom code with a definitive diagnosis code**

Codes for signs and symptoms may be reported in addition to a related definitive diagnosis when the sign or symptom is not routinely associated with that diagnosis, such as the various signs and symptoms associated with complex syndromes. The definitive diagnosis code should be sequenced before the symptom code.

Signs or symptoms that are associated routinely with a disease process should not be assigned as additional codes, unless otherwise instructed by the classification.

ICD-10-CM Official Guidelines for Coding and Reporting
2014
Page 64 of 117
Courtesy of the Centers for Disease Control and Prevention, www.cdc.gov

c.   Combination codes that include symptoms

ICD-10-CM contains a number of combination codes that identify both the definitive diagnosis and common symptoms of that diagnosis. When using one of these combination codes, an additional code should not be assigned for the symptom.

d.   Repeated falls

Code R29.6, Repeated falls, is for use for encounters when a patient has recently fallen and the reason for the fall is being investigated.

Code Z91.81, History of falling, is for use when a patient has fallen in the past and is at risk for future falls. When appropriate, both codes R29.6 and Z91.81 may be assigned together.

e.   Coma scale

The coma scale codes (R40.2-) can be used in conjunction with traumatic brain injury codes, acute cerebrovascular disease or sequelae of cerebrovascular disease codes. These codes are primarily for use by trauma registries, but they may be used in any setting where this information is collected. The coma scale codes should be sequenced after the diagnosis code(s).

These codes, one from each subcategory, are needed to complete the scale. The 7th character indicates when the scale was recorded. The 7th character should match for all three codes.

At a minimum, report the initial score documented on presentation at your facility. This may be a score from the emergency medicine technician (EMT) or in the emergency department. If desired, a facility may choose to capture multiple coma scale scores.

Assign code R40.24, Glasgow coma scale, total score, when only the total score is documented in the medical record and not the individual score(s).

f.   Functional quadriplegia

Functional quadriplegia (code R53.2) is the lack of ability to use one's limbs or to ambulate due to extreme debility. It is not associated with neurologic deficit or injury, and code R53.2 should not be used for cases of neurologic quadriplegia. It should only be assigned if functional quadriplegia is specifically documented in the medical record.

g.   SIRS due to Non-Infectious Process

The systemic inflammatory response syndrome (SIRS) can develop as a result of certain non-infectious disease processes, such as trauma, malignant neoplasm, or pancreatitis. When SIRS is documented with a noninfectious condition, and no subsequent infection is documented, the code for the underlying condition, such as an injury, should be assigned, followed by code R65.10, Systemic inflammatory response syndrome (SIRS) of non-infectious origin without acute organ dysfunction, or code R65.11, Systemic inflammatory response syndrome (SIRS) of non-infectious origin with acute organ dysfunction. If an associated acute organ dysfunction is documented, the appropriate code(s) for the specific type of organ dysfunction(s) should be assigned in addition to code R65.11. If acute organ dysfunction is documented, but it cannot be determined if the acute organ dysfunction is associated with SIRS or due to another condition (e.g., directly due to the trauma), the provider should be queried.

h.   Death NOS

Code R99, Ill-defined and unknown cause of mortality, is only for use in the very limited circumstance when a patient who has already died is brought into an emergency department or other healthcare facility and is pronounced dead upon arrival. It does not represent the discharge disposition of death.

19.   Chapter 19: Injury, poisoning, and certain other consequences of external causes (S00-T88)

a.   Application of 7th Characters in Chapter 19

Most categories in chapter 19 have a 7th character requirement for each applicable code. Most categories in this chapter have three 7th character values (with the exception of fractures): A, initial encounter, D, subsequent encounter and S, sequela. Categories for traumatic fractures have additional 7th character values.

7th character "A", initial encounter is used while the patient is receiving active treatment for the condition. Examples of active treatment are: surgical treatment, emergency department encounter, and evaluation and treatment by a new physician.

7th character "D" subsequent encounter is used for encounters after the patient has received active treatment of the condition and is receiving routine care for the condition during the healing or recovery phase. Examples of subsequent care are: cast change or removal, removal of external or internal fixation device, medication adjustment, other aftercare and follow up visits following treatment of the injury or condition.

The aftercare Z codes should not be used for aftercare for conditions such as injuries or poisonings, where 7th characters are provided to identify subsequent care. For example, for aftercare of an injury, assign the acute injury code with the 7th character "D" (subsequent encounter).

7th character "S", sequela, is for use for complications or conditions that arise as a direct result of a condition, such as scar formation after a burn. The scars are sequelae of the burn. When using 7th character "S", it is necessary to use both the injury code that precipitated the sequela and the code for the sequela itself. The "S" is added only to the injury code, not the sequela code. The 7th character "S" identifies the injury responsible for the sequela. The specific type of sequela (e.g. scar) is sequenced first, followed by the injury code.

b.   Coding of Injuries

When coding injuries, assign separate codes for each injury unless a combination code is provided, in which case the combination code is assigned. Code T07, Unspecified multiple injuries should not be assigned in the inpatient setting unless information for a more specific code is not available. Traumatic injury codes (S00-T14.9) are not to be used for normal, healing surgical wounds or to identify complications of surgical wounds.

The code for the most serious injury, as determined by the provider and the focus of treatment, is sequenced first.

1)   Superficial injuries

Superficial injuries such as abrasions or contusions are not coded when associated with more severe injuries of the same site.

2)   Primary injury with damage to nerves/blood vessels

When a primary injury results in minor damage to peripheral nerves or blood vessels, the primary injury is sequenced first with additional code(s) for injuries to nerves and spinal cord (such as category S04), and/or injury to blood vessels (such as category S15). When the primary injury is to the blood vessels or nerves, that injury should be sequenced first.

c.   Coding of Traumatic Fractures

The principles of multiple coding of injuries should be followed in coding fractures. Fractures of specified sites are coded individually by site in accordance with both the provisions within categories S02, S12,

S22, S32, S42, S49, S52, S59, S62, S72, S79, S82, S89, S92 and the level of detail furnished by medical record content.

A fracture not indicated as open or closed should be coded to closed. A fracture not indicated whether displaced or not displaced should be coded to displaced.

More specific guidelines are as follows:

1)   **Initial vs. Subsequent Encounter for Fractures**

Traumatic fractures are coded using the appropriate 7th character for initial encounter (A, B, C) while the patient is receiving active treatment for the fracture.   Examples of active treatment are: surgical treatment, emergency department encounter, and evaluation and treatment by a new physician. The appropriate 7th character for initial encounter should also be assigned for a patient who delayed seeking treatment for the fracture or nonunion.

Fractures are coded using the appropriate 7th character for subsequent care for encounters after the patient has completed active treatment of the fracture and is receiving routine care for the fracture during the healing or recovery phase. Examples of fracture aftercare are: cast change or removal, removal of external or internal fixation device, medication adjustment, and follow-up visits following fracture treatment.

Care for complications of surgical treatment for fracture repairs during the healing or recovery phase should be coded with the appropriate complication codes.

Care of complications of fractures, such as malunion and nonunion, should be reported with the appropriate 7th character for subsequent care with nonunion (K, M, N,) or subsequent care with malunion (P, Q, R).

A code from category M80, not a traumatic fracture code, should be used for any patient with known osteoporosis who suffers a fracture, even if the patient had a minor fall or trauma, if that fall or trauma would not usually break a normal, healthy bone.
See Section I.C.13. Osteoporosis.

The aftercare Z codes should not be used for aftercare for traumatic fractures. For aftercare of a traumatic fracture, assign the acute fracture code with the appropriate 7th character.

ICD-10-CM Official Guidelines for Coding and Reporting
2014
Page 68 of 117
Courtesy of the Centers for Disease Control and Prevention, www.cdc.gov

2) Multiple fractures sequencing

Multiple fractures are sequenced in accordance with the severity of the fracture.

d. Coding of Burns and Corrosions

The ICD-10-CM makes a distinction between burns and corrosions. The burn codes are for thermal burns, except sunburns, that come from a heat source, such as a fire or hot appliance. The burn codes are also for burns resulting from electricity and radiation. Corrosions are burns due to chemicals. The guidelines are the same for burns and corrosions.

Current burns (T20-T25) are classified by depth, extent and by agent (X code). Burns are classified by depth as first degree (erythema), second degree (blistering), and third degree (full-thickness involvement). Burns of the eye and internal organs (T26-T28) are classified by site, but not by degree.

1) Sequencing of burn and related condition codes

Sequence first the code that reflects the highest degree of burn when more than one burn is present.

a. When the reason for the admission or encounter is for treatment of external multiple burns, sequence first the code that reflects the burn of the highest degree.

b. When a patient has both internal and external burns, the circumstances of admission govern the selection of the principal diagnosis or first-listed diagnosis.

c. When a patient is admitted for burn injuries and other related conditions such as smoke inhalation and/or respiratory failure, the circumstances of admission govern the selection of the principal or first-listed diagnosis.

2) Burns of the same local site

Classify burns of the same local site (three-character category level, T20-T28) but of different degrees to the subcategory identifying the highest degree recorded in the diagnosis.

3) Non-healing burns

Non-healing burns are coded as acute burns.
Necrosis of burned skin should be coded as a non-healed burn.

4) **Infected Burn**

For any documented infected burn site, use an additional code for the infection.

5) **Assign separate codes for each burn site**

When coding burns, assign separate codes for each burn site. Category T30, Burn and corrosion, body region unspecified is extremely vague and should rarely be used.

6) **Burns and Corrosions Classified According to Extent of Body Surface Involved**

Assign codes from category T31, Burns classified according to extent of body surface involved, or T32, Corrosions classified according to extent of body surface involved, when the site of the burn is not specified or when there is a need for additional data. It is advisable to use category T31 as additional coding when needed to provide data for evaluating burn mortality, such as that needed by burn units. It is also advisable to use category T31 as an additional code for reporting purposes when there is mention of a third-degree burn involving 20 percent or more of the body surface.

Categories T31 and T32 are based on the classic "rule of nines" in estimating body surface involved: head and neck are assigned nine percent, each arm nine percent, each leg 18 percent, the anterior trunk 18 percent, posterior trunk 18 percent, and genitalia one percent. Providers may change these percentage assignments where necessary to accommodate infants and children who have proportionately larger heads than adults, and patients who have large buttocks, thighs, or abdomen that involve burns.

7) **Encounters for treatment of sequela of burns**

Encounters for the treatment of the late effects of burns or corrosions (i.e., scars or joint contractures) should be coded with a burn or corrosion code with the 7th character "S" for sequela.

8) **Sequelae with a late effect code and current burn**

When appropriate, both a code for a current burn or corrosion with 7th character "A" or "D" and a burn or corrosion code with 7th character "S" may be assigned on the same record (when both a current burn and sequelae of an old burn exist). Burns and corrosions do not heal at the same rate and a current healing wound may still exist with sequela of a healed burn or corrosion.

9) Use of an external cause code with burns and corrosions

An external cause code should be used with burns and corrosions to identify the source and intent of the burn, as well as the place where it occurred.

e. Adverse Effects, Poisoning, Underdosing and Toxic Effects

Codes in categories T36-T65 are combination codes that include the substance that was taken as well as the intent. No additional external cause code is required for poisonings, toxic effects, adverse effects and underdosing codes.

1) Do not code directly from the Table of Drugs

Do not code directly from the Table of Drugs and Chemicals. Always refer back to the Tabular List.

2) Use as many codes as necessary to describe

Use as many codes as necessary to describe completely all drugs, medicinal or biological substances.

3) If the same code would describe the causative agent

If the same code would describe the causative agent for more than one adverse reaction, poisoning, toxic effect or underdosing, assign the code only once.

4) If two or more drugs, medicinal or biological substances

If two or more drugs, medicinal or biological substances are reported, code each individually unless **a** combination code is listed in the Table of Drugs and Chemicals.

5) The occurrence of drug toxicity is classified in ICD-10-CM as follows:

(a) Adverse Effect

When coding an adverse effect of a drug that has been correctly prescribed and properly administered, assign the appropriate code for the nature of the adverse effect followed by the appropriate code for the adverse effect of the drug (T36-T50). The code for the drug should have a 5th or 6th character "5" (for example T36.0X5-) Examples of the nature of an adverse effect are tachycardia, delirium, gastrointestinal hemorrhaging, vomiting, hypokalemia, hepatitis, renal failure, or respiratory failure.

(b) **Poisoning**

When coding a poisoning or reaction to the improper use of a medication (e.g., overdose, wrong substance given or taken in error, wrong route of administration), first assign the appropriate code from categories T36-T50. The poisoning codes have an associated intent as their 5th or 6th character (accidental, intentional self-harm, assault and undetermined. Use additional code(s) for all manifestations of poisonings.

If there is also a diagnosis of abuse or dependence of the substance, the abuse or dependence is assigned as an additional code.

Examples of poisoning include:

(i) Error was made in drug prescription

Errors made in drug prescription or in the administration of the drug by provider, nurse, patient, or other person.

(ii) Overdose of a drug intentionally taken

If an overdose of a drug was intentionally taken or administered and resulted in drug toxicity, it would be coded as a poisoning.

(iii) Nonprescribed drug taken with correctly prescribed and properly administered drug

If a nonprescribed drug or medicinal agent was taken in combination with a correctly prescribed and properly administered drug, any drug toxicity or other reaction resulting from the interaction of the two drugs would be classified as a poisoning.

(iv) Interaction of drug(s) and alcohol

When a reaction results from the interaction of a drug(s) and alcohol, this would be classified as poisoning.

See Section I.C.4. if poisoning is the result of insulin pump malfunctions.

(c) **Underdosing**

Underdosing refers to taking less of a medication than is prescribed by a provider or a manufacturer's instruction. For underdosing, assign the code from categories T36-T50 (fifth or sixth character "6").

Codes for underdosing should never be assigned as principal or first-listed codes. If a patient has a relapse or exacerbation of the medical condition for which the drug is prescribed because of the reduction in dose, then the medical condition itself should be coded.

Noncompliance (Z91.12-, Z91.13-) or complication of care (Y63.6-Y63.9) codes are to be used with an underdosing code to indicate intent, if known.

(d) **Toxic Effects**

When a harmful substance is ingested or comes in contact with a person, this is classified as a toxic effect. The toxic effect codes are in categories T51-T65.

Toxic effect codes have an associated intent: accidental, intentional self-harm, assault and undetermined.

f. Adult and child abuse, neglect and other maltreatment

Sequence first the appropriate code from categories T74.- (Adult and child abuse, neglect and other maltreatment, confirmed) or T76.- (Adult and child abuse, neglect and other maltreatment, suspected) for abuse, neglect and other maltreatment, followed by any accompanying mental health or injury code(s).

If the documentation in the medical record states abuse or neglect it is coded as confirmed (T74.-). It is coded as suspected if it is documented as suspected (T76.-).

For cases of confirmed abuse or neglect an external cause code from the assault section (X92-Y08) should be added to identify the cause of any physical injuries. A perpetrator code (Y07) should be added when the perpetrator of the abuse is known. For suspected cases of abuse or neglect, do not report external cause or perpetrator code.

If a suspected case of abuse, neglect or mistreatment is ruled out during an encounter code Z04.71, Encounter for examination and observation following alleged physical adult abuse, ruled out, or code Z04.72, Encounter for examination and observation following alleged child physical abuse, ruled out, should be used, not a code from T76.

If a suspected case of alleged rape or sexual abuse is ruled out during an encounter code Z04.41, Encounter for examination and observation following alleged physical adult abuse, ruled out, or code Z04.42, Encounter for examination and observation following alleged rape or sexual abuse, ruled out, should be used, not a code from T76.
See Section I.C.15. Abuse in a pregnant patient.

g. Complications of care

1) General guidelines for complications of care

(a) Documentation of complications of care
See Section I.B.16. for information on documentation of complications of care.

2) Pain due to medical devices
Pain associated with devices, implants or grafts left in a surgical site (for example painful hip prosthesis) is assigned to the appropriate code(s) found in Chapter 19, Injury, poisoning, and certain other consequences of external causes. Specific codes for pain due to medical devices are found in the T code section of the ICD-10-CM. Use additional code(s) from category G89 to identify acute or chronic pain due to presence of the device, implant or graft (G89.18 or G89.28).

3) Transplant complications

(a) Transplant complications other than kidney
Codes under category T86, Complications of transplanted organs and tissues, are for use for both complications and rejection of transplanted organs. A transplant complication code is only assigned if the complication affects the function of the transplanted organ. Two codes are required to fully describe a transplant complication: the appropriate code from category T86 and a secondary code that identifies the complication.

Pre-existing conditions or conditions that develop after the transplant are not coded as complications unless they affect the function of the transplanted organs.

See I.C.21. for transplant organ removal status
See I.C.2. for malignant neoplasm associated with transplanted organ.

    (b)   **Kidney transplant complications**

Patients who have undergone kidney transplant may still have some form of chronic kidney disease (CKD) because the kidney transplant may not fully restore kidney function. Code T86.1- should be assigned for documented complications of a kidney transplant, such as transplant failure or rejection or other transplant complication. Code T86.1- should not be assigned for post kidney transplant patients who have chronic kidney (CKD) unless a transplant complication such as transplant failure or rejection is documented. If the documentation is unclear as to whether the patient has a complication of the transplant, query the provider.

Conditions that affect the function of the transplanted kidney, other than CKD, should be assigned a code from subcategory T86.1, Complications of transplanted organ, Kidney, and a secondary code that identifies the complication.

For patients with CKD following a kidney transplant, but who do not have a complication such as failure or rejection, *see section I.C.14. Chronic kidney disease and kidney transplant status*.

4)   Complication codes that include the external cause

As with certain other T codes, some of the complications of care codes have the external cause included in the code. The code includes the nature of the complication as well as the type of procedure that caused the complication. No external cause code indicating the type of procedure is necessary for these codes.

5)   Complications of care codes within the body system chapters

Intraoperative and postprocedural complication codes are found within the body system chapters with codes specific to the organs and structures of that body system. These codes should be sequenced first, followed by a code(s) for the specific complication, if applicable.

20. Chapter 20: External Causes of Morbidity (V0̲0̲-Y99)

The external causes of morbidity codes should never be sequenced as the first-listed or principal diagnosis.

External cause codes are intended to provide data for injury research and evaluation of injury prevention strategies. These codes capture how the injury or health condition happened (cause), the intent (unintentional or accidental; or intentional, such as suicide or assault), the place where the event occurred the activity of the patient at the time of the event, and the person's status (e.g., civilian, military).

There is no national requirement for mandatory ICD-10-CM external cause code reporting. Unless a provider is subject to a state-based external cause code reporting mandate or these codes are required by a particular payer, reporting of ICD-10-CM codes in Chapter 20, External Causes of Morbidity, is not required. In the absence of a mandatory reporting requirement, providers are encouraged to voluntarily report external cause codes, as they provide valuable data for injury research and evaluation of injury prevention strategies.

a. General External Cause Coding Guidelines

1) Used with any code in the range of A00.0-T88.9, Z00-Z99

An external cause code may be used with any code in the range of A00.0-T88.9, Z00-Z99, classification that is a health condition due to an external cause. Though they are most applicable to injuries, they are also valid for use with such things as infections or diseases due to an external source, and other health conditions, such as a heart attack that occurs during strenuous physical activity.

2) External cause code used for length of treatment

Assign the external cause code, with the appropriate 7th character (initial encounter, subsequent encounter or sequela) for each encounter for which the injury or condition is being treated.

3) Use the full range of external cause codes

Use the full range of external cause codes to completely describe the cause, the intent, the place of occurrence, and if applicable, the activity of the patient at the time of the event, and the patient's status, for all injuries, and other health conditions due to an external cause.

4)   Assign as many external cause codes as necessary

Assign as many external cause codes as necessary to fully explain each cause. If only one external code can be recorded, assign the code most related to the principal diagnosis.

5)   The selection of the appropriate external cause code

The selection of the appropriate external cause code is guided by the Alphabetic Index of External Causes and by Inclusion and Exclusion notes in the Tabular List.

6)   External cause code can never be a principal diagnosis

An external cause code can never be a principal (first-listed) diagnosis.

7)   Combination external cause codes

Certain of the external cause codes are combination codes that identify sequential events that result in an injury, such as a fall which results in striking against an object. The injury may be due to either event or both. The combination external cause code used should correspond to the sequence of events regardless of which caused the most serious injury.

8)   No external cause code needed in certain circumstances

No external cause code from Chapter 20 is needed if the external cause and intent are included in a code from another chapter (e.g. T36.0X1- Poisoning by penicillins, accidental (unintentional)).

b.   Place of Occurrence Guideline

Codes from category Y92, Place of occurrence of the external cause, are secondary codes for use after other external cause codes to identify the location of the patient at the time of injury or other condition.

A place of occurrence code is used only once, at the initial encounter for treatment. No 7th characters are used for Y92. Only one code from Y92 should be recorded on a medical record.

Do not use place of occurrence code Y92.9 if the place is not stated or is not applicable.

c.   Activity Code

Assign a code from category Y93, Activity code, to describe the activity of the patient at the time the injury or other health condition occurred.

An activity code is used only once, at the initial encounter for treatment. Only one code from Y93 should be recorded on a medical record.

The activity codes are not applicable to poisonings, adverse effects, misadventures or sequela .

Do not assign Y93.9, Unspecified activity, if the activity is not stated.

A code from category Y93 is appropriate for use with external cause and intent codes if identifying the activity provides additional information about the event.

d.   Place of Occurrence, Activity, and Status Codes Used with other External Cause Code

When applicable, place of occurrence, activity, and external cause status codes are sequenced after the main external cause code(s). Regardless of the number of external cause codes assigned, there should be only one place of occurrence code, one activity code, and one external cause status code assigned to an encounter.

e.   If the Reporting Format Limits the Number of External Cause Codes

If the reporting format limits the number of external cause codes that can be used in reporting clinical data, report the code for the cause/intent most related to the principal diagnosis. If the format permits capture of additional external cause codes, the cause/intent, including medical misadventures, of the additional events should be reported rather than the codes for place, activity, or external status.

f.   Multiple External Cause Coding Guidelines

More than one external cause code is required to fully describe the external cause of an illness or injury. The assignment of external cause codes should be sequenced in the following priority:

If two or more events cause separate injuries, an external cause code should be assigned for each cause. The first-listed external cause code will be selected in the following order:

External codes for child and adult abuse take priority over all other external cause codes.

See Section I.C.19., Child and Adult abuse guidelines.

External cause codes for terrorism events take priority over all other external cause codes except child and adult abuse.

External cause codes for cataclysmic events take priority over all other external cause codes except child and adult abuse and terrorism.

External cause codes for transport accidents take priority over all other external cause codes except cataclysmic events, child and adult abuse and terrorism.

Activity and external cause status codes are assigned following all causal (intent) external cause codes.

The first-listed external cause code should correspond to the cause of the most serious diagnosis due to an assault, accident, or self-harm, following the order of hierarchy listed above.

g. Child and Adult Abuse Guideline

Adult and child abuse, neglect and maltreatment are classified as assault. Any of the assault codes may be used to indicate the external cause of any injury resulting from the confirmed abuse.

For confirmed cases of abuse, neglect and maltreatment, when the perpetrator is known, a code from Y07, Perpetrator of maltreatment and neglect, should accompany any other assault codes.

See Section I.C.19. Adult and child abuse, neglect and other maltreatment

h. Unknown or Undetermined Intent Guideline

If the intent (accident, self-harm, assault) of the cause of an injury or other condition is unknown or unspecified, code the intent as accidental intent. All transport accident categories assume accidental intent.

1) Use of undetermined intent

External cause codes for events of undetermined intent are only for use if the documentation in the record specifies that the intent cannot be determined.

i. **Sequelae (Late Effects) of External Cause Guidelines**

1) **Sequelae external cause codes**

Sequela are reported using the external cause code with the 7th character "S" for sequela. These codes should be used with any report of a late effect or sequela resulting from a previous injury.

2) **Sequela external cause code with a related current injury**

A sequela external cause code should never be used with a related current nature of injury code.

3) **Use of sequela external cause codes for subsequent visits**

Use a late effect external cause code for subsequent visits when a late effect of the initial injury is being treated. Do not use a late effect external cause code for subsequent visits for follow-up care (e.g., to assess healing, to receive rehabilitative therapy) of the injury when no late effect of the injury has been documented.

j. **Terrorism Guidelines**

1) **Cause of injury identified by the Federal Government (FBI) as terrorism**

When the cause of an injury is identified by the Federal Government (FBI) as terrorism, the first-listed external cause code should be a code from category Y38, Terrorism. The definition of terrorism employed by the FBI is found at the inclusion note at the beginning of category Y38. Use additional code for place of occurrence (Y92.-). More than one Y38 code may be assigned if the injury is the result of more than one mechanism of terrorism.

2) **Cause of an injury is suspected to be the result of terrorism**

When the cause of an injury is suspected to be the result of terrorism a code from category Y38 should not be assigned. Suspected cases should be classified as assault.

3) **Code Y38.9, Terrorism, secondary effects**

Assign code Y38.9, Terrorism, secondary effects, for conditions occurring subsequent to the terrorist event. This code should not be assigned for conditions that are due to the initial terrorist act.

It is acceptable to assign code Y38.9 with another code from Y38 if there is an injury due to the initial terrorist event and an injury that is a subsequent result of the terrorist event.

k. External cause status

A code from category Y99, External cause status, should be assigned whenever any other external cause code is assigned for an encounter, including an Activity code, except for the events noted below. Assign a code from category Y99, External cause status, to indicate the work status of the person at the time the event occurred. The status code indicates whether the event occurred during military activity, whether a non-military person was at work, whether an individual including a student or volunteer was involved in a non-work activity at the time of the causal event.

A code from Y99, External cause status, should be assigned, when applicable, with other external cause codes, such as transport accidents and falls. The external cause status codes are not applicable to poisonings, adverse effects, misadventures or late effects.
Do not assign a code from category Y99 if no other external cause codes (cause, activity) are applicable for the encounter.

An external cause status code is used only once, at the initial encounter for treatment. Only one code from Y99 should be recorded on a medical record.

Do not assign code Y99.9, Unspecified external cause status, if the status is not stated.

21. Chapter 21: Factors influencing health status and contact with health services (Z00-Z99)

Note: The chapter specific guidelines provide additional information about the use of Z codes for specified encounters.

a. Use of Z codes in any healthcare setting

Z codes are for use in any healthcare setting. Z codes may be used as either a first-listed (principal diagnosis code in the inpatient setting) or secondary code, depending on the circumstances of the encounter. Certain Z codes may only be used as first-listed or principal diagnosis.

b. Z Codes indicate a reason for an encounter

Z codes are not procedure codes. A corresponding procedure code must accompany a Z code to describe any procedure performed.

c.   **Categories of Z Codes**

1)   **Contact/Exposure**

Category Z20 indicates contact with, and suspected exposure to, communicable diseases. These codes are for patients who do not show any sign or symptom of a disease but are suspected to have been exposed to it by close personal contact with an infected individual or are in an area where a disease is epidemic.

Category Z77, indicates contact with and suspected exposures hazardous to health.

Contact/exposure codes may be used as a first-listed code to explain an encounter for testing, or, more commonly, as a secondary code to identify a potential risk.

2)   **Inoculations and vaccinations**

Code Z23 is for encounters for inoculations and vaccinations. It indicates that a patient is being seen to receive a prophylactic inoculation against a disease. Procedure codes are required to identify the actual administration of the injection and the type(s) of immunizations given. Code Z23 may be used as a secondary code if the inoculation is given as a routine part of preventive health care, such as a well-baby visit.

3)   **Status**

Status codes indicate that a patient is either a carrier of a disease or has the sequelae or residual of a past disease or condition. This includes such things as the presence of prosthetic or mechanical devices resulting from past treatment. A status code is informative, because the status may affect the course of treatment and its outcome. A status code is distinct from a history code. The history code indicates that the patient no longer has the condition.

A status code should not be used with a diagnosis code from one of the body system chapters, if the diagnosis code includes the information provided by the status code. For example, code Z94.1, Heart transplant status, should not be used with a code from subcategory T86.2, Complications of heart transplant. The status code does not provide additional information. The complication code indicates that the patient is a heart transplant patient.

For encounters for weaning from a mechanical ventilator, assign a code from subcategory J96.1, Chronic respiratory failure, followed by code Z99.11, Dependence on respirator [ventilator] status.

The status Z codes/categories are:

Z14   Genetic carrier

Genetic carrier status indicates that a person carries a gene, associated with a particular disease, which may be passed to offspring who may develop that disease. The person does not have the disease and is not at risk of developing the disease.

Z15   Genetic susceptibility to disease

Genetic susceptibility indicates that a person has a gene that increases the risk of that person developing the disease.

Codes from category Z15 should not be used as principal or first-listed codes. If the patient has the condition to which he/she is susceptible, and that condition is the reason for the encounter, the code for the current condition should be sequenced first. If the patient is being seen for follow-up after completed treatment for this condition, and the condition no longer exists, a follow-up code should be sequenced first, followed by the appropriate personal history and genetic susceptibility codes. If the purpose of the encounter is genetic counseling associated with procreative management, code Z31.5, Encounter for genetic counseling, should be assigned as the first-listed code, followed by a code from category Z15. Additional codes should be assigned for any applicable family or personal history.

Z16   Resistance to antimicrobial drugs

This code indicates that a patient has a condition that is resistant to antimicrobial drug treatment. Sequence the infection code first.

Z17   Estrogen receptor status

Z18   Retained foreign body fragments

Z21   Asymptomatic HIV infection status

This code indicates that a patient has tested positive for HIV but has manifested no signs or symptoms of the disease.

Z22   Carrier of infectious disease

Carrier status indicates that a person harbors the specific organisms of a disease without manifest

	symptoms and is capable of transmitting the infection.
Z28.3	Underimmunization status
Z33.1	Pregnant state, incidental
	This code is a secondary code only for use when the pregnancy is in no way complicating the reason for visit. Otherwise, a code from the obstetric chapter is required.
Z66	Do not resuscitate
	This code may be used when it is documented by the provider that a patient is on do not resuscitate status at any time during the stay.
Z67	Blood type
Z68	Body mass index (BMI)
Z74.01	Bed confinement status
Z76.82	Awaiting organ transplant status
Z78	Other specified health status
	Code Z78.1, Physical restraint status, may be used when it is documented by the provider that a patient has been put in restraints during the current encounter. Please note that this code should not be reported when it is documented by the provider that a patient is temporarily restrained during a procedure.
Z79	Long-term (current) drug therapy
	Codes from this category indicate a patient's continuous use of a prescribed drug (including such things as aspirin therapy) for the long-term treatment of a condition or for prophylactic use. It is not for use for patients who have addictions to drugs. This subcategory is not for use of medications for detoxification or maintenance programs to prevent withdrawal symptoms in patients with drug dependence (e.g., methadone maintenance for opiate dependence). Assign the appropriate code for the drug dependence instead.
	Assign a code from Z79 if the patient is receiving a medication for an extended period as a prophylactic measure (such as for the prevention of deep vein thrombosis) or as treatment of a chronic condition (such as arthritis) or a disease requiring a lengthy course of treatment (such as cancer). Do not assign a code from category Z79 for medication being administered for a brief period of time to treat an acute illness or injury (such as a course of antibiotics to treat acute bronchitis).

Z88	Allergy status to drugs, medicaments and biological substances
	Except: Z88.9, Allergy status to unspecified drugs, medicaments and biological substances status
Z89	Acquired absence of limb
Z90	Acquired absence of organs, not elsewhere classified
Z91.0-	Allergy status, other than to drugs and biological substances
Z92.82	Status post administration of tPA (rtPA) in a different facility within the last 24 hours prior to admission to a current facility

Assign code Z92.82, Status post administration of tPA (rtPA) in a different facility within the last 24 hours prior to admission to current facility, as a secondary diagnosis when a patient is received by transfer into a facility and documentation indicates they were administered tissue plasminogen activator (tPA) within the last 24 hours prior to admission to the current facility.

This guideline applies even if the patient is still receiving the tPA at the time they are received into the current facility.

The appropriate code for the condition for which the tPA was administered (such as cerebrovascular disease or myocardial infarction) should be assigned first.

Code Z92.82 is only applicable to the receiving facility record and not to the transferring facility record.

Z93	Artificial opening status
Z94	Transplanted organ and tissue status
Z95	Presence of cardiac and vascular implants and grafts
Z96	Presence of other functional implants
Z97	Presence of other devices
Z98	Other postprocedural states

Assign code Z98.85, Transplanted organ removal status, to indicate that a transplanted organ has been previously removed. This code should not be assigned for the encounter in which the transplanted organ is removed. The complication necessitating removal of the transplant organ should be assigned for that encounter.

See section I.C19. for information on the coding of organ transplant complications.

Z99   Dependence on enabling machines and devices, not elsewhere classified

Note: Categories Z89-Z90 and Z93-Z99 are for use only if there are no complications or malfunctions of the organ or tissue replaced, the amputation site or the equipment on which the patient is dependent.

4) **History (of)**

There are two types of history Z codes, personal and family. Personal history codes explain a patient's past medical condition that no longer exists and is not receiving any treatment, but that has the potential for recurrence, and therefore may require continued monitoring.

Family history codes are for use when a patient has a family member(s) who has had a particular disease that causes the patient to be at higher risk of also contracting the disease.

Personal history codes may be used in conjunction with follow-up codes and family history codes may be used in conjunction with screening codes to explain the need for a test or procedure. History codes are also acceptable on any medical record regardless of the reason for visit. A history of an illness, even if no longer present, is important information that may alter the type of treatment ordered.

The history Z code categories are:

Z80   Family history of primary malignant neoplasm

Z81   Family history of mental and behavioral disorders

Z82   Family history of certain disabilities and chronic diseases (leading to disablement)

Z83   Family history of other specific disorders

Z84   Family history of other conditions

Z85   Personal history of malignant neoplasm

Z86   Personal history of certain other diseases

Z87   Personal history of other diseases and conditions

Z91.4-   Personal history of psychological trauma, not elsewhere classified

Z91.5   Personal history of self-harm

Z91.8-   Other specified personal risk factors, not elsewhere classified

Exception:

Z91.83, Wandering in diseases classified elsewhere

Z92   Personal history of medical treatment
        Except: Z92.0, Personal history of contraception
        Except: Z92.82, Status post administration of tPA
        (rtPA) in a different facility within the last 24 hours
        prior to admission to a current facility

5)   **Screening**

Screening is the testing for disease or disease precursors in seemingly well individuals so that early detection and treatment can be provided for those who test positive for the disease (e.g., screening mammogram).

The testing of a person to rule out or confirm a suspected diagnosis because the patient has some sign or symptom is a diagnostic examination, not a screening. In these cases, the sign or symptom is used to explain the reason for the test.

A screening code may be a first-listed code if the reason for the visit is specifically the screening exam. It may also be used as an additional code if the screening is done during an office visit for other health problems. A screening code is not necessary if the screening is inherent to a routine examination, such as a pap smear done during a routine pelvic examination.

Should a condition be discovered during the screening then the code for the condition may be assigned as an additional diagnosis.

The Z code indicates that a screening exam is planned. A procedure code is required to confirm that the screening was performed.

The screening Z codes/categories:
Z11   Encounter for screening for infectious and parasitic
        diseases
Z12   Encounter for screening for malignant neoplasms
Z13   Encounter for screening for other diseases and
        disorders
        Except: Z13.9, Encounter for screening, unspecified
Z36   Encounter for antenatal screening for mother

6)   **Observation**

There are two observation Z code categories. They are for use in very limited circumstances when a person is being observed for a suspected condition that is ruled out. The observation codes are not for use if an injury or illness or any signs or symptoms related to the suspected condition are present. In such cases the diagnosis/symptom code is used with the corresponding external cause code.

The observation codes are to be used as principal diagnosis only. Additional codes may be used in addition to the observation code but only if they are unrelated to the suspected condition being observed.

Codes from subcategory Z03.7, Encounter for suspected maternal and fetal conditions ruled out, may either be used as a first-listed or as an additional code assignment depending on the case. They are for use in very limited circumstances on a maternal record when an encounter is for a suspected maternal or fetal condition that is ruled out during that encounter (for example, a maternal or fetal condition may be suspected due to an abnormal test result). These codes should not be used when the condition is confirmed. In those cases, the confirmed condition should be coded. In addition, these codes are not for use if an illness or any signs or symptoms related to the suspected condition or problem are present. In such cases the diagnosis/symptom code is used.

Additional codes may be used in addition to the code from subcategory Z03.7, but only if they are unrelated to the suspected condition being evaluated.

Codes from subcategory Z03.7 may not be used for encounters for antenatal screening of mother. *See Section I.C.21. Screening.*

For encounters for suspected fetal condition that are inconclusive following testing and evaluation, assign the appropriate code from category O35, O36, O40 or O41.
The observation Z code categories:
Z03   Encounter for medical observation for suspected diseases and conditions ruled out
Z04   Encounter for examination and observation for other reasons
             Except: Z04.9, Encounter for examination and observation for unspecified reason

7)   **Aftercare**

Aftercare visit codes cover situations when the initial treatment of a disease has been performed and the patient requires continued care during the healing or recovery phase, or for the long-term consequences of the disease. The aftercare Z code should not be used if treatment is directed at a current, acute disease. The diagnosis code is to be used in these cases. Exceptions to this rule are codes Z51.0, Encounter for antineoplastic radiation therapy, and codes from subcategory Z51.1, Encounter for antineoplastic chemotherapy and immunotherapy. These codes are to be first-listed, followed by the diagnosis code when a patient's encounter is solely to receive radiation therapy, chemotherapy, or immunotherapy for the treatment of a neoplasm. If the reason for the encounter is more than one type of antineoplastic therapy, code Z51.0 and a code from subcategory Z51.1 may be assigned together, in which case one of these codes would be reported as a secondary diagnosis.

The aftercare Z codes should also not be used for aftercare for injuries. For aftercare of an injury, assign the acute injury code with the appropriate 7th character (for subsequent encounter).

The aftercare codes are generally first-listed to explain the specific reason for the encounter. An aftercare code may be used as an additional code when some type of aftercare is provided in addition to the reason for admission and no diagnosis code is applicable. An example of this would be the closure of a colostomy during an encounter for treatment of another condition.

Aftercare codes should be used in conjunction with other aftercare codes or diagnosis codes to provide better detail on the specifics of an aftercare encounter visit, unless otherwise directed by the classification. Should a patient receive multiple types of antineoplastic therapy during the same encounter, code Z51.0, Encounter for antineoplastic radiation therapy, and codes from subcategory Z51.1, Encounter for antineoplastic chemotherapy and immunotherapy, may be used together on a record. The sequencing of multiple aftercare codes depends on the circumstances of the encounter.

Certain aftercare Z code categories need a secondary diagnosis code to describe the resolving condition or sequelae. For others, the condition is included in the code title.

Additional Z code aftercare category terms include fitting and adjustment, and attention to artificial openings.

Status Z codes may be used with aftercare Z codes to indicate the nature of the aftercare. For example code Z95.1, Presence of aortocoronary bypass graft, may be used with code Z48.812,

Encounter for surgical aftercare following surgery on the circulatory system, to indicate the surgery for which the aftercare is being performed. A status code should not be used when the aftercare code indicates the type of status, such as using Z43.0, Encounter for attention to tracheostomy, with Z93.0, Tracheostomy status.

The aftercare Z category/codes:

Z42	Encounter for plastic and reconstructive surgery following medical procedure or healed injury
Z43	Encounter for attention to artificial openings
Z44	Encounter for fitting and adjustment of external prosthetic device
Z45	Encounter for adjustment and management of implanted device
Z46	Encounter for fitting and adjustment of other devices
Z47	Orthopedic aftercare
Z48	Encounter for other postprocedural aftercare
Z49	Encounter for care involving renal dialysis
Z51	Encounter for other aftercare

8) **Follow-up**

The follow-up codes are used to explain continuing surveillance following completed treatment of a disease, condition, or injury. They imply that the condition has been fully treated and no longer exists. They should not be confused with aftercare codes, or injury codes with a 7th character for subsequent encounter, that explain ongoing care of a healing condition or its sequelae. Follow-up codes may be used in conjunction with history codes to provide the full picture of the healed condition and its treatment. The follow-up code is sequenced first, followed by the history code.

A follow-up code may be used to explain multiple visits. Should a condition be found to have recurred on the follow-up visit, then the diagnosis code for the condition should be assigned in place of the follow-up code.

The follow-up Z code categories:

Z08	Encounter for follow-up examination after completed treatment for malignant neoplasm
Z09	Encounter for follow-up examination after completed treatment for conditions other than malignant neoplasm
Z39	Encounter for maternal postpartum care and examination

9) **Donor**

Codes in category Z52, Donors of organs and tissues, are used for living individuals who are donating blood or other body tissue. These codes are only for individuals donating for others, not for self-donations. They are not used to identify cadaveric donations.

10) **Counseling**

Counseling Z codes are used when a patient or family member receives assistance in the aftermath of an illness or injury, or when support is required in coping with family or social problems. They are not used in conjunction with a diagnosis code when the counseling component of care is considered integral to standard treatment.

The counseling Z codes/categories:

Z30.0-   Encounter for general counseling and advice on contraception
Z31.5   Encounter for genetic counseling
Z31.6-   Encounter for general counseling and advice on procreation
Z32.2   Encounter for childbirth instruction
Z32.3   Encounter for childcare instruction
Z69   Encounter for mental health services for victim and perpetrator of abuse
Z70   Counseling related to sexual attitude, behavior and orientation
Z71   Persons encountering health services for other counseling and medical advice, not elsewhere classified
Z76.81   Expectant mother prebirth pediatrician visit

11) **Encounters for Obstetrical and Reproductive Services**

See Section I.C.15. Pregnancy, Childbirth, and the Puerperium, for further instruction on the use of these codes.

Z codes for pregnancy are for use in those circumstances when none of the problems or complications included in the codes from the Obstetrics chapter exist (a routine prenatal visit or postpartum care). Codes in category Z34, Encounter for supervision of normal pregnancy, are always first-listed and are not to be used with any other code from the OB chapter.

Codes in category Z3A, Weeks of gestation, may be assigned to provide additional information about the pregnancy. **The date of the admission should be used to determine weeks of**

gestation for inpatient admissions that encompass more than one gestational week.

The outcome of delivery, category Z37, should be included on all maternal delivery records. It is always a secondary code. Codes in category Z37 should not be used on the newborn record.

Z codes for family planning (contraceptive) or procreative management and counseling should be included on an obstetric record either during the pregnancy or the postpartum stage, if applicable.

Z codes/categories for obstetrical and reproductive services:

Z30	Encounter for contraceptive management
Z31	Encounter for procreative management
Z32.2	Encounter for childbirth instruction
Z32.3	Encounter for childcare instruction
Z33	Pregnant state
Z34	Encounter for supervision of normal pregnancy
Z36	Encounter for antenatal screening of mother
Z3A	Weeks of gestation
Z37	Outcome of delivery
Z39	Encounter for maternal postpartum care and examination
Z76.81	Expectant mother prebirth pediatrician visit

12) Newborns and Infants

See Section I.C.16. Newborn (Perinatal) Guidelines, for further instruction on the use of these codes.

Newborn Z codes/categories:

Z76.1	Encounter for health supervision and care of foundling
Z00.1-	Encounter for routine child health examination
Z38	Liveborn infants according to place of birth and type of delivery

13) Routine and administrative examinations

The Z codes allow for the description of encounters for routine examinations, such as, a general check-up, or, examinations for administrative purposes, such as, a pre-employment physical. The codes are not to be used if the examination is for diagnosis of a suspected condition or for treatment purposes. In such cases the diagnosis code is used. During a routine exam, should a diagnosis or condition be discovered, it should be coded as an additional code. Pre-existing and chronic conditions and history codes may also be included as additional codes as long as the examination is for administrative purposes and not focused on any particular condition.

Some of the codes for routine health examinations distinguish between "with" and "without" abnormal findings. Code assignment depends on the information that is known at the time the encounter is being coded. For example, if no abnormal findings were found during the examination, but the encounter is being coded before test results are back, it is acceptable to assign the code for "without abnormal findings." When assigning a code for "with abnormal findings," additional code(s) should be assigned to identify the specific abnormal finding(s).

Pre-operative examination and pre-procedural laboratory examination Z codes are for use only in those situations when a patient is being cleared for a procedure or surgery and no treatment is given.

The Z codes/categories for routine and administrative examinations:

Z00	Encounter for general examination without complaint, suspected or reported diagnosis
Z01	Encounter for other special examination without complaint, suspected or reported diagnosis
Z02	Encounter for administrative examination Except: Z02.9, Encounter for administrative examinations, unspecified
Z32.0-	Encounter for pregnancy test

14) Miscellaneous Z codes

The miscellaneous Z codes capture a number of other health care encounters that do not fall into one of the other categories. Certain of these codes identify the reason for the encounter; others are for use as additional codes that provide useful information on circumstances that may affect a patient's care and treatment.

Prophylactic Organ Removal

For encounters specifically for prophylactic removal of an organ (such as prophylactic removal of breasts due to a genetic susceptibility to cancer or a family history of cancer), the principal or first-listed code should be a code from category Z40, Encounter for prophylactic surgery, followed by the appropriate codes to identify the associated risk factor (such as genetic susceptibility or family history).

If the patient has a malignancy of one site and is having prophylactic removal at another site to prevent either a new primary malignancy or metastatic disease, a code for the malignancy should also be assigned in addition to a code from subcategory Z40.0, Encounter for prophylactic surgery for risk factors related to malignant neoplasms. A Z40.0 code should not be assigned if the patient is having organ removal for treatment of a malignancy, such as the removal of the testes for the treatment of prostate cancer.

Miscellaneous Z codes/categories:

Z28	Immunization not carried out
	Except: Z28.3, Underimmunization status
Z40	Encounter for prophylactic surgery
Z41	Encounter for procedures for purposes other than remedying health state
	Except: Z41.9, Encounter for procedure for purposes other than remedying health state, unspecified
Z53	Persons encountering health services for specific procedures and treatment, not carried out
Z55	Problems related to education and literacy
Z56	Problems related to employment and unemployment
Z57	Occupational exposure to risk factors
Z58	Problems related to physical environment
Z59	Problems related to housing and economic circumstances
Z60	Problems related to social environment
Z62	Problems related to upbringing
Z63	Other problems related to primary support group, including family circumstances
Z64	Problems related to certain psychosocial circumstances
Z65	Problems related to other psychosocial circumstances
Z72	Problems related to lifestyle
Z73	Problems related to life management difficulty
Z74	Problems related to care provider dependency
	Except: Z74.01, Bed confinement status
Z75	Problems related to medical facilities and other health care
Z76.0	Encounter for issue of repeat prescription
Z76.3	Healthy person accompanying sick person
Z76.4	Other boarder to healthcare facility

Z76.5	Malingerer [conscious simulation]
Z91.1-	Patient's noncompliance with medical treatment and regimen
Z91.83	Wandering in diseases classified elsewhere
Z91.89	Other specified personal risk factors, not elsewhere classified

15) Nonspecific Z codes

Certain Z codes are so non-specific, or potentially redundant with other codes in the classification, that there can be little justification for their use in the inpatient setting. Their use in the outpatient setting should be limited to those instances when there is no further documentation to permit more precise coding. Otherwise, any sign or symptom or any other reason for visit that is captured in another code should be used.

Nonspecific Z codes/categories:

Z02.9	Encounter for administrative examinations, unspecified
Z04.9	Encounter for examination and observation for unspecified reason
Z13.9	Encounter for screening, unspecified
Z41.9	Encounter for procedure for purposes other than remedying health state, unspecified
Z52.9	Donor of unspecified organ or tissue
Z86.59	Personal history of other mental and behavioral disorders
Z88.9	Allergy status to unspecified drugs, medicaments and biological substances status
Z92.0	Personal history of contraception

16) Z Codes That May Only be Principal/First-Listed Diagnosis

The following Z codes/categories may only be reported as the principal/first-listed diagnosis, except when there are multiple encounters on the same day and the medical records for the encounters are combined:

Z00	Encounter for general examination without complaint, suspected or reported diagnosis
Z01	Encounter for other special examination without complaint, suspected or reported diagnosis
Z02	Encounter for administrative examination
Z03	Encounter for medical observation for suspected diseases and conditions ruled out

Z04	Encounter for examination and observation for other reasons
Z33.2	Encounter for elective termination of pregnancy
Z31.81	Encounter for male factor infertility in female patient
Z31.82	Encounter for Rh incompatibility status
Z31.83	Encounter for assisted reproductive fertility procedure cycle
Z31.84	Encounter for fertility preservation procedure
Z34	Encounter for supervision of normal pregnancy
Z39	Encounter for maternal postpartum care and examination
Z38	Liveborn infants according to place of birth and type of delivery
Z42	Encounter for plastic and reconstructive surgery following medical procedure or healed injury
Z51.0	Encounter for antineoplastic radiation therapy
Z51.1-	Encounter for antineoplastic chemotherapy and immunotherapy
Z52	Donors of organs and tissues Except: Z52.9, Donor of unspecified organ or tissue
Z76.1	Encounter for health supervision and care of foundling
Z76.2	Encounter for health supervision and care of other healthy infant and child
Z99.12	Encounter for respirator [ventilator] dependence during power failure

Section II. Selection of Principal Diagnosis

The circumstances of inpatient admission always govern the selection of principal diagnosis. The principal diagnosis is defined in the Uniform Hospital Discharge Data Set (UHDDS) as "that condition established after study to be chiefly responsible for occasioning the admission of the patient to the hospital for care."

The UHDDS definitions are used by hospitals to report inpatient data elements in a standardized manner. These data elements and their definitions can be found in the July 31, 1985, Federal Register (Vol. 50, No, 147), pp. 31038-40.

Since that time the application of the UHDDS definitions has been expanded to include all non-outpatient settings (acute care, short term, long term care and psychiatric hospitals; home health agencies; rehab facilities; nursing homes, etc).

In determining principal diagnosis, coding conventions in the ICD-10-CM, the Tabular List and Alphabetic Index take precedence over these official coding guidelines.
(See Section I.A., Conventions for the ICD-10-CM)

The importance of consistent, complete documentation in the medical record cannot be overemphasized. Without such documentation the application of all coding guidelines is a difficult, if not impossible, task.

A. Codes for symptoms, signs, and ill-defined conditions

Codes for symptoms, signs, and ill-defined conditions from Chapter 18 are not to be used as principal diagnosis when a related definitive diagnosis has been established.

B. Two or more interrelated conditions, each potentially meeting the definition for principal diagnosis.

When there are two or more interrelated conditions (such as diseases in the same ICD-10-CM chapter or manifestations characteristically associated with a certain disease) potentially meeting the definition of principal diagnosis, either condition may be sequenced first, unless the circumstances of the admission, the therapy provided, the Tabular List, or the Alphabetic Index indicate otherwise.

C. Two or more diagnoses that equally meet the definition for principal diagnosis

In the unusual instance when two or more diagnoses equally meet the criteria for principal diagnosis as determined by the circumstances of admission, diagnostic workup and/or therapy provided, and the Alphabetic Index, Tabular List, or another coding guidelines does not provide sequencing direction, any one of the diagnoses may be sequenced first.

D. Two or more comparative or contrasting conditions

In those rare instances when two or more contrasting or comparative diagnoses are documented as "either/or" (or similar terminology), they are coded as if the diagnoses were confirmed and the diagnoses are sequenced according to the circumstances of the admission. If no further determination can be made as to which diagnosis should be principal, either diagnosis may be sequenced first.

E. A symptom(s) followed by contrasting/comparative diagnoses

When a symptom(s) is followed by contrasting/comparative diagnoses, the symptom code is sequenced first. **However, if the symptom code is integral to the conditions listed, no code for the symptom is reported.** All the contrasting/comparative diagnoses should be coded as additional diagnoses.

F. Original treatment plan not carried out

Sequence as the principal diagnosis the condition, which after study occasioned the admission to the hospital, even though treatment may not have been carried out due to unforeseen circumstances.

G. Complications of surgery and other medical care

When the admission is for treatment of a complication resulting from surgery or other medical care, the complication code is sequenced as the principal diagnosis. If the complication is classified to the T80-T88 series and the code lacks the necessary specificity in describing the complication, an additional code for the specific complication should be assigned.

H. Uncertain Diagnosis

If the diagnosis documented at the time of discharge is qualified as "probable", "suspected", "likely", "questionable", "possible", or "still to be ruled out", or other similar terms indicating uncertainty, code the condition as if it existed or was established. The bases for these guidelines are the diagnostic workup, arrangements for further workup or observation, and initial therapeutic approach that correspond most closely with the established diagnosis.

Note: This guideline is applicable only to inpatient admissions to short-term, acute, long-term care and psychiatric hospitals.

I. Admission from Observation Unit

1. Admission Following Medical Observation

When a patient is admitted to an observation unit for a medical condition, which either worsens or does not improve, and is subsequently admitted as an inpatient of the same hospital for this same medical condition, the principal diagnosis would be the medical condition which led to the hospital admission.

2. Admission Following Post-Operative Observation

When a patient is admitted to an observation unit to monitor a condition (or complication) that develops following outpatient surgery, and then is subsequently admitted as an inpatient of the same hospital, hospitals should apply the Uniform Hospital Discharge Data Set (UHDDS) definition of principal diagnosis as "that condition established after study to be chiefly responsible for occasioning the admission of the patient to the hospital for care."

J. Admission from Outpatient Surgery

When a patient receives surgery in the hospital's outpatient surgery department and is subsequently admitted for continuing inpatient care at the same hospital, the following guidelines should be followed in selecting the principal diagnosis for the inpatient admission:

- If the reason for the inpatient admission is a complication, assign the complication as the principal diagnosis.

- If no complication, or other condition, is documented as the reason for the inpatient admission, assign the reason for the outpatient surgery as the principal diagnosis.
- If the reason for the inpatient admission is another condition unrelated to the surgery, assign the unrelated condition as the principal diagnosis.

K. Admissions/Encounters for Rehabilitation

When the purpose for the admission/encounter is rehabilitation, sequence first the code for the condition for which the service is being performed. For example, for an admission/encounter for rehabilitation for right-sided dominant hemiplegia following a cerebrovascular infarction, report code I69.351, Hemiplegia and hemiparesis following cerebral infarction affecting right dominant side, as the first-listed or principal diagnosis.

If the condition for which the rehabilitation service is no longer present, report the appropriate aftercare code as the first-listed or principal diagnosis. For example, if a patient with severe degenerative osteoarthritis of the hip, underwent hip replacement and the current encounter/admission is for rehabilitation, report code Z47.1, Aftercare following joint replacement surgery, as the first-listed or principal diagnosis.

See Section I.C.21.c.7, Factors influencing health states and contact with health services, Aftercare.

Section III. Reporting Additional Diagnoses

GENERAL RULES FOR OTHER (ADDITIONAL) DIAGNOSES

For reporting purposes the definition for "other diagnoses" is interpreted as additional conditions that affect patient care in terms of requiring:

   clinical evaluation; or
   therapeutic treatment; or
   diagnostic procedures; or
   extended length of hospital stay; or
   increased nursing care and/or monitoring

The UHDDS item #11-b defines Other Diagnoses as "all conditions that coexist at the time of admission, that develop subsequently, or that affect the treatment received and/or the length of stay. Diagnoses that relate to an earlier episode which have no bearing on the current hospital stay are to be excluded." UHDDS definitions apply to inpatients in acute care, short-term, long term care and psychiatric hospital setting. The UHDDS definitions are used by acute care short-term hospitals to report inpatient data elements in a standardized manner. These data elements and their definitions can be found in the July 31, 1985, Federal Register (Vol. 50, No, 147), pp. 31038-40.

Since that time the application of the UHDDS definitions has been expanded to include all non-outpatient settings (acute care, short term, long term care and psychiatric hospitals; home health agencies; rehab facilities; nursing homes, etc).

The following guidelines are to be applied in designating "other diagnoses" when neither the Alphabetic Index nor the Tabular List in ICD-10-CM provide direction. The listing of the diagnoses in the patient record is the responsibility of the attending provider.

A. Previous conditions

If the provider has included a diagnosis in the final diagnostic statement, such as the discharge summary or the face sheet, it should ordinarily be coded. Some providers include in the diagnostic statement resolved conditions or diagnoses and status-post procedures from previous admission that have no bearing on the current stay. Such conditions are not to be reported and are coded only if required by hospital policy.

However, history codes (categories Z80-Z87) may be used as secondary codes if the historical condition or family history has an impact on current care or influences treatment.

B. Abnormal findings

Abnormal findings (laboratory, x-ray, pathologic, and other diagnostic results) are not coded and reported unless the provider indicates their clinical significance. If the findings are outside the normal range and the attending provider has ordered other tests to evaluate the condition or prescribed treatment, it is appropriate to ask the provider whether the abnormal finding should be added.

Please note: This differs from the coding practices in the outpatient setting for coding encounters for diagnostic tests that have been interpreted by a provider.

C. Uncertain Diagnosis

If the diagnosis documented at the time of discharge is qualified as "probable", "suspected", "likely", "questionable", "possible", or "still to be ruled out" or other similar terms indicating uncertainty, code the condition as if it existed or was established. The bases for these guidelines are the diagnostic workup, arrangements for further workup or observation, and initial therapeutic approach that correspond most closely with the established diagnosis.

Note: This guideline is applicable only to inpatient admissions to short-term, acute, long-term care and psychiatric hospitals.

Section IV. Diagnostic Coding and Reporting Guidelines for Outpatient Services

These coding guidelines for outpatient diagnoses have been approved for use by hospitals/ providers in coding and reporting hospital-based outpatient services and provider-based office visits.

Information about the use of certain abbreviations, punctuation, symbols, and other conventions used in the ICD-10-CM Tabular List (code numbers and titles), can be found in Section IA of these guidelines, under "Conventions Used in the Tabular List." **Section I.B. contains general guidelines that apply to the entire classification. Section I.C. contains chapter-specific guidelines that correspond to the chapters as they are arranged in the classification.** Information about the correct sequence to use in finding a code is also described in Section I.

The terms encounter and visit are often used interchangeably in describing outpatient service contacts and, therefore, appear together in these guidelines without distinguishing one from the other.

Though the conventions and general guidelines apply to all settings, coding guidelines for outpatient and provider reporting of diagnoses will vary in a number of instances from those for inpatient diagnoses, recognizing that:

> The Uniform Hospital Discharge Data Set (UHDDS) definition of principal diagnosis applies only to inpatients in acute, short-term, long-term care and psychiatric hospitals.

> Coding guidelines for inconclusive diagnoses (probable, suspected, rule out, etc.) were developed for inpatient reporting and do not apply to outpatients.

A. Selection of first-listed condition

> In the outpatient setting, the term first-listed diagnosis is used in lieu of principal diagnosis.

> In determining the first-listed diagnosis the coding conventions of ICD-10-CM, as well as the general and disease specific guidelines take precedence over the outpatient guidelines.

> Diagnoses often are not established at the time of the initial encounter/visit. It may take two or more visits before the diagnosis is confirmed.

> The most critical rule involves beginning the search for the correct code assignment through the Alphabetic Index. Never begin searching initially in the Tabular List as this will lead to coding errors.

1. **Outpatient Surgery**

   When a patient presents for outpatient surgery (same day surgery), code the reason for the surgery as the first-listed diagnosis (reason for the encounter), even if the surgery is not performed due to a contraindication.

2. **Observation Stay**

   When a patient is admitted for observation for a medical condition, assign a code for the medical condition as the first-listed diagnosis.

   When a patient presents for outpatient surgery and develops complications requiring admission to observation, code the reason for the surgery as the first reported diagnosis (reason for the encounter), followed by codes for the complications as secondary diagnoses.

B. Codes from A00.0 through T88.9, Z00-Z99

The appropriate code(s) from A00.0 through T88.9, Z00-Z99 must be used to identify diagnoses, symptoms, conditions, problems, complaints, or other reason(s) for the encounter/visit.

C. Accurate reporting of ICD-10-CM diagnosis codes

For accurate reporting of ICD-10-CM diagnosis codes, the documentation should describe the patient's condition, using terminology which includes specific diagnoses as well as symptoms, problems, or reasons for the encounter. There are ICD-10-CM codes to describe all of these.

D. Codes that describe symptoms and signs

Codes that describe symptoms and signs, as opposed to diagnoses, are acceptable for reporting purposes when a diagnosis has not been established (confirmed) by the provider. Chapter 18 of ICD-10-CM, Symptoms, Signs, and Abnormal Clinical and Laboratory Findings Not Elsewhere Classified (codes R00-R99) contain many, but not all codes for symptoms.

E. Encounters for circumstances other than a disease or injury

ICD-10-CM provides codes to deal with encounters for circumstances other than a disease or injury. The Factors Influencing Health Status and Contact with Health Services codes (Z00-Z99) are provided to deal with occasions when circumstances other than a disease or injury are recorded as diagnosis or problems.
See Section I.C.21. Factors influencing health status and contact with health services.

F. Level of Detail in Coding

1. **ICD-10-CM codes with 3, 4, 5, 6 or 7 characters**

   ICD-10-CM is composed of codes with 3, 4, 5, 6 or 7 characters. Codes with three characters are included in ICD-10-CM as the heading of a category of codes that may be further subdivided by the use of fourth, fifth, sixth or seventh characters to provide greater specificity.

2. Use of full number of *characters* required for a code

A three-character code is to be used only if it is not further subdivided. A code is invalid if it has not been coded to the full number of characters required for that code, including the 7th character, if applicable.

G. ICD-10-CM code for the diagnosis, condition, problem, or other reason for encounter/visit

List first the ICD-10-CM code for the diagnosis, condition, problem, or other reason for encounter/visit shown in the medical record to be chiefly responsible for the services provided. List additional codes that describe any coexisting conditions. In some cases the first-listed diagnosis may be a symptom when a diagnosis has not been established (confirmed) by the physician.

H. Uncertain diagnosis

Do not code diagnoses documented as "probable", "suspected," "questionable," "rule out," or "working diagnosis" or other similar terms indicating uncertainty. Rather, code the condition(s) to the highest degree of certainty for that encounter/visit, such as symptoms, signs, abnormal test results, or other reason for the visit.

Please note: This differs from the coding practices used by short-term, acute care, long-term care and psychiatric hospitals.

I. Chronic diseases

Chronic diseases treated on an ongoing basis may be coded and reported as many times as the patient receives treatment and care for the condition(s)

J. Code all documented conditions that coexist

Code all documented conditions that coexist at the time of the encounter/visit, and require or affect patient care treatment or management. Do not code conditions that were previously treated and no longer exist. However, history codes (categories Z80-Z87) may be used as secondary codes if the historical condition or family history has an impact on current care or influences treatment.

K. Patients receiving diagnostic services only

For patients receiving diagnostic services only during an encounter/visit, sequence first the diagnosis, condition, problem, or other reason for encounter/visit shown in the medical record to be chiefly responsible for the outpatient services provided during the encounter/visit. Codes for other diagnoses (e.g., chronic conditions) may be sequenced as additional diagnoses.

For encounters for routine laboratory/radiology testing in the absence of any signs, symptoms, or associated diagnosis, assign Z01.89, Encounter for other specified

Courtesy of the Centers for Disease Control and Prevention, www.cdc.gov

special examinations. If routine testing is performed during the same encounter as a test to evaluate a sign, symptom, or diagnosis, it is appropriate to assign both the **Z** code and the code describing the reason for the non-routine test.

For outpatient encounters for diagnostic tests that have been interpreted by a physician, and the final report is available at the time of coding, code any confirmed or definitive diagnosis(es) documented in the interpretation. Do not code related signs and symptoms as additional diagnoses.

Please note: This differs from the coding practice in the hospital inpatient setting regarding abnormal findings on test results.

L. Patients receiving therapeutic services only

For patients receiving therapeutic services only during an encounter/visit, sequence first the diagnosis, condition, problem, or other reason for encounter/visit shown in the medical record to be chiefly responsible for the outpatient services provided during the encounter/visit. Codes for other diagnoses (e.g., chronic conditions) may be sequenced as additional diagnoses.

The only exception to this rule is that when the primary reason for the admission/encounter is chemotherapy or radiation therapy, the appropriate Z code for the service is listed first, and the diagnosis or problem for which the service is being performed listed second.

M. Patients receiving preoperative evaluations only

For patients receiving preoperative evaluations only, sequence first a code from subcategory Z01.81, Encounter for pre-procedural examinations, to describe the pre-op consultations. Assign a code for the condition to describe the reason for the surgery as an additional diagnosis. Code also any findings related to the pre-op evaluation.

N. Ambulatory surgery

For ambulatory surgery, code the diagnosis for which the surgery was performed. If the postoperative diagnosis is known to be different from the preoperative diagnosis at the time the diagnosis is confirmed, select the postoperative diagnosis for coding, since it is the most definitive.

O. Routine outpatient prenatal visits

See Section I.C.15. Routine outpatient prenatal visits.

P. Encounters for general medical examinations with abnormal findings

The subcategories for encounters for general medical examinations, Z00.0-, provide codes for with and without abnormal findings. Should a general medical examination result in an abnormal finding, the code for general medical examination with abnormal finding should be assigned as the first-listed diagnosis. A secondary code for the abnormal finding should also be coded.

Q. Encounters for routine health screenings

See Section I.C.21. Factors influencing health status and contact with health services, Screening

Appendix I
Present on Admission Reporting Guidelines

Introduction

These guidelines are to be used as a supplement to the *ICD-10-CM Official Guidelines for Coding and Reporting* to facilitate the assignment of the Present on Admission (POA) indicator for each diagnosis and external cause of injury code reported on claim forms (UB-04 and 837 Institutional).

These guidelines are not intended to replace any guidelines in the main body of the *ICD-10-CM Official Guidelines for Coding and Reporting*. The POA guidelines are not intended to provide guidance on when a condition should be coded, but rather, how to apply the POA indicator to the final set of diagnosis codes that have been assigned in accordance with Sections I, II, and III of the official coding guidelines. Subsequent to the assignment of the ICD-10-CM codes, the POA indicator should then be assigned to those conditions that have been coded.

As stated in the Introduction to the ICD-10-CM Official Guidelines for Coding and Reporting, a joint effort between the healthcare provider and the coder is essential to achieve complete and accurate documentation, code assignment, and reporting of diagnoses and procedures. The importance of consistent, complete documentation in the medical record cannot be overemphasized. Medical record documentation from any provider involved in the care and treatment of the patient may be used to support the determination of whether a condition was present on admission or not. In the context of the official coding guidelines, the term "provider" means a physician or any qualified healthcare practitioner who is legally accountable for establishing the patient's diagnosis.

These guidelines are not a substitute for the provider's clinical judgment as to the determination of whether a condition was/was not present on admission. The provider should be queried regarding issues related to the linking of signs/symptoms, timing of test results, and the timing of findings.

General Reporting Requirements

All claims involving inpatient admissions to general acute care hospitals or other facilities that are subject to a law or regulation mandating collection of present on admission information.

Present on admission is defined as present at the time the order for inpatient admission occurs -- conditions that develop during an outpatient encounter, including emergency department, observation, or outpatient surgery, are considered as present on admission.

POA indicator is assigned to principal and secondary diagnoses (as defined in Section II of the Official Guidelines for Coding and Reporting) and the external cause of injury codes.

Issues related to inconsistent, missing, conflicting or unclear documentation must still be resolved by the provider.

If a condition would not be coded and reported based on UHDDS definitions and current official coding guidelines, then the POA indicator would not be reported.

Reporting Options
    Y - Yes
    N - No
    U - Unknown
    W – Clinically undetermined
    Unreported/Not used   – (Exempt from POA reporting)

Reporting Definitions
    Y = present at the time of inpatient admission
    N = not present at the time of inpatient admission
    U = documentation is insufficient to determine if condition is present on admission
    W = provider is unable to clinically determine whether condition was present on admission or not

Timeframe for POA Identification and Documentation

There is no required timeframe as to when a provider (per the definition of "provider" used in these guidelines) must identify or document a condition to be present on admission. In some clinical situations, it may not be possible for a provider to make a definitive diagnosis (or a condition may not be recognized or reported by the patient) for a period of time after admission. In some cases it may be several days before the provider arrives at a definitive diagnosis. This does not mean that the condition was not present on admission. Determination of whether the condition was present on admission or not will be based on the applicable POA guideline as identified in this document, or on the provider's best clinical judgment.

If at the time of code assignment the documentation is unclear as to whether a condition was present on admission or not, it is appropriate to query the provider for clarification.

Assigning the POA Indicator

Condition is on the "Exempt from Reporting" list
    Leave the "present on admission" field blank if the condition is on the list of ICD-10-CM codes for which this field is not applicable. This is the only circumstance in which the field may be left blank.

POA Explicitly Documented
    Assign Y for any condition the provider explicitly documents as being present on admission.

ICD-10-CM Official Guidelines for Coding and Reporting
2014
Page 108 of 117
Courtesy of the Centers for Disease Control and Prevention, www.cdc.gov

Assign N for any condition the provider explicitly documents as not present at the time of admission.

Conditions diagnosed prior to inpatient admission
Assign "Y" for conditions that were diagnosed prior to admission (example: hypertension, diabetes mellitus, asthma)

Conditions diagnosed during the admission but clearly present before admission
Assign "Y" for conditions diagnosed during the admission that were clearly present but not diagnosed until after admission occurred.

Diagnoses subsequently confirmed after admission are considered present on admission if at the time of admission they are documented as suspected, possible, rule out, differential diagnosis, or constitute an underlying cause of a symptom that is present at the time of admission.

Condition develops during outpatient encounter prior to inpatient admission
Assign Y for any condition that develops during an outpatient encounter prior to a written order for inpatient admission.

Documentation does not indicate whether condition was present on admission
Assign "U" when the medical record documentation is unclear as to whether the condition was present on admission. "U" should not be routinely assigned and used only in very limited circumstances. Coders are encouraged to query the providers when the documentation is unclear.

Documentation states that it cannot be determined whether the condition was or was not present on admission
Assign "W" when the medical record documentation indicates that it cannot be clinically determined whether or not the condition was present on admission.

Chronic condition with acute exacerbation during the admission
If a single code identifies both the chronic condition and the acute exacerbation, see POA guidelines pertaining to combination codes.

If a single code only identifies the chronic condition and not the acute exacerbation (e.g., acute exacerbation of chronic leukemia), assign "Y."

Conditions documented as possible, probable, suspected, or rule out at the time of discharge
If the final diagnosis contains a possible, probable, suspected, or rule out diagnosis, and this diagnosis was based on signs, symptoms or clinical findings suspected at the time of inpatient admission, assign "Y."

If the final diagnosis contains a possible, probable, suspected, or rule out diagnosis, and this diagnosis was based on signs, symptoms or clinical findings that were not present on admission, assign "N".

ICD-10-CM Official Guidelines for Coding and Reporting
2014
Page 109 of 117
Courtesy of the Centers for Disease Control and Prevention, www.cdc.gov

Conditions documented as impending or threatened at the time of discharge

If the final diagnosis contains an impending or threatened diagnosis, and this diagnosis is based on symptoms or clinical findings that were present on admission, assign "Y".

If the final diagnosis contains an impending or threatened diagnosis, and this diagnosis is based on symptoms or clinical findings that were not present on admission, assign "N".

Acute and Chronic Conditions

Assign "Y" for acute conditions that are present at time of admission and N for acute conditions that are not present at time of admission.

Assign "Y" for chronic conditions, even though the condition may not be diagnosed until after admission.

If a single code identifies both an acute and chronic condition, see the POA guidelines for combination codes.

Combination Codes

Assign "N" if any part of the combination code was not present on admission (e.g., COPD with acute exacerbation and the exacerbation was not present on admission; gastric ulcer that does not start bleeding until after admission; asthma patient develops status asthmaticus after admission)

Assign "Y" if all parts of the combination code were present on admission (e.g., patient with acute prostatitis admitted with hematuria)

If the final diagnosis includes comparative or contrasting diagnoses, and both were present, or suspected, at the time of admission, assign "Y".

For infection codes that include the causal organism, assign "Y" if the infection (or signs of the infection) was present on admission, even though the culture results may not be known until after admission (e.g., patient is admitted with pneumonia and the provider documents pseudomonas as the causal organism a few days later).

Same Diagnosis Code for Two or More Conditions

When the same ICD-10-CM diagnosis code applies to two or more conditions during the same encounter (e.g. two separate conditions classified to the same ICD-10-CM diagnosis code):

Assign "Y" if all conditions represented by the single ICD-10-CM code were present on admission (e.g. bilateral unspecified age-related cataracts).

Assign "N" if any of the conditions represented by the single ICD-10-CM code was not present on admission (e.g. traumatic secondary and recurrent hemorrhage and seroma is assigned to a single code T79.2, but only one of the conditions was present on admission).

Obstetrical conditions

Whether or not the patient delivers during the current hospitalization does not affect assignment of the POA indicator. The determining factor for POA assignment is whether the pregnancy complication or obstetrical condition described by the code was present at the time of admission or not.

If the pregnancy complication or obstetrical condition was present on admission (e.g., patient admitted in preterm labor), assign "Y".

If the pregnancy complication or obstetrical condition was not present on admission (e.g., 2nd degree laceration during delivery, postpartum hemorrhage that occurred during current hospitalization, fetal distress develops after admission), assign "N".

If the obstetrical code includes more than one diagnosis and any of the diagnoses identified by the code were not present on admission assign "N".
   (e.g., Category O11, Pre-existing hypertension with pre-eclampsia)

Perinatal conditions

Newborns are not considered to be admitted until after birth. Therefore, any condition present at birth or that developed in utero is considered present at admission and should be assigned "Y". This includes conditions that occur during delivery (e.g., injury during delivery, meconium aspiration, exposure to streptococcus B in the vaginal canal).

Congenital conditions and anomalies

Assign "Y" for congenital conditions and anomalies except for categories Q00-Q99, Congenital anomalies, which are on the exempt list. Congenital conditions are always considered present on admission.

External cause of injury codes

Assign "Y" for any external cause code representing an external cause of morbidity that occurred prior to inpatient admission (e.g., patient fell out of bed at home, patient fell out of bed in emergency room prior to admission)

Assign "N" for any external cause code representing an external cause of morbidity that occurred during inpatient hospitalization (e.g., patient fell out of hospital bed during hospital stay, patient experienced an adverse reaction to a medication administered after inpatient admission)

Categories and Codes
Exempt from
Diagnosis Present on Admission Requirement

Note: "Diagnosis present on admission" for these code categories are exempt because they represent circumstances regarding the healthcare encounter or factors influencing health status that do not represent a current disease or injury or are always present on admission

B90–B94, Sequelae of infectious and parasitic diseases

E64,   Sequelae of malnutrition and other nutritional deficiencies

I25.2, Old myocardial infarction

I69,   Sequelae of cerebrovascular disease

O09,   Supervision of high risk pregnancy

O66.5, Attempted application of vacuum extractor and forceps

O80,   Encounter for full-term uncomplicated delivery

O94,   Sequelae of complication of pregnancy, childbirth, and the puerperium

P00, Newborn (suspected to be) affected by maternal conditions that may be unrelated to present pregnancy

Q00 – Q99, Congenital malformations, deformations and chromosomal abnormalities

S00-T88.9, Injury, poisoning and certain other consequences of external causes with 7th character representing subsequent encounter or sequela

V00- V09, Pedestrian injured in transport accident

      Except V00.81-, Accident with wheelchair (powered)

           V00.83-, Accident with motorized mobility scooter

V10-V19, Pedal cycle rider injured in transport accident

V20-V29, Motorcycle rider injured in transport accident

V30-V39, Occupant of three-wheeled motor vehicle injured in transport accident

V40-V49, Car occupant injured in transport accident

V50-V59, Occupant of pick-up truck or van injured in transport accident

V60-V69, Occupant of heavy transport vehicle injured in transport accident

V70-V79, Bus occupant injured in transport accident

V80-V89, Other land transport accidents

V90-V94, Water transport accidents

V95-V97, Air and space transport accidents

V98-V99, Other and unspecified transport accidents

W09, Fall on and from playground equipment

W14, Fall from tree

W15, Fall from cliff

W17.0, Fall into well

W17.1, Fall into storm drain or manhole

W18.01 Striking against sports equipment with subsequent fall

W21, Striking against or struck by sports equipment

W30, Contact with agricultural machinery

W31, Contact with other and unspecified machinery

W32-W34, Accidental handgun discharge and malfunction

W35- W40, Exposure to inanimate mechanical forces

W52, Crushed, pushed or stepped on by crowd or human stampede

W56, Contact with nonvenomous marine animal

W58, Contact with crocodile or alligator

W61, Contact with birds (domestic) (wild)

W62, Contact with nonvenomous amphibians

W89, Exposure to man-made visible and ultraviolet light

X02, Exposure to controlled fire in building or structure

X03, Exposure to controlled fire, not in building or structure

X04, Exposure to ignition of highly flammable material

X52, Prolonged stay in weightless environment

X71, Intentional self-harm by drowning and submersion

> Except X71.0-, Intentional self-harm by drowning and submersion while in bath tub

X72, Intentional self-harm by handgun discharge

X73, Intentional self-harm by rifle, shotgun and larger firearm discharge

X74, Intentional self-harm by other and unspecified firearm and gun discharge

X75, Intentional self-harm by explosive material

X76, Intentional self-harm by smoke, fire and flames

X77, Intentional self-harm by steam, hot vapors and hot objects

X81,   Intentional self-harm by jumping or lying in front of moving object

X82,   Intentional self-harm by crashing of motor vehicle

X83,   Intentional self-harm by other specified means

Y03,   Assault by crashing of motor vehicle

Y07,   Perpetrator of assault, maltreatment and neglect

Y08.8, Assault by strike by sports equipment

Y21,   Drowning and submersion, undetermined intent

Y22,   Handgun discharge, undetermined intent

Y23,   Rifle, shotgun and larger firearm discharge, undetermined intent

Y24,   Other and unspecified firearm discharge, undetermined intent

Y30,   Falling, jumping or pushed from a high place, undetermined intent

Y32,   Assault by crashing of motor vehicle, undetermined intent

Y37,   Military operations

Y36,   Operations of war

Y92,   Place of occurrence of the external cause

Y93,   Activity code

Y99,   External cause status

Z00,   Encounter for general examination without complaint, suspected or reported diagnosis

Z01,   Encounter for other special examination without complaint, suspected or reported diagnosis

Z02,   Encounter for administrative examination

Z03,   Encounter for medical observation for suspected diseases and conditions ruled out

Z08,   Encounter for follow-up examination following completed treatment for malignant neoplasm

Z09,   Encounter for follow-up examination after completed treatment for conditions other than malignant neoplasm

Z11,   Encounter for screening for infectious and parasitic diseases

Z11.8, Encounter for screening for other infectious and parasitic diseases

Z12,   Encounter for screening for malignant neoplasms

Z13,   Encounter for screening for other diseases and disorders

Z13.4, Encounter for screening for certain developmental disorders in childhood

Z13.5, Encounter for screening for eye and ear disorders

Z13.6, Encounter for screening for cardiovascular disorders

ICD-10-CM Official Guidelines for Coding and Reporting
2014
Page 114 of 117
Courtesy of the Centers for Disease Control and Prevention, www.cdc.gov

Z13.83, Encounter for screening for respiratory disorder NEC

Z13.89, Encounter for screening for other disorder

Z13.89, Encounter for screening for other disorder

Z14,   Genetic carrier

Z15,   Genetic susceptibility to disease

Z17,   Estrogen receptor status

Z18,   Retained foreign body fragments

Z22,   Carrier of infectious disease

Z23,   Encounter for immunization

Z28,   Immunization not carried out and underimmunization status

Z28.3, Underimmunization status

Z30,   Encounter for contraceptive management

Z31,   Encounter for procreative management

Z34,   Encounter for supervision of normal pregnancy

Z36,   Encounter for antenatal screening of mother

Z37,   Outcome of delivery

Z38,   Liveborn infants according to place of birth and type of delivery

Z39, Encounter for maternal postpartum care and examination

Z41, Encounter for procedures for purposes other than remedying health state

Z42, Encounter for plastic and reconstructive surgery following medical procedure or healed injury

Z43, Encounter for attention to artificial openings

Z44, Encounter for fitting and adjustment of external prosthetic device

Z45, Encounter for adjustment and management of implanted device

Z46, Encounter for fitting and adjustment of other devices

Z47.8, Encounter for other orthopedic aftercare

Z49, Encounter for care involving renal dialysis

Z51, Encounter for other aftercare

Z51.5, Encounter for palliative care

Z51.8, Encounter for other specified aftercare

Z52,   Donors of organs and tissues

Z59,   Problems related to housing and economic circumstances

Z63, Other problems related to primary support group, including family circumstances

Z65, Problems related to other psychosocial circumstances

Z65.8 Other specified problems related to psychosocial circumstances

Z67.1 – Z67.9 Blood type

Z68, Body mass index (BMI)

Z72, Problems related to lifestyle

Z74.01, Bed confinement status

Z76, Persons encountering health services in other circumstances

Z77.110- Z77.128, Environmental pollution and hazards in the physical environment

Z78, Other specified health status

Z79, Long term (current) drug therapy

Z80, Family history of primary malignant neoplasm

Z81, Family history of mental and behavioral disorders

Z82, Family history of certain disabilities and chronic diseases (leading to disablement)

Z83, Family history of other specific disorders

Z84, Family history of other conditions

Z85, Personal history of primary malignant neoplasm

Z86, Personal history of certain other diseases

Z87, Personal history of other diseases and conditions

Z87.828, Personal history of other (healed) physical injury and trauma

Z87.891, Personal history of nicotine dependence

Z88, Allergy status to drugs, medicaments and biological substances

Z89, Acquired absence of limb

Z90.710, Acquired absence of both cervix and uterus

Z91.0, Allergy status, other than to drugs and biological substances
Z91.4, Personal history of psychological trauma, not elsewhere classified

Z91.5, Personal history of self-harm

Z91.8, Other specified risk factors, not elsewhere classified

Z92, Personal history of medical treatment

Z93, Artificial opening status

Z94, Transplanted organ and tissue status

Z95, Presence of cardiac and vascular implants and grafts

Z97, Presence of other devices

Z98,   Other postprocedural states

Z99,   Dependence on enabling machines and devices, not elsewhere classified

APPENDIX D

ICD-10-PCS Official Guidelines for Coding

and Reporting

2014

The Centers for Medicare and Medicaid Services (CMS) and the National Center for Health Statistics (NCHS), two departments within the U.S. Federal Government's Department of Health and Human Services (DHHS) provide the following guidelines for coding and reporting using the International Classification of Diseases, 10th Revision, Procedure Coding System (ICD-10-PCS). These guidelines should be used as a companion document to the official version of the ICD-10-PCS as published on the CMS website. The ICD-10-PCS is a procedure classification published by the United States for classifying procedures performed in hospital inpatient health care settings.

These guidelines have been approved by the four organizations that make up the Cooperating Parties for the ICD-10-PCS: the American Hospital Association (AHA), the American Health Information Management Association (AHIMA), CMS, and NCHS.

These guidelines are a set of rules that have been developed to accompany and complement the official conventions and instructions provided within the ICD-10-PCS itself. The instructions and conventions of the classification take precedence over guidelines. These guidelines are based on the coding and sequencing instructions in the Tables, Index and Definitions of ICD-10-PCS, but provide additional instruction. Adherence to these guidelines when assigning ICD-10-PCS procedure codes is required under the Health Insurance Portability and Accountability Act (HIPAA). The procedure codes have been adopted under HIPAA for hospital inpatient healthcare settings. A joint effort between the healthcare provider and the coder is essential to achieve complete and accurate documentation, code assignment, and reporting of diagnoses and procedures. These guidelines have been developed to assist both the healthcare provider and the coder in identifying those procedures that are to be reported. The importance of consistent, complete documentation in the medical record cannot be overemphasized. Without such documentation accurate coding cannot be achieved.

Table of Contents

Conventions

A1

ICD-10-PCS codes are composed of seven characters. Each character is an axis of classification that specifies information about the procedure performed. Within a defined code range, a character specifies the same type of information in that axis of classification.

Example: The fifth axis of classification specifies the approach in sections 0 through 4 and 7 through 9 of the system.

A2

One of 34 possible values can be assigned to each axis of classification in the seven-character code: they are the numbers 0 through 9 and the alphabet (except I and O because they are easily confused with the numbers 1 and 0). The number of unique values used in an axis of classification differs as needed.

Example: Where the fifth axis of classification specifies the approach, seven different approach values are currently used to specify the approach.

A3

The valid values for an axis of classification can be added to as needed.

Example: If a significantly distinct type of device is used in a new procedure, a new device value can be added to the system.

A4

As with words in their context, the meaning of any single value is a combination of its axis of classification and any preceding values on which it may be dependent.

Example: The meaning of a body part value in the Medical and Surgical section is always dependent on the body system value. The body part value 0 in the Central Nervous body system specifies Brain and the body part value 0 in the Peripheral Nervous body system specifies Cervical Plexus.

A5

As the system is expanded to become increasingly detailed, over time more values will depend on preceding values for their meaning.

Example: In the Lower Joints body system, the device value 3 in the root operation Insertion specifies Infusion Device and the device value 3 in the root operation Replacement specifies Ceramic Synthetic Substitute.

A6

The purpose of the alphabetic index is to locate the appropriate table that contains all information necessary to construct a procedure code. The PCS Tables should always be consulted to find the most appropriate valid code.

A7

It is not required to consult the index first before proceeding to the tables to complete the code. A valid code may be chosen directly from the tables.

A8

All seven characters must be specified to be a valid code. If the documentation is incomplete for coding purposes, the physician should be queried for the necessary information.

A9

Within a PCS table, valid codes include all combinations of choices in characters 4 through 7 contained in the same row of the table. In the example below, 0JHT3VZ is a valid code, and 0JHW3VZ is *not* a valid code.

Section: 0 Medical and Surgical
Body System: J Subcutaneous Tissue and Fascia
Operation: H Insertion: Putting in a nonbiological appliance that monitors, assists, performs, or prevents a physiological function but does not physically take the place of a body part

Body Part	Approach	Device	Qualifier
S Subcutaneous Tissue and Fascia, Head and Neck V Subcutaneous Tissue and Fascia, Upper Extremity W Subcutaneous Tissue and Fascia, Lower Extremity	0 Open 3 Percutaneous	1 Radioactive Element 3 Infusion Device	Z No Qualifier
T Subcutaneous Tissue and Fascia, Trunk	0 Open 3 Percutaneous	1 Radioactive Element 3 Infusion Device V Infusion Pump	Z No Qualifier

A10

"And," when used in a code description, means "and/or."
Example: Lower Arm and Wrist Muscle means lower arm and/or wrist muscle.

A11

Many of the terms used to construct PCS codes are defined within the system. It is the coder's responsibility to determine what the documentation in the medical record equates to in the PCS definitions. The physician is not expected to use the terms used in PCS code descriptions, nor is the coder required to query the physician when the correlation between the documentation and the defined PCS terms is clear.
Example: When the physician documents "partial resection" the coder can independently correlate "partial resection" to the root operation Excision without querying the physician for clarification.

Medical and Surgical Section Guidelines (section 0)

B2. Body System

General guidelines
B2.1a
The procedure codes in the general anatomical regions body systems should only be used when the procedure is performed on an anatomical region rather than a specific body part (e.g., root operations Control and Detachment, Drainage of a body cavity) or on the rare occasion when no information is available to support assignment of a code to a specific body part.
Example: Control of postoperative hemorrhage is coded to the root operation Control found in the general anatomical regions body systems.

B2.1b
Where the general body part values "upper" and "lower" are provided as an option in the Upper Arteries, Lower Arteries, Upper Veins, Lower Veins, Muscles and Tendons body systems, "upper" or "lower "specifies body parts located above or below the diaphragm respectively.
Example: Vein body parts above the diaphragm are found in the Upper Veins body system; vein body parts below the diaphragm are found in the Lower Veins body system.

B3. Root Operation

General guidelines
B3.1a
In order to determine the appropriate root operation, the full definition of the root operation as contained in the PCS Tables must be applied.

B3.1b
Components of a procedure specified in the root operation definition and explanation are not coded separately. Procedural steps necessary to reach the operative site and close the operative site, including anastomosis of a tubular body part, are also not coded separately.
Example: Resection of a joint as part of a joint replacement procedure is included in the root operation definition of Replacement and is not coded separately. Laparotomy performed to reach the site of an open liver biopsy is not coded separately. In a resection of sigmoid colon with anastomosis of descending colon to rectum, the anastomosis is not coded separately.

Multiple procedures
B3.2
During the same operative episode, multiple procedures are coded if:
a.   The same root operation is performed on different body parts as defined by distinct values of the body part character.
         Example: Diagnostic excision of liver and pancreas are coded separately.
b.   The same root operation is repeated at different body sites that are included in the same body part value.
         Example: Excision of the sartorius muscle and excision of the gracilis muscle are both included in the upper leg muscle body part value, and multiple procedures are coded.
c.   Multiple root operations with distinct objectives are performed on the same body part.
         Example: Destruction of sigmoid lesion and bypass of sigmoid colon are coded separately.
d.   The intended root operation is attempted using one approach, but is converted to a different approach.
         Example: Laparoscopic cholecystectomy converted to an open cholecystectomy is coded as percutaneous endoscopic Inspection and open Resection.

Discontinued procedures
B3.3
If the intended procedure is discontinued, code the procedure to the root operation performed. If a procedure is discontinued before any other root operation is performed, code the root operation Inspection of the body part or anatomical region inspected.
Example: A planned aortic valve replacement procedure is discontinued after the initial thoracotomy and before any incision is made in the heart muscle, when the patient

becomes hemodynamically unstable. This procedure is coded as an open Inspection of the mediastinum.

Biopsy procedures
B3.4a
Biopsy procedures are coded using the root operations Excision, Extraction, or Drainage and the qualifier Diagnostic. The qualifier Diagnostic is used only for biopsies.
Examples: Fine needle aspiration biopsy of lung is coded to the root operation Drainage with the qualifier Diagnostic. Biopsy of bone marrow is coded to the root operation Extraction with the qualifier Diagnostic. Lymph node sampling for biopsy is coded to the root operation Excision with the qualifier Diagnostic.

Biopsy followed by more definitive treatment
B3.4b
If a diagnostic Excision, Extraction, or Drainage procedure (biopsy) is followed by a more definitive procedure, such as Destruction, Excision or Resection at the same procedure site, both the biopsy and the more definitive treatment are coded.
Example: Biopsy of breast followed by partial mastectomy at the same procedure site, both the biopsy and the partial mastectomy procedure are coded.

Overlapping body layers
B3.5
If the root operations Excision, Repair or Inspection are performed on overlapping layers of the musculoskeletal system, the body part specifying the deepest layer is coded.
Example: Excisional debridement that includes skin and subcutaneous tissue and muscle is coded to the muscle body part.

Bypass procedures
B3.6a
Bypass procedures are coded by identifying the body part bypassed "from" and the body part bypassed "to." The fourth character body part specifies the body part bypassed from, and the qualifier specifies the body part bypassed to.
Example: Bypass from stomach to jejunum, stomach is the body part and jejunum is the qualifier.

B3.6b
Coronary arteries are classified by number of distinct sites treated, rather than number of coronary arteries or anatomic name of a coronary artery (e.g., left anterior descending). Coronary artery bypass procedures are coded differently than other bypass procedures as described in the previous guideline. Rather than identifying the body part bypassed from, the body part identifies the number of coronary artery sites bypassed to, and the qualifier specifies the vessel bypassed from.
Example: Aortocoronary artery bypass of one site on the left anterior descending coronary artery and one site on the obtuse marginal coronary artery is classified in the body part axis of classification as two coronary artery sites and the qualifier specifies the aorta as the body part bypassed from.

B3.6c

If multiple coronary artery sites are bypassed, a separate procedure is coded for each coronary artery site that uses a different device and/or qualifier.

Example: Aortocoronary artery bypass and internal mammary coronary artery bypass are coded separately.

Control vs. more definitive root operations
B3.7

The root operation Control is defined as, "Stopping, or attempting to stop, postprocedural bleeding." If an attempt to stop postprocedural bleeding is initially unsuccessful, and to stop the bleeding requires performing any of the definitive root operations Bypass, Detachment, Excision, Extraction, Reposition, Replacement, or Resection, then that root operation is coded instead of Control.

Example: Resection of spleen to stop postprocedural bleeding is coded to Resection instead of Control.

Excision vs. Resection
B3.8

PCS contains specific body parts for anatomical subdivisions of a body part, such as lobes of the lungs or liver and regions of the intestine. Resection of the specific body part is coded whenever all of the body part is cut out or off, rather than coding Excision of a less specific body part.

Example: Left upper lung lobectomy is coded to Resection of Upper Lung Lobe, Left rather than Excision of Lung, Left.

Excision for graft
B3.9

If an autograft is obtained from a different body part in order to complete the objective of the procedure, a separate procedure is coded.

Example: Coronary bypass with excision of saphenous vein graft, excision of saphenous vein is coded separately.

Fusion procedures of the spine
B3.10a

The body part coded for a spinal vertebral joint(s) rendered immobile by a spinal fusion procedure is classified by the level of the spine (e.g. thoracic). There are distinct body part values for a single vertebral joint and for multiple vertebral joints at each spinal level.

Example: Body part values specify Lumbar Vertebral Joint, Lumbar Vertebral Joints, 2 or More and Lumbosacral Vertebral Joint.

B3.10b

If multiple vertebral joints are fused, a separate procedure is coded for each vertebral joint that uses a different device and/or qualifier.

Example: Fusion of lumbar vertebral joint, posterior approach, anterior column and fusion of lumbar vertebral joint, posterior approach, posterior column are coded separately.

B3.10c

Combinations of devices and materials are often used on a vertebral joint to render the joint immobile. When combinations of devices are used on the same vertebral joint, the device value coded for the procedure is as follows:

- If an interbody fusion device is used to render the joint immobile (alone or containing other material like bone graft), the procedure is coded with the device value Interbody Fusion Device
- If bone graft is the *only* device used to render the joint immobile, the procedure is coded with the device value Nonautologous Tissue Substitute or Autologous Tissue Substitute
- If a mixture of autologous and nonautologous bone graft (with or without biological or synthetic extenders or binders) is used to render the joint immobile, code the procedure with the device value Autologous Tissue Substitute

Examples: Fusion of a vertebral joint using a cage style interbody fusion device containing morsellized bone graft is coded to the device Interbody Fusion Device.

Fusion of a vertebral joint using a bone dowel interbody fusion device made of cadaver bone and packed with a mixture of local morsellized bone and demineralized bone matrix is coded to the device Interbody Fusion Device.

Fusion of a vertebral joint using both autologous bone graft and bone bank bone graft is coded to the device Autologous Tissue Substitute.

Inspection procedures

B3.11a

Inspection of a body part(s) performed in order to achieve the objective of a procedure is not coded separately.

Example: Fiberoptic bronchoscopy performed for irrigation of bronchus, only the irrigation procedure is coded.

B3.11b

If multiple tubular body parts are inspected, the most distal body part inspected is coded. If multiple non-tubular body parts in a region are inspected, the body part that specifies the entire area inspected is coded.

Examples: Cystoureteroscopy with inspection of bladder and ureters is coded to the ureter body part value.

Exploratory laparotomy with general inspection of abdominal contents is coded to the peritoneal cavity body part value.

B3.11c

When both an Inspection procedure and another procedure are performed on the same body part during the same episode, if the Inspection procedure is performed using a different approach than the other procedure, the Inspection procedure is coded separately.

Example: Endoscopic Inspection of the duodenum is coded separately when open Excision of the duodenum is performed during the same procedural episode.

Occlusion vs. Restriction for vessel embolization procedures
B3.12
If the objective of an embolization procedure is to completely close a vessel, the root operation Occlusion is coded. If the objective of an embolization procedure is to narrow the lumen of a vessel, the root operation Restriction is coded.
Examples: Tumor embolization is coded to the root operation Occlusion, because the objective of the procedure is to cut off the blood supply to the vessel.
Embolization of a cerebral aneurysm is coded to the root operation Restriction, because the objective of the procedure is not to close off the vessel entirely, but to narrow the lumen of the vessel at the site of the aneurysm where it is abnormally wide.

Release procedures
B3.13
In the root operation Release, the body part value coded is the body part being freed and not the tissue being manipulated or cut to free the body part.
Example: Lysis of intestinal adhesions is coded to the specific intestine body part value.

Release vs. Division
B3.14
If the sole objective of the procedure is freeing a body part without cutting the body part, the root operation is Release. If the sole objective of the procedure is separating or transecting a body part, the root operation is Division.
Examples: Freeing a nerve root from surrounding scar tissue to relieve pain is coded to the root operation Release. Severing a nerve root to relieve pain is coded to the root operation Division.

Reposition for fracture treatment
B3.15
Reduction of a displaced fracture is coded to the root operation Reposition and the application of a cast or splint in conjunction with the Reposition procedure is not coded separately. Treatment of a nondisplaced fracture is coded to the procedure performed.
Examples: Putting a pin in a nondisplaced fracture is coded to the root operation Insertion.
Casting of a nondisplaced fracture is coded to the root operation Immobilization in the Placement section.

Transplantation vs. Administration
B3.16
Putting in a mature and functioning living body part taken from another individual or animal is coded to the root operation Transplantation. Putting in autologous or nonautologous cells is coded to the Administration section.
Example: Putting in autologous or nonautologous bone marrow, pancreatic islet cells or stem cells is coded to the Administration section.

B4. Body Part

General guidelines
B4.1a
If a procedure is performed on a portion of a body part that does not have a separate body part value, code the body part value corresponding to the whole body part.
Example: A procedure performed on the alveolar process of the mandible is coded to the mandible body part.

B4.1b
If the prefix "peri" is combined with a body part to identify the site of the procedure, the procedure is coded to the body part named.
Example: A procedure site identified as perirenal is coded to the kidney body part.

Branches of body parts
B4.2
Where a specific branch of a body part does not have its own body part value in PCS, the body part is coded to the closest proximal branch that has a specific body part value.
Example: A procedure performed on the mandibular branch of the trigeminal nerve is coded to the trigeminal nerve body part value.

Bilateral body part values
B4.3
Bilateral body part values are available for a limited number of body parts. If the identical procedure is performed on contralateral body parts, and a bilateral body part value exists for that body part, a single procedure is coded using the bilateral body part value. If no bilateral body part value exists, each procedure is coded separately using the appropriate body part value.
Example: The identical procedure performed on both fallopian tubes is coded once using the body part value Fallopian Tube, Bilateral. The identical procedure performed on both knee joints is coded twice using the body part values Knee Joint, Right and Knee Joint, Left.

Coronary arteries
B4.4
The coronary arteries are classified as a single body part that is further specified by number of sites treated and not by name or number of arteries. Separate body part values are used to specify the number of sites treated when the same procedure is performed on multiple sites in the coronary arteries.
Examples: Angioplasty of two distinct sites in the left anterior descending coronary artery with placement of two stents is coded as Dilation of Coronary Arteries, Two Sites, with Intraluminal Device.
Angioplasty of two distinct sites in the left anterior descending coronary artery, one with stent placed and one without, is coded separately as Dilation of Coronary Artery, One Site with Intraluminal Device, and Dilation of Coronary Artery, One Site with no device.

Tendons, ligaments, bursae and fascia near a joint
B4.5
Procedures performed on tendons, ligaments, bursae and fascia supporting a joint are coded to the body part in the respective body system that is the focus of the procedure. Procedures performed on joint structures themselves are coded to the body part in the joint body systems.
Example: Repair of the anterior cruciate ligament of the knee is coded to the knee bursae and ligament body part in the bursae and ligaments body system. Knee arthroscopy with shaving of articular cartilage is coded to the knee joint body part in the Lower Joints body system.

Skin, subcutaneous tissue and fascia overlying a joint
B4.6
If a procedure is performed on the skin, subcutaneous tissue or fascia overlying a joint, the procedure is coded to the following body part:
- Shoulder is coded to Upper Arm
- Elbow is coded to Lower Arm
- Wrist is coded to Lower Arm
- Hip is coded to Upper Leg
- Knee is coded to Lower Leg
- Ankle is coded to Foot

Fingers and toes
B4.7
If a body system does not contain a separate body part value for fingers, procedures performed on the fingers are coded to the body part value for the hand. If a body system does not contain a separate body part value for toes, procedures performed on the toes are coded to the body part value for the foot.
Example: Excision of finger muscle is coded to one of the hand muscle body part values in the Muscles body system.

Upper and lower intestinal tract
B4.8
In the Gastrointestinal body system, the general body part values Upper Intestinal Tract and Lower Intestinal Tract are provided as an option for the root operations Change, Inspection, Removal and Revision. Upper Intestinal Tract includes the portion of the gastrointestinal tract from the esophagus down to and including the duodenum, and Lower Intestinal Tract includes the portion of the gastrointestinal tract from the jejunum down to and including the rectum and anus.
Example: In the root operation Change table, change of a device in the jejunum is coded using the body part Lower Intestinal Tract.

B5. Approach

Open approach with percutaneous endoscopic assistance
B5.2
Procedures performed using the open approach with percutaneous endoscopic assistance are coded to the approach Open.
Example: Laparoscopic-assisted sigmoidectomy is coded to the approach Open.

External approach
B5.3a
Procedures performed within an orifice on structures that are visible without the aid of any instrumentation are coded to the approach External.
Example: Resection of tonsils is coded to the approach External.

B5.3b
Procedures performed indirectly by the application of external force through the intervening body layers are coded to the approach External.
Example: Closed reduction of fracture is coded to the approach External.

Percutaneous procedure via device
B5.4
Procedures performed percutaneously via a device placed for the procedure are coded to the approach Percutaneous.
Example: Fragmentation of kidney stone performed via percutaneous nephrostomy is coded to the approach Percutaneous.

B6. Device

General guidelines
B6.1a
A device is coded only if a device remains after the procedure is completed. If no device remains, the device value No Device is coded.

B6.1b
Materials such as sutures, ligatures, radiological markers and temporary post-operative wound drains are considered integral to the performance of a procedure and are not coded as devices.

B6.1c
Procedures performed on a device only and not on a body part are specified in the root operations Change, Irrigation, Removal and Revision, and are coded to the procedure performed.
Example: Irrigation of percutaneous nephrostomy tube is coded to the root operation Irrigation of indwelling device in the Administration section.

Drainage device
B6.2
A separate procedure to put in a drainage device is coded to the root operation Drainage with the device value Drainage Device.

C. Obstetrics Section

Products of conception
C1
Procedures performed on the products of conception are coded to the Obstetrics section. Procedures performed on the pregnant female other than the products of conception are coded to the appropriate root operation in the Medical and Surgical section.
Example: Amniocentesis is coded to the products of conception body part in the Obstetrics section. Repair of obstetric urethral laceration is coded to the urethra body part in the Medical and Surgical section.

Procedures following delivery or abortion
C2
Procedures performed following a delivery or abortion for curettage of the endometrium or evacuation of retained products of conception are all coded in the Obstetrics section, to the root operation Extraction and the body part Products of Conception, Retained. Diagnostic or therapeutic dilation and curettage performed during times other than the postpartum or post-abortion period are all coded in the Medical and Surgical section, to the root operation Extraction and the body part Endometrium.

Selection of Principal Procedure

The following instructions should be applied in the selection of principal procedure and clarification on the importance of the relation to the principal diagnosis when more than one procedure is performed:

1. Procedure performed for definitive treatment of both principal diagnosis and secondary diagnosis

      a. Sequence procedure performed for definitive treatment most related to principal diagnosis as principal procedure.

2. Procedure performed for definitive treatment and diagnostic procedures performed for both principal diagnosis and secondary diagnosis

      a. Sequence procedure performed for definitive treatment most related to principal diagnosis as principal procedure

3. A diagnostic procedure was performed for the principal diagnosis and a procedure is performed for definitive treatment of a secondary diagnosis.

      a. Sequence diagnostic procedure as principal procedure, since the procedure most related to the principal diagnosis takes precedence.

4. No procedures performed that are related to principal diagnosis; procedures performed for definitive treatment and diagnostic procedures were performed for secondary diagnosis

      a. Sequence procedure performed for definitive treatment of secondary diagnosis as principal procedure, since there are no procedures (definitive or nondefinitive treatment) related to principal diagnosis.